THE OLDER WOMAN

THE OLDER WOMAN

Lavender Rose or Gray Panther

Edited By

MARIE MARSCHALL FULLER

Texas Woman's University
Denton, Texas

and

CORA ANN MARTIN

Center for Studies in Aging
North Texas State University
Denton, Texas

CHARLES   C   THOMAS • PUBLISHER
Springfield • Illinois • U.S.A.

Published and Distributed Throughout the World by
CHARLES C THOMAS • PUBLISHER
Bannerstone House
301-327 East Lawrence Avenue, Springfield, Illinois, U.S.A.

© *1980, by* CHARLES C THOMAS • PUBLISHER
ISBN 0-398-03974-7
Library of Congress Catalog Card Number: 79-26514

With **THOMAS BOOKS** *careful attention is given to all details of
manufacturing and design. It is the Publisher's desire to present books that
are satisfactory as to their physical qualities and artistic possibilities and
appropriate for their particular use.* **THOMAS BOOKS** *will be true to those
laws of quality that assure a good name and good will.*

Printed in the United States of America
V-OO-2

*HQ
1064
U5
O43*

Library of Congress Cataloging in Publication Data
Main entry under title:
The Older Woman.

 1. Aged women--United States--Addresses, essays,
lectures. 2. Aged women--United States--Social condi-
tions--Addresses, essays, lectures. 3. Socialization--
Addresses, essays, lectures. 4. Aged women--United
States--Political activity. I. Fuller, Marie Marschall.
II. Martin, Cora Ann.
HQ1064.U5043   301.43'5   79-26514
ISBN 0-398-03974-7

DEDICATED TO OUR MOTHERS AND AUNTS
VANGUARD OF THE FUTURE

PREFACE

SINCE it is better to be male than female and to be young than old in our society, perhaps it is not surprising that persons who are both female and old, and therefore doubly devalued, have been on the periphery of attention in social science. However, the extent of the neglect is shocking. Surveying the literature in gerontology and women's studies as the most likely source of information on older women, the reader might well come to the conclusion that 6 percent of our society, the percent of females sixty-five years of age and over, is invisible. The editors of this reader teach courses in both gerontology and women's studies; yet, when we first started looking for articles to include in the anthology, we were surprised to find so few studies of older women. We later discovered that, in some cases, the titles of articles obscured the fact that older women were being written about, and in some, one had to examine the characteristics of the sample to discover that the authors were discussing, for the most part, women, in a vocabulary limited by the generic "he" and older "person." Indeed, one could make the argument that most of gerontological literature is about older women, and that older men are the ones who are missing. We, however, prefer to argue that, for a variety of reasons explicated in our introduction, older women have been and remain to a large degree "unseen."

We made an initial decision to limit our readings to the women sixty-five years of age and older, but we have not always found it possible to honor this. Women do not, after all, exist in discrete categories arbitrarily selected by social scientists. The "older woman" in age-segregated housing is usually defined (because of HUD rules) as 62 years of age and older, for economic studies as 65 years of age and older (because of social security regulations), and for educational studies we found the "older woman" returning to school is in her thirties! Needless to say, we found it necessary to violate our "rule" on occasion.

Sadly, we frequently had to select articles which talked about The Older Woman as though all older women were the same — thus violating one of our major premises of the great variety of older women. We have even been guilty of this "homogenization" ourselves, but the title of this book is meant to emphasize the differences among older women by identifying the polar extremes of the aggressive gray panther or the retiring lavender rose. In fact, a lifetime of accumulated differences in socialization experiences, education, income, health, and opportunities might suggest that older women exhibit greater differences than similarities.

We have made an attempt to survey literature from many fields and have decided to limit articles to ones published in the 1970s, and with the exception of a few cases, data from the seventies. Although the historical value of earlier literature is recognized, social change is occurring so rapidly that we believe this limitation will make the reader maximally useful to our colleagues and students. Trying to develop a well-rounded anthology, we have found that gaps of information exist in some areas, for example, religion — surely an important aspect of the lives of many older women — while in other areas, such as economics, an abundance of fine articles dictated hard choices to be made.

Since the majority of older women are not members of an ethnic/racial minority, we have deliberately chosen, in this first reader on the older woman, to concentrate on them. Even within this category, socialization experiences, as we have suggested, produce wide variations. If cultural differences are added, the variations become too great to be adequately addressed here. However, just as we found it difficult to always stay within our defined parameters of age, time, etc., so we also have some articles that have racial/ethnic variations in the subjects for comparative purposes.*

This volume attempts to bring together from scattered sources a current description of the lives of older women, their special problems, and the needs that set them apart both from younger women and from men in the same age cohort. We begin with a profile of the older woman in America in the 1970s: her numbers, her diversity, her employment patterns, marital situation, friendship patterns, living arrangements, etc. A section follows on socialization in which we point out that the roles and value systems to which the older woman was socialized in the early 1900s may not prepare her for the quite different world of today. However, socialization is an unending process, and while the initial socialization and continuing circumstances of some older women may create difficulty in adjusting to a changed

---

*For the reader interested in ethnic/racial differences, we suggest the bibliography, "Ethnic Background and the Older Woman" in *Past Sixty: The Older Woman in Print and Film*, (Hollenshead, Katz, and Ingersoll, comp. Ann Arbor: Institute of Gerontology, The University of Michigan-Wayne State University, 1978).

world, other women, forced by diverse socialization experiences and personality characteristics, display remarkable resilience in old age.

Biological differences between men and women are undeniable; however, a large body of fallacies has grown up around some of the particular aspects of being a woman. In the reader we have presented articles that deal with the more obvious of these: sex, menopause, attitudes toward health and mental health. (The word "hysteria," which has come to mean "unmanageable fear or emotional excess," derives from "hyster" for uterus — a rather telling comment on the presumed tie between being female and irrational behavior.)

Social bonds that tie older women into meaningful interpersonal relationships become the topic of the next section. Older women have launched their children and probably had lengthy marriages that, perhaps, have ended with the death of their husbands, but many family and friendship networks remain.

A broader pattern of relationships with the various institutions of society (family, economy, politics, religion, and education) impact older women's lives, and the articles in the section on Women and Society's Institutions examine these relationships.

Next there is a section presenting a variety of life-styles of older women. The selections presented do not exhaust the spectrum that describes the circumstances of older women but suggest some of the variations.

Finally, we present articles that look at the women who is old tomorrow — ourselves. What will the world be like for us? Healthier, with more education, better economic status, having participated in the political process and been a part of the labor force — what can we expect? Our authors suggest things will be better, though different. It is projected that the "younging" of the old will soon result in age 75 being the lower limits of "old." In 25 years, not only will we have to address ourselves to different topics, different problems, and different solutions, even our age limits will be changed.

We assume that this reader will be most useful for undergraduate classes in women's studies (where the older woman is often invisible) and in gerontology (where, though constantly present in the numerical majority, she is often obscured). More and more we discover that our colleagues are teaching courses on the older woman; we think that they will find it a great convenience to have these articles compiled. In addition, many people in disciplines that serve or work with older women as clients, students, subjects, or friends should find the articles of considerable interest: home economics, human development, sociology, psychology, counseling, social work, nursing — and a myriad of others. Libraries increasingly have special collections on women or aging, and the book will fill a gap in that literature.

In making selections we kept the undergraduate student in mind, but we believe the book will be useful also for graduate students, professionals, the growing number of middle-aged and older women who are becoming conscious of their special status, and the men whose sympathies are enlisted for older women.

INTRODUCTION

CAN you imagine an anthropologist discovering a new tribe and, in writing up the field notes, *ignoring 59 percent of the tribe?* That is exactly what two major government-sponsored (and of course tax-supported) longitudinal studies in gerontology, the National Institute on Childhood and Adult Development Study of older people[1] and the Veterans Administration study of Spanish War Veterans have done. Both used only older male subjects.

Can you imagine an anthropologist observing the tribe and *failing to note sex differences?* Yet that is what many of the studies in aging do. The size of the sample is noted, but apparently the researchers are reluctant to admit sex bias in the sample — so numbers of each sex are not reported.

Can you imagine an anthropologist visiting a tribe and *not seeing age differences?* Examples abound; although some of the latest books are adding sections on middle age and aging, a discussion of socialization frequently ends with young adult roles. Volume after volume of major feminist works treat all women as though age were not a significant category or as though women were ageless.

They are not few in number; there were some 13,288,000 older women in America in 1975 — or 12.1 percent of all females.[2] How did 13+ million women become invisible to social scientists, gerontologists, sociologists, economists, psychologists, women's studies scholars, and others? Of course women are not invisible — just largely ignored or obscured in the reporting of data.

Surely it is not intentional nor necessarily a lack of concern for the plight of some older women. Rather we who study may be captives of our own social milieu. After some consideration, we thought of a variety of reasons to explain this situation. They can be classified into two categories. There are reasons related to the nature of science, research, and theory. Further we believe there are a number of social

---

[1]Recently the sample has been enlarged to include women.

[2]Tables 1.1 and 1.2, p. 5, from *A Statistical Portrait of Women in the United States.* Bureau of the Census, Current Population Reports, Special Studies: Series P-23, No. 58, April 1976.

factors that may contribute to the problem.

Numerous points come to mind that are related to science, research, and theory. First, while social science seeks the development of general principles and regularities of human behavior, this search for universals may bias perception, emphasizing what is generally true rather than specifically different and therefore an exception to the general rule. Thus a search for propositions about older people in general may lead to tunnel vision, noting similarities among the aged but obscuring possible sex differences.

Second, most of the theories that guide research and suggest variables to investigate focus on a narrow spectrum of the total life cycle and are largely blind to age and sex differences in human behavior. With some exceptions, such as Eric Erickson's developmental theory that considers the life cycle, theorists have described early growth, perhaps to adulthood, and stopped as though development were arrested at that stage and no further change occurred. Similarly, theories (even Erickson's) have ignored sex differences or assumed they did not exist; limitations of the theories by age and sex factors have been neither stressed nor addressed.

Third, availability of research subjects on university campuses and limited research funds to seek subjects elsewhere often lead to an age bias in the samples. Without the obliging, captive college student, much of what is published would disappear in psychology, sociology, women's studies, and other "people-oriented" disciplines. How much college students and older women have in common is unknown — but we suspect it is limited.

Fourth, the norm for *statistical* analysis has been male, presuming that his characteristics described the larger units of which he was a part. For example, the head of household for the United States Census Bureau records has been male — if one was present and old enough — regardless of the occupations or incomes of the spouses, even if the husband was an invalid supported by his wife. (We understand the fact has been the cause of much embarrassment for some perceptive census officials and modification to include an element of choice is planned for the next census).

Fifth, many of the *topics* of interest to serious scholars, such as the division of labor, governmental processes, religion as an institution, economic forces — topics of importance to society — have not been characterized by the presence of older women in positions of power. There have been few Golda Meiers.

Sixth, the language that builds our thoughts has limited bricks. Women's libbers have become hoarse making that point. It is true that use of the generic expressions of "mankind," "he," and "his" — meaning everyone — inclines the viewer to focus on aspects that best square with the vocabulary of his (see!) thoughts. Did you visualize a woman when you read the word *mankind?*

Possibly a seventh, though we think the point debatable, is the high proportion of male theorists, researchers, and professors. Female investigators, the product of socialization by male mentors, seem little more perceptive than their male colleagues except for those sensitized to the problem, most notably those in the women's studies area. Not too atypical, unfortunately, in the gerontological literature was a study reported by a female author in which she repeatedly talked about the widow and "his" role orientations.

Social factors also promote the neglect of the older woman in studies. One such may be that the *visibility* of the older woman is limited by transportation and living patterns. Sunday morning church services, not a frequent subject of social science interest, may be the time of the greatest concentration of older women in public.

A second social reason is that older women simply were not present in large numbers until recently. Through most of history, though some individuals lived long lives, large groups of old people did not exist. Life spans in general were short and females died in large numbers in childbirth, of its complications, or simply from the extreme hardships of living. In 1900 men outnumbered women in the 65+ ages; by 1974 there were 143 women for each 100 men of those ages.[3]

Regardless of the validity of our suppositions for the reasons of the neglect of the older woman in scientific literature, one fact is clear — she is neglected. *The Older Woman: Lavender Rose or Gray Panther* proposes to redress this situation.

The framework within which we have chosen to present our articles has two major divisions. In the first three sections of the book, we look at the older woman in close focus, as her socialization and biology influence her life and as society views her. Beginning with statistical descriptions of older women and followed by research-supported generalizations, we next present articles that examine the older woman as a product of socialization forces and the considerable influence of biology on her life. In the next three sections of the book we examine the older woman in the matrix of the social structure — the social bonds that weave her into the social fabric of the institutions of society and her resulting life-styles. The final section is a look into the future.

---

[3]Blanch Williams. *Profile of the Elderly Woman.* (See Part I of this book).

More specifically, Section I includes a statistical description of the older woman. As interesting as statistics are to those of us who are social scientists, they only provide a structure for our profile and lack substance. Substance is added by a number of interesting articles that examine some of the multi-faceted aspects of older women today, creating a more complete picture of the older woman.

In Section II we look at the socialization process, by which we mean the way in which people learn to behave so those around them approve their behavior because they live up to society's expectations. Socialization is a particularly critical variable when one looks at the older woman. How has she been taught to behave and are these behaviors adaptive to her current life circumstances? We highlight some of the experiences that produce the variability that we observe in older women today: the gray panthers, the lavender roses, and the vast majority who fall somewhere in between.

Section III is devoted to some of the fallacies that have grown up around the biological differences between men and women. The more obvious, of course, are related to sex, but some of the more vicious relate to the emotional stability and intellectual capacity of women. What has aging got to do with this? According to some views, aging can be dated from the time of a biological crisis (menopause), which has the curious effect of rendering the mature woman a sexual neuter while at the same time creating a creature of psychological and mental instability. Ben Franklin, far from agreeing, advocated the special rewards of choosing older women as lovers and listed eight reasons for their superiority, nor did he think their mental abilities declined. He speaks appreciatively in his letter to his sister, "Consideration for the Old Folks," of the continued mental acuity with which at least one old lady controlled her social milieu.

In Section IV we move to a consideration of the older woman in the matrix of her social relationships. Considerable research attests to the continued importance of social bonding and the ability of the older woman to preserve old and forge new bonds. The accumulating evidence of the increasing number of old age marriages and their high success rate is an example of this social bonding. Not only marriage but also friends and other family bonds maintain their importance to the older woman.

More problematic, at least based on the evidence we were able to discover, is the relationship between the older woman and the traditional institutions of society, considered in Section V. Both successes and failures of the older woman vis-à-vis the economic system are well documented. To a lesser degree the relationship of the older woman to the institution of the family has been the subject of social scientists' concern. There is beginning to emerge political consciousness among older women, as witness Maggie Kuhn, and this political involvement is being documented. Religion as an institution has been of particular importance in the lives of many older women and much of the support for the religious institution has come from older women. Yet nowhere in the gerontological literature nor in women's studies did we find recognition of that fact. Education is a curious case since from the perspective of educators any woman 30 years of age and older is an "older woman." These "older women" are returning to school in record numbers, but so are many of their sisters 65 and older. The impact of this has yet to be measured.

In Section VI we examine a sampling of the variety of life-styles that characterize the older woman. Increasingly, this life-style means living alone. In March 1974, 4.5 million older women lived alone and it is estimated that by 1990 this number will grow by two-thirds.[4] This change in the composition of households is reflected in the change of life-styles among the elderly women with increasing numbers living in public or private multi-unit housing for the elderly, single room occupancy hotels, and other "protected environments" of age-segregated communities.

The final section forecasts the position of the aged in the world of tomorrow. We present the views of two gerontologists as they try to visualize the future.

The anthology, taken as a whole, both demonstrates what we know about older women and where knowledge is needed. We would like to add a caution. Older women are changing. Better educated, more economically secure, more politically involved, more personally competent — new problems will emerge as old ones are solved. For example, we believe that the older women of the future will have had to work out new forms of personal support systems as more often they will be living alone with a smaller kin network. Social policy must keep up with the changing older woman.

---

[4]*Ibid.*

ACKNOWLEDGMENTS

WHILE many people deserve our appreciation for their encouragement and suggestions, some are due special thanks: Jean Marie Coyle, whose enthusiasm and initial bibliographic work helped get us started; Elizabeth Almquist, who tested an early version of the book in a class she taught on the older woman for the Center for Studies in Aging and made useful comments; Cynthia Carolyn Fuller, who cheerfully handled technical aspects; and Sherry Ross and Phyllis Eccleston who were invaluable throughout.

M.M.F.
C.A.M.

ACKNOWLEDGMENTS

CONTENTS

                                                                    Page

Preface vii

Introduction xi

Part I. PROFILE OF THE OLDER WOMAN

Chapter

1. A PROFILE OF THE ELDERLY WOMAN 5
   Blanch Williams

2. OLDER WOMEN: AN EXAMINATION OF POPULAR STEREO-
   TYPES AND RESEARCH EVIDENCE 9
   Barbara Payne and Frank Whittington

3. ON GROWING OLDER FEMALE: AN INTERVIEW WITH
   TISH SOMMERS 31

4. WOMEN IN STUDIES OF AGING: A CRITIQUE AND
   SUGGESTION 35
   Diane Beeson

5. DO SPECIAL FOLKS NEED SPECIAL STROKES? COUN-
   SELING OLDER WOMEN: A PERSPECTIVE 45
   Jane Berry

6. MABEL, YOU DON'T BELONG HERE 50
   Carol-Grace Toussie

Part II. SOCIALIZATION

7. LAVENDER ROSE OR GRAY PANTHER 55
   Cora A. Martin

8. THE SOCIALIZATION PROCESS OF WOMEN 59
   Chrysee Kline

9. A CRABBIT OLD WOMAN WROTE THIS 71
   Author unknown

Chapter *Page*

Part III. BIOLOGICAL FACTS AND FALLACIES

10. My Crabbed Age.. 75
    Faith Baldwin

11. Benjamin Franklin and Geropsychiatry:
    Vignettes for the Bicentennial Year................. 79
    Virginia T. Sherr

12. Sex and the Senior Citizen 88
    Norman M. Lobsenz

13. The Case For and Against Estrogen Therapy......... 99
    Edward A. Graber and Hugh R. K. Barber

Part IV. SOCIAL BONDS

14. Older Persons' Perceptions of Their Marriages 113
    Nick Stinnett, Linda M. Carter, and
    James E. Montgomery

15. A New Look at Older Marriages..................... 124
    Walter C. McKain

16. Attitudinal Orientation of Wives Toward
    Their Husband's Retirement 137
    Alfred P. Fengler

17. Living as a Widow: Only the Name's the Same 151
    Edward Wakin

18. Relationships Between the Elderly and
    Their Adult Children 158
    Elizabeth S. Johnson and Barbara J. Bursk

19. The Elderly Widow and Her Family, Neighbors,
    and Friends 170
    Greg Arling

20. Sex Differences in Intimate Friendships
    of Old Age 190
    Edward A. Powers and Gordon L. Bultena

Part V. WOMEN AND SOCIETY'S INSTITUTIONS

21. Mother and Daughter Back in School 209

Chapter *Page*

22. WHY IS WOMEN'S LIB IGNORING OLD WOMEN? 211
   Myrna I. Lewis and Robert N. Butler
23. GRASS-ROOTS GRAY POWER 223
   Maggie Kuhn
24. LEGAL ISSUES INVOLVING THE OLDER WOMAN............. 228
   Rosemary Redmond
25. FORECAST OF WOMEN'S RETIREMENT INCOME: CLOUDY
   AND COLDER; 25 PERCENT CHANCE OF POVERTY 234
   Merton C. Bernstein
26. SOCIAL SECURITY: A WOMAN'S VIEWPOINT................ 247
   Tish Sommers
27. RELIGION AND THE OLDER WOMAN 262
   Letitia T. Alston and Jon P. Alston
28. RELIGION AND AGING IN A LONGITUDINAL PANEL 279
   Dan Blazer and Erdman Palmore

Part VI. ALTERNATIVE LIFE STYLES

29. COMMUNAL LIFE-STYLES FOR THE OLD................... 289
   Arlie Russell Hochschild
30. OLDER WOMEN IN SINGLE ROOM OCCUPANT (SRO)
   HOTELS: A SEATTLE PROFILE 304
   Maureen Lally et al.
31. IT'S TOUGH TO BE OLD................................ 317
   Aloyse Hahn

Part VII. LOOKING AHEAD: OLD TOMORROW

32. THE FUTURE STATUS OF THE AGED 323
   Erdman Palmore
33. THE AGED IN THE YEAR 2025 332
   Bernice L. Neugarten

THE OLDER WOMAN

Part I

Profile of the Older Woman

INTRODUCTION

If older women were scarce and rich their opportunities would be different from those facing most older women today. Thus basic to any study of the older woman is a description of the commonalities and diversity of the millions of individuals in that category. However, we need to know not only demographic facts to understand her position in today's social structure, we must also take into account the beliefs held in common about the older woman.

Demographic characteristics such as education, occupation, health, marital status, and income affect the circumstances of her life. Conventional wisdom also sets parameters that limit the older woman's life opportunities. Such wisdom may be useful when it is true; the difficulty is that much of it is based on false assumptions and incomplete information.

It is often said that older people (and particularly older women) become "non-persons" in our youth-oriented society. The first step away from this must, surely, be understanding. As we learn to distinguish the varieties of older women, to disentangle myth from reality, we find ourselves reacting to them as persons. We come to understand aging women among our own friends and relatives. In our relationships with others outside our immediate circle — patients, clients, colleagues — we develop empathy. We have taken the first step in letting older women emerge as the persons they are.

The selection of articles in Part I addresses these issues. First, we present a statistical profile of the older woman in the 1970s. The next three selections examine some of the social myths and truths about the older woman. The fifth article demonstrates how this knowledge can be useful in working with older people. The final selection makes the point that all little old ladies do not sit in rocking chairs; some of them handicap the horses!

Among the older population, almost 60 percent are women — no small minority. Blanch Williams (Chapter 1) draws a profile of the elderly woman in the first article in this section. Thirteen million strong, her numbers are exploding at a rate more than twice that of

3

the general population. About four-fifths of female children will live to join her ranks. The "typical" older woman today is white, poor or near poor, and single — usually after more than a quarter century of marriage. She is likely to stay single since older women far outnumber older men. Her education stopped before high school graduation and she is not in the labor force. We do, however, want to enter a note of caution by suggesting that changes can be expected in the women who will be old by the end of this century. But that will be the topic of a later section in the book.

In Chapter 2, Barbara Payne and Frank Whittington compare research evidence with the popular stereotypes of the older woman. Social beliefs about health and longevity, marital status and family roles, and leisure activities of older women are addressed. Most of the stereotypes should be written with invisible ink, to disappear in the light of evidence. Some, however, seem to be true. With Payne and Whittington the reader may explore the complexities of reality, separating those social beliefs based on evidence — and therefore useful — from those perpetuating myths that are harmful.

While ageism affects both men and women, women may be more vulnerable, claims Tish Sommers (Chapter 3), discussing growing older as a female. A lifetime as a homemaker and volunteer worker brings praise but neither monetary reward, social security, nor retirement benefits. She contends that the poorest segment of our society is the 7.5 million widows and single women over 65 years of age. The picture remains depressingly dark as displaced homemakers struggle in a social world needing the light of legislative reform.

Diane Beeson (Chapter 4) challenges the position of both gerontologists and feminist writers on male and female experiences of aging. In this interesting, thought-provoking article she illustrates a point we made earlier: reality construction is often in the eye of the beholder!

Wrinkles and sagging chins, few employment opportunities, limited economic resources, unmet sexual needs, shaky self-confidence — any or all may send older women to counselors who should be trained to react with sensitivity and understanding, pleads Jane Berry (Chapter 5). She stresses the challenge of counseling older women who were born too soon for opportunities open to today's young woman and who may be reacting with resentment. The kind of understanding Berry requests is applicable when working with older women in any relationship. It is remarkably well exemplified in our final selection by a nurse, Carol-Grace Toussie, who demonstrates (Chapter 6) the kind of understanding we all hope to receive — at ninety or before.

Chapter 1

A PROFILE OF THE ELDERLY WOMAN*

BLANCH WILLIAMS

As of July 1, 1974, there were an estimated 12.8 million women 65 and over residing in the United States. These women constituted 6% of the total population, 12% of all women, and 59% of the older population.

Over the past several decades, the gains in life expectancy have been greater for women than for men. As a consequence, women have become an increasing majority among the elderly. In 1900, there were actually fewer women than men in the 65+ age group (98 women per 100 men), but by 1974 this relationship had reversed to the extent that there were 143 women per 100 men.

In fact, between 1960 and 1974, the number of older women increased 42% compared with 18% for the total population and 32% for the older population. If the assumptions underlying the current Bureau of the Census projections of population trends to the year 2000 are borne out, there will be 18.6 million older women by the turn of the next century. By then, women 65+ will constitute 7% of the total population and will outnumber elderly men by a margin of 154 to 100.

Life Expectancy

Average life expectancy is a statistical measure that reflects the remaining lifetime in years of persons who have attained a given age. In the United States, there are significant differences in average expectation of life by sex.

Older women have a longer life expectancy than do older men and, in general, white women live longer than women of other races. In 1973, life expectancy for women at age 65 was 17.2 years (17.3 for whites and 16.2 years for others), 4.1 years longer than their male counterparts. Assuming that the 1973 death rates do not change in the future, 80% of female children will live to age 65.

*From *Aging*:12-13, Nov-Dec 1975.

This higher life expectancy results from the considerably lower mortality rates for women compared to men. Furthermore, the difference between these rates by sex has increased significantly in recent years. In 1940, the overall death rate for men 65 to 74 years was 29% higher than the comparable rate for women. By 1974, provisional figures show that the mortality rate for men was over 90% higher than for women in this age group. However, between 1940 and 1974 the mortality rate for both sexes decreased.

Three-fourths of the deaths among the elderly of both sexes are caused by heart disease, cancer, or stroke; and heart disease alone is the reported cause of nearly half of all deaths among this age group. There are differences by sex in the relative frequency of these three causes, however. The mortality rate due to heart disease is over twice as high for men 65 to 74 years old as for women; for cancer, the rate is four-fifths higher; while for stroke, it is only one-third higher for men than for women of these ages.

Geographic Distribution

Geographically, older women are distributed in a pattern similar to the total population. However, they are somewhat more likely to live either in the central cities of large metropolitan areas or outside these areas altogether and less likely than the population as a whole to reside in suburban areas. Two States — New York and California — have more than one million elderly women and five states — Florida, Illinois, Ohio, Pennsylvania, and Texas — have more than half a million. Together these seven populous States account for almost half of the elderly women.

Race

Among the 12.8 million elderly women, 11.8 million, or 91%, were white; one million, or 8%, were black; and about 100,000, or less than 1%, were members of other racial groups such as Orientals or American Indians. Persons of Spanish origin, most of whom are white, accounted for about 215,000, or 2%, of the elderly female population.

Education

Elderly women have had fewer years of schooling than younger women who are remaining in school longer than their forebears. Over two-thirds of the women 25 to 64 years old in 1974 had at least a high school education and 11% had completed at least four years of college. These proportions were considerably less for women 65 and older. Only one-third had a high school education and 6% were college graduates. For older men, the proportions were 31% with a high school diploma and 9% with college degrees. Half of the women 65 to 74 years of age in 1974 had completed 9.8 years of school and half of those 75 and over had completed 8.7 years. As the present younger women become the older women by the turn of the Twenty-first century, over half of these older women will have at least a high school education.

Employment

Among noninstitutionalized women 65 and older, about one in 13 was either working or actively looking for work compared to one in five for men of that same age group, as of August 1975. This low participation rate has been declining slowly for the last 15 years for elderly women who are single, widowed, or divorced, while it has been increasing slowly during this period for elderly women who are living with their husbands.

Income

In 1974, half of the more than 1.1 million families headed by an older woman received incomes of $7,723 or less, an increase of 25.6% over 1973. However, after adjusting for the 11% rise in the Consumer Price Index during this period, the real income of these families increased 13.2% over 1973. Nearly 112,000 of the families (10.1%) had less than $3,000 in total cash income, about a fifth of older female-headed families (19%) received between $10,000 and $14,999, and 18% had incomes $15,000 or more.

The five million older women living alone or with nonrelatives did not do as well as families headed by an older woman. Their median income rose from $2,642 in 1973 to $2,869 in 1974, an increase of 8.6% in money income. Because of rising prices, the buying power of this group dropped about 2.1%. More than a fifth of the individuals (21.3%) received incomes of less than $2,000 and more than 1.9 million, or 38%, had less than $2,500. At the upper end of the income scale, 197,000, or 3.9%, had incomes between $10,000 and $14,999 and about 76,000, or 1.5%, had incomes of $15,000 or more.

About 144,000, or 13%, of families headed by an elderly woman reported incomes below the poverty level in 1974. For older women who lived alone or with nonrelatives, the number and proportion below the poverty level was much higher, 1.7 million and 33.2 percent, respectively. The number of these poor families and individuals did not decrease significantly between 1973 and 1974. However the number of elderly poor has decreased considerably in recent years, primarily due to increases of over 80 percent in Social Security benefits since 1970.

Marital Status

Because of differences in death rates for elderly men and women, and because husbands tend to be older than their wives, women are much more likely to be widowed than are men. In 1974, more than half, or 6.3 million women 65+ were widows, while only 39% were married.

Living Arrangements

Approximately 5% of the elderly live in institutions, primarily nursing homes. According to a recent survey by the National Center for Health Statistics, nearly three-fourths of the elderly residents of these homes were women.

Among noninstitutionalized elderly men, over three-fourths are still living with their wives and only 17% live alone or with nonrelatives. However, the longer life expectancy of women has created an entirely different set of living arrangements. Among the 12.1 million noninstitutionalized elderly women, as of March 1974, over one-third (4.5 million) lived alone and a similar proportion lived with their husbands. Most of the remaining elderly women lived with family members other than their husbands.

The greater life expectancy of women and the growing tendency in America for extended or multigeneration families to split up into several households has caused a tremendous spurt in the number headed by elderly women. In 1974, there were 5.8 million such households. If recent trends in household formation continue, the Bureau of the Census estimates that the total number will increase about one-third by 1990. During the same period, the number of households headed by elderly women will increase by more than one-half and the number who live alone will grow by over two-thirds.

Chapter 2

OLDER WOMEN: AN EXAMINATION OF POPULAR STEREOTYPES AND RESEARCH EVIDENCE*

BARBARA PAYNE AND FRANK WHITTINGTON

The older woman in our society is socially devalued and is subject to a number of harmful, negative stereotypes that picture her as sick, sexless, uninvolved except for church work, and alone. Moreover, when researchers study the aged, they too often fail to analyze the data for females separately from that of males, thus glossing over the differences and losing valuable information. It is possible, however, using data from studies which have used sex as an independent variable, to demythologize the older woman somewhat by separating the characteristics which are uniquely female from those of males and those common to the sexes. This paper, then, examines stereotypical images of the older women in three major areas: (1) health and longevity; (2) marital status and family roles; and (3) leisure activity. Several unresolved questions and areas for future research are suggested, and the implication of this analysis for such research is discussed.

IT is a sociological commonplace that in American society women have been considered less socially valuable than men, just as the aged are believed to be less worthy than the young. Consequently, the older woman, burdened with more negative stereotypes than any other age-sex group, is often viewed as one of society's least socially important members. Since negative attitudes usually lead to differential treatment, and because they occupy different roles and statuses throughout life, older men and women might be expected to exhibit different characteristics and behavior. It is also quite likely that they experience different aging trajectories, or at least experience them differently.

The older woman not only suffers from social prejudice but from a certain scientific indifference as well. Researchers purporting to study the problems or characteristics of the aged ought to view males and

---

*From *Social Problems*, 23:488-504, 1976.

9

females as separate subgroups of the older population, at least for research purposes. Unfortunately, an assumption of homogeneity appears to have been the implicit guide for much of the research which has been done in the field of aging. There are, however, enough studies which have employed sex as an independent variable to allow the separation of some of the characteristics and social patterns which are uniquely female from those of males and the specification of those common to both sexes. It is also possible to test certain of the stereotypes concerning the older woman by surveying these findings for supportive or contradictory evidence.

This paper, then, will examine several "old woman" stereotypes in light of available evidence in three areas of research: (1) health and longevity; (2) marital status and family roles; and (3) leisure activity, including voluntary associations, religious participation, and volunteering.[1] It will conclude with a specification of several unresolved questions about older women which suggest areas for future investigation and will outline certain implications of the present analysis for such research.

Health and Longevity

Stereotype: Older Women Have More Health Problems — Both Real and Imaginary — Than Older Men

The greater longevity of women in all industrialized countries is a well-documented and generally well-known fact.[2] Reasons for this important difference are less well understood, however. One possible explanation is that females are biologically superior to males. For example, Rose and Bell (1971) argue that historically women lived shorter lives than men due to a harsher social and physical environment and a particularly high mortality in childbirth. However, with the coming of better health care and improved living conditions for all, the innate superiority of females was allowed to surface so that now they greatly outlive men.

This reasoning, however, seems to overlook the oft-noted finding that women, especially older women, are less healthy than men. Riley and Foner (1968) report that women over 65 experience more days per

---

[1]These were selected because they represent topics on which significant research relevant to stereotypes of older women has been reported.

[2]Brotman (1973) reports that in the United States expectancy at birth is 74.0 years for females and 66.6 years for males, a difference of 7.4 years. By age 65, the differential has diminished but remains a significant 3.5 years.

year of restricted activity, more days of bed-disability, more doctor's visits, and higher expenditures for health care than do men of the same age.[3] If the aged female is, indeed, less healthy than her male counterpart, how then does she manage to survive longer? At least two possible explanations can be drawn from research reports from the Duke longitudinal study of aging.[4]

One resolution of the paradox of women's greater longevity and poorer health rests on the argument that women are *not* less healthy than men but do have a greater tendency than men to underrate their health and to seek medical care more readily. This argument is strongly related to the stereotypical notion that women, especially old women, are often hypochondriacs, constantly complaining about their imaginary illnesses. Its corollary assumption holds that men often overrate their health or ignore health problems in an attempt to fulfill a sociocultural expectation that men ought to be strong, healthy, and stoical in the face of pain (Maddox, 1964). This might explain findings that women are less healthy than men if such findings are based on self-reported health status. An analysis of the Duke panel data by Dovenmuehle, Busse, and Newman (1961) found that, in terms of physician-rated health and functioning, there was no significant difference between older males and females — an observation that came from a cross-sectional analysis of longitudinal data carried out by Heyman and Jeffers (1963) also indicates that changes in physical functioning were not significantly related to sex. That is, the decline in health status experienced by women was little different from that of men. Both of these findings were based on actual physical examinations and physicians' ratings of health status. Moreover, the individual's own subjective assessment of his health status also was considered, Heyman and Jeffers reported that changes in self-assessed health status did not vary significantly by sex. In addition, Maddox and Douglass (1973) observed no significant differences between males and females with regard to over or underestimation. They did report, however, that the overly optimistic group tended to

---

[3]Older women also have a higher incidence of both acute and chronic illnesses than older men, although the men are found to have a greater number of physical impairments, a situation almost wholly attributable to their higher injury rate.

[4]Since all studies discussed in this section employ data from the Duke panel, it seems appropriate before detailing these positions to discuss briefly the study design. Conceived as an exploratory, comprehensive, multidisciplinary investigation, the research commenced in 1955 with initial interviews of 271 non-institutionalized community volunteers between 60 and 94 years old. It has continued to retest the survivors at periodic intervals of approximately two to three years. The original panel, though not a random sample, was created to reflect the age, sex, racial, and socioeconomic distributions of the elderly population in Durham, North Carolina. Approximately 52 percent of the panel were females, and all data were available by sex.

be male and the overly pessimistic group female, although these ten-
dencies were not significant. On the basis of the evidence from analyses of the Duke data, then, it appears that neither objective nor
subjective physical health differentiates between the sexes. While there
may exist a slight tendency among aged women to underrate their
health, it certainly fails to justify stereotyping them as hypochondriacs.

An alternative hypothesis which emphasizes environmental rather
than constitutional differences holds that women have greater longevity because they work in less dangerous and less stressful occupations, are less subject to violent death due to war, homicide, suicide,
or accident, smoke less than men, and so on (Palmore and Jeffers,
1971). To test the relative importance of social, psychological, and
physical factors for longevity, Palmore (1969a; 1969b; 1974) conducted
a series of analyses of data from the Duke panel.[5] He dichotomized the
sex groups into two age cohorts (60-69 and 70+) enabling comparisons
between age-sex categories. The significant predictor variables for
men under 70 proved to be, in order of strength, amount of cigarette
smoking, cardiovascular disease, and work satisfaction, while for the
older men cardiovascular disease was the strongest predictor, followed
by work satisfaction and health self-rating. Physical factors, then, are
strongly implicated for both groups of men, although the significant
presence of work satisfaction "seems to indicate the continuing importance of meaningful social roles for the longevity of older men"
(Palmore, 1974). Among the younger women, cardiovascular disease
and physical function are equally strong predictors, while happiness,
performance IQ, and socioeconomic status are significant for those
over 70. Thus, the pattern for the women in their 60s, as for the
younger men, is one in which physical variables are salient. But in
contrast to their male counterparts, women surviving past 70 show
little dependence on health measures; rather, their longevity seems
contingent on psychological and social variables.

In a similar sort of analysis, Pfeiffer (1970) observed a somewhat
different pattern. He found that, although the sexes were similar on
some variables, economics appeared to be more critical overall for
males since their current financial status not only ranked first among

---

[5]He was attempting to improve upon actuarial predictions of life expectancy (which are
normally based only on age, race, and sex) by employing a number of social,
psychological, and physical variables as predictors of longevity within a multiple
regression framework. Because the technique was refined for each new analysis and
because Palmore states that the more recent refinement allows an increased number of
variables and cases to be used in the regression and substantially increases the amount
of variance explained, only these latest findings will be considered.

the men but failed to attain significance altogether for the females.[6] Marital status appeared to be more important for older females than for the older males, with married individuals benefitting in terms of added years of life, although the finding seems to contradict the fact that mortality of single persons is more marked for males than for females (Speigelman, 1963). Rose (1971) speculates upon the possibilities "that health as a selective factor for entry into marriage plays a less important role for females than for males, or that single life is less dangerous for women than for men," because of the single male's high rate of violent death. Presumably, however, the older male is less subject to situations (war, crime, etc.) which fuel this statistic, and might, therefore, find single life more agreeable than do older women. Yet the most striking difference revealed by this analysis is the importance of IQ as an influence on the older female's longevity. Pfeiffer does not try to explain this finding and neither will an attempt be made here. It does, however, offer an interesting contrast between the sexes, one which, coupled with Palmore's identification of performance IQ as a significant predictor among women over 70, deserves further study.

Marital Status and Family Roles

Stereotype: Older Women are Usually Either Widowed or Never-married

While most older women are widowed (53 percent), a relatively large number (38 percent) are married and only about 9 percent have never married or are divorced. These figures are in stark contrast to those for males, however, which reveal that 77 percent of older men are married and that fewer than 16 percent are widowed (U.S. Department of Health, Education and Welfare, 1973). Obviously these disparities are indicative of the longevity differential between women and men, but they also reflect the higher rates of remarriage for men after both divorce and widowhood and the fact that, as at all ages, older men tend to marry women younger than themselves.

But whatever her marital status, there are stereotypical images and

---

[6]The strongest predictors of female longevity among older women were: (1) IQ; (2) perception of health change; (3) marital status; (4) physical functioning rating; and (5) change in financial status. For the older men, the factors which were significantly correlated with longevity included: (1) financial status; (2) perception of health change; (3) physical functioning rating; (4) change in financial status; (5) marital status.

expectations attached to each role the older woman is called upon to perform. To explore the relationship between image and reality, the discussion now turns its focus to aspects of the older woman's performance of one major marital role — that of sex partner[7] and the post-marital role of widow.

Sexual Behavior of the Older Woman

Stereotype: The Older Woman is Both Sexually Inactive and Sexually Uninterested

One of the most persistent and pernicious stereotypes of older women is that of asexuality.[8] While it is true that age is the most important factor affecting the frequency of sexual activity for both sexes, there is ample evidence to topple this widely-held myth. For instance, Masters and Johnson (1966) describe the biological changes experienced by older females which are related to sexual activity and point out that none of these changes prevent or even inhibit a rewarding sex life. They report that their research demonstrates that "the aging female is fully capable of sexual performance at orgasmic response levels." However, as Peterson and Payne (1975:63) point out, "Both Kinsey [1948; 1953] and Masters and Johnson [1966] suggest that how a woman reacts sexually in the later years may be a matter of her sexual history. Those women who have had sexually rewarding marriages move through the menopausal and post-menopausal years with little change in frequency of or interest in sex. On the other hand if a woman had an unsatisfactory sexual life, she may welcome her advanced years as an excuse to forget sex." Furthermore, the extent of heterosexual activity of the aging woman is determined by the availability of a partner and, unlike for the aging male, is determined by her partner's sexual capacity, not hers.

Reports from the Duke longitudinal study reveal some interesting differences between the older men and women in sexual interest and activity. Older men of all ages were found to exhibit greater interest in sex, both in terms of incidence and degree, and to report more sexual activity than women. The age-related pattern for both sexes, however, was one of gradual decline in both interest and activity. By the mid-seventies, the discrepancy in sexual interest between females and males, so apparent during the sixties, has been greatly reduced, al-

---

[7]Certainly, the role of sex partner is not necessarily limited to marriage, but the term "marital" is employed in the absence of a more general one.

[8]Of course, this applies to both males and females but is at least partially offset for males by their competing image as "dirty old men."

though men still maintain much higher levels of activity than women. This activity differential was found to be largely a function of marital status, however. That is, although the married and unmarried men were little different in level of sexual interest or activity, unmarried females, deprived of a socially acceptable sex partner, had a very low incidence of sexual activity relative to their married counterparts. It is interesting to note, however, that marital status had little effect on the older woman's *interest* in sex (Verwoerdt, Pfeiffer and Wang, 1969). Although neither married nor unmarried women reported a high degree of sexual interest, the two most common reasons given for cessation of intercourse were death and impotence of the husband. Moreover, the older men agreed, giving their own impotence, *not* their wives' lack of interest, as the primary reason for the discontinuation of sexual activity (Pfeiffer, Verwoerdt and Wang, 1968). In short, ". . . the extent of an aging woman's sexual activity and interest depends heavily on the availability to her of a societally sanctioned, sexually capable partner" (Pfeiffer and Davis, 1972).

Most women must expect to spend a major portion of their lives as widows without access to partners. This is due in large measure to the shorter life expectancy of men, but it is also due to the fact that women at all ages tend to marry older men. For example, Carter and Glick (1970) found that age was the most powerful factor in the process of marital selection. They point out that three out of four American husbands are older than their wives and that the age differential increases from 2.5 years for first-marriage couples to 6-10 years for couples remarrying after age 55. McKain (1969) found that, among 100 couples over 60, husbands were older than their wives in 85 percent of the cases and that the age disparity ranged from two to eighteen years. For this reason, Pfeiffer (1969) warns that ". . . to exhort [older women] to an active sexual life when none is available would be cruel advice indeed." This interpretation assumes, however, that older women will continue to be culturally defined as inappropriate mates or sex partners for younger men.

Older Widows

Stereotype: The Older Woman is a Happily Married "Wife for Life" (Hers, Not His) Who, Even in Widowhood, Retains a Sense of Personal Identity Based on that of Her Sainted Husband

Just as those older women who are married seem to experience marriage in different ways, some of which are not altogether pleasant,[9] so do widows respond to the trauma of widowhood in various ways. Nevertheless, the disproportionate number of widowed elderly females has generated much research on this topic, including that of Lopata (1973) and Blau (1973), and some regularities and relationships have become apparent.

Lopata points out that getting married is a *rite de passage* from girlhood to womanhood and thus is highly significant to the identity development of most women. Therefore, the female who gains her major identity and self-esteem from the marital role, experiences more loss at widowhood than at retirement. The converse is true for the male, however, whose personal and social identity is more dependent on the work role (Blau, 1973). Moreover, the extent and direction of a widow's identity crisis is affected by her educational level and by the social class location achieved in marriage. According to Lopata, those widows with higher education and those from working class marriages experienced less of a crisis. These findings reflect the fact that in American society women are socialized to be wives and mothers and not to have alternative identities available at any stage of life. As a consequence, women are affected by marriage more than men. Being a wife and being the wife of a particular man whose involvements reflexively give importance to his woman is still the focus of life for most women.

The concept of the female as a poor financial manager is reinforced by the reported stress experienced by the widows of Lopata's sample when they were faced with financial decisions. In the process of bereavement, widows tended to feel incompetent to deal with crises and serious problems, such as financial matters and major social decisions (Lopata, 1973), a situation which likely reflects the long exclusion of women from formal and informal training in money management. Although most older widows work outside the home at some time during their adult life, the findings of both Blau and Lopata reinforce

---

[9]Peterson and Payne (1975), in a review of a number of studies of marital satisfaction, developed a typology of marriages which discriminates between the different marital experiences of older women: (1) long-duration first marriages which were contracted before age 25; (2) middle-age marriages contracted after the first marriage was broken by divorce or death; and (3) retirement marriages which were contracted after age 60. Women in Type 1 marriages tend to experience decreased marital satisfaction in late life. Blood and Wolfe (1960) found that only 6 percent of the respondent wives were fully satisfied with marriage after 20 years or longer and that the trends of dissatisfaction continue. Based on this finding and that of Pineo (1961) showing a negative correlation between duration of marriage and marital satisfaction, women in Type 2 (middle age) and Type 3 (retirement) marriages would be expected to experience greater satisfaction than those in Type 1 marriages. McKain's (1969) analysis of 100 retirement marriages tends to support this assumption, since 75 percent of the marriages he studied were successful and highly rewarding to both husbands and wives.

the image of the older woman as an "uncommitted" worker whose work career has been erratic and related primarily to the family welfare or economic necessity. At least for this generation of older women, the wife-mother roles have taken precedence over the worker role, and, in fact, the idea of commitment to a professional or work role appears inconsistent with the older women's image of the female role.

On the other hand, most widows learn to live alone, often for the first time in their lives, and few older widows reported that they would like to remarry. Although many complained of loneliness, they also confessed a great enjoyment of their new-found independence and freedom (Lopata, 1973). Such expressions seem contradictory of the myth that all widows want to remarry so they can continue the "wife" role. The findings suggest, however, that most older women are adequately socialized to the wife role as the appropriate and primary adult role for the female, but that they usually achieve this early in life as young women. Once the woman has met this social expectation — changing from Miss to Mrs. — widowhood does not strip her of this achievement, but frees her to experience the independence denied at earlier periods in her life. This may in fact be a form of liberation her younger sisters cannot achieve.

The older the woman at widowhood, the more likely she is to have known her present friends prior to the death of the husband; that is, older widows continue to see old friends who are still married, or at least consider these people to be friends (Lopata, 1973). Blau also observes that widowhood not only affects the friendship participation of males and females in a different fashion, but it has a different impact on women under seventy than it does on women over seventy. Widowhood has adverse effects *only* when it places a person in a position different from that of most of his age-sex peers. Thus, older couples, being different from their age-sex peers who are mostly widows, therefore, have less friendship participation with them. Older widows then, because they are similar to most of their friends, are in a better position for continuing friendship ties than is commonly believed, better even than married persons of the same age.

Leisure

Stereotype: The Older Woman is Often Depicted as a Pleasantly Plump Granny Who Spends Her Time in a Rocking Chair Knitting or Sewing

Accompanying the increase in life expectancy achieved in this century has been an increase in leisure time for adults. These gains in leisure time have come mainly among skilled and semi-skilled workers, persons over 60 years of age, and women, but the adults with the most free time are women over 60. Yet, the image of the rocker-bound granny hardly squares with that of a Foster Grandmother or a Gray Panther. The impact of increased, and sometimes forced, leisure on the social behavior of old people, especially women, and the way in which they structure their "bulk non-work time" are areas of much needed research. Although existing research tends to focus on a determination of the negative changes in leisure activities and habits that accompany aging and not on the voluntary structuring of leisure for self-fulfillment (Dumazedier, 1974:92-93), there are a few studies which yield some insight into sex differences in the use of leisure time.

DeGrazia (1961) and the National Recreation Survey (1962) report that hours spent on various leisure activities other than reading was not significantly different for the sexes, although women spent slightly more time than men reading and on household duties. However, both Havighurst's Kansas City Adult Study (1961) and Payne's study of adult leisure behavior in the Eastern United States (1973) found that in general the favorite activity of women involved formal and informal associations and reading, while men preferred sports, fishing and gardening. Additional sex differences in these studies are reflected in the following: (1) formal associations lose attractiveness for men as age changes from 40 to 70 though not among women until they reach the 60s; (2) informal groups are most attractive to men in the 50-60 age group but are equally attractive at all ages to women; (3) there is a sharp falling away from participation in sports for men in their 60s; and (4) in general, people in their 60s favor the more solitary activities of gardening and manual-manipulative projects, e.g., sewing and handcrafts for women and shopcrafts for men (Havighurst, 1961; Payne, 1973).

Payne also observed that women highly ranked such activities as church and volunteer work, gardening, cooking, playing with children, television viewing, and radio listening. Furthermore, most older women still prefer the activity they enjoyed most five years ago and expect little change in preference during the next five years. Women's liberation advocates point out that these are the activities which the female has been socialized to enjoy most; that is, they are normative leisure activities for the female.

Pfeiffer and Davis' study (1971) on the use of leisure at middle life is important in focusing on the potential problems adults will be experiencing in leisure. They observed that more men than women would still work even if they did not have to, that they derive more satisfaction from work than from leisure activities. As the percentage of women employed outside the home increases, we can expect this observed sex difference to become less. Women were found to complain of too little free time between the ages of 46 and 55 which is traditionally regarded as the crisis period for women due to the menopause, the "empty nest" syndrome, and the possibility for middle age employment. In contrast, the crisis for men seems to come immediately following retirement, between 66 and 71 years of age, when they complained of too *much* time.

Obviously, there are a variety of styles for the organization of leisure time and a wide range of possible activities from which to choose. One such style is that of participation in voluntary associations, and after a brief discussion of general sex differences relative to such participation, two specific types — religious and volunteer — will be examined.

Voluntary Association Participation

Stereotype: Older Women Participate in Few Voluntary Associations Other Than the Church

The proliferation and diffusion of voluntary associations accompanying urbanization, particularly in the United States, have led to the generalization by many sociologists that we are a nation of joiners. Although the present population of older people has been a part of this urban social development, only about 4 percent of them report a significant amount of participation in voluntary associations (Riley and Foner, 1968). Most studies relating sex to membership and participation in voluntary associations have found men to hold more membership and to participate more than women (Lynd and Lynd, 1937; Komarovsky, 1946; Wright and Hyman, 1958; Babchuk and Booth, 1969). However, Hausknecht (1962), in an analysis and comparison of two major national surveys, the AIPO and NORC, reports that men and women join associations in equal numbers. Lundberg, et al. (1934), Bushee (1945), and Mayo (1950) found that women participate as much or more than men. The conflict in the research findings results from variations in what types of groups are included as voluntary associations, e.g. inclusion/exclusion of unions, church and church groups, etc.

Types of membership are consistently reported to vary by sex. Women belong to more religious or "do goodism" organizations (service-oriented voluntarism) than men (see, for example, Fichter, 1954; Argyle, 1959; Schuyler, 1959; and Lazerwitz, 1961). Some organizations, many of which are church-related, restrict membership to one sex, and the variation reflects cultural definitions of what is appropriate for men and what for women. Therefore, a greater number of men than women belong to civic and service organizations which include Lions, Kiwanis and certain lodges and fraternal organizations like the Shriners because these organizations are functional for men's occupations and careers (Hausknecht, 1962).

Researchers noting the effect of age on participation have found that membership and participation increase into the middle years and then decline. The decline is less for women than for men and is related to socio-economic status (Foskett, 1955; Payne, Payne and Reddy, 1972). In France, Dumazedier (1974) reports that although men are more likely to belong to political associations, trade unions, friendly societies, and charitable organizations (38 percent vs. 18 percent), women are more likely to be active participants. These sex differentials may be due to the fact that many memberships held by older people tend to be those also held in the middle years which have persisted into late life. Although continued emeritus or retired-benefit membership exists in professional and labor union organizations, the disengagement that takes place is most likely to be from formal organizations related to work. Participation in religious, civic, and fraternal organizations declines least.

Religious Participation

Stereotype: Women are More Religious Than Men at Every Stage of the Life Cycle and Particularly so in Old Age

Although religion is generally assumed to become increasingly important with old age, research data are limited in the use of the sex variable, since major studies of religion and aging have generally neglected sex differences (Glock, 1962; Moberg, 1965; Glock, Ringer and Barbee, 1967; Stark, 1968; Bahr, 1968). However, most of the research evidence does support the popular notion that women are more religious than men in every stage of the life cycle. Church attendance is generally maintained at a high level among old people in their 60s but becomes less regular with advanced old age. Furthermore, older women regardless of marital status are more active in church participation than men (Albrecht, 1958). Although regular attendance for both sexes drops at age 75 and continues to decline, it declines more for women than men (Taietz and Larson, 1956; Cumming and Henry, 1961; Orbach, 1961).

Several studies which focused on the meaning of religion in the lives of the elderly report that fewer women than men say that religion does not mean much to them, and that a majority of the women reported religion was the most important thing in their lives (Taves and Hanson, 1963). In a study of adult patterns of leisure, older women were the only group of respondents that ranked church and church work as a favorite leisure activity (Payne, 1974).

These studies generally support the stereotype of the increased religiosity of older women and their reliance upon the church for social activity. Dumazedier's summary of a number of French and American studies demonstrates that the rate of religious participation continues for Americans after retirement, while it declines for the older French person. But, even so, religion is more important to the older French women than men, and fewer older women withdraw from participation than men (Dumazedier, 1974).

Volunteering

Stereotype: The Typical Service Volunteer is a Vigorous, Young, or Middle-aged Woman

The worth and talents of the older adult volunteer are receiving national attention as many agencies and organizations incorporate volunteer positions for the elderly into their formal structures. By 1980 the older volunteer is expected to make up an increasing portion of the $30 billion estimated to be contributed annually by volunteers to the economy (Wolozin, 1968). A 1974 Harris Poll reported that 20 percent of people over 65 were engaged in volunteer service of some type and that an additional 10 percent said that they were interested in volunteer activity (Havighurst, 1975). While there is no precise count, it is generally estimated that women constitute a majority of the estimated 50 million American volunteers (Perlis, 1975). Sex role differences in volunteer activity throughout the life cycle and the disproportionate number of females in the older age group lead us to conclude that older women and men might be expected to experience volunteering differently.

In reviewing the literature on the volunteer, we found no studies of older volunteers which were restricted to one sex. Although all studies reported that the older volunteers were overwhelmingly female and widowed (60 to 80 percent), sex differences in volunteer behavior (activity) are either not found to be significant or they are ignored (Monk and Cryns, 1974; Rosenblatt, 1964; Dye, et al., 1973; Carp, 1968; Babic, 1972). One exception, the Sainer and Zander (1971) study of *Serve* (a research and demonstration project), found that, unlike the females, the majority of the male volunteers had had no previous volunteer or civic work experience. In addition, more women than men served in senior centers, hospitals, and homes for the aged. The older women seemed to view volunteering as an expressive role, i.e., helping others, doing good. In contrast, the men were concerned with finding a substitute for work and being useful, which reflects an instrumental role gratification in volunteering. Women, however, dropped out sooner than men and gave fewer extra hours.

Payne (1975) also reports that women seem to continue to experience volunteering as they always have, as expressive or socio-emotional rather than instrumental. However, in some of the new settings for older volunteering such as the Shepherd's Center in Kansas City, women are finding in volunteer roles the values and social status normally associated with work; that is, volunteer roles are becoming instrumental roles for the women also. In such contexts women report volunteer satisfaction and positive attitudes toward volunteering that were not experienced in earlier years. No longer is volunteering just the giving of free service but is now the acquisition of a new social status and self-fulfillment.[10]

CONCLUSION

The preceding examination of a number of popular stereotypes about older women suggests several conclusions. First, it seems clear that most of the stereotypes discussed characterize older women in very negative terms and that most, if not all, originate within the dominant American culture. That is, the popular view of older women as weak, ineffective, inactive, asexual old maids or widows is deeply rooted in the American image of both older people and women. Both are groups which have traditionally fared quite badly in

---

[10]However, as the number of volunteer programs for and recruitment of older people (especially women) are accelerated, warnings have been raised that some of these programs could be just another subtle form of sexist exploitation designed to extract free labor from women, in this case older women.

this country's social and economic marketplace and which continue to suffer discrimination motivated, at least in part, by such negative stereotypical images. Since this kind of discrimination often reinforces the stereotype, and given the dual disadvantage of being old and female, it is not surprising that older women have reaped a double whirlwind of negative stereotypes.

It has also been clearly demonstrated that most of the stereotypes analyzed above are patently false and grossly misleading. Certainly, our review of the research evidence reveals that older women are not significantly weaker, sicker or more hypochondriacal than older men. We have shown that the older woman is not devoid of either sexual feeling or satisfaction, that widowhood is not necessarily a social and emotional grave for older women, that leisure time is not always spent inactively or in lonely solitude, and that new roles, such as volunteer work, are emerging which promise a new kind of psychological payoff for older women. We have also found, however, that not all stereotypes of older women are entirely invalid. For example, it is true that association with religious organizations and participation in church related activities are still the overwhelming norm among this generation of older women. This, of course, does not justify stereotyping all older women as religious; it merely demonstrates a fundamental truth about stereotypes — that there is often a kernel of truth, and sometimes a statistical norm, at the core of most of them.

Not all stereotypes are totally culturally based and promulgated, however. Many researchers have directly and indirectly contributed to their popular acceptance. For example, our review points up two important methodological failings of much of the research on older people which can produce false or misleading findings. The first is that of ignoring a basic rule of social research which is, "To describe the whole is not always to describe the parts." The strategy to aggregating data may sometimes be deemed necessary, but such an approach, when reason exists to suspect subgroup differences, is liable to have spurious results. This is especially true, it seems, with respect to the sex classification. Commonalities are certainly apparent, but so many differences abound that the researcher of aging ignores them at his peril. The second and related notion is expressed in Rashi Fein's (1965) dictum: "Always we shall compare." That is, a single observation is of limited utility until it is compared with a standard. Thus, it has become commonplace now to decry cross-sectional research in favor of the superior longitudinal design. Likewise, information about one category is not fully meaningful until it has been measured against similar data on its comparison group. Knowledge of widows, then, without accompanying facts about widowers is, at best, incomplete. The real danger, however, is that of committing the logical fallacy of ascribing observed-group traits to the unobserved group. Moreover, when sex is employed as an independent variable, it is often treated as a demographic characteristic merely to be controlled. In reality, however, sex is more than just a physical distinction; it is also a sociological shorthand which can be used to symbolize the complex of social differences between women and men. This means that by holding sex constant, one actually is seeking to approximate the different social statuses and role expectations of the two sexes. Ryder (1965), Riley, Johnson and Foner (1972), and others have pointed up the necessity of treating age as a sociological variable and not just a controllable nuisance; the same holds true for sex. It is proposed, then, that future research on aging not only include women in its samples but also pay attention to the similarities and differences which become apparent when the sexes are compared.

There are, in addition, a number of other steps which researchers can take to avoid contributing to stereotypical images of older women. First, many older studies need to be replicated, but the research instruments employed must be carefully examined for bias reflecting cultural stereotypes of older women. In both these and newly-conceived investigations researchers must handle their findings in a scientifically rigorous manner, taking care to avoid easy generalizations. Just as older people are not a homogeneous group, neither are older women. As noted above, investigators too often focus on broadly defined groups, neglecting the sometimes contradictory patterns of subpopulations in favor of aggregate uniformity. This strategy may deliver an economical overview of the situation, but it also may mask crucial information. In fact, our own conclusions are open to question at this point because of this weakness in nearly all the data we cited. It is necessary, therefore, to include in the analysis such social and demographic variables as race, rural-urban residence, socioeconomic status, and education which are employed to subdivide the sex groups according to relevant criteria.

The review also raises a number of substantive issues and suggests several fruitful avenues for additional research on older women. First, it is clear that longevity for both males and females depends on a combination of physical and environmental influences, although the mix is not the same for both sexes. Not so clear are the meanings which should be attached to some of the predictor variables and relationships, if any, between them. For instance, to what factors might the happiness which contributed to long life among the older females be attributed? To continuing intellectual capacity? To socioeconomic security? And if the link between cigarette smoking and heart disease, apparent for males under 70, is so well known, why is cardiovascular disease, apparently an important predictor, unaccompanied by the smoking variable among the older men and the younger women? Plainly, further work is needed (perhaps with a path analysis design) to clarify the interrelations of the predictor variables. Until relationships between physical factors (like cardiovascular disease) and social and psychological factors (like cigarette smoking) can be specified for both males and females, it will be difficult to determine with certainty why women live longer than men.

Research in the area of marital statuses and roles has centered on the aged female's adaptation to widowhood. Little, if any, effort has been made to study widowers, probably because of the stereotyped view that males encounter little difficulty in adjusting to this new situation. After all, if the wife's death occurs prior to his retirement, the husband still maintains the work role as a major compensation for loss of the marital role. He is also seen as more likely to remarry and to do so without delay. The fact is that so little actual research has been done that few of these assertions can be supported. Research is also needed on occupants of the other marital statuses — divorcees, single never-married persons, intact couples, and aged newlyweds.

Cultural changes which become socially and psychologically imprinted upon a younger cohort are inevitably destined to be transmitted in some form through the age strata as the cohort grows older. Such changes are certain to have some immediate effect on older cohorts as well. It is, thus, a reasonable assumption, given the present revolution in sexual attitudes and habits among the young, that the sexual relationships of future generations of older persons will be vastly different from those of today's elderly. Given the observed trend of a gradual lessening of sexual desire among the aged, long-term longitudinal studies of changing sexual habits among the elderly are needed to determine the effects of cultural and generational changes relative to the effects associated with the aging process.

Several other topics also seem ripe for investigation. One is the changing roles and involvement of the older woman in religious organizations. Is she beginning to assume a more active leadership function in church activities, and what effect would such a trend have on male participation? One might also wonder whether ever-increasing amounts of leisure time for males coupled with the growing economic participation of women might bring the male and female to old age with a more similar approach to leisure activities. Or, will more leisure for everyone open up new leisure opportunities which may lead the sexes in different directions? Will the increasing number of women retiring from jobs at 62 or 65 choose retirement patterns similar to, or different from, those of men?

Belonging to voluntary associations other than church is less widespread among old people than for other age groups in the population. This lower rate of participation might be due to an exclusion of older people from active membership and leadership roles, or it might be a response of the older people to the social expectation that they turn these roles over to younger people. However, low participation rates may be due to cohort-specific negative attitudes toward voluntary associations themselves. Thus, studies are needed which will document both the nature of those attitudes and the changing character of the available roles. Additional research questions raised by Riley and Foner (1968) in their summary of research on voluntary associations are also significant. What changes have been occurring in association membership among older people? What are the implications of membership for individuals: does it stimulate their interest, provide them with new friends, afford opportunities to serve community goals? In addition, studies are needed which link the participation of men and women in all non-work activities — religious, recreational, and voluntary — throughout the life cycle. For it is these sorts of activities which, in old age, provide role continuity and help structure lives.

Finally, it seems reasonable to expect that the dramatic cultural changes which continue to occur will cause future cohorts of older women to differ markedly from the present generation. These changes are probably best exemplified by the liberationist goal of providing women with equal access to all social roles and statuses and reducing the differential in role performance and expectations. It is understandable that the initial focus of the movement would be directed toward the major life roles of younger women who dominate the movement. However, recently attention has begun to be paid to the peculiar position of older women and the double standard of aging in our society. Moreover, as the contemporary younger woman grows older, she may expect to continue in old age to experience the advantages she has gained as a young woman but will likely find her hard-won liberation being eroded by age discrimination and replaced by a new form of bondage. If so, today's liberationist could be tomorrow's Gray Panther, and the phrase, "Granny, get your gun!" might presage a completion of the liberation of women and the beginning of the liberation of the elders.

REFERENCES

Albrecht, Ruth
1958 "The meaning of religion to the older person." Pp. 53-70 in Delton L. Scudder (ed.), Organized Religion and the Older Person. Gainesville: University of Florida Press.

Argyle, Michael
1959 Religious Behavior. Glencoe, Illinois: The Free Press.

Babchuk, Nicholas and Alan Booth
1969 "Voluntary association membership: a longitudinal analysis." American Sociological Review 34(February):31-45.

Babic, Anna L.
1972 "The older volunteer: expectations and satisfactions." Gerontologist (Spring):87-90.

Bahr, Howard M.
1970 "Aging and religious disaffiliation." Social Forces 49(September):59-71.

Blau, Zena Smith
1973 Old Age in a Changing Society. New York: New Viewpoints.

Blood, Robert O., Jr., and Donald N. Wolfe
1960 Husbands and Wives: The Dynamics of Married Living. Glencoe, Illinois: The Free Press.

Brotman, Herman B.
1973 "Who are the aging?" Pp. 21-39 in Ewald W. Busse and Eric Pfeiffer (eds.), Mental Illness in Later Life. Washington, D.C.: American Psychiatric Association.

Bushee, Frederick A.
1945 "Social organization in a small city." American Journal of Sociology 51:217-226.

Carp, Frances M.
1968 "Differences among older workers, volunteers, and persons who are neither." Journal of Gerontology 23(October):497-501.

Carter, Hugh and Paul C. Glick
1970 Marriage and Divorce: A Social and Economic Study. Cambridge, Mass: Harvard University Press.

Cumming, Elaine and William E. Henry
1961 Growing Old. New York: Basic Books.

de Grazia, Sebastian
1961 "The uses of time." Pp. 113-154 in Robert W. Kleemier (ed.) Aging and Leisure. New York: Oxford University Press.

Dovenmuehle, Robert H., Ewald W. Busse, and Gustave Newman
1961 "Physical problems of older people." Journal of the American Geriatrics Society 9:208-217.

Dumazedier, Joffre
1974 Sociology of Leisure. Trans. Marea A. McKenzie. New York: Elsevier.

Dye, David, Mortimer Goodman, Melvin Roth, Nina Bley, and Kathryn Jensen
1973 "The older volunteer compared to the non-volunteer." Gerontologist 13(Summer):215-218.

Fein, Rashi
1965 "An economic and social profile of the Negro American." Daedalus 94(Fall):815-846.

Fichter, Joseph
    1954 Social Relations in the Urban Parish. Chicago: University of Chicago Press.
Foskett, John M.
    1955 "Social structure and social participation." American Sociological Review 20(August):431-438.
Glock, Charles Y.
    1962 "On the study of religious commitment." Religious Education, Research Supplement 57:98-110.
Glock, Charles, Benjamin B. Ringer, and Earl Barbee
    1967 To Comfort and To Challenge: A Dilemma of the Contemporary Church. Berkeley: University of California Press.
Hausknecht, Murray
    1962 The Joiners: A Sociological Description of Voluntary Association Membership in the United States. New York: Bedminster Press.
Havighurst, Robert J.
    1961 "The nature and values of meaningful freetime activity." In Robert W. Kleemeir (ed.), Aging and Leisure. New York: Oxford University Press.
    1975 "The future aged: the use of time and money." Gerontologist 15(February, Part II):10-15.
Heyman, Dorothy K. and Frances C. Jeffers
    1963 "Effect of time lapse on consistency of self-health and medical evaluations of elderly persons." Journal of Gerontology 18(April):160-164.
Kinsey, A. C., W. B. Pomeroy, and C. R. Martin
    1948 Sexual Behavior in the Human Male. Philadelphia: W. B. Saunders.
Kinsey, A. C., W. B. Pomeroy, C. R. Martin, and P. H. Gebhard
    1953 Sexual Behavior in the Human Female. Philadelphia: W. B. Saunders.
Komarovsky, Mirra
    1946 "The voluntary associations of urban dwellers." American Sociological Review 11(December):686-698.
Lazerwitz, Bernard
    1961 "Some factors associated with variation in church attendance." Social Forces 39(May):301-309.
Lopata, Helena Znaniecki
    1973 Widowhood in an American City. Cambridge, Mass.: Schenkman.
Lundberg, George A., Mirra Komorovsky, and Mary A. McInery
    1934 Leisure: A Suburban Study. New York: Columbia University Press.
Lynd, Robert S. and Helen M. Lynd
    1937 Middletown in Transition. New York: Harcourt.
Maddox, George L.
    1964 "Self-assessment of health status." Journal of Chronic Diseases 17(January):449-460.
Maddox, George L. and Elizabeth B. Douglass
    1973 "Self-assessment of health." Journal of Health and Social Behavior 14(March):87-93.
Masters, William H. and Virginia E. Johnson
    1966 Human Sexual Response. Boston: Little, Brown & Company.
Mayo, Selz C.
    1950 "Age profiles of social participation in rural areas of Wake County, N.C." Rural Sociology 15:242-251.
McKain, Walter C.
    1969 Retirement Marriages. Storrs, Conn.: Storrs Agricultural Experiment

Station, Monograph 3(January).

Moberg, David O.
1965 "Religiosity of old age." Gerontologist 5(June):78-87.

Monk, Abraham and Arthur G. Cryns
1974 "Predictors of voluntaristic intent among the aged." Gerontologist 14(October):425-429.

Orbach, Harold L.
1961 "Aging and religion: a study of church attendance in the Detroit metropolitan area." Geriatrics 16:530-540.

Outdoor Recreation Resources Review Commission
1962 National Recreation Survey, Study Report 19. Washington, D.C.: Government Printing Office.

Palmore, Erdman B.
1969a "Physical, mental, and social factors in predicting longevity." Gerontologist 9(Summer):103-108.
1969b "Predicting longevity: a follow-up controlling for age." Gerontologist 9(Winter):247-250.
1974 "Predicting longevity: a new method." Pp. 281-285 in Erdman Palmore (ed.), Normal Aging II. Durham, North Carolina: Duke University Press.

Palmore, Erdman and Frances C. Jeffers
1971 Prediction of Life Span. Lexington, Mass.: Heath Lexington Books.

Payne, Barbara P.
1973a "Adult patterns of leisure in the Piedmont region." Unpublished report for National Park Service.
1973b "Age differences in the meaning of leisure activities." Paper presented at the Annual Meeting of the Gerontological Society, Miami Beach, Florida.
1975 "The elderly woman volunteer: sex differences in role continuity." Paper presented at the Annual Meeting of the Society for the Study of Social Problems, San Francisco, California.

Payne, Raymond, Barbara P. Payne, and Richard Reddy
1972 "Social background and role determinants of individual participation in organized voluntary action." Pp. 207-250 in David H. Smith, Richard D. Reddy, and Burt R. Baldwin (eds.), Voluntary Action Research. Lexington, Mass.: D. C. Heath Company.

Perlis, Leo
1975 "The role of the volunteer." Interaction 3(February).

Peterson, James A. and Barbara Payne
1975 Love in the Later Years. New York: Association Press.

Pfeiffer, Eric
1969 "Sexual behavior in old age." Pp. 151-162 in Ewald W. Busse and Eric Pfeiffer (eds.), Behavior and Adaptation in Late Life. Boston: Little, Brown & Company.
1970 "Survival in old age: physical, psychological, and social correlates of longevity." Journal of the American Geriatrics Society 18(April):273-285.

Pfeiffer, Eric and Glenn C. Davis
1971 "The use of leisure time in middle life." Gerontologist 11:187-195.
1972 "Determinants of sexual behavior in middle and old age." Journal of the American Geriatrics Society 20:151-158.

Pfeiffer, Eric, Adriaan Verwoerdt, and Hsioh-Shan Wang
1968 "Sexual behavior in aged men and women." Archives for General Psychiatry 19:756-758.

Pineo, Peter C.
1961 "Disenchantment in the later years of marriage." Marriage and Family Living 23:3-11.
Riley, Matilda White and Anne Foner (eds.)
1968 Aging and Society. Vol. 1: An Inventory of Research Findings. New York: Russell Sage Foundation.
Riley, Matilda White, Marilyn Johnson and Anne Foner (eds.)
1972 Aging and Society. Vol. 3: A Sociology of Age Stratification. New York: Russell Sage Foundation.
Rose, Charles L.
1971 "Critiques of longevity studies." Pp. 13-29 in Erdmore Palmore and Frances C. Jeffers (eds.), Prediction of Life Span. Lexington, Mass.: Heath Lexington Books.
Rose, Charles L. and Benjamin Bell
1971 Predicting Longevity. Lexington, Mass.: Heath Lexington Books.
Rosenblatt, A.
1964 "Older people in the Lower Eastside: their interest in employment and volunteer activities and their general characteristics." New York: Community Service Society of New York.
Ryder, Norman B.
1965 "The cohort in the study of social change." American Sociological Review 30(December):843-861.
Sainer, Janet S. and Mary L. Zander
1971 Serve: Older Volunteers in Community Service. New York: Community Service Society of New York.
Schuyler, Joseph
1959 "Religious observance differentials by age and sex in northern parish." American Catholic Sociological Review 20:124-131.
Spiegelman, Mortimer
1963 "The changing demographic spectrum and its implications for health." Eugenics Quarterly 10:161-174.
Stark, Rodney
1968 "Age and faith: a changing outlook or an old process." Sociological Analysis 29:1-10.
Taietz, Philip and I. F. Larson
1956 "Social participation and old age." Rural Sociology 21:229-238.
Taves, Marvin and G. D. Hanson
1963 "Seventeen hundred elderly citizens." In Arnold Rose (ed.), Aging in Minnesota. Minneapolis: University of Minnesota Press.
U.S. Department of Health, Education and Welfare
1973 New Facts About Older Americans. Washington, D.C.: U.S. Government Printing Office.
Verwoerdt, Adriaan, Eric Pfeiffer, and Hsioh-Shan Wang
1969 "Sexual behavior in senescence." Geriatrics 24:137-154.
Wolozin, H.
1968 "Volunteer manpower in the U.S. federal programs for the development of human resources." A compendium of papers submitted. Washington: 90th Congress, 2nd Session.
Wright, Charles R. and Herbert H. Hyman
1958 "Voluntary association memberships of American adults: evidence from national surveys." American Sociological Review 23:284-294.

Chapter 3

ON GROWING OLDER FEMALE:
AN INTERVIEW WITH TISH SOMMERS*

The Displaced Homemaker and Forced Retirement

THE displaced homemaker is one of an undetermined but growing number of women who have experienced a sudden personal and economic dislocation, due to divorce or the death of her husband and the departure of children from the home.

She has been laid-off from her occupation just as much as an auto worker, but without any unemployment insurance, pension or union benefit. Not considered elderly, she is not yet eligible for Social Security or Medicare.

There are 1.1 million formerly married women under 60, without minor children, who are not in the labor force. In addition, there are 6.1 million married women, under 60, without minor children, who are not in the labor force. If the husbands of these women died or left them, a very large number would be displaced homemakers.

Thus, in effect, thousands of women experience retirement at a much earlier age than men. The dependent homemaker never had much status on her own account at any time, but what she pulled together to create her selfhood usually crashes in the middle years. The empty nest syndrome is a crisis of identity similar to the one men face on retirement, coupled with the hush-hush personal trauma of what is called "the change." If she loses her husband "forced retirement" becomes even more complete. She finds herself without a clearly defined place in society to replace the status she had as a homemaker.

Divorce has doubled in the past 10 years, often leaving older women caught in the middle as marriage as an institution comes under severe strain. The most frequent estimate is that one in three marriages fails, and one fourth of the divorces filed are after more than 15 years of marriage. The trend in divorce legislation is toward no fault dissolution. Irretrievable breakdown is now grounds for divorce in 25 States and only five States remain which do not have some form of no-fault

*From *Aging:11*-12, Nov-Dec, 1975.

divorce. Most women in my generation (I'm 60) bought the social contract of man the breadwinner and woman the homemaker. We set aside our ability to earn a living in the family interest, and relied upon the breadwinner for security. Then, at an age when we cannot easily start afresh, we learn that the rules of the game have been changed, and the contract is no longer viable. Divorce, especially after 25 years of marriage or more, is another form of forced retirement for many women.

In most cases an older woman's investment in that marriage is wiped out with the consent decree.

Barriers to Reentering the Job Market

As part of the backlash against women, judges are saying, "You want equality — go out and get a job." But an older woman who has adapted herself to the dependent's role is not psychologically or practically able to compete. Whether she suddenly hits the job market because of widowhood, divorce, or the unemployment of her husband she faces an alien and hostile world. At first, most of us don't recognize age discrimination when it hits us. We can't admit that we're getting old. But after we've been turned down a few times we begin to think we're over-the-hill, and soon that's where we are. Another self-fulfilling prophesy.

After long years of homemaking, a woman would find herself at a decided disadvantage, despite the Age Discrimination in Employment Act of 1967. In a tight job market, only the exceptional woman will break through the combined barrier of age and sex.

The Double Standard

There is, in practice, a *double standard of aging*. This is most obvious in mating practices. Young women are complaining loudly about being treated as sex objects, but who worries about being treated as that when you are already an obsolete sex object, as every passing man makes it perfectly clear? At an age when men are often at their most attractive, a woman is often a has-been. She finds it difficult to remarry, since men in her age group tend to marry down in age and there are insufficient numbers of eligible "older men."

The differences in aging patterns for men and women are most dramatically revealed in suicide rates. Faced with job discrimination, often unable to find a new marriage partner, and convinced that they are no longer "sexually" attractive, the number of women committing suicide peaks around 55, then declines, while with males, the rate continues to rise, until past 65, it is far more frequent among men than women.

So, the patterns of aging for men and women have significant differences. Women hit mandatory retirement earlier, but live longer. For us, the heavy problems are already upon us in our forties and fifties. If we're not married, especially. Yet, at this age we seem to fall between the cracks of most social programs.

An underlying problem is sexism, compounded by ageism. Consider woman's traditional role — motherhood. If staying at home and caring for children is so important to the fabric of American society, wouldn't you think there would be some reward at the end of the line? But a homemaker receives not one penny of social security of her own, nor are her years of unpaid work taken into account in the amount she receives as a dependent. Nor will her volunteer efforts, extolled to the skies as essential to maintain charitable programs, bring one penny of retirement benefits. Economically speaking, women are punished for having performed what society defines as women's role. The impact becomes greater each decade of our lives.

The Elderly Woman

At the stroke of 65 both men and women lose their sexual identity (if not their right to sex). We join a new category — the senior citizen — and few take note that we will remain men and women. While ageism affects both genders, women because of prolonged economic and psychological effects of sexism, are the most vulnerable, especially economically.

As women move forward from dependency to self-sufficiency there must be greater attention to those women caught in the middle. The 7.5 million widows and single women over 65 constitute the poorest segment of our society. In 1970, half of these women had yearly incomes of $1,888 or *less*. That proposed 5% ceiling on Social Security cost-of-living increases would have come out of their hides.

At the very least these women deserve freedom from economic want and adequate medical care in their final years.

Legislative Reforms Needed

In the first place we need some legislative changes that will bring homemakers under social security in their own names, because dependency affords many pitfalls. Women should be eligible for income maintenance because they have earned it, not because they are dependents. There are a number of bills that have been introduced to this effect. The most far reaching proposal is called the Fraser Plan. It would consider marriage a partnership and provide an option for yearly sharing of benefits similar to the joint income tax. Legislation along this line is currently in preparation.

Second, Displaced Homemaker Bills have been introduced in this session, authored by Rep. Yvonne Brathwaite Burke (H.R. 7003) and Sen. John Tunney (S. 2353). This legislation addresses those women caught in the black out area of social legislation. The bills offer job training and jobs which build upon a homemaker's skills, to provide needed community services. In addition, they would create service centers designed to assist the homemaker to develop a new life for herself.

Similar legislation was enacted in California on Sept. 2, which establishes a demonstration displaced homemaker's center.

The middle years are crucial in a woman's life cycle. If she is able to develop self-respect, independence, and the ability to cope, she is far more likely to be self-sufficient in the years to come. This is *preventive care* in the most fundamental sense, and to those who emphasize costs of alternative programs, here is the best way to save money. The current situation in which displaced homemakers are either left to sink or swim, and paid exploitive wages at exploitive jobs just lays the basis for more costly welfare and services later on.

Chapter 4

WOMEN IN STUDIES OF AGING: A CRITIQUE AND SUGGESTION*

DIANE BEESON

The tendency of social gerontologists to compare the male and female experiences of aging is examined. The conclusion that aging is more problematic and traumatic for men than for women is discussed. A contrasting view, expressed in feminist writings and supported in some measure by demographic and statistical data, is presented. The divergence between these two positions is shown to be related to theoretical and methodological assumptions. The social gerontologists' use of role theory is a major focus of the critique. A phenomenological approach is suggested as more appropriate for probing the private sphere in which much of the female experience is defined.

SOCIAL gerontology, following similar trends in other social sciences, is giving increasing attention to female subjects. This is an appropriate development since gerontology, like other social sciences, has tended to focus predominantly on male subjects (Birren et al., 1963:7; Holmes and Jorgensen, 1971). In order to suggest directions for research on aging women, this paper will critically examine the treatment of women in some important studies.

I will show that when women have been included as subjects their experience of aging has frequently been compared to that of men and evaluated as less problematic, less traumatic, and their difficulties seen as more easily resolved. This view contrasts sharply with nonacademic writings on aging. I will show that the discrepancy is related to theoretical and methodological assumptions, and propose an approach which is essential if social gerontologists are to fill the gaps now extant in the field.

*From *Social Problems*, 23:52-59, 1975.
The research for this chapter was partially supported by NIH Training Grant No. HD 00238 from the National Institute of Child Health and Human Development.

Evaluations of Aging as Experienced by Men and Women

Retirement is seen by many gerontologists as "the most crucial life change requiring a major adjustment of the older person" (Atchley, 1973:103). However, such evaluations actually refer only to male persons, as Atchley (1973:105) clarifies by adding, "Although most women have had work experience, their orientation to work is apparently not strong enough to cause any significant problems in retirement."

Retirement has received more attention than any issue related to later life because of assumptions about its salience for men. Women who retire have been neglected because of parallel assumptions about the relative unimportance of work in their lives. Such a position is made explicit in the work of Cumming and Henry (1961), authors of disengagement theory, who on the basis of 36 working women in their Kansas City sample concluded:

> Retirement is not an important problem for women because . . . working seems to make little difference to them. It is as though they add work to their lives the way they would add a club membership (Cumming and Henry, 1961:144).

Although their sample included twenty unmarried women they further concluded that work

> does not express the whole woman in the way that work no matter how uncongenial tends to express the whole man. . . . The basic division of labor between men and women assigns to the woman the task of sociability, of keeping the social system she belongs to free of tension, of maintaining the system's integrity against disruptive inner disturbances (Cumming and Henry, 1961:144).

Twelve years later, Zena Blau states her similar evaluation in this way:

> Retirement . . . deprives a man of the respect accorded the breadwinner in the American family and constrains him to assume a role similar to that of a woman. In this respect, retirement is a more demoralizing experience for men than for women. Women may choose to work, but according to cultural prescription they are not obliged to do so (Blau, 1973:29).

Role theory has led sociologists from various perspectives to see retirement as relatively non-problematic for women, yet as severely disturbing for men. Burgess (1960:20) speaks of the retired older man and his wife as "imprisoned in a roleless role." He finds that

This is doubly true of the husband, because a woman as long as she is physically able retains the role and satisfactions of homemaker (Burgess, 1960:20).

Working women facing the transition of retirement are not considered at all. Work is recognized as a source of identity in our society only for males by Cavan (1962) and Hansen et al. (1965) as well. Hansen (1965:316) explains

> For an adult in our society, employment is of obvious importance as a source of income. Particularly for males, work has additional significance in that it serves as one of the fundamental bases for an adult social identity.

Assumptions of this nature have been so powerful that they have rarely been tested directly, yet evidence which challenges them is beginning to emerge. For example, in 1967 Lowenthal, Berkman and Associates found in their San Francisco study that retired women were more likely to be psychiatrically impaired than retired men.

In a recent report of one of the few longitudinal studies of retirement, and one of the few studies of retirement to include women respondents, Streib and Schneider (1971) came to two conclusions which challenge previous assumptions and findings of gerontologists. First, they concluded that retirement does not have the "broad negative consequences for the older person" that they had expected (Streib and Schneider, 1971:163). (In this case they are actually referring to male persons.) They found a "more positive set of consequences than had been hypothesized." Second, they reported

> more surprising is the fact that women who retire report a sharper increase in feelings of uselessness than do their retired male counterparts. This finding certainly suggests that further research is needed to examine the stereotyped idea that the male retiree will find it harder to occupy his time than the older woman who retires (Streib and Schneider, 1971:161).

It is clear that assumptions by gerontologists which dismiss problems of women and overestimate the problematic nature of the male experience have existed and still persist around the issue of retirement.

The major transition of the aging woman has long been considered to be widowhood. Let us briefly examine the assumptions and conclusions about the significance of this experience. One cannot help but notice the common practice among gerontologists of comparing widowhood for women to retirement for men. The purpose of such a comparison is not clear, but the conclusion is invariably one which dismisses widowhood for women as less significant than retirement for men. Remarkably, widowhood is sometimes even evaluated as a welcome transition, while again emphasizing the traumatic nature of the so-called male equivalent — retirement.

Cumming and Henry (1961:156) argue in comparing widowhood for women to retirement for men:

> On the whole, resolutions of these problems of disengagement are much easier for women than for men. . . . Integrating herself into both the larger society and small social systems without a husband is a problem, but a relatively easy one for a widow. In the first place, widowhood is an honored state. . . . Finally widows have a ready-made peer group and there is reason to believe that they join this very happily. There is, in fact, some evidence in our interviews of considerable frustration among some married women over being *unable* to join the society of widows, a frustration especially true of wives of retired husbands.

Generally, disengagement theorists argue that women have a "smoother passage" made possible apparently because aging for them begins earlier and lasts longer.

Similar assumptions remain dominant in current work. In 1973 Zena Blau writes:

> Though widowhood, like retirement, signifies the involuntary loss of a significant role, it does not have the invidious implications for the social position of older people that retirement does. . . . Retirement threatens the individual's self-esteem, whereas no similar threat is inherent in widowhood. Retirement, more so than widowhood, lessens opportunities for daily social contacts and is therefore more demoralizing (Blau, 1973:32).

Moving even further along the theoretical spectrum from functionalism, Cavan (1962) has also felt it necessary to compare the aging experiences of men and women and concluded that widowhood is recognized to be a severely disturbing transition, but for the widow in contrast to the retiring male she finds that the culture has devised several appropriate self-images including the grandparent role which is essentially a maternal one and therefore presents more difficulty for the grandfather.

Even loss of a spouse is considered most devastating when the surviving partner is male. Cumming and Henry, (1961:160) for example, argue that women are better able than men to establish "quasi-relationships" and

> better able to live alone because they are in command of the necessary domestic skills and it is appropriate for them to exercise them. This is not so for men; even when they are good at housework, they

are ashamed of it.

Thus we have numerous judgments of the woman's experience as "smoother," "less demoralizing" and "easier." There is little or no empirical basis for these conclusions. The justification in each case is essentially theoretical. Some form of role theory provides the basis for each evaluation.

Another View

Students of aging cannot help but be struck by the contrast between journalistic and scholarly accounts of the female experience of aging. Susan Sontag's (1972) article, "The Double Standard of Aging," powerfully documents how cultural differences work to the disadvantage of women. Lynn Caine's (1974) book *Widow* describes her own experience of widowhood in terms of grief, loneliness, financial problems, and changes in self-conception bearing little resemblance to social-psychological insights offered in gerontological literature.[1]

Readers of women's publications find articles that emphasize economic and social-psychological problems and issues that are rarely mentioned in gerontological literature. These articles include discussions of inequities in social security legislation. Major complaints are that homemakers receive no benefits for their own work. They qualify as dependents only after 20 years of marriage to the same man. Widows under sixty without dependent children receive no benefits (Ahern, 1974). Another major problem of older women, noted by Berquist (1973), is re-entry into the paid labor force after years as homemakers. Sex discrimination is compounded by age discrimination and she argues that confidence is usually low even where older women have credentials that are adequate or better than those of competing males.

Social gerontologists have contributed very little to the understanding of the universal phenomenon of female menopause. Neugarten's (Neugarten et al., 1963) work raised interesting questions about differences in the meaning of menopause for older and younger women. Bart's work (1971) elaborated on the social elements in depression among middle-aged women which may contribute to or be confused with symptoms of menopause. Yet such issues are little researched and more attention has probably been given the question of whether or not there is such a thing as "male menopause." In an effort to understand their experience older women are now turning to each other, rather than to the experts, by forming "menopause rap

---

[1]Lopata's (1973) recent book is a major contribution and an important exception.

groups."

A double standard of physical attractiveness that creates anxiety in women decades before it is an issue for men has also received attention (Brabec, 1974) in popular women's publications. The absence of attention to many of these issues in gerontological literature has been observed by the Coordinator of the Task Force on Older Women of the National Organization of Women (Sommers, 1974). As a partial explanation she has suggested the tendency of our culture to be more concerned with "those who rise and fall, than those who never rise at all."

One might be tempted to explain the discrepancy between the issues addressed in non-academic writings and those recognized in gerontological literature as the difference between propaganda and scholarship. The difficulty with this explanation is that special problems of older women such as greater poverty (Butler and Lewis, 1973:90), increased prevalence of living alone and higher incidence of institutionalization (Brotman, 1974:250), disadvantage for remarriage (Butler and Lewis, 1973:91), and even symbolic denigration (Arnoff, 1974) are confirmed by statistical and demographic evidence. Somehow these differences do not show up in theoretical statements, nor do they often lead to generalizations by scholars about the situation of aging women.

Conscious discrimination against women by scholars, particularly in a field where women have been active, is not an adequate explanation. Theoretical and methodological styles have worked to perpetuate dominant culture values even where women have received attention. These values may accurately be labeled as sexist or androcentrist. Theoretical and methodological fashions which facilitate these values or at least fail to expose them must be recognized if we are to avoid sexism in research.

Theoretical and Methodological Issues

Theoretical orientations vary among gerontologists who express concern for the problematic nature of masculine transitions while dismissing the feminine experience as non-problematic. Those who consider themselves symbolic interactionists often fall into the same trap as functionalists when interactionists draw upon role theory so that they see one-sided·causation in what is actually a dialectical process between actors and their social world. Dominant social values are mistakenly assumed to be synonymous with subjective experience. Such a view might be called the "oversocialized conception of women."[2]

This emphasis on one aspect of the process of reality construction becomes more misleading as the group under consideration is more powerless. All classes or groups do not contribute equally to the dominant value systems or definitions of reality. Traditional sex roles can be expected to be more in line with the subjective experience of males since they have more power in defining male and female relationships.

Here the link between theoretical assumptions and methodologies becomes important. Studies, particularly in survey research, which have perpetuated the emphasis on the aging male by revealing the subtleties and difficulties of his problems while remaining unresponsive to problems of older women are studies where the categories of experience to be investigated have been predefined by the researchers. This structuring of the problem has the effect of preventing definitions of reality other than those anticipated by the researcher from emerging clearly and fully, even in empirical work. Mueller (1970) points out that the predefinitions which form the standard political language assure maintenance of the dominant value system. When this language is used by social scientists it functions in the same way. Sociologists' failure to explore the semantic field of their subjects works against those who have the smallest roles in constructing both popular and scholarly predefinitions. Aging women are good examples of such powerless subjects.

Mueller (1970) notes in discussing the social stratification of language, it "is the medium containing possibilities for the perpetuation and generation of symbols contrary to predefinitions imposed from above." He uses the example of the difference between public and private spheres to demonstrate the effect of a given language on social integration. Public language, he argues, is an expression of official symbols and predefinitions while private language is the expression of individualized needs and privatized meanings.

Gerontologists have tended to use a version of public language to describe the aging process, particularly when they use role theory. This perspective has assured that counter symbols and definitions, insofar as they may exist among widows or aging women, are not examined. The public world at this point in history is predominantly a male one and the private world predominantly female, and public predefinitions today speak disproportionately to the male experience.

Those sociologists who have chosen to focus their work on the

---

[2]The problem is similar to what Wrong (1961) has called "The Oversocialized Conception of Man."

subjectively perceived, micro level of social life — the other side of the dialectic from the normative, objectively structured — come to different conclusions about the meaning of various experiences. Berger and Kellner (1970) have elaborated this approach. From this interpretive, phenomenological perspective, sometimes called the microsociology of knowledge, not only roles but *worlds* are explored. Berger and Kellner see marriage as involving a step into a new world. It is a social arrangement that creates for the individual the sort of order in which one can experience his or her life making sense, particularly in a highly mobile society. From this perspective "marriage is a crucial nomic instrumentality in our society . . . a dramatic act in which two strangers come together and redefine themselves" (Berger and Kellner, 1970:53).

These authors have not explicitly compared widowhood and retirement or other typically masculine and feminine transitions related to aging, but one can see that their perspective logically leads to a contrasting view of the relative importance to identity of these transitions from that found in most gerontological literature. Berger and Kellner contend, for example, that in our society large numbers of people are content with a situation in which public involvements such as work have little subjective importance. They turn to the private sphere for experiences of self-realization. This emphasis challenges the simplistic conclusions that emerge from rigid interpretations of role theory and socialization suggestive that retirement is easy for women and difficult for men.[3] It also helps explain why recent empirical work (Streib and Schneider, 1971) has not supported this earlier view.

Mueller (1970) has called attempts semantically to structure the world of meaning for certain class or group members by more powerful groups or institutions "repressive communication." Social scientists may, particularly in studying powerless groups such as the aged, and especially aged women, be guilty of repressive communication. The only way to avoid this problem is to explore the symbolic world of the subjects without a prior commitment to specific concepts and definitions of the situation. The symbols and privatized meanings as they are shared among members of the group under study must be allowed to penetrate the symbols and definitions of the social scientist

---

[3]But phenomenology may be subject to sexist use. Berger and Kellner (1970) have been criticized for failing to recognize the consequences of power differentials in defining a relationship, particularly in marriage (Grether, 1975). Their work is entirely theoretical, however, and my position is that the methodology implicit in phenomenology leads toward discovering rather than obscuring power differentials where they exist.

if we are to understand the group accurately.

Today the women's movement, even among older women, is organizing and articulating issues and problems that have existed for years. Many of the concerns these women share indicate their rejection of the dominant value system. To decipher such cleavages before they gain widespread and loud expression requires special sensitivity. This sensitivity can be most easily achieved by initially abandoning theoretical assumptions about what should be happening, as well as leaving behind predefined variables, categories and definitions in favor of an inductive exploration of the symbolic world of the aging woman.

REFERENCES

Ahern, Dee Dee
    1974 "Social security — a gross misnomer, especially for women." Prime Time
    2:1(January): 11-14.
Arnoff, Craig
    1974 "Old age in prime time." Journal of Communication 24:4(Autumn): 86-87.
Atchley, Robert C.
    1972 The Social Forces in Later Life: An Introduction to Social Gerontology.
    Belmont, California: Wadsworth Publishing Company.
Bart, Pauline
    1971 "Depression in middle-aged women." Pp. 99-117 in Vivian Gornick and
    Barbara K. Moran (eds.), Woman in Sexist Society. New York: Basic Books.
Berger, Peter L. and Hansfried Kellner
    1970 "Marriage and the construction of reality." Pp. 49-72 in Recent Sociology
    No. 2: Patterns of Communicative Behavior. London: Macmillan Company.
Berquist, Laura
    1973 "Recycling lives." MS (August): 59-105.
Birren, James W., Robert N. Butler, Samuel W. Greenhouse, Louis Sokoloff, and
    Marian R. Yarrow
    1963 Human Aging: A Biological and Behavioral Study. Bethesda, Maryland:
    Public Health Service, National Institute of Mental Health, U. S. Department of
    Health, Education and Welfare.
Blau, Zena Smith
    1973 Old Age in a Changing Society. New York: New Viewpoints.
Brabec, Bette Dewing
    1974 "Being our age and learning to like it." Prime Time 2:1(January): 5-6.
Brotman, Herman B.
    1974 "The fastest growing minority: The aging." American Journal of Public
    Health 64:3(March): 251.
Burgess, Ernest W.
    1960 "Aging in western culture." In E. W. Burgess (ed.), Aging in Western
    Societies. Chicago: University of Chicago Press.
Butler, Robert N. and Myrna I. Lewis
    1973 Aging and Mental Health: Positive Psychosocial Approaches. St. Louis: C.

V. Mosby.

Caine, Lynn
1974 Widow. New York: William Morrow and Company, Inc.

Cavan, Ruth S.
1962 "Self and role in adjustment during old age." Pp. 526-536 in Arnold M. Rose (ed.), Human Behavior and Social Processes. Boston: Houghton Mifflin Company.

Cumming, Elaine and William H. Henry
1961 Growing Old: The Process of Disengagement. New York: Basic Books.

Grether, Judith K.
1975 "Berger and Kellner's social construction of marriage: A critique and feminist commentary." Paper presented at the Annual Meetings of the Pacific Sociological Association, Victoria, B.C., April.

Hansen, Gary D., Samuel Yoshioka, Marvin J. Taves, and Francis Caro
1965 "Older people in the Midwest: conditions and attitudes." Pp. 311-322 in Arnold M. Rose and Warren A. Peterson (eds.), Older People and Their Social World. Philadelphia: F. A. Davis Company.

Holmes, Douglas S. and Bruce W. Jorgensen
1971 "Do personality and social psychologists study men more than women?" Government Reports Announcements, December 25.

Lopata, Helena Znaniecki
1973 Widowhood in an American City. Cambridge, Mass.: Schenkman Publishing Company.

Lowenthal, Marjorie Fiske, Paul L. Berkman, and Associates
1967 Aging and Mental Disorder in San Francisco: A Social Psychiatric Study. San Francisco: Jossey-Bass.

Mueller, Claus
1970 "Notes on the repression of communicative behavior." Pp. 101-113 in Hans Peter Dreitzel (ed.), Recent Sociology No. 2: Patterns of Communicative Behavior. London: Macmillan Company.

Neugarten, Bernice L., Vivian Wood, Ruth Kraines, and Barbara Loomis
1963 "Women's attitudes toward the menopause." Vita Humana 6:140-151.

Sommers, Tish
1974 "The compounding impact of age on sex." Civil Rights Digest 7:1(Fall): 3-9.

Sontag, Susan
1972 "The double standard of aging." Saturday Review of the Society September 23:29-38.

Streib, Gordon F. and Clement J. Schneider, S.J.
1971 Retirement in American Society: Impact and Process, Ithaca: Cornell University Press.

Wrong, Dennis H.
1961 "The oversocialized conception of man in modern sociology." American Sociological Review, 26:2(April): 183-193.

Chapter 5

DO SPECIAL FOLKS NEED SPECIAL STROKES? COUNSELING OLDER WOMEN: A PERSPECTIVE*

JANE BERRY

OLDER women are beginning to receive the attention of both practitioners and researchers — a concern long overdue. Counseling, guidance, placement, and related services are increasingly needed by the rapidly rising number of persons in their middle and later years. Momentum has been gathering for some time and it would seem that we are on the verge of recognizing a full-blown movement that will respond to the pressures and problems of aging in contemporary society.

Counselors are becoming more aware of the needs and special dilemmas of older women. Generally speaking, the challenge of counseling older women centers on those seeking new careers in mid-life and those facing the additional pressures of feeling really "over the hill." This article briefly delineates the major problems of the latter group and suggests ways that counselors can be increasingly effective in their efforts to understand and work with these women.

Old is Ugly

The concerns and anxieties of many older women today tend to be frequently and subtly reinforced by our pervasive societal climate that glorifies youth and particularly young women. Young is beautiful and old is ugly. Even young children are often heard to repeat the unattractive labels reserved for old ladies, grandmas, and other older women.

Appearance and health and their obvious interrelationship are special problems of the older woman. She feels that she no longer is attractive to others as before. She is on guard not to betray signs or symptoms of age and the very anxiousness produced by these efforts contributes to the tenseness and nervousness observed in some older women.

There are the real problems of job seeking and employment. Protective legislation designed to militate against age discrimination is far from effective in the market place. Many employers are caught up with the youth-is-beautiful syndrome. Most have been socialized to see the pretty in youth and wish to sustain this image in the employment surroundings for which they are responsible. This is frequently an unconscious response and therefore difficult to combat.

For many older women today, an additional problem is the "new message." The new education and employment opportunities for younger women that have been fostered by the women's movement of the past decade have often tended to arouse resentment of older women who are unhappy about what they have missed. Such women are frequently heard to say "I was born too soon." They consider themselves somehow to have missed out on the horizons that are evident for the younger women with whom they come in contact.

The Retirement Blues

Another problem of older women is the retirement blues. Many older women who have been active in business, industry, and education resent their enforced leisure and the life-style that occurs when one "drops out of the mainstream."

Hobbies, volunteer work, community involvement, frequently prescribed for the older women, are not always a panacea for all older women. This is particularly the case for women who have been active intellectually and have not developed any particular skills or interests that translate readily into what needs doing in the community.

For example, many senior citizen centers may need volunteers, but such effort may not appeal to some older women. In this connection it is pertinent to point out the problem within the problem. Reduced to simple terms, the fact is that some older women do not find other older people attractive. They want to be with younger people. They report that they are depressed by being around "old folks."

Certainly not all older women are disheartened and disturbed by retirement. There are many examples of women who have retired, developed new horizons, and report they are happy. What makes the difference? Research, careful case studies, and other investigative work to assess the attitudes of women who have had responsible positions and are faced with the "phase out" or lessened position and prestige can provide the understandings and insights needed to counsel with today's older women.

The recent economic crisis may have several long-range consequences that will affect the employment possibilities and retirement plans of older women. For example, enforcement of early retirement to reduce personnel costs, a practice utilized by a number of companies and organizations during the past years, has resulted in a counter movement. Some elderly workers are now agitating against rules that permit early retirement and require it at sixty-five.

Several well-known economists are also taking a long-range look and recognizing that by 1985 there will be fewer Americans in their late 40s and 50s than there are today. These economists are advocating policies that would keep competent older workers on the job after 65. They even go so far as to suggest retirement in phases — which would amount to lessening responsibilities and working hours between ages 65 and 72.

Partners and Families

Older women may be widowed, divorced, or simply have outgrown a marriage partner of long standing. In this instance, they may be afraid to consider separation or divorce for economic reasons or because they fear they would not be able to attract another man. Thus, they elect to stay in the marriage, but still have problems related to fulfillment or the psychological and physiological aging of husband or partner. Some older women trapped in these circumstances take the medical way out: they develop psychosomatically related ailments that will further inhibit their functioning and limit potential for more satisfying outlets and activities.

Sexual problems and needs of the older women are beginning to be understood more fully and even talked about in polite society. Again, such problems may be related to the young-is-beautiful syndrome. Wrinkles, ankle skin puffs, and sagging chins are not considered particularly pleasing.

Problems of older women are frequently economic. Resources may be very limited, with little or no extra for travel or other distractions.

The grown children of the older women can be a source of pleasure or pain, or both, and the problems resulting from these relationships may be priority problems for a number of older women who seek the assistance of a counselor.

Counselors and Older Women

Specialization, sensitivity, empathy, and examination of the counselor's own perceptions of and attitudes toward aging are priorities.

Particular attention is essential to the glorification of youth and beauty in our culture and its demeaning and debilitating influence on the older women.

Counselors will find assistance in the life-span concept that attempts to integrate the age phases of a woman's life. In this connection counselors will want to concentrate on problems and expectations of both the mid-career and the older woman life-span periods.

Much has been learned about the self-confidence problems of older women in connection with the continuing education efforts of many institutions in recent years. Many individuals associated with such programs are an excellent intramural resource for special training seminars on problems encountered in counseling older women.

Medical knowledge concerning aging and the interrelationship of the psychological and physiological balance should be included in sophisticated in-service training programs for counselors working with older women. Adult development curricula in counselor education programs should contain specialized material pertaining to the dilemmas and problems confronted by older women.

The Older Americans Act, which has provided programs and services for older men and women, is being reviewed, revised, and expanded with a view to providing more service and experimental programs as well as training programs for counselors and support personnel. Certainly, there can be opportunities for demonstration programs designed for meeting the special needs of mid-career and older women.

Advocate organizations for older persons are growing rapidly and representatives of such groups as Gray Panthers, American Association of Retired Persons, and the NOW Task Force on Older Women may be utilized as resource persons for state and local counselor association meetings. Such programs can be designed to provide an opportunity for first-hand exploration of the feelings of anger many women tend to experience at being older and particularly at being an "older woman."

The need is urgent for increased insight and honesty in counseling the older woman. Older women are troubled about being older women. Many regard it as not a good thing to be. Many feel that if you have to be older, it is better to be a man. Somehow society seems to offer more esteem for older males.

The main message for counselors of older women is to keep up with a number of new and emerging developments in the larger society that can affect future work with older women. APGA has a committee on aging that is focusing attention on counseling the older person. There are an increasing number of indications that consciousness is being raised.

Counselors' awareness and advocacy regarding older women will depend on more than training programs. Counselors can make a significant difference in the lives of their older women clients by: understanding the special feelings and needs of aging women; keeping up with the contributions of sociology and other social sciences related to aging; and becoming catalysts who interpret problems of older women to the larger community with a view to changing old attitudes that damn the old as ugly.

Chapter 6

MABEL, YOU DON'T BELONG HERE*

CAROL-GRACE TOUSSIE

MS. Mabel Maye Harrison, a hospital is no place for you!

After 91 years your back is so bent that I tower head and shoulders above you although I am only five feet tall. Your wizened face, spindly legs, skinny arms, and spidery fingers make us fear that you'll disintegrate if exposed to the air too long. Yet how sharp your mind is.

Wobbling around with a cane almost up to your chin, you've managed 30 years of perfect attendance at the race track. The racing forms and receipts in your purse show your favorites to the date of your admission.

"I don't win as much as I used to," you admit. "It's probably my eyesight that's going. After all, it's not as if I were still 70." Right on, Ms. Harrison!

A fall brought you to the hospital from the hotel you've called home for 40 years, and an isolated episode of premature ventricular contractions sent you to the coronary care unit. How disgusted you are with CCU nurses and doctors for making you miss your beloved horse races.

"The maid waxed the floor too much — there's nothing wrong with my heart," you insist.

It turns out that you are right. Your left shoulder and arm pain is due to your sprained shoulder, but the purplish black blotches which cover that side make you look battered and pathetic. You've never had angina nor broken a bone in your life.

You don't ask for much, but you know exactly what will make you comfortable. "Hand me my cane!" you bark. "And don't call me *Mrs.* Harrison. My name is *Miss* Mabel Maye Harrison." You badger each of us for reassurance that you are going to be all right. "I've got so much to live for . . . and just think of the hotel gossip I'm missing, not to mention the races!"

---

*From *American Journal of Nursing,* 73:2059, Dec. 1973. ©1973. Reproduced with permission.

You hate the telemetry box hung like a medallion around your neck. "I feel like a cat that's going to be drowned," you grumble, and stoop over so far to prove your point that you barely reach my waist. Now the box is attached to your handbag, which you never allow more than a foot away from you.

Five days after admission, you are ready for discharge to your hotel. Grudgingly and reluctantly, you have come to accept us. The "service" in the cardiac intensive care unit is "pretty good," you allow, and as long as you can watch television, you'll put up with all that blood pressure and cardiogram "nonsense."

You have flatly refused suggestions to move to a senior citizens' apartment complex. Give up the races and nightly dinners at the Post and Coach Restaurant? NEVER! For you, a spinster who supported her parents through two world wars, New York City streets and subways present no peril.

You laboriously inch your way into your clothes before discharge. You have come to enjoy the assistance you've received because you seemed so fragile, but now you are finally convinced that I'm only watching in order to assess your level of independence in dressing. You do well.

"I'm foxy," you confide, showing the cotton purse pinned to your ancient lace girdle. "I keep most of my money for the track here and just a dollar or so in my handbag in case I have to give something to a mugger."

Being transported in a wheelchair frightens and infuriates you. "No college boy is going to push me around!" you announce. "Medications? Why? WHY?"

We all hesitate to send you home alone, although we know the competent visiting nurse and occupational therapist will be seeing you tomorrow. One moment you are "absolutely unable" to use your bruised arm. The next moment you are busily fluffing up your gray hair with the same arm. "I've got to look good for the gang back at the hotel — have to brush my hair straight up. It gives me more height that way."

In parting, you inform us that you are going out to dinner tonight as usual. Only the top of your brushed-up hair is visible over the back of your wheelchair as you disappear through the double doors of the CCU. "It's a lucky thing!" you call back, "I'll be in time for my beauty parlor appointment."

Slim chance our visiting nurse has of finding you home tomorrow if the races are on. (When the visiting nurse did visit Mabel Harrison, she found this note taped to the door: "Sorry I'm not home. Went to have my whiskers waxed off. — M. Harrison.")

I think of the woman who shared your hospital room. At 60, she has walled herself within her apartment and trembles at the mention of going for a walk. Like a timid deer, she is startled whenever someone enters the room. She clutches at us for comfort and sits with her hand on her pulse, "always waiting for the palpitations to come." She has lived through only the first thousand deaths she must face before her eyes close forever on the faded pictures of her dead family.

In the few days we knew you, Ms. Harrison, your spunk and spirit became symbols of strength, independence, and beauty in old age. God bless you, Miss Mabel Maye Harrison, and hit the Daily Double tomorrow!

Part II

Socialization

INTRODUCTION

When an infant is born, parents and other relatives begin to teach the child the behavior and skills which will help it cope effectively with the world in which it lives. This process of socialization, or building into the individual the skills, values, beliefs, and behavior needed in the society, is a life-long process of continual growth and adaptation to changing circumstances. In all societies males and females are expected to behave in different ways — and they learn the appropriate way early in life. If socialization is to be effective in equipping the individual for successful living, the training must be based upon some assumption about the nature of the world in which the child will live and grow. Although it is doubtful if most parents articulate their assumptions about the world of the present and their projections about the world in future years, nevertheless socialization proceeds upon some basis — possibly the world of the parents' childhood.

Today's older women were children in the early 1900s. Any woman born in that period can vividly describe the first automobile she ever saw. Telephone, telegraph, radio, air conditioning, mass transportation, television, and the home freezer would not be commonplace for many years. The world of the early 1900s did not appear too different from the years of the previous century and certainly was more similar in many ways to that period than to the changed world of recent years. Women were socialized to cook, sew, wash, iron, can, make quilts, care for children, bake bread, boil home-made jam. They were taught to be dependent upon men, father or husband, who braved the larger world beyond the home, earning the living and negotiating whatever business was necessary. Thus the skills, values, and attitudes appropriate for that time would not be the same needed by the older woman facing a world alone today. Many widows of today spent the *first night alone in their lives* after the death of their husbands, having gone from home with parents and siblings to a home with husband and, later, children.

Socialized for dependence and facing a world where independence would be a valuable asset, today's older woman has a variety of prob-

lems and experiences addressed by the articles in this section on socialization. The two articles examine the variety of socialization experiences of women and emphasize the outcomes. They point out that
the characteristics of aged women must be taken into account if programs are to be successful in meeting their needs. The poem illustrates the usual socialization of a woman of this period.

Chapter 7 carries the title of this book, as it was written by one of
the editors. Cora Martin discussed the "flowering" of the lavender
roses and the trauma experienced when they must face the world
alone. Though the qualities stressed as desirable in a woman today
may not be as different from earlier generations as some people would
like to think, the author foresees a future in which independent
women will have different skills and different needs and are likely to
take action to improve their lot. Policy makers may have to work with
a different woman indeed.

Discussing the socialization of women in Chapter 8, Chrysee Kline
argues that the various roles occupied by women as they progress
through life, alternating, mixing, or dropping employment-related
and home-related roles, predisposes to flexibility. Whether this flexibility, developed throughout the life cycle, provides a basis for a
smooth transition to old age for women is debatable and conflicting
viewpoints are evaluated.

Chapter 9 illustrates the product: the perfectly socialized women of
the cohort born around the turn of the century. She reviews her life in
terms of her relations to others and her family roles.

Chapter 7

LAVENDER ROSE OR GRAY PANTHER?

CORA A. MARTIN

LAVENDER Rose or Gray Panther? The title is
designed to call attention to two extremes of life-styles that characterize the older women.

You see, we need different kinds of programs and services for roses
and panthers. And if we are going to be planners, preparing for the
aged in our society, we need to know something about who the aged
are, who they will be, and how they get to be the way they are.

We can make good predictions about the older people of 2000 or
2010 because we already know a lot about them. They will be largely
women. If we look at the way women have been (and are being)
socialized we might get some clues as to the kinds of programs they
will need.

First, let us look at the process of socialization as it has affected the
women who are "old" today. By socialization I mean the process by
which we learn to act so that people around us approve of our behavior because we live up to society's expectations. They say, "You
are a nice woman" not, "You are an aggressive female."

Socialization continues throughout the life cycle. We are continually learning new roles. But early socialization is very important and,
since our culture is more or less consistent, it reinforces the lessons of
childhood with expectations for similar behavior later. For example,
society taught little girls in the early 1900s to be nice, obedient, quiet
little girls. In the 1920s, they were expected to be respectable married
women, devoting their energies to having contented husbands and
well-behaved children. In the 70s we expect them to be nice old ladies.
We have created, in this age group, a garden of lavender roses.

Of course, not all have thus bloomed. There were, after all, the
flappers of the 20s. But most of them settled down in the 30s and
followed the pattern. These older women often have a very hard time
as widows (which most are by this time), dealing with the impersonal
social system which characterizes today's society. They always had a
father, or a husband, or at least a brother or son to buffer them from

*From *Aging*:28-30, July-Aug. 1978.

the outside world. But now they don't. They must cope alone with an impersonal system which often terrifies them and of which they are always suspicious.

My friends working for social security tell me that they often find widows who have never written a check, who have no idea of how much money was in the estate, who know nothing about money management. They are vulnerable to fraud and do not know what benefits are due them. They are suspicious of "government" and tend to see any benefits as a handout. Will older women always be this vulnerable?

I think the answer is a resounding no, but I'm not sure when we can expect the change from more roses to more panthers.

Let us briefly examine the traditional role of women in our society and how it is changing.

Traditionally we have expected girls to be gentle, nonaggressive, noncompetitive, dependent and emotional. Girls are sent to school but it is made clear to them that their main purpose in life is to be a wife and mother. Jobs are necessary but they are never primary. They serve to make some money before marriage for a big wedding; perhaps, after marriage in the early years to help accumulate enough capital to buy a new house, or to put a husband through school; then there is a period of "nesting." When the last child goes to school, the wife/mother often returns to the labor force to make "extra" money for the needs — or luxuries — of the family, to send children through college, etc. Finally comes retirement. But even retirement for women has usually been adjusted so that they can leave the labor force earlier than men (at reduced retirement benefits, of course) thus retiring at the same time as their husbands. Even the end of their working career is tied to their husband's departure from the work force, not their own ability or desire to continue to make a contribution.

Some excerpts from a widely used psychology text published in 1974 prove the point. In *Adulthood and Aging,* Douglas Kimmel describes the personality development of women:

> Because of women's investment in the marriage relationship, because of their history of assessing themselves by others' responses, and because they really do perceive reality in interpersonal terms, they overwhelmingly define and evaluate identity and femininity within the context of marriage.
>
> Passivity in the sense of indrawing, or evolving a rich, empathic, intuitive inner life — in contrast to activity directed outward — may be a necessary part of the personality equipment of healthy women. . . . Certainly not all women are passive and not all men are aggressive; but at this point in time in our society these characteris-

tics seem to stand out as differential aspects of femininity and masculinity.

Kimmel seems to say not only that this is the state of affairs but that it is the preferred state: It is "healthy." What will happen when these dependent, "healthy" women are widowed?

Another author, while supporting the point of view that these qualities are expected of women, questions whether or not they are "healthy." He says:

> The cost in terms of always having to assume a dependent, secondary role is most telling on some women. To assume some responsibility, to assert their independence, to respond aggressively to a problem are all unfeminine and interpreted as attempts to challenge the male's authority. Woman's role becomes that of an object to be admired and used by men; she is there to meet his needs as mistress, mother, and housekeeper. If she questions this role and challenges the limits placed upon her, she is demeaned, ridiculed, and if perchance successful, immediately defined as "not a real woman." (F. McKinney, R. Lorion, M. Zax, *Effective Behavior and Human Development*, p. 138.)

These expectations of what women should be are being presented to college students today. They are certainly descriptive of those 80+ today. Their needs are financial management training, protective services, and "helping" programs of various kinds.

But the winds of change are blowing, if not always through psychology texts. Cartoonists are more attuned to the times than some psychologists! One of my favorite strips is Peanuts. In one, Lucy, reading a composition to her class, says:

> And so World War II came to an end. My grandmother left her job in the defense plant and went to work for the telephone company. We need to study the lives of great women like my grandmother. Talk to your own grandmother today. Ask her questions. You'll find she knows more than peanut butter cookies! Thank you!

My generation has had much of the same childhood socialization as our mothers but it was attenuated by the social upheaval of the great depression. Then WWII encouraged women to leave the household and join the labor force. And, though there was a mass exodus by most women from that force as the war ended, in 1974, 53 percent of women between 45 and 54 were working. Most of us were or had been married (more than 90 percent) yet, increasingly, we find ourselves at midlife living in one-person households. We are learning independence. We, the middle aged group, are less ruled by the traditional concept of the woman's place, yet we have not moved as far as many have supposed. We still value the traditional womanly virtues and are reluctant to appear aggressive or competitive — despite the "assertive" training of the more liberal feminists among us. Of course, this has some good payoffs. We have fewer heart attacks and other stress-related illnesses than our male counterparts and live longer.

As we, the coming generation of aged, arrive on the scene, our first needs are not likely to be for the mastery of the rudiments of financial management or protective agencies. We probably will need to be taught the rudiments of political activism. Robert Butler points out "There is a sturdy and hopefully growing group of old women who are undaunted and look to life with enthusiasm. Old women will not accept their bleak lot forever because they have the brains, money, and voting strength to do something about it." So planners for programs for the aged for the years 2000+, look alive! You are going to have to adjust your planning for us.

GRAY PANTHERS, HERE WE COME.

Chapter 8

THE SOCIALIZATION PROCESS
OF WOMEN*

Chrysee Kline

LITERATURE dealing with the occupational involvement of Americans has for the most part been based on male work history, and, except for very recent working generations, neglects the substantially different pattern of women (see, for example, Hughes, 1958; de Grazia, 1964; Kreps, 1971). Jackson has commented that this reflects "an implicit assumption that the working roles of women are relatively unimportant and that retirement is not a significant stage for women" (Jackson, 1971).

With few exceptions, some of which are noted below, retirement studies that include women do so only in relation to their reactions as wives toward the retirement of their husbands (Heyman & Jeffers, 1968).

Career Development

Cumming's (1974) position, too, is that women's basic difference from men lies in having experienced a much "smoother" life cycle:

> Disengagement from central life roles is basically different for women than for men, perhaps because women's roles are essentially unchanged from girlhood to death. In the course of their lives, women are asked to give up only pieces of their core socioemotional roles or to change their details. Their transitions are therefore easier . . .

Others have reported on informative studies concerning work roles of women. Lopata and Steinhart (1971) studied work experiences of metropolitan Chicago widows aged 50 or over and succeeded in demonstrating the marginality of older women vis-à-vis the occupational structure of the society. Most typical of the respondents was an "inflexible work history involving routinized and directed jobs handled passively." The average subject had a very uneven employment history and had dropped out of the labor market several times during her life, withdrawing to the home to perform the roles of wife, mother, and housewife. In general, however, the work histories of these older women reflect frequent engagement in the work world. Most of those respondents who had continuous or almost continuous work histories shared several characteristics: they spent relatively few years in marriage, entering late in life and/or being widowed or separated; they had no children or only one offspring; and they moved around frequently. The jobs they took were the ones available conveniently at the time they were looking, with no program of career-type succession. Part-time work was common after retirement.

Despite the heavy use of the working world during their life cycle, the older women interviewed in Chicago did not place much value on the role of worker in the list of social roles most often performed by women. The role of worker is not assigned major importance by widows, women who never married, and those who never performed the role of mother. The American culture, locating women in the home as wives and mothers, has had so strong an influence on housewives (Lopata, 1971a) and widows (Lopata, 1972) as to prevent the roles of worker, citizen, and even friend from reaching the top three positions in a six-rank scale of importance.

While Williams and Wirth (1965) do not discuss the differential career development of men and women, they do consider differences between their career patterns. Although they give attention to homemaking as the primary career role of women, they fail to specify career patterns in terms of an acceptance of work as a primary or secondary mode of validating identity. This distinction seems crucial, because many who work are unable and/or unwilling to work full-time consistently throughout the year.

Roles

The basic notion of the concept of role, as employed in this paper, is focused on descriptive real life roles such as parent, spouse, worker, retiree, widow. Involved in these roles and many others which older persons enact are three basic conceptual distinctions: the normative, the behavioral, the interactional. A role is always associated with a position in a social structure, organization, or group. These positions are normatively defined, and these norms establish expectations for what is appropriate behavior to the role. A second major dimension is the behavioral or performance aspect. This component is what a person does in enacting a certain role or set of roles. Almost all roles are interactional, encompassing "both the behaving organism and the expectancies which the perceived organism has regarding his behavior" (Steinmann, 1963) — that is, they involve some kind of social exchange with other persons who are, i.e., parent, child, spouse, worker, supervisor.

Each person normally has several roles to enact because of the various positions occupied in the different institutional aspects of the social structure. In the context of role theory, the enactment of these multiple roles is considered to be the primary basis for most of a person's behavior, attitudes, values, prestige, and personal integration. The "role theory perspective," as defined by Biddle and Thomas (1966) is:

> ... a limited social determinism that ascribes much but rarely all of the variance of real-life behavior to the operation of immediate or past external influences. Such influences include prescriptive framework of demands and rules, the behavior of others as it facilitates or hinders and rewards or punishes the person, the positions of which the person is a member, and the individual's own understanding of, and reactions to these factors.

The problem of analyzing roles at any stage of the life cycle is complicated by the fact that the person has a number of intersecting and overlapping roles which must be undertaken — sometimes simultaneously and sometimes sequentially, according to the expectations of that particular situation. This problem is accentuated for the female who, according to Atchley (1972), is under greater pressure to assume a number of conflicting roles throughout the life cycle than is the male. For the female, the various roles of worker, housewife, and mother occupy different priority positions at different points throughout the life cycle. Although the male's "role set," or "complement of role specializations" (Biddle & Thomas, 1966) throughout the life cycle also typically consists of a number of rôles, the role of worker consistently occupies the greatest area of "role space."

The reasons for the predominance of the role of worker are twofold: (1) it is the one role which most frequently takes precedence over other roles, and (2) the one which derives greater societal rewards relative to rewards from other male roles (Palmore, 1965).

Work Role

Historical tables of United States labor force participation rates (Gallaway, 1965) suggest a much greater degree of fluctuation in importance of the work role for today's aged woman. A female born in 1900, for example, probably entered the labor force during or immediately after finishing high school, then retired to her home to bear and rear children, perhaps re-entered employment outside the home during World War II, and then exited again. The Women's Bureau reported that about 9 out of 10 women work outside the home sometime during their lives, whether they marry or not. Marriage and the presence of children tend to curtail employment, while widowhood, divorce, and the decrease of family responsibilities tend to attract into the work force (Women's Bureau, 1969). During 1973, the highest proportion of women in the labor force was between 20 and 24 years of age (61%). After this there is a sudden drop in the proportion of women who are working, followed by an upswing until the high of 53.4% between the ages of 45 and 54 years. (U. S. Dept. of Commerce, 1974, Table 543).

Other recent trends show that among married women aged 25 to 44 living with their husbands, the proportion in the labor force increased by 41% between 1960 and 1973, from 33.1% to 46.4%, and among wives between the ages of 45 and 64 years, the proportion of workers increased similarly (U. S. Dept. of Commerce, 1974, Table 545). One important consideration, however, is that the employment figures of women in the labor force often camouflage a minimal level of involvement. Only 42% of those women who worked some time in 1967 did so full time the year round (Women's Bureau, 1969). Thus, despite strong indication that women will continue to increase their number of years of work involvement over the life cycle, and despite a seeming gradual change in attitude of the traditional culture toward women's roles, the intermittent nature of the female work career will most likely continue, and the work cycles of women will remain clearly distinguishable from those of men.

Lopata (1966) maintains the social role of housewife has a unique cycle compared to other roles, involving relatively little anticipatory socialization, very brief time devoted to the "becoming" stage, and a rather compressed and early peak. It can be performed during the major part of the life cycle of a woman, yet "its entrance, modifications, and cessation are usually not a consequence of its own characteristics or rhythm but of those of other roles." She goes on to explain that some women never become "inside-located," so that the return to work or other community involvement (of married women) after the birth of the children is rapid and complete. Women who have placed themselves in the home and for whom the housewife role became important may be attracted to the outside or forced out of the inside by a feeling of obligation to help in the financial support of the family, or through crises such as widowhood. Those who do not go out completely, but do so part time, include women who have never cut off ties with the outside, or who develop new lines of connection.

They most frequently combine both orientations through the addition of some outside role, such as part-time worker, without letting such identification grow into a total commitment. Most of the aforementioned Chicago interviewees, even those who had full time employment outside of the home, expressed an "inside" identity.

Housewife Role

The "shrinking circle" stage in the social role of housewife starts when the first child is married or has left home and is very difficult for women who have invested their lives in that role and who do not have alternative sources for the focusing of identity. According to Lopata (1966), the "shrinking" of the "circle" removes many of the sources of prestige without any choice or control on the part of the woman whose identity is bound with it. No matter how well she performs it, how many and how important are the persons for whom it is performed, or how significant is the role in the lives of recipients, modern society automatically decreases the ability of the role of housewife to serve as a center of relations. Thus, "the housewife ceases to perform the role at a high plateau level, long before capacity to carry out its duties decreases, providing a reason or excuse for its cessation." Changes in the role come basically and primarily from changes in characteristics of the circle prior to any changes in her which could provide justification for decreasing functionality. Furthermore, the shrinking of the role importance of housewife and mother cannot always lead to a shift of self and of role-focus to a concentration of the role of wife, if such an emphasis was absent, since the husband tends still to be highly involved in the role of worker.

Also, according to Lopata (1966), for those aging women who have survived the "shrinking circle" stage, fewer decision-making problems, a lack of pressure from demanding and often conflicting roles, satisfaction with past performance of the role of housewife and with the products of the role of mother, and prior adjustment to the lack of centrality in the lives of children can all contribute to a relatively high degree of satisfaction in the later years. For those who are not widows, the focal nature of the role of wife may be increased with the retirement, or "fade out," from occupational roles on the part of the spouse. Widowhood is more likely to occur for females than for males (Lopata, 1972); at any point during the life cycle, death of a spouse could cause a major transformation in the social role of housewife and could demand a role realignment.

Thus, the life cycle of a human being can be seen as involving shifts in the components of his or her role cluster, when new ones are added and old ones dropped, and when shifts occur in the location of each role in the cluster. The general attitude which seems to pervade the gerontological literature is that while circumstances and family composition may vary over time, the female's identification with the roles of wife, mother, homemaker, and worker remains unchanged throughout her adult life.

Retirement Role

The facts *are*, however, that the female is constantly undergoing modifications in the characteristics of each assigned role as she enters different stages of the life cycle or changes her definition of the role, in response to events external to the person. Heyman (1970) remarks that while some wives may retire as many as three different times during a lifetime, these retirements obviously differ from the "retirement" of a man who at a relatively advanced age and with declining physical health is facing a single, final separation from his central life role as a wage-earner and principal provider for his family. The male is faced with loss of what has heretofore been conceived as a permanent work role, reduced economic resources, and necessity for role realignment and the need for new role opportunities. For today's elderly women, on the other hand, retirement may have begun quite early in her lifetime and have recurred periodically.

There currently exists considerable disagreement as to the impact of retirement upon the male. Miller's (1965) identity crisis theory suggests that retirement in and of itself negatively influences the quality of one's life, while Atchley's (1971) identity continuity theory posits that work is not necessarily at the top of several roles on which one's identity rests and that its removal is not regarded negatively by most retired people. However, there is a general consensus in the literature that retirement rarely poses any problems for women because "she is merely giving up a secondary role in favor of the primary roles of housewife, mother, and grandmother" (Palmore, 1965).

Role Continuity and Discontinuity

The writer would agree with Lowenthal and Berkman (1967) that "adjustment to the later stages of life may be more gradual for women than for men," and with McEwan and Sheldon (1969) that "women tend to be more satisfied at retirement than men," but would not attribute the positive adjustment to the static nature of women's roles from girlhood to grave. Rather, it appears that the impact of socialization on American women creates *impermanence* in the form of role loss and repeated adjustment to change in the life situation — and that this socialization process facilitates adjustment of women to old age.

Our society defines "permanence" as having a long-lasting, viable social and economic role. While it appears that this "permanence" is relatively accessible to at least middle-majority males, for women it is tenuous and thwarted. Women of all educational, geographical, and economic positions have been subjected to changes produced by our modern industrial society. Increasing mobility, for example, has changed the complexion of American society in the diminution of the extended family structure in its varied form as well as its demands upon individuals. The striving of women for permanence is dead-ended numerous times during the life cycle, resulting in role *dis*continuity or change in life situation. This striving for permanence is periodically redirected until old age when societal roles for the aged, both male and female, are further withdrawn.

Failure to attain permanence is exhibited throughout the entire social life cycle of women. Role losses impede attaining permanence before facing the impermanence impact of old age. Symbols of permanence that are thwarted, resulting in role discontinuity and changes in life situation, are numerous.

As stated by Steinman (1963), the feminine role is "not only ill-defined, but full of contradictions, ambiguities, and inconsistencies. Education, for instance, prepared women for membership in the labor force; yet many parents still raise their daughters with a view of marriage rather than furthering their personal development through employment. The women who are processed through the educational system and then marry experience a strong role discontinuity, as described by Decter (1971). For the woman who disbands her work role to give priority to roles of mother and housewife, there is discontinuity when the children leave home or become increasingly independent of home and parents. Another role discontinuity to consider is the disrupted marital status such as widowhood. In 1968, the wife was the surviving spouse in 70% of all marriages broken by the death of one partner (Lopata, 1971b). Although men also suffer the loss of husband role through widowhood, the loss is experienced by fewer numbers of men and is not coupled with financial loss due to widowhood.

Thus, role discontinuity and change in life situation are more likely suffered by women than men. Adjustments to the discontinuities are imposed on women by society through the socialization process.

It is suggested here, then, that precisely because women *are* subjected to repeated role discontinuities and changes in life situation to which they adjust, the final adjustment to old age is made more easily by them.

Readjustment Theory

Cottrell (1942) maintains that an individual will make a facile adjustment to a role change to the extent that he has undergone anticipatory preparation for that role situation. Women have had considerable experience in adjusting to age-linked changes (children leaving home, menopause) and have therefore become accustomed to change and impermanence. Thus, women are not as devastated as men are likely to be when old age, another impermanence, separates them from the productive, involved, financially independent world of middle age; and the adoption of new roles and the giving up of middle-age roles should be relatively more facile for women than for men. If this theory of repeated readjustment fosters adjustment to old age for women more readily than for men is valid, one should be able to demonstrate that the process of adjustment to aging, especially as it reflects a response to impermanence or discontinuity, is different for men than for women.

Mulvey (1963) organized what data she had found on characteristics of women's vocational behavior into seven career patterns, defined in terms of a career with and without marriage, and with and without work. Her study of women between the ages of 50 and 60 years concludes that high life satisfaction is associated with career patterns marked by: (1) return to career after children entered school ("interrupted-work primary"), (2) entry upon deferred career ("delayed-work secondary"), (3) contribution of talent and time to volunteer activities when children were young ("stable homemaking-work secondary"), (4) continuous and simultaneous homemaking and working. The vocational behavior of women who displayed the least degree of life satisfaction was characterized by a single, continuous role of either homemaker or worker over the adult life-span. The woman with a greater degree of life satisfaction has experienced more discontinuity and change of primary roles over the lifetime.

Dunkle (1972) reanalyzed data from Schooler's (1969) study of non-institutionalized elderly to investigate the relationship of length of time at residential location, distance moved, change in marital status, and change in position within the labor force to morale in old age. The value of her work in application to this paper's hypothesis is greatly enhanced by the inclusion of sex differentiation in her sample. Her results show that 47.1% of the men experiencing only a small degree of change in residence, marital status, and work involvement have high morale, while 51.8% of those men who have experienced a considerable amount of change over the life cycle display high morale, a difference of 4.3 percentage points; 6.3% more women who display a large amount of change over their lives have high morale than the women characterized by stability in residence, marital status, and work involvement. Furthermore, Dunkle's data show that almost twice as many women as men experience change with relation to the tested variables.

With admittedly weak measures in the sense that the data were not originally intended for this purpose, Dunkle's study suggests that women are socialized differently from men such that they were in the past more likely to experience discontinuity and impermanence, and that women, in fact, are better able to adjust in old age as a result of this past impermanence in life situations. It seems, therefore, that if discontinuity could be shown to be positively associated with adjustment to old age as measured by morale, there would be important implications for a theory of successful aging, based on discontinuity and impermanence over the life cycle.

Work and Leisure Patterns

Probably the most feasible method of building an option for discontinuity into our societal structure would be to revamp our current work and leisure patterns. Kreps (1971) points out:

> The individual's choice seems to have little to do with how much he works. At any point in time, institutional arrangements largely dictate the terms of nonworking time, i.e., when it occurs and who receives it.

Compulsory retirement at age 65 is one example; the statutory 40-hour week, as well as negotiated vacation plans, help to standardize the length of the workyear. It is important to raise the question of worker preference: preference as to how much free time one would elect, under any given income status; and preference as to when that free time would be taken. "For there may be ways to bend the institutions to the workers' wishes, once they are known" (Kreps, 1971).

Little is known about people's perceptions of the worth of free time; certainly, there is no evidence on the price that will be paid for time off. Most important, there is the question of whether leisure becomes more or less valuable as one grows older. Research might indicate that retirement in the optional years has the effect of conferring leisure on man when he least wants it — a curious inversion of the notion that youth is wasted on the young. The total number of workers involved in career changes during middle age or later worklife might increase, moreover, if such changes were made to be viable alternatives to present continuous cycles of employment.

Senator Mondale (Special Committee on Aging, 1969), a member of the Senate Special Committee on Aging, called for the altering of traditional work lifetime patterns, including institution of sabbaticals, phased retirement, trial retirement, and part-time work arrangements for those near retirement years. Such experiments, however, have been limited. For most elderly males, retirement, whether compulsory or voluntary, has provided the first opportunity for considerable amounts of leisure time throughout all of the adult years. It is no wonder then that renouncing the primary work role and substituting new roles for which there has been little change for "rehearsal" presents difficulty for the male.

Lopata and Steinhart (1971) suggest it might be valuable for our society to assume that few persons actually benefit from working in one occupation for more than perhaps 10 years, and that, with some exceptions, those who do produce diminishing returns for the organization. More efficient methods of education could then be introduced to retrain people at the end of each "natural cycle" of involvement in a particular occupation. We still lack adequate re-engagement procedures in the work world, because of a myth that modern workers work continuously and have steady careers from education to retirement. This fiction does not reflect lives of men, let alone women.

Career Flexibility

Recently, important strides are beginning to be made in liberating women to engage in meaningful employment and in liberating society at large to make positions of power available to women. Perhaps the seeming goal to attain the same rigid, life-long role to which most males in our society are now subjected should be reconsidered by women's activist groups. If the theory that impermanence and discontinuity over the adult life cycle exert a direct effect upon positive adjustment to old age is valid, then a new system of career flexibility should be adopted as the new battle cry by men and women alike.

REFERENCES

Atchley, R. C. Retirement and leisure participation: Continuity or crisis? *Gerontologist*, 1971, *11* (1:1), 13-17.

Atchley, R. C. Role changes in later life. In R. C. Atchley (Ed.), *The social forces in later life*. Wadsworth, Belmont, CA, 1972.

Biddle, B. J. & Thomas, E. J. (Eds.) *Role theory: Concepts and research*. Wiley & Sons, New York, 1966.

Cottrell, L. S., Jr. The adjustment of the individual to his age and sex roles. *American Sociological Review*, 1942, *7*, 617-622.

Cumming, M. E. New thoughts on the theory of disengagement. In R. Kastenbaum (Ed.), *New thoughts on old age*. Springer, New York, 1964.

Decter, M. *The liberated woman and other Americans*. Coward, McCann, & Geoghegan, New York, 1971.

deGrazia, S. *Of time, work and leisure*. Anchor Books, Garden City, NY, 1964.

Dunkel, R. E. Life experiences of women and old age. Paper presented at 25th annual meeting of Gerontological Society, San Juan, Dec. 17-21, 1972.

Gallaway, L. E. *The retirement decision: An exploratory essay*. Report No. 9. USDHEW, Washington, 1965.

Heyman, D. K. Does a wife retire? *Gerontologist*, 1970, *10*, 54-56.

Heyman, D. K., & Jeffers, F. C. Wives and retirement: A pilot study. *Journal of Gerontology*, 1968, *23*, 488-496.

Hughes, E. C. *Men and their work*. Free Press, Glencoe, IL, 1958.

Jackson, J. J. Negro aged: Toward needed research in social gerontology. *Gerontologist*, 1971, *11*, 52-57.

Kreps, J. M. Career options after fifty: Suggested research. *Gerontologist* 1971, *11* (1:2), 4-8.

Lopata, H. Z. The life cycle of the social role of the housewife. *Sociology & Social Research*, 1966, *51*, 5-22.

Lopata, H. Z. *Occupation: Housewife*. Oxford Press, New York, 1971.(a)

Lopata, H. Z. Widows as a minority group. *Gerontologist* 1971, *11* (1:2), 22-27.(b)

Lopata, H. Z. *Widowhood in an American city*. Schenkman, Boston, 1972.

Lopata, H. Z. & Steinhart, F. Work histories of American urban women. *Gerontologist*, 1971, *11*, (4:2), 27-36.

Lowenthal, M. F., & Berkman, P. *Aging and mental disorder in San Francisco*. Jossey-Bass, San Francisco, 1967.

McEwan, P. J. M., & Sheldon, A. P. Patterns of retirement. *Journal of Geriatric Psychiatry*, 1969, *3*, 35-54.

Miller, S. J. The social dilemma of the aging leisure participant. In A. M. Rose & W. A. Peterson (Eds.), *Older people and their social world*. Davis, Philadelphia, 1965.

Mulvey, M. C. Psychological and sociological factors in prediction of career patterns of women. *Genetic Psychological Monographs*, No. 68, 1963.

Palmore, E. B. Differences in the retirement patterns of men and women. *Gerontologist*, 1965, *5*, 4-8.

Schooler, K. K. The relationship between social interaction and moral of the elderly as a function of environmental characteristics. *Gerontologist*, 1969, *9*, 25-29.

Special Committee on Aging. The federal role in encouraging preretirement counselling and new work lifetime patterns. Hearing before the Subcommittee on Retirement and the Individual of the Special Committee on Aging, U. S.

Senate, 91st Congress, 1st Session, July 25, 1969.

Steinmann, A. A study of the concept of the feminine role of 51 middle class American families. *Genetic Psychological Monographs*, No. 67, 1963.

U. S. Dept. of Commerce, Bureau of the Census. *Statistical abstracts of the U. S.* Washington, 1974.

Williams, R. H., & Wirths, C. G. *Lives through the years.* Atherton Press, New York, 1965.

Women's Bureau. *1969 Handbook on women workers*, Bull. No. 294, U. S. Dept. of Labor, Washington, 1969.

Chapter 9

A CRABBIT OLD WOMAN WROTE THIS

AUTHOR UNKNOWN

IT appeared when the old lady died in the geriatric ward of Ashludie Hospital, near Dundee, that she had left nothing of value; then the nurse going through her possessions found a poem.

The quality of this so impressed the staff that copies were duplicated and distributed to every nurse in the hospital.

When one of the nurses, 35 year old Vertha Rainey, moved to nurse geriatric patients in Braid Valley Hospital, Ballymena, she took her copy with her and the poem — the old lady's only bequest to posterity — has since appeared in a Christmas edition of the "Beacon House News," magazine of the Northern Ireland Association for Mental Health, and also in Barrow Hospital's "The Barrow Broadsheet."

> What do you see nurses, what do you see?
> Are you thinking when you are looking at me
> A crabbit old woman, not very wise
> Uncertain of habit, with far away eyes,
> Who dribbles her food and makes no reply
> When you say in a loud voice — "I do wish you'd try."
> Who seems not to notice the things that you do,
> And forever is losing a stocking or shoe.
> Who unresisting or not, lets you do as you will,
> With bathing and feeding, the long day to fill.
> Is that what you are thinking, is that what you see?
> Then open your eyes, nurse, you're not looking at me.
> I'll tell you who I am as I sit here so still
> As I use at your bidding, as I eat at your will.
> I'm a small child of ten with a father and mother.
> Brothers and sisters, who love one another,
> A young girl of sixteen with wings on her feet,
> Dreaming that soon now a lover she'll meet.
> A bride soon at twenty — my heart gives a leap,
> Remembering the vows that I promised to keep,
> At twenty-five now I have young of my own,
> Who need me to build a secure, happy home.

A woman of thirty, my young now grow fast
Bound to each other with ties that should last.
At forty, my young sons have grown and are gone,
But my man's beside me to see I don't mourn.
At fifty once more babies play round my knee,
Again we know children, my loved one and me.

Dark days are upon me, my husband is dead,
I look at the future, I shudder with dread,
For my young are all rearing young of their own,
And I think of the years and the love that I've known.
I'm an old woman now and nature is cruel.
"Tis her just to make old age look like a fool."
The body it crumbles, grace and vigor depart.
There is now a stone where I once had a heart.
But inside this old carcass a young girl still dwells,
And now and again my battered heart swells.
I remember the joys, I remember the pain,
And I'm loving and living life over again,
I think of the years all too few — gone too fast,
And accept the stark fact that nothing can last.
So open your eyes, nurses, open and see
Not a crabbit old woman, look closer — see ME!

Part III

Biological Facts and Fallacies

INTRODUCTION

The insults of aging — the physiological malfunctionings of the organism — are an unfortunate aspect of aging for most of the human race. By the age of 65, about three-fourths of people have one or more chronic conditions. One of the interesting, and still not satisfactorily explained, biological phenomena is the greater longevity of women. Indeed, the whole area of biological aging is characterized by much research, yet there is still much disagreement on what "causes" aging. One of the reasons research in this area is popular is that all of us would like to live to be one hundred — in good health and full possession of our faculties. We would like to escape the insults of aging.

The biological processes of aging differ little when the subjects are women or men. Both seem to have cardiovascular systems that wear out in the same way — though perhaps at somewhat different rates. Similarly, sensory loss is common to both as are various other accumulated pathologies of aging. Menopause, at least as a readily recognizable physiological event, is, however, unique to women, and it is usually associated with aging. Sexual interest also has been allegedly different for men and women throughout their lives and in the past it has been assumed that women lose interest in sex sooner than men. A third area in which there have been alleged differences between men and women has been in connection with mental health. Many writers assert that neurosis, pathological dependency, hysteria, and various other mental "illnesses" have been associated with menopause in the aging woman. We have chosen some provocative articles that will bring into focus some of the biological facts and fallacies about these three areas of the life of the aging woman.

Chapter 10 sets the stage by giving the perspective of an articulate older woman. Faith Baldwin, who resents being imprisoned in her aging body, enumerates many of the insults she suffers — though not gladly. Certainly her mental health is excellent.

Some have claimed that all knowledge is a footnote to Aristotle. One could almost make the same claim for Benjamin Franklin. In a delightful article (Chapter 11), Virginia Sherr reminds us of the value that Dr. Franklin assigned to older women as lovers; he certainly did not dismiss them as sexual partners because of age. Sherr also concurs in his advice about life-styles as he writes his sister about an older relative. She adds some interesting information addressed to a medical audience about therapeutic measures for older people.

In Chapter 12, Norman Lobsenz summarizes the literature on sexuality and aging. He also makes the point that —

> Clearly, there is more to sexuality after 65 than just the act of sex. For a man, there is the satisfaction of feeling still masculine; for a woman, still feminine; for both, still being wanted and needed. There is the comforting warmth of physical nearness, the pleasure of companionship. There is the rewarding emotional intimacy of shared joys.

This is a clear statement of the breadth of sexuality for old or young. We would wish every older woman its joys!

Chapter 13, by Edward Graber and Hugh Barber, deals with menopause and presents the case for and against estrogen therapy. This unresolved question has importance for all women past menopause, and this thoughtful article should prove helpful in making up one's mind.

We are aware that these few articles have not adequately treated the intricate subject of the health of older women. We hope they have spoken to some of the facts and tenacious fallacies held by many of us in some degree and that they will stimulate a more positive attitude toward the biological changes of aging.

Chapter 10

MY CRABBÈD AGE*

FAITH BALDWIN

Y ESTERDAY my daughter returned from a trip to the village and presented me with a lightweight cane. This is either the beginning or end of an era. I am, to be sure, humiliatingly unsteady, but have managed for the last five years by holding on to uncomplaining furniture, a friend, or relative. I take exception to Robert Browning, who invited us to grow old along with him. He was 29 when he wrote that in his poem, "Pippa Passes," and he lived to be 70. I have sometimes wondered how he felt, if during the geriatric years he glanced at those lines.

Personally, I am tired of the how-to-grow-old-gracefully books, the articles extolling the sunset years, and the admonitions delivered in doctors' offices. I am quite aware that there are those from 70 to 100 who crash happily about, agile as the chamois, paragons of usefulness and creativity, objects of admiration, often living efficiently alone; although most of the centenarians are in nursing homes, often appearing on TV surrounded by candles and reporters. There are writers, musicians, actors, and others who have survived to my age, and longer, yet appear to function without effort.

Me, I don't.

The actual number of years I've been around causes me no trauma nor tantrum. I once enjoyed revealing my age publicly, but when my audience, be it composed of one person or hundreds, stopped saying, "You don't look it," and took to exclaiming, "God bless you," I ceased to volunteer this information, unless asked. After a time, no one asked; they didn't have to.

Years are all right and survival splendid, but what these bring to us is not usually what it's cracked up to be. The books say "wisdom." Well, perhaps in some cases, but in mine, it's simply knowledge — everyone has to acquire a certain amount from childhood. We learn early what no means; and are told why. Another thing we are expected to attain is serenity — a marvelous faculty that I've not possessed since, possibly, the age of two-and-a-half.

As for becoming mellow, this word astonishes me; it sounds like something overripe.

Only rare people have assumed early the proper attitudes, to say nothing of selecting organic foods, avoiding excesses, shunning alcohol, tobacco, anxiety, and panic, thus keeping a low profile and blood pressure so diligently that it showed when they became four score and ten. Most of us scramble to undo, or not do, too late. Remember, as the twig is bent . . .

Up until five years ago, I was merry as a grig. Then I began to receive in hospitals and examining rooms all the sensible guidelines: Be patient, adjust, accept, adapt; and some suggested, "Just be glad you have all your buttons."

Who *knows* that? To be sure I am no more forgetful than my children, no more absentminded than I was at 40. But no one on earth is privy to my buttons. I've never had a buttoned-down mind. Upstairs in the drawer of an old lampstand I have a button box — and who's to say what's in it?

Pleasant people ask me, "How are you able to write of contemporary matters?" This is a curious question; I am contemporary, I've always been. Everyone living at, or in, any age has to be — except the geniuses who were ahead of their eras. As I am no longer able to lurk about listening to strangers talk in trains, planes, and restaurants, nor lose myself in crowds with my ears open, nor go to parties and mind other people's vocal business, nor receive their unwitting confidences, I keep up with the times in other ways. There are basics in each generation that do not alter, and I have an excellent memory. I can recall my childhood, my children's, and my grandchildren's, and I have outside knowledge of what is known as *now*, thanks to radio, television, books, newspapers, and magazines. It is not difficult to comprehend new *mores* — some of which were current in 1920 — nor the current argot, so I remain contemporary. I wrote my first book in 1920, and except for a few period novels I have written, two that ended with World War I, and one that began in 1860, I have remained with today; however, I'm not contemporary in the use of certain words or phrases. I grew bored with those from the time I heard them uttered behind the barn or read them on fences. I am not contemporary in my avoidance of explicitizing situations. (That's a made-up word and I'm proud of it.) Such situations have been around for centuries, so what's novel about them except that now everything can be said, told, or shouted from the literary housetops?

And yet all I've seen and experienced has not extinguished my hopes for the world and its inheritors, the young.

I wouldn't choose to be young again if I had to relive the years, but I'd like to be, say, 35 and know, at that age, what I've learned since.

What I mind is not my age but the insistence that all is sweetness and light, as one rides off into the sunset or, more accurately, stumbles downhill. Also, I dislike the handicaps, the figurative straitjacket, the destruction of mobility, the lessening of sight, the distressing necessity of having to look after myself, as well-wishers bid me. I've always looked after myself but not in the tedious ways — be careful of stairs and of what you eat, don't sit in drafts, nor get your feet wet . . . be sure to rest!

All this bugs me. I resent not just being old, not even growing older, but the disabilities and prohibitions. I have a few friends of my own age; only two admit to resentment.

It's just not done, according to Mr. Browning.

However, I must endeavor to be grateful for the buttons — and the ability to see, if through a glass darkly. I must be thankful for the power to walk at all, with or without a cane, and to hear as well as I ever have, and also the ability to laugh, mostly at myself, and to enjoy such pleasures as are possible.

My paternal grandmother, who spent many years in what is now called Old China, used to tell me in what reverence the old were held. Every Chinese girl, ruled by her mother-in-law, yearned to be old, a matriarch, the venerable and absolute boss lady. I don't know if this reverence is extant anywhere on earth now. But most countries are concerned about their aged, in terms of health care, food, recreation, and money. But they are also aware that, thanks to advances in medicine, too many people are living too long. I think at this point reverence goes out the window and resignation comes in.

Resignation; that's another guideline for the faltering feet I am not resigned to. I haven't worn a hat in years, but if I owned one, I'd put it on and take it off to the many adventurous ancients going on cruises, bus tours, platforms, and talk shows. If you removed all the little bottles of nitroglycerin they stow away in pockets and handbags, you could blow up a small section of the world. But more power to them; may they live for as long as it pleases them.

After two cataract operations, after recovery, and proper glasses, I looked in the mirror and screamed. As it took some time before I could have surgery, I had not seen myself clearly for several years. Of course, I'd long been conscious of the fact that I was no longer 18 and haven't been for decades, except in the stubborn inner-self that never grows up.

Well, there are sneaky, and expensive, ways to fight the battle we must eventually lose — plastic surgeons, new medication, trips to rejuvenation centers, cosmeticians, prescribed nutrition, moderate exercise, and, of course, thinking positively.

I'm not fighting. I am unregenerate and lazy; all my life I've shied away from the strenuous and avoided regimes.

So I'm complaining; I think it's time someone did. I can't believe I'm the only person of my age group who isn't resigned and abhors the "Brace up, you're only 80" suggestion that adds, "also, the best is yet to come."

Balderdash!

I cannot alter my physical disabilities, so I'll live with them — but I don't have to like it; and I do have one regret. There are so many people I'd like to meet, so many places I'd like to see.

But long ago I learned to leave the table a trifle hungry. This is good discipline for the figure and, perhaps, the spirit.

Chapter 11

BENJAMIN FRANKLIN AND GEROPSYCHIATRY: VIGNETTES FOR THE BICENTENNIAL YEAR*

Virginia T. Sherr

It is timely in this Bicentennial year for readers of a journal devoted to geriatrics to refer to the wisdom of an older leader of the Revolution of 1776. So provocative was his thinking that Dr. Benjamin Franklin might well have inspired today's writers in the field, as demonstrated by relevant gleanings from articles in the recent literature.

PRACTICING geriatric psychiatry in 1776 might have been a difficult way to make a living because, at that time, relatively few citizens reached 65 years of age. Even the elder statesmen of the revolution were in the young middle-age category by today's standards. General George Washington was 44 years old in 1776. Daniel Morgan was 43; Benjamin Rush was 31; Thomas Jefferson was 33; and John Hancock was 39 years old. General Israel Putnam, who because of his years was nicknamed "Old Put," left his plow in a field and went to Bunker Hill at the advanced age of 58.

Who was there, then, wise with experience and a full life whom we today would consider geriatric? Benjamin Franklin qualifies. He was 70 years old at the signing of the Declaration of Independence; he was a prolific writer, scientist, and humanist — a true multidisciplinarian. Perhaps of all the men named, he would least likely be astonished at the world today; as a matter of fact, he foresaw much of what since has become history. His 1751 remarks on the future American population was prophetic: "There are supposed to be now upward of one million English souls in North America (although it is thought scarce 80,000 have been brought over by sea). This million doubling, suppose but once in 25 years, will in another century be more than the people of England and the greatest number of Englishmen will be on this side of the water. . . ." (1). Look what has happened recently.

---

*From *Journal of the American Geriatrics Society,* 24:447-451, 1976.

The overall United States 1970 census was somewhat over 203 million and the 1974 census was 211 million. Thus, in four years' time, there was an 8-million increase in the population.

In this century alone, there has been roughly a seven-fold increase from the 3 million people who were 65 or older in 1900, up to 22 million in 1974. These older people now constitute 10.3 percent of our population. The average lifespan for women went from 48 years in 1900 to 75 years in 1973, an increase of 56 percent; for men, the lifespan went from 46 years in 1900 to 68 years in 1973, an increase of only 46 percent. The census report notes that while there were 134 women for every 100 men in the entire older age group (60 and up), the ratio of women to men rose steadily with age to the point that there were and are over 200 women to every 100 men for subgroup 85 years and over (2).

Sexual Activity

Ben Franklin's creative mind may well have anticipated this dilemma for older women. What is to be done when women outnumber male peers two to one? In his "Old Mistresses Apologue" Franklin pointed out what may become a possible solution to the statistical imbalance. In essence, he felt that older women and young men are ideally suited for one another. Many of these arguments would brand him a male chauvinist in today's world, but he enumerated eight reasons why old women make good lovers:

1. Because as they (older women) have more knowledge of the World and their Minds are better stor'd with Observations, their Conversation is more improving and more lastingly agreable.

2. Because when Women cease to be handsome, they study to be good. To maintain their Influence over Men, they supply the Diminution of Beauty by an Augmentation of Utility. They learn to do a 1000 Services small and great, and are the most tender and useful of all Friends when you are sick. Thus they continue amiable. And hence there is hardly such a thing to be found as an old Woman who is not a good Woman.

3. Because there is no hazard of Children, which irregularly produc'd may be attended with much Inconvenience.

4. Because thro' more Experience, they are more prudent and discreet in conducting an Intrigue to prevent Suspicion. The Commerce with them is therefore safer with regard to your Reputation. And with regard to theirs, if the Affair should happen to be known, considerate People might be rather inclin'd to excuse an old Woman who would kindly take care of a young Man, form his Manners by

her good Counsels, and prevent his ruining his Health and Fortune amongst mercenary Prostitutes.

5. Because in every Animal that walks upright, the Deficiency of the Fluids that fill the Muscles appears first in the highest Part: The Face first grows lank and wrinkled; then the Neck; then the Breast and Arms; the lower Parts continuing to the last as plump as ever: So that covering all above with a Basket, and regarding only what is below the Girdle, it is impossible of two Women to know an old from a young one. And as in the dark all Cats are grey, the Pleasure of corporal Enjoyment with an old Woman is at least equal, and frequently superior, every Knack being by Practice capable of Improvement.

6. Because the Sin is less. The debauching a Virgin may be her Ruin, and make her for Life unhappy.

7. Because the Compunction is less. The having made a young Girl miserable may give you frequent bitter Reflections; none of which can attend the making an old Woman happy.

8thly and Lastly. They are so grateful!! (3).

Owing to his interest in related problems, Ben Franklin's library of today surely might include references from recent issues of this and other journals. For example, in this Bicentennial Year, sexuality as related to aging is becoming acknowledged as a real issue. It is not only a question of whether geriatric sex is a myth or a miracle, as discussed in a recent issue of the Journal of the American Geriatrics Society (4). It also is a matter of personal autonomy, civil rights and the politics of a climate which tends to impose on older people that they are in a futureless, stereotyped position. It is the issue of the right to expect tender, loving skin — a need of every one from birth to death — an especially great need at the two extremities of life. The issue is not just of the right of residents to have intercourse in nursing homes, but of the loss of the expectation by self and by caretakers of one's ever again fulfilling oneself as an intimately valuable being. What greater loss could there be?

Enlightened medical consultants to nursing homes now are obtaining a sexuality history in their intake interviews with new guests (4). One consultant found "most of the ladies still interested and about one-half of the men interested." Norman West (4) made five observations: 1) sexual desire and activity exist in a significant number of the elderly; 2) aged persons are quite willing to substitute modified forms of sexual activity as needed; 3) if they have lost desire or function, they can come to accept this fact without becoming upset and obsessed by it; 4) sex and high moral values are closely associated and pure self-gratification is of little interest; and 5) older peoples' experience has been that sex in itself is not purely mechanical or physiologic and the important component is love. Sex is seen as an expression of love and not just a self-satisfying exercise.

Lifestyle

Providing institutionalized older people with their usual beverage and food is another area we are just fully appreciating. A recent article in the Journal of the American Geriatrics Society promotes the therapeutic value of "soul food" for aged residents of institutions (5). Soul food now means anyone's familiar cultural gastronomic specialty, and it does not have to be served daily to treat the inner spirit. One day a week of corn beef and cabbage, or bagels and lox, or black-eyed peas and ham hocks, or rigatoni with tomato sauce may be enough to refresh the taste buds of an ethnic minority in an institution. People not only enjoy this but see the nod in their directions, culturally, as evidence of respect for their life styles and customs.

The Bicentennial era is becoming comfortable also with the idea of alcohol as a social stimulant for the institutionalized elderly. Dr. Franklin wrote that it must have been Noah who first appreciated the importance of wine over water: "That virtue and safety in Wine-bibbings's found. While all that drinks water deserves to be drown'd. So for safety and honesty put the glass round" (3). In regard to the safety factor, modern medical literature does not seem to support the belief that ill people are always physically helped by their evening cocktail; in fact, this may aggravate some physical problems in a few. However, the use of a social hour and wine with meals to promote social awareness and to create a climate of honest or meaningful interaction between older people has begun to flourish and may become a vital part of milieu therapy for the majority of older adults in residential homes. Again, the availability of this familiar offering allows social flexibility, as well as an appropriate bow to the older guest's lifestyle, precious as that is to each person.

Sudden lifestyle change can be risky. Do physicians realize how much is demanded of an octogenarian in asking him to re-orient himself overnight to institutional living? What we often interpret as psychotic, agitated behavior on the part of a nursing-home guest may well be the outward manifestation of a clash of lifestyles. For the sake of a longer and more comfortable quality of life, the challenge is to gear our institutions to people and not try to force people to fit rigid preconceived programs (6). Benjamin Franklin once wrote a letter, "Consideration for the Old Folks," to his sister:

Dear Sister, I wrote a few lines to you yesterday, but omitted to answer yours relating to sister Dowse. As *having their own way* is one of the greatest comforts of life to old people, I think their friends should endeavor to accommodate them in that, as well as in anything else. When they have long lived in a house, it becomes natural to them; they are almost as closely connected with it as the tortoise with his shell; they die if you tear them out of it; old folks and old trees, if you remove them it is ten to one that you kill them; so let our good old sister be no more importuned on that head. We are growing old fast ourselves and shall expect the same kind of indulgences; if we give them, we shall have a right to receive them in our turn.

And as to her few fine things, I think she is in the right not to sell them, and for that reason she gives, that they will fetch but little; when that little is spent, they would be of no further use to her; but perhaps the expectation of possessing them at her death may make that person tender and careful of her, and helpful to her to the amount, of ten times their value. If so, they are put to the best use they possibly can be.

I hope you visit sister as often as your affairs will permit, and afford her what assistance and comfort you can in her present situation. Old age, infirmities, and poverty, joined, are affliction enough. The neglect and slights of friends and near relations should never be added. People in her circumstances are apt to suspect this sometimes without cause; *appearances* should therefore be attended to, in our conduct toward them, as well as *realities*. I write by this post to cousin Williams to continue his care, which I doubt not he will do. (7)

One of the key points in this letter is the last one: "Appearances should therefore be attended to, as well as realities." To the health professional, this means that one must be careful not to convey to the older client even the appearance of dealing him out of a decision-making role (unless it is mandatory, and then that should be discussed directly with the patient). The appearance of treating him as a second-class citizen or the appearance of not dealing with him as an individual should be avoided. Doctors sometimes are guilty, inadvertently, of establishing an inaccurate, but fatal verdict of "senility" or "hopelessness" or "incompetence" by their style of handling aged clients. For example, many physicians, when an aged client is referred to them, leave him in the waiting room while the family is interviewed, seeing him only after the family has had its say. Just as serious is the fact that many physicians initially see the aged client at the same time as the family. Much more pertinent information and the true mental state of the older client can be elicited clearly when the client sees the physician first; this allows him to view the doctor as his ally, *his* doctor, and not as an authoritative reinforcer of the social impotence he fears. In the presence of his family, he may withdraw emotionally. The doctor's taking the family aside to talk can create in the patient a hopeless, depressed self-view and an angry suspiciousness of the physician based on reality. Why not avoid the "appearance" of a conspiracy as well as the reality?

Therapeutic Measures

Benjamin Franklin, natural philosopher, as the eighteenth century called its scientists, was intrigued by gadgets and any new ideas which would benefit the people. He would have been delighted with the EMI Scanner (CCT, Computerized Transaxial Tomography) which we now have in the Bicentennial era. Here at last, is a noninvasive tool with which we can almost see the brain. For 1976, physicians will be using the EMI scan to evaluate more accurately their organically brain-impaired patients.

In the past, curable cases of normal-pressure hydrocephalus may have remained unidentified because doctors did not have conviction in their ability to diagnose this brain-killing condition without resorting to a pneumoencephalogram — a test which is exhausting to both patient and pocketbook, and fraught with the possibility of serious complications. But now, increasing numbers of aged people with organic brain impairment, including many who are admitted to private or state psychiatric hospitals, will be able to undergo the safe scan procedure. This group includes especially the victims of "cerebrovascular accidents" (one thinks of Poor Richard's "little strokes fell great oaks"), of repeated transient ischemic attacks, of focal neurologic symptoms or of the classic triad of normal-pressure hydrocephalus (incontinence, dementia and ataxia). The scan easily picks up such abnormalities as ventricular enlargement, cerebral hemorrhages, tumors, or cerebral atrophy.

In Philadelphia, the cost of the individual scan is about $200.00. Medicare should fund 80 percent of this, with "65 Special" paying most of the remainder. The possibility of diagnosing a reversible brain syndrome is well worth the expense. Much of the time, those who work with the organically brain-impaired must be content with treating an individual and his disability so that health and the quality of life are maintained as long as possible. To find a reversible organic brain disorder is a therapeutic ideal. To offer relief to a person with a surgically curable brain disorder, such as normal-pressure hydrocephalus, would be a triumphant way to celebrate this year.

The 1976 report by Jacobs et al. (8) on the diagnosis and treatment of normal-pressure hydrocephalus (NPH) is a Bicentennial gift for patients with early brain impairment. This work augurs well for preventive psychoneurologic intervention (9). When the NPH triad appears in a middle-aged or older person with normal cerebrospinal fluid pressure, the patient may experience great relief if surgery permits the fluid to drain into the atrium, or the peritoneal or pleural spaces. In the past, the failure rate for this shunt procedure (including a few fatalities) has been abysmal. Many psychiatrists have taken a dim view of shunting because they see the surviving failures, not the successes. However, Jacobs et al. identified clinical symptoms which enable reliable prediction as to who will be a successful candidate for shunting. Motor signs are the most valuable. Gait dyspraxia similar to drunken walking and signs of parkinsonism were common preoperatively in those who showed the greatest improvement after shunting. Those who improved the most had all three cardinal symptoms, but every successful patient had motor involvement; those without motor signs did poorly. In all cases, the pneumoencephalograms showed enlarged ventricles, but none showed cerebral atrophy or cerebrospinal fluid obstruction. There was a significant correlation between the length of illness and the outcome. The best responders had symptoms for less than three years. Most patients improved within one month after the shunting operation, many in just a few days. Some improved slowly in six months. When relief occurred, there was often dramatic reversal of the dementia and all other related symptoms with the exception of tremor which, when present, frequently still required *l*-dopa therapy. The most hopeful finding for psychiatrists was that the severity of the dementia was of no consistent value in predicting the response to surgery. Again, with this knowledge and with results of the EMI scan, there is a new avenue of hope for these brain-impaired patients.

Poor Richard was fond of saying, "A little neglect may breed great mischief." With the goal of preventive care, multidisciplinary teams (mobile out-reach units) and home health visitors have pioneered in habilitative geropsychiatric and social medicine. It is clear that such intervention is valuable to the client to prevent unnecessary admission to an institution. Being present in the personal habitat of the referred older person also allows an interviewer to observe ecologically the psychologic symptoms. Often these are found to be simply adaptive maneuvers in impossible life situations. Such observations permit social engineering, combined with good medical and psychiatric care, to constitute the successful preventive steps.

A recent report by Dawson and English (10), of McMaster University Medical Centre, relating to a program of psychiatric consultancy in a home for the aged, speaks for the importance of mobility and out-reach to prevent neglect. "By successfully handling requests for service from a home for the aged, the team established a consultative relationship and then a six-month teaching program centered on problems by the home's staff in group sessions. Results included a drop in requests for direct service, the establishment of group programs for the residents, and an increase in the home's willingness to accept and deal with disturbed behavior without resort to hospitalization."

Franklin's "a little neglect" aphorism relates also to discoveries about the effect of prolonged immobilization, especially in the aged. Physicians who have seen elderly patients in exercise groups may have thought that fun was the only benefit. However, Michael Miller (11) has noted the development of bizarre motor disorders which seem to prohibit walking in elderly persons undergoing prolonged immobilization (e.g., those in restraints because of fractures). This strange, helpless-appearing motor behavior may cause mislabeling of the patients as senile or psychotic. Luckily, with regular exercise, the bizarre motor signs clear up.

Many writers have promoted the judicious use of drugs for the elderly. However, Ben Franklin once said, "He's the best physician who knows the worthlessness of most medicines" (12). There are two medicines which may represent both points of view. Gerovital H3, the highly publicized youth drug, was studied by Zwerling et al. (13) in a double-blind test; unfortunately, there seemed to be no mental or physical beneifts in hospitalized geriatric patients. However, cyclandelate (400 mg four times daily) fared better in a study by Peter Hall in England (14). His 21 patients with cerebral arteriosclerosis were treated for 12 months in a double-blind study with crossover of drug and placebo after six months. Tests of memory, manual dexterity, and comprehension showed significant improvement with cyclandelate. In contrast to the effect of placebo, no measurable intellectual decline occurred during cyclandelate therapy. 1976 will tell us if this promise is fulfilled.

Comment

The challenge for 1976's older people and those helping them is similar to that faced by Dr. Franklin's peers 200 years ago when they rebelled against being programmed without representation. Older people tend to be treated, and have traditionally accepted being treated, like second-class citizens. As a group, they are very poor, inadequately nourished, stereotyped, and neglected as citizens. Their spokespersons are few, although such representatives are becoming more vocal. Dr. Franklin said, "They that can give up essential liberty to obtain a little temporary safety, deserve neither liberty nor safety." Perhaps it is our job therapeutically to assist older people in reasonable risk-taking, in appropriate rebelling. We need caution against the development in ourselves of an attitude similar to that taken by King George III, that their revolts are merely insurrections to be put down. Let us be careful to encourage and respect older adults' full range of emotional expression and group activism as a step toward their growth and sense of independence, for their and our future years.

REFERENCES

1. Goodman NG (Editor): A Benjamin Franklin Reader. New York, TY Crowell Co, 1945, p. 335.
2. Census Bureau Report: Estimates of Size and Characteristics of Older Population in 1974 — Projections to Year 2000, (abstr.) Am Geriatrics Soc Newsletter 4: August, 1976.
3. Cady EH (Editor): Literature of the Early Republic, (2nd ed.). Holt, Rinehart and Winston, Inc, 1969, pp. 404-406.
4. West ND: Sex in geriatrics: myth or miracle?, J Am Geriatrics Soc 23: 551, 1975.
5. Boykin LS: Soul foods for some older Americans, J. Am Geriatrics Soc 23: 380, 1975.
6. Wolk RL and Reingold J: The course of life for old people, J Am Geriatrics Soc 23: 376, 1975.
7. Reference 1, pp. 746-747.
8. Jacobs L, Conti D, Kinkel W et al.: "Normal-pressure" hydrocephalus, JAMA 235: 510, 1976.
9. Sugar O: Meanwhile, back at the bedside, JAMA 235: 534, 1976.
10. Dawson D and English C: Psychiatric consultation and teaching in a home for the aged, Hosp & Commun Psych 26: 509, 1975.
11. Miller MB: Iatrogenic and nurisgenic effects of prolonged immobilization of the ill aged, J Am Geriatrics Soc 23: 360, 1975.
12. Reference 1, p. 297.
13. Zwerling I, Plutchik R, Hotz M et al.: Effects of a procaine preparation (Gerovital H3) in hospitalized geriatric patients: a double-blind study, J Am Geriatrics Soc 23: 355, 1975.
14. Hall P: Cyclandelate in the treatment of cerebral arteriosclerosis, J Am Geriatrics Soc 24: 41, 1976.

Chapter 12

SEX AND THE SENIOR CITIZEN*

NORMAN M. LOBSENZ

A WRITER looking for a funny ending to his interview with Bob Hope asked the comedian recently if he thought there was still sex after 65. "You bet," said Hope, "and awfully good, too. *(Pause for a beat of exquisite timing.)* Especially the one in the fall."

The image of geriatric love-making seems always good for a laugh. A few years ago, Dr. Mary Calderone, executive director of SIECUS, the Sex Information and Education Council of the U.S., and one of the nation's leading authorities on sex education, was answering questions from an audience of Chicago high-schoolers. When one daring teen-ager asked, "How old are you, are you married, and are you still doing it?" the students broke into giggles. Dr. Calderone was characteristically forthright. When the laughter died down, she said, "The answer to the first part of that question is 64, and the answer to the other two is yes." Then she added, "Young people do not have a monopoly on sexuality. It is with you all your life."

Indeed, every medical study conducted during recent years indicates that there is no physiological reason why older men and women in reasonably good health should not have — and be able to have — an active and satisfying sex life. Yet, despite increasing scientific evidence to the contrary, our culture continues to foster the belief that by the time one is in his or her 60's, sex is neither necessary nor possible. Or if it *does* occur, it is somehow not quite normal. Or that it certainly isn't nice for the old folks to be indulging in it.

In a time of ever more tolerant attitudes toward sexual self-determination for everyone else, why this puritanical approach to "senior citizens"? Some of the reasons may stem from long-dormant Oedipal fears and incest taboos associated with the idea of sexual expression on the part of parental figures, from remnants of childhood's disbelief that one's mother and father — and by extension any older person — actually ever make love. Manhattan psychotherapist

---

*From *The New York Times Magazine*, 28-31, Jan. 29, 1974. Copyright © 1974 by Norman Lobsenz. Reprinted by permission.

Dr. Leah Schaefer reports, for example, that none of the women she interviewed for a book on sex could accept with any equanimity the idea of their own parents engaging in intercourse.

Another source of sexual puritanism toward the aged is the clichés of a youth-fixated society. Given the movie-television-advertising stereotype that sexuality exists only in and for beautiful people with firm flesh and agile bodies, the notion of older persons enjoying it — wrinkles, flabbiness and all — seems at first ludicrous and then repugnant.

For the 20 million Americans over 65 these attitudes present formidable problems. Having been conditioned to believe erroneously that sexual performance declines to the vanishing point with age, or that sexual exertion is dangerous to their health, many older pesons tend to give up sex more or less completely.

Others shut off sexual feelings out of shame and embarrassment about having them. Doctors and counselors report that when older people *do* admit to having sexual desires, they often apologize for having such "undignified" or even "depraved" sensations. Dr. Joseph T. Freeman, a Pennsylvania gerontologist who has written for medical textbooks on the sexual aspects of aging, cites the case of an 84-year-old man who complained to his physician about the frequent demands for intercourse made by his 79-year-old wife. The husband was able to meet them, Freeman writes, but felt that this activity was "not natural for such an old man and woman." Another couple in their early 70's had continued to make love at least once a day; yet both believed, says Freeman, "that they were doing something unnatural . . . an expression of some abnormal inclination."

Some older people fear the ridicule or censure of younger persons if they show signs of still being interested in sex. Children and even grandchildren disapprove, make them feel guilty. I was told of a recently remarried 78-year-old man whose daughter greets him every morning with a derisive "How did it go last night?" A Florida psychiatrist reported two instances where children tried to commit their parents to a mental institution because they had moved in with friends of the opposite sex. It's not just coincidence that we never refer to even the most profligate youth as a "dirty young man," but are quick to label any older person who shows some interest in sex as a "dirty old man." (One California septuagenarian struck back with a bumper sticker on his sports car: "I'm not a dirty old man, I'm a sexy senior citizen.")

The D.O.M. label is applied with even greater vehemence if the aging man or woman is involved with a much younger person, although there's no reason why love or sex should be age-segregated. May-December relationships can and do flourish. It is true that in many such cases the attraction is not necessarily romantic: Younger women often marry older men — and younger men often marry older women — for their money, fame, power, wisdom, or out of neurotic needs.

Yet if this general climate of deprecation hampers sexual expression for married older persons, it creates far greater obstacles for two-thirds of those men and women over 65 who never wed or are widowed or divorced. And because of a combination of demographics and cultural standards, women are affected more seriously.

To begin with — thanks to a longer life expectancy, plus the fact that women are usually younger than their husbands — older women outnumber older men. According to the latest available statistics from the Department of Health, Education and Welfare, for every 100 people in the over-65 age bracket, 57 are women. Moreover, two-thirds of them are widows, and there are three times as many widows as widowers. In terms of sheer availability of partners, therefore, older men have a far better statistical opportunity for sex.

Social custom offers men a similar advantage. It's much easier for an older man to find a wife than for an older woman to find a husband (in a typical year, 35,000 such men and only 16,000 such women will wed) largely because he retains the male prerogatives. He's more likely to take the sexual initiative. Age is not deemed to make as much difference to his looks. It is more acceptable for him to wed a young wife than for an older woman to wed a young man.

Moreover, *non*marital sex is more available to men than to women. Since one tends to follow in old age the cultural patterns of one's youth, today's over-65's — who grew up when "illicit" sex was a serious transgression — cannot easily accept the idea of such relationships. Even so, men are still freer to pursue them. Dr. Eric Pfeiffer, head of Duke University's Center for the Study of Aging and Human Development, reports that close to 90 per cent of the women interviewed for its long-term study of geriatric sex behavior had stopped having intercourse when their husbands became ill, impotent or died. "By contrast," reports Dr. Pfeiffer, "marital status had little or no effect on the incidence of sexual activity among elderly men."

The "double standard" he grew up with — permitting greater sexual freedom to men — enables the older man to purchase sex without the guilt or social disapproval that it would create for the older women. (And from a purely practical viewpoint, there are far more women who will sleep for money with an older man than there are men who will do the same for an older woman.) Similarly, it is morally easier for an older man to accept the idea of an affair, or some other variety of an "illicit" relationship.

However, this attitude may be changing. Dr. Paul Glick, senior demographer with the population division of the U.S. Census Bureau, has reported that more than 18,000 couples over 65 listed themselves in the last census as unmarried and living together. This is surely a vast underestimate of the actual number. Those who deal with older persons — gerontologists, counselors, retirement-community administrators — say that the aged are increasingly pairing off in long-term affairs. For some, it is a purely practical matter, a way to preserve maximum Social Security income and to keep the "widow's benefits" from company or union pensions — payments that are usually cut off if a woman remarries. (It also cuts down interference from children worried about the possibility of losing their inheritance if a parent remarries.) For others, it may be an "unmarriage of convenience," a way of sharing chores, alleviating loneliness. But for a growing number of older couples, living together is seen as a logical solution to their desire for emotional closeness and sexual expression.

They do not take the step easily. Struggling with guilt, many seek guidance from ministers who themselves must struggle to sort out the conflict among legalities, religious principles and compassion. For example, the Rev. Dr. Benton Gaskell, minister of the Pilgrim United Church in Pomona, Calif., whose congregation of more than 2,000 people includes a high percentage of over-65's, told of a couple, both widowed, who came to him for help.

"They were in their 70's," he said, "and living together clandestinely because they couldn't afford to marry since they would lose pension income. They said they felt 'faithless' to their late spouses, never knew what to tell their children or friends, and were in spiritual distress over their predicament. They asked me to ease their guilt by solemnizing their union in the sight of God."

For Dr. Gaskell, the plea presented a quandary. A minister may not conduct a marriage ceremony if there is no marriage license. Nor could he compromise the church. Yet he could not turn away the couple's plea. After consultation with his staff, Dr. Gaskell fashioned a ritual which enabled him formally to bless the couple's "union." With this emotional support, the couple were able to live together openly. "I don't know what they told friends or family," says Dr. Gaskell, "and I don't care. I know what they told me. 'We feel better about ourselves now,' they said. 'It makes us feel our relationship is all right.' "

Are our sexual drives and capacities really so persistent and long-lasting? From time to time a scientist returns from such Shangri-Las as Hunza, Soviet Georgia or an Andean village in Ecuador with reports of virile octogenarians. Dr. Alexander Leaf of the Harvard Medical School, who has been to all three of these centers of longevity, recently reported that he was convinced that "a vigorous life — sexual activity included — was possible for at least 100 years. . . ." Occasionally, too a charismatic elder offers similar evidence: a Chaplin, a Picasso, a Senator Thurmond fathering children late in life; or Somerset Maugham complaining, in his 80's, that "one loses one's looks and desirability yet the desire itself remains."

But is that also true of the typical older man or woman? To echo Dr. Calderone, the answer is yes — and much of the sexual indignity the aged suffer could be eased if the biological facts were better known. The three most significant studies of geriatric sexual behavior have been made by Kinsey, Duke's Center for the Study of Aging, and Masters and Johnson. In each, the findings clearly show that men and women in a state of general good health are physiologically able to have a satisfying sex life well into their 70's, 80's and beyond. The studies also indicate that those who were most active sexually during youth and middle age usually retain their vigor and interest longer into old age.

Though Kinsey interviewed only a small number of older persons, his was the pioneering survey. It showed for the first time that four out of five men over the age of 60 were capable of intercourse, and that there was no evidence of sexual decline in women until much later in life. The Duke studies, which have been conducted on a continuing basis for 20 years, are unique in that researchers have been able to follow the trend of sexuality in aging individuals over a sustained time period. One fascinating result was evidence that 15 percent of men and women studied showed a steady *rising* rate of sexual interest and activity as they got older.

While such a complex survey as Duke's cannot be simplistically summarized, the main findings indicate that two out of three men are sexually active past 65, and one out of five is still active in his 80's. And though activity may decline, interest remains: About half of the 80- and 90-year-olds reported a moderate degree of interest. The story is somewhat different for women. "In their 60's," writes Duke's Dr. Eric Pfeiffer, "about one in three reports sexual interest while only one in five is actually having sex. However, their rates of interest and activity don't seem to fall off with increasing age." There are several obvious explanations for the lower activity rate for women: the lack of available men, a greater reluctance to accept nonmarital sex, more anxiety over physical appearance, and a willingness to believe that sex is, or should be, ended after menopause.

Dr. William Masters and Virginia Johnson not only interviewed the aged, but also clinically monitored their sexual performance. For one thing, this helped to discount faulty memory, wishful thinking, bragging or its converse, embarrassed understatement. For another, it provided the first detailed picture of the older body's physiological sexual reactions. Masters and Johnson found that a man's capacity for erection and climax, and a woman's capacity for orgasm, were slowed but not terminated by the aging process. "Inevitably," they say, "all physical responses are slowed. . . . A man can't run around the block as fast as he could 20 or 30 years previously. Yet the simple fact that his sexual functioning is but one more element of his total physiologic functioning may never occur to him."

Thus, it takes the older man longer to achieve a full erection and to reach a climax. He experiences fewer genital spasms, and there is a reduction in both the force and amount of his ejaculation. It takes him longer before he can have another erection. None of this, however, detracts from the pleasure an older man experiences in intercourse.

Yet many men, Masters and Johnson point out, interpret such slowing-down as the sign of inevitable sexual bankruptcy. The fear of impotency itself then further inhibits their sexual functioning. Some men react to this threat to their masculinity by rationalizing that it is time to "give up" sex, that it should not be that "important" any more. (Similarly, women who have never been quite emotionally comfortable with their sexuality find aging an excuse to avoid it — "We're too old for that sort of thing now.") Still, an older man's sexual performance can be particularly satisfying to both himself and his partner just *because* he can maintain an erection for a longer period of time before climaxing. Indeed, if they do not talk themselves out of it, say Masters and Johnson, older couples "can and should continue unencumbered sexual functioning indefinitely."

A similar set of physiological changes occurs in the older woman. There is less lubrication and elasticity of the vagina. The tissues lining it become thin and more easily irritated. The uterine contractions that accompany orgasm may become spasmic and painful. Fortunately, all these symptoms can be eased or counteracted by hormonal treatment. The older woman, write Masters and Johnson, "is fully capable of sexual performance at orgasmic response levels."

Medical literature offers numerous case histories of women who not only are orgasmic in their 60s, and 70s, but of women who *became* orgasmic for the first time during those years.

In addition to the three major studies, a number of limited surveys confirm this continued sexuality of the aged. Some show, for example, that men past 65 can average four climaxes a month for many years; others show that many men and women without a sexual partner, or whose spouse is unable or unwilling to have a physical relationship, masturbate regularly. One of the more intriguing experiments was conducted by psychiatrist Dr. Charles Fisher at the Sleep Laboratory of New York's Mount Sinai Hospital. He developed techniques to detect and measure penile erection during REM sleep — when the characteristic "rapid eye movement" signals that the sleeper is dreaming. Twenty-one men, aged 71 to 96, spent several nights connected to an EEG recorder and a penile "strain gauge." During REM sleep, three-quarters of them (including the 96-year-old) developed erections. The dreams they later described all revolved around sexual themes.

Every day, 4,000 more Americans reach the age of 65, and they can expect an average of 15 more years of life. What is truly distressing is that those who deal with the rapidly growing number of older persons — family and friends, doctors and social workers, staffs of old-age homes — are either unaware of the data proving the sexual interest and capability of the aged or cannot psychologically accept it. Just as Freud's findings about childhood sexuality met enormous emotional resistance at first, so are the discoveries about sexuality in the aged. Some authorities manage to reject them altogether. For example, a current book, "How to Deal with Aging and the Elderly," states: "Most persons lose interest somewhere along the line. . . . A normal development is a displacement of passionate physical sexual relations for a deeper marital relationship that revolves more about . . . philosophical thought about the hereafter."

This sort of attitude cuts older persons off from reassuring information, deprives them of helpful guidance, and reinforces their own sense of shame for still having sexual feelings. Dr. Laura Singer-Magdoff, a New York therapist and former president of the American Association of Marriage and Family Counselors, recently included the topic of sexuality in a talk she gave to a group of older persons. "A gray-haired woman about 70 came up to me with tears in her eyes," the counselor recalled, "She said it was the first time anyone had discussed sex in old age as if it were a normal thing."

The men and women in nursing and old-age homes are probably

the most deprived on this score. Their environment is almost totally desexualized: It is considered progress when dining or recreation halls and residential wings are not sex-segregated. Privacy is virtually non-existent: the administrator of one Delaware convalescent home told me that her staff respected patients' privacy, but added that "we run a bed-check every two hours to make sure they are all right." Only a minority of institutions make an effort to provide areas where a couple can be alone together even to talk, much less to court. Dr. Calderone cites an instance in which one home forbade any unmarried man and woman to watch television together late in the evening. Even married couples may be separated; some state institutions segregate them, or permit the sexes to mix only under "supervision." If only one spouse is in a home, the other seldom has the right to privacy during a visit. A vigorous woman of 71 recently complained to the director of a convalescent home because there was neither the opportunity nor the facility for her to have a sexual relationship with her husband, who was a patient there. "He entered the home to be cared for during his recovery from a serious eye operation," the woman said. "I can't take care of him properly at home. But there is nothing else wrong with him, no reason why we cannot make love. Yet when I come to visit him we must meet only in 'public' areas. Even if we *could* be alone in his room, there's only a narrow hospital bed there. When I suggested to the home's director that he put at least a three-quarter bed in my husband's room, the man looked at me as if I were some sort of sexual monster."

"Society tends to say," observes Dr. Calderone, " 'You should be finished with sex — especially since trying to meet your sexual needs adds to the bother of looking after you.' " Thus staff members, from administrators to attendants, for the most part avoid any reference to the idea that their residents may have sexual needs or even feelings. An older person who evidences them in any way is often reproved, or considered sick or depraved — the "dirty old man" label again.

In its 15 years of existence, the American Nursing Home Association, which includes 7,000 public and private facilities, has never scheduled a discussion of sexuality at any of its meetings. A spokeswoman said the American Association of Homes for the Aging was "concerned" about residents' sexual rights — the A.A.H.A. is in the process of drawing up a "Patient's Bill of Rights" which includes privacy — but added that the topic was "sort of taboo, people don't like to think about it, and since it isn't a front-line issue, we don't concentrate on it." (In fairness, some distinctions should be drawn. Many homes care for the chronically ill, for whom sex is not an issue.

Publicly supported homes operate under legislative restrictions. Some privately supported ones have large budgets and trained staffs, while others are short of money, facilities and trained personnel. Some reflect conservative community mores, or the conventional attitudes of their administrators. And all believe they have to deal with problems far more important than geriatric sexuality.)

Nevertheless, some small progress is being made. According to Hannah Weiner, a sociologist and head of a counseling group called SOMA (Services to Ongoing Mature Aging), this can range from establishing beauty parlors in old-age homes to scheduling talks on sex by gynecologists and urologists. A few homes now set aside small lounges where one or two couples can talk or have tea. Too, SOMA has had an encouraging response from institutions to the "sexuality and aging" seminars it conducts.

But no amount of frills or lectures can substitute for privacy, and certainly not for a more understanding approach. "Those are needed most," says Jacob Reingold, executive director of the modern 600-guest Hebrew Home for the Aged on the banks of the Hudson in New York City. An energetic and empathic man, Mr. Reingold once shocked a nurse who came running to him to report that an elderly couple were making love in the woman's room. "What should I do?" the nurse asked frantically. Answered Mr. Reingold: "Tiptoe gently out so you don't disturb them."

Recently a Canadian doctor suggested that all old-age homes should set aside "petting rooms." But privacy is important, Mr. Reingold points out, not so much to isolate affection or intimacy as to give it legitimacy. "Because of their cultural background," he says, "older people tend to separate what's 'right' in public from what's 'right' in private. So a woman rebuffs a man's overtures, or a man turns a blind eye to a little flirting — but I think they would act differently if there weren't so many witnesses. They are caught in a bind. Either they behave 'acceptably' and miss out on emotional satisfactions, or feel they must run the risk of disapproval and embarrassment."

We may be slowly acclimating ourselves to the idea that there is sexuality after 65, but we are still a long way from actively helping older people to express it fully, or to deal with their feelings about it. This is the opinion of Dr. Robert N. Butler, a Washington, D.C., psychiatrist and an expert in the mental health of the aging. "Aging & Mental Health," which he has written with Myrna I. Lewis, a mental-health specialist, calls for "positive psychosocial approaches" to the question. "What we need," the authors say, "is a campaign of sex education for the aged. For example, techniques of intercourse especially pertinent to the needs of older people should be clarified. Thus, sex in the morning may be preferable for those who fatigue easily at night. Certain coital positions may make intercourse more feasible for those who are crippled by arthritis."

Butler feels doctors have a responsibility to be more specific about the sexual effects of medical problems. A man or woman with a heart condition, for instance, ought to know that a coronary attack during sex occurs much less often than the patient may fear is the case. "If a person is taking nitroglycerine pills as medication," says Butler, "there's no reason he can't take one *before* beginning intercourse, as a precautionary measure to ease his concern. A woman who experiences vaginal discomfort should be encouraged to have hormonal replacement therapy, even in her older years. A man facing a prostatectomy should be reassured that the likelihood of impotence resulting is comparatively small. And if a doctor has a choice among the varying techniques for that surgery, he should consider the sexual effects in making his decision."

Butler also inveighs against the indiscriminate dosing of old people with tranquilizers and antidepressants, often just to make them "easier to handle." One of the pills' side effects is to cut sexual drive and inhibit ejaculation. "The average doctor," says Butler, "does not really think sex matters in old age." For example, a 72-year-old man recently asked his physician's help just before he planned to remarry. During the past two or three years, the man had experienced lessened potency. Occasionally he could not achieve an erection at all. He wondered if he could be given hormone pills or an injection that would help him. "The woman I'm going to marry is a wonderful person, and I don't want to embarrass or disappoint her," the man said. Instead of examining the man to see if anything could be done medically to aid him, the doctor dismissed the idea as not worth bothering about. "If she's a wonderful woman," he pontificated, "she'll understand."

But sexual activity can actually be therapeutic for an older person. "There is some evidence," says Butler, "that it helps arthritics by increasing adrenal-gland output of cortisone. The sex act also helps to reduce psychological tension."

But though Butler and other experts believe that much can be done to improve the physical aspects of sex for the aged, they emphasize that, in the best sense, older persons should be encouraged to explore the broader emotional limits of sexuality. Researchers focus on quantitative questions — outlet, frequency, response. They seldom, seek answers to qualitative questions — needs, desires, hopes.

"Perhaps I am romanticizing," Butler says, "but old age may be the time to make sex a work of art. It would be tragic if older persons seek merely to recapture the physical sensations of their younger days. Age offers the opportunity to view sex as intimate communication in its best sense."

Clearly, there is more to sexuality after 65 than just the act of sex. For a man, there is the satisfaction of feeling still masculine; for a woman, still feminine; for both, still being wanted and needed. There is the comforting warmth of physical nearness, the pleasure of companionship. There is the rewarding emotional intimacy of shared joys. All we need, the song says, is love, love, love. Do not those who are older need it as much as any of us?

Chapter 13

THE CASE FOR AND AGAINST ESTROGEN THERAPY*

EDWARD A. GRABER AND HUGH R. K. BARBER

ADVERTISEMENTS for estrogen frequently show a middle-aged woman in the kitchen being kissed by a middle-aged man. The implication obviously is that this happy state results because she has had an adequate daily dose of estrogen.

Estrogens should be and have been prescribed for more than 35 years for menopausal women for severe symptoms of estrogen withdrawal. However, a few gynecologists have suggested that the menopause is a deficiency disease, and that estrogen should be given from the onset of the menopause until death to reverse this abnormality. Thus, automatically one would remain young, healthy, sexually attractive, desirable, youthful, and sensuous. Their therapeutic enthusiasm and evangelistic preaching in the lay press is based on assumptions that cannot be scientifically substantiated.

Facts about the prophylactic use of estrogen must be examined in the light of presently known facts.

Aging cannot be prevented by estrogens. The aging process is governed by many factors other than estrogens — heredity, environment, diet, illness, physical and emotional stress, and most significantly one's genes. Look at a patient's mother and father and you will get a better idea of the aging potential of a woman than by looking at her vaginal smear.

Aging is a chronic disease which ultimately none survives. As cells get older, they lose their ability to regenerate efficiently. There is a loss of ability to manufacture adequate protein, and the ability to reproduce normal DNA and RNA diminishes, as does enzyme activity. An upset in cell programming produces excessive mutations which the body probably rejects as foreign material and begins to destroy (autoimmunization). Collagen is not replenished as one gets older and it loses its elasticity. This tends to interfere with the free flow of nourishment to cells. As a result, millions of cells that are not re-

*From *American Journal of Nursing,* 75:1766-1771. ©1975. Reproduced with permission.

placed die daily.

Women place great importance on the appearances of their skin in the menopausal years. Aging shows especially in areas which are exposed to sunlight. If older women would just not try to get tan, they would appear much younger.

The skin wrinkles because of elasticity loss due to insoluble collagen hardening, decreased acid mucopolysaccharides, the effects of a lower level of hyaluronic acid, and digestion of the elastase in the skin's elastic fibers. Estrogen does not in any way retard these changes.

Aging also produces changes in glands other than the ovary with attendant effects: an irreplaceable loss of muscle mass; loss in weight of the spleen, liver, and kidneys; and a diminished oxygen uptake by the brain, as well as destruction of nonreplaceable neural tissue. None of these changes will be reversed by estrogen.

The only aging tissues that respond to estrogens are the breasts, vagina, uterus, and base of the bladder, probably due to estrogen receptors present in these areas. These receptors appear to be proteins that attract and bind specifically with estrogens.

One of the great fallacies promulgated by the group calling the menopause a "deficiency disease" is that the ovarian hormone is suddenly shut off when menstruation ceases. In the postmenopausal woman the metabolites of estrogen excreted in the urine are in the lower range of menstruating women (1). Analysis of serum or urine 15 years after the onset of the menopause showed estrogenic activity in 50 percent of women (2).

The postmenopausal ovary continues to secrete some estrogen so long as follicular or thecal cells are present. When these finally disappear, the main circulating estrogen is estrone. The postmenopausal ovary secretes dehydroepiandrosterone, androstenedione, and testosterone from its stroma. These are contributed to the plasma pool and added to the contributions from the adrenal. This is followed by peripheral conversion of androstenedione to estrone. Where this conversion occurs is not known, but aromatization occurs in the adrenal and gonadal tissue.

The important point is that many women still have adequate endogenous estrogen for many years after the cessation of menstruation (3). Routine replacement may do a little good at the risk of doing a lot of harm. The role of estrogen deficiency in most menopausal women has been exaggerated, to say the least. Enzyme histochemistry indicates ovarian steroidogenesis as long as 25 years postmenopause. The primary sites are the ovarian stromal cells and the hilus cells.

Arteriosclerosis

Another widely discussed facet of aging is the role of estrogens in the prevention of generalized arteriosclerosis and coronary artery disease. There is no definitive, statistically valid study, as yet, to demonstrate that estrogen prevents coronary artery disease. Although estrogens may decrease serum cholesterol values, this drug also increases serum phospholipids and the ratio of alpha to beta lipoproteins. Lowered cholesterol *per se* is not a reliable atherogenic index, and in most studies has no effect on mortality figures. There are no controlled studies that substantiate the claim that arteriosclerosis is prevented by the use of prophylactic estrogen.

Everyone has arteriosclerosis. It begins in early childhood and what it does depends on how fast it progresses and what complications are superimposed. An individual's genes and chromosomes, diet, physical and emotional stresses, and a host of superimposed factors — diabetes, hypertension, kidney pathology, metabolic, endocrine, and fat-mobilizing status, liver disease, obesity, drugs, culture, trauma, physical exercise, blood flow dynamics, and others — all determine the course of arteriosclerosis, not the estrogens taken during one's 50s or 60s. The disease is well on its way by then (4).

Hypertension

There is equal ambivalence about hypertension. All physicians see hypertension in innumerable women with normal levels of estrogen. To what extent are emotional factors, suppressed anxiety, fear, anger, and irritability major factors in the production of hypertension? Is not some hypertension due to diminished blood supply to the kidney or to other factors which stimulate the juxtoglomerular cells, increasing the supply of renin and angiotension? What about obesity and hypertension?

It is estimated that at age 50, 30 percent of women are significantly overweight. Is this not an important factor? What about the rise in incidence of diabetes in this age group? What about genetic background, culture, occupation, chronic pyelonephritis and so many other etiologic factors? Why hypertension is automatically and unequivocally related to estrogen deprivation by some physicians without their taking into account all the other important factors cannot be explained. How well do they explain Taylor's results indicating that the incidence of hypertension in the castrate is no greater than that of the noncastrate population (5)?

Osteoporosis

Osteoporosis continues to be a special area in which exaggerated claims are made regarding the merits of postmenopausal estrogen. There is no argument that symptomatic improvement does occur in many postmenopausal women with osteoporosis who are given estrogen. Reports indicate estrogens given to halt the progress of osteoporosis benefit the condition for 4 to 20 months (6).

Estrogen probably acts by diminishing the calcium lost through the kidney, and in some unknown manner temporarily helps many of these patients. What is objectionable is the prejudicial manner in which the subject is often presented in the literature: lack of estrogen causes osteoporosis — give estrogen to prevent it — give estrogen and cure it.

Facts do not bear out these statements. If estrogen lack causes osteoporosis, why should it occur in only 20 to 25 percent of the postmenopausal female population? On examination, the osteoporotic female has a normal serum alkaline phosphatase, indicating a normal rate of bone formation, and a normal urinary hydroxyproline, indicating normal bone absorption.

Osteoporosis can occur in young women with normal estrogen levels. It is seen in conjunction with a markedly sedentary life (bedridden patients), protein deficiency, lack of dietary calcium, diminished vitamin intake, lack of gastric acidity, diminished parathyroid efficiency, diminished blood supply to bone, hyperthyroidism, cortisone excess, longstanding diabetes, acromegaly, cirrhosis of the liver, multiple myeloma, leukemia, and, finally, there is idiopathic osteoporosis. Why don't these also enter into the picture in the postmenopausal woman? Why is her osteoporosis entirely different and due to lack of estrogen alone?

A low protein low calcium diet in a sedentary aged person is the most significant factor in producing osteoporosis. Estrogen alone without correction of protein and calcium intake will do little to help over the long term. A negative nitrogen balance makes it difficult for the osteoblasts to lay down the necessary osseous matrix. So, all the above factors must be investigated if one is to be successful in preventing or treating osteoporosis. The answer is not in estrogen alone.

To recommend estrogens for all postmenopausal women to prevent osteoporosis if there are no signs or symptoms of marked estrogen deficiency is not only imprudent, but scientifically fallacious. There are no prospective studies to show that prophylactic estrogen prevents osteoporosis. Studies do indicate that women experiencing the menopause at age 30 do not develop osteoporosis for about 28 years, while those beginning menopause at age 50, who will develop osteoporosis, will do so in five to six years (7). Obviously, factors other than estrogen deprivation are of significance. It is well known that bone density decreases with linear age. It starts at about age 35 (when there is still adequate estrogen) and decreases at a rate of 10 percent a decade. This occurs, incidentally, in all animals.

The only acceptable prophylactic treatment of osteoporosis is muscular exercise, calcium, fluoride, vitamin D, and a high protein diet. After three years of such a regimen, actual improvement of bone matrix has been seen in the spine on x-ray. To sum up, the kindest thing that can be said about the proponents of estrogen is that they have excessive therapeutic enthusiasm. Patients with a hereditary predisposition, incapacitating disease, poor diets, and other endogenous or exogenous factors will still get osteoporosis. It occurs earlier and more severely in some women than others, but in the vast majority it never reaches a level of severity to become a problem.

Cancer

Estrogen produced cancer in mice over 20 years ago. Since then, there has been an unwarranted fear that estrogen would produce similar pathology in the human female. There is no definitive evidence that estrogen causes cancer in nonsusceptible individuals.

One point, however, must be considered. There is no way of knowing who will develop genital cancer. Further, there is no doubt that cancer of the endometrium and breast are estrogen-dependent in many instances.

The consensus of all gynecological authorities is that estrogens are contraindicated in all women with previous or concomitant breast or endometrial malignancy. As a result, physicians who endorse routine estrogen replacement therapy (ERT) advocate that patients be seen frequently for meticulous examinations for possible neoplasm.

There is no doubt that many women have been on estrogen therapy for 10 or more years and have not developed genital malignancy. There is no evidence, however, that malignant growth cannot be triggered by estrogens in women who have a genetic susceptibility.

Several investigators have shown a 16-21 percent rate of carcinoma of the endometrium (10 to 15 times greater than the general population) in women who had estrogen-secreting ovarian tumors (3.8).

Gusberg also reported carcinoma of the uterus in 20 women who had prolonged and persistent stimulation of the endometrium by estrogen. Novak documented four cases of endometrial carcinoma in 33 women with prolonged estrogen administration (2). There are also reports of increased endometrial carcinoma with persistent unopposed estrogen, such as is found in Stein-Leventhal syndrome and cirrhosis of the liver (1). Until these reports are adequately explained, it behooves one to proceed with circumspection.

It is postulated by many gynecologists and endocrinologists that persistent, prolonged, uninterrupted stimulation of the endometrium by estrogen may be the triggering factor in producing endometrial carcinoma in women who have a particular constellation that predisposes to uterine cancer. On this basis, most physicians prescribing estrogens postmenopausally advocate that the drug be used cyclically. Yet Davis, an advocate of ERT, states that cyclic estrogen is not desirable in the postmenopausal woman. He maintains that if this hormone is given continuously (his method of choice), it stimulates the growth of the endometrium for a time, following which it regresses and remains inactive. Cyclic therapy, he contends, provokes uterine bleeding; since this may be indicative of endometrial malignancy it usually mandates a D and C. Many unnecessary operations, he says, can be prevented if continuous therapy is practiced (1).

The disagreement about even the method of administration of estrogenic hormone simply reflects the uncertainty and lack of firm facts upon which to base a sound therapeutic regimen. One can only speculate as to which method is correct and, indeed, whether the use of estrogen is justified at all in most instances.

Some gynecologists advocate the use of estrogen-androgen combinations. This, they maintain, diminishes the incidence of hormonal uterine bleeding. There is little evidence, however, that these hormones work synergistically to produce the hoped-for result. A combination of estrogen and progesterone is now in vogue. It is maintained that with progesterone the endometrium is shed monthly and there is less chance of endometrial hyperplasia due to unopposed estrogen. This obviously makes sense, but many women do not find monthly bleeding at age 60 very attractive (9).

Twenty percent of women receiving ovarian hormone (without additional hormones) postmenopausally will bleed vaginally. The American Cancer Society has done a remarkable job of instilling the idea that abnormal vaginal bleeding is related to possible cancer, so even if an explanation for bleeding in those taking ovarian hormone is offered, there still is marked alarm or, at best, uneasiness on the part of the patient. Whether the physician admits it or not, he is also weighing the odds as to whether the bleeding is or is not significant. He is never sure. This one complication alone makes routine estrogen administration most unattractive to many patients and physicians.

Almost 50 percent of women with endometrial carcinoma have endometrial hyperplasia prior to or in conjunction with their tumor (10). This probably indicates unphysiological estrogen activity, either endogenous or exogenous. Neoplasia occurs most frequently in hormone-stimulated organs rather than in resting ones. While cancer is not caused by activity of the organ, the addition of such other factors as gene mutation, virus, radiation, or other carcinogens may be sufficient to trigger the process of the stimulated organ and act as a trap for the carcinogens.

The complex of obesity, hypertension, menstrual abnormality, and diabetes is frequently found in conjunction with endometrial carcinoma. Abnormal estrogen constellations frequently accompany this picture. If patients are followed long enough, it is not unusual to see in them a progression of endometrial changes through hyperplasia, anaplasia, carcinoma in situ, and finally invasive cancer.

The relationship between breast cancer and estrogen has been questioned. A marked increase in breast cancer in men who were given stilbestrol for prostatic cancer is reported. Further, there are practically no reports of breast cancer in prepubertal girls. It would seem, therefore, that there must be some underlying relationship between estrogen and breast malignancy.

There is no doubt that the senile breast can be changed to a functionally mature state by estrogens. Any abnormality in the enzyme mechanism of older women affecting estrogen metabolism may predispose them in an abormal response in the atrophic, aging breast. It has been shown that with ovarian ablative or hormone therapy used in conjunction with metastatic breast cancer the carcinoma regressed only when there was an increase in urinary estriol (9). Can there be a connection between abnormal estrogen metabolism in certain people and breast cancer?

In summary, there is still a great gap in our knowledge of the relationship between estrogen and cancer. It seems to be premature, with the lack of definite evidence, to give estrogens to all women automatically, just because they enter the menopause.

Measuring Response

Attempts have been made to exploit the value of the vaginal smear in following the therapeutic response to estrogens. While the smear, euphemistically called the "femininity index," has certain value, one should treat the patient, not the smear. It is merely a laboratory aid. The total reaction of the patient is much more important. In many instances a patient's response is good in spite of a poor vaginal smear; other patients are seen with a good vaginal response and a poor · general reaction.

The maturation count does not always reflect the patient's true estrogen level. Not only is it the result of the interplay with other hormones, but other extraneous factors enter into it. This includes a multitude of factors, among them vaginitis, end organ sensitivity, diabetes, uterine myoma, uterine polyps, local medication, endometrial hyperplasia, digitalis, hepatic insufficiency, adrenal hormones, tetracycline, vitamin A deficiency, use of pessaries and other vaginal foreign bodies, and genital malignancy. All these may increase cornification and mislead.

Further, there is no unanimity as to what constitutes a normal smear for the menopausal patient. What some consider normal on the basis of some arbitrary criteria can be subject to erroneous interpretation, since smear reports are somewhat subjective and are read differently by a number of respected cytopathologists. To exploit the vaginal cornification index as the scientific method of treating the menopause is at best an exaggeration.

In truth, only 20 percent of vaginal smears are atrophic 10 years after the onset of the menopause. If one accepts this as the criterion for treatment, 80 percent of the patients treated routinely with estrogen at the menopause are exposed to estrogen unnecessarily.

Psychiatric Disorder

Despite statements to the contrary, estrogens do not overcome true psychiatric abnormalities of the menopause. Sturgis states that people with marked depression or other significant emotional difficulties manifested at the time of the menopause are basically psychoneurotic or even psychotic (1).

The average woman at about 50 whose children have left home, who feels without purpose in life, and who cannot find work of interest to keep her emotionally and intellectually satisfied may use illness consciously or unconsciously to gain attention from her family or friends. Headaches, fatigue, depression, insomnia, and other psychosomatic symptoms occur.

Those of us who have had experience with these women know that sympathy, support, explanation, and, at times, consultation with a member of the family can correct the situation. We also know that if there is a good marriage, security, a psychiatrically well-adjusted female, and adequate education as to the physiology of the menopause, there are few emotionally "sick" menopausal patients. There is no reason to equate sickness with the menopause in the large majority of women.

When a menopausal patient is emotionally ill, psychiatric treatment is much more efficacious than estrogen. If estrogen is administered, it has slight anabolic activity and may give an occasional patient a feeling of well-being. Also there is the psychological reaction of having something done to help, but to assume that estrogen will make a woman happy or help her adjust to a difficult life situation is thoroughly unrealistic.

If one is looking for an anabolic agent, testosterone, methandrostenedione, and other synthetic testosterone derivatives are much more effective. However, protein intake must be adequate regardless of the drug used. Protein intake must exceed nitrogen excretion in the feces, urine, and other discharges before anabolism takes place. Unfortunately, many disturbed patients do not eat an adequate diet so that, again, estrogen is not the answer. *The Medical Letter* which reviews medical research stated unequivocally in a 1973 issue that estrogens have no demonstrable effect on anxiety, depression, or any other type of emotional symptoms.

When Do Estrogens Help?

Estrogens are excellent drugs when indicated, but one must be aware of their pluses and minuses. They can relieve three symptoms: flushes, sweats, and atrophic vaginitis.

Medication should be given when specifically indicated. We also must add that there is a sense of well-being that some patients find gratifying. Unfortunately, the "lift" is not a continuous or lasting phenomenon, and the price of complications may be too high.

Why some 50 percent of menopausal patients get hot flushes is unknown. In these patients the follicle stimulating hormone level (FSH) rises about 15 times and the luteal hormone 2 to 4 times, which estrogen controls. When the patient is gradually weaned off the drug, she gets along well without medication in approximately 6 to 12 months.

What are the hazards of estrogen? *The Medical Letter* of January 19, 1973, points out that side effects include spotting, menorrhagia, breast tenderness, fluid retention and edema, and stimulation of the metabolic activity of the breast and uterus. Other side effects include impaired glucose tolerance, increased fluid retention in the presence of liver or cardiac disease, increased predisposition to thromboembolism, and nausea and vomiting associated with some types of estrogens. Estrogens are contraindicated with previous vasculitis or thrombophlebitis. Estrogens may trigger hypertrophic osteoarthritis and ulcerative colitis.

Estrogen may also trigger hypertension because it causes an increase in renin substrate and an increase in the net renin activity. Uterine fibroids or other estrogen-dependent tumors may increase in size. Abdominal discomfort and menstrual-like cramps are frequent complaints. Finally, one must add the expense and inconvenience of taking medication daily.

We wish to make one point particularly clear. We are not against the use of estrogen. The drug is an excellent one to be used on indication. Some of the indications for which it is generally advocated are borderline in the opinion of many competent gynecologists.

The entire picture of routine postmenopausal estrogen therapy is in a state of complete confusion. Until cogent evidence is developed to back up the convictions of the advocates of "estrogen forever," we must proceed with circumspection and caution. We need less passion, fewer theoretical hypotheses, and more facts.

REFERENCES

1. STURGIS, S. H. Hormone therapy in menopause. *Human Sexuality* 3:69, 1969.
2. NOVAK, E. R. Postmenopausal endometrial hyperplasia. *Am. J. Obstet. Gynecol.* 71:1312-1321, June 1956.
3. MCLENNAN, M. T., and MCLENNAN, C. E. Estrogenic status of menstruating and menopausal women assessed by cervicovaginal smears. *Obstet. Gynecol.* 37:325-331, Feb. 1971.
4. PARISH, H. M., and Others. Time interval between castration in premenopausal women and the development of excessive coronary atherosclerosis. *Am. J. Obstet. Gynecol.* 99:155, 1967.
5. TAYLOR, E. S. Estrogens. *Obstet. Gynecol. Survey.* 26:442, 1971.
6. LIN, T. J., and SO-BOSITA, J. L. Pitfalls in interpretation of estrogenic effect in post-menopausal women. *Am. J. Obstet. Gynecol.* 114:929-931, Dec. 1, 1972.
7. MATTINGLY, R. F., and HUANG, W. Y. Steroidogenesis in the menopausal and postmenopausal ovary. *Am. J. Obstet. Gynecol.* 103:679-693, Mar. 1, 1969.
8. POLIAK, A., and Others. Estrogen synthesis in castrated women. *Am. J. Obstet. Gynecol.* 110:377-379, June 1, 1971.
9. PLOTZ, E. J., and FRIEDLANDER, R. L. Endocrinology in women over 65 years of age. *Clin. Obstet. Gynecol.* 10:466-480, Sept. 1967.
10. SPEERT, H. Premalignant phase of endometrial carcinoma. *Cancer* 5:927-944, Sept. 1952.

Part IV

Social Bonds

INTRODUCTION

A network of relationships tie individuals into a social world, providing a source of meaning and stability in life. For women, these bonds frequently are composed of relationships with family and friends rather than occupational ties. In fact her relationships with others become the definition of a woman's place in life, and she will be introduced as someone's wife, someone's mother more often than on any basis of her own personal achievement in spheres beyond primary relationships. Unlike a man, typically the woman's name changes with her relationships as she moves from the position of the daughter of one man to the wife of another. Rarely is a man introduced as the husband of his wife; usually his occupational role is foremost. Even if a woman holds a professional position, she is usually identified by placing her within a family relationship.

Marriage is a singular event for celebration in our society — which illustrates its importance. Photographs in the newspaper, a series of parties honoring the bride, and a procession of gifts may emphasize the event. No other achievement in her life will draw forth such tributes as her wedding.

In a few years after marriage, several children may require most of the hours of the day spent in loving, grooming, feeding, training, or nursing them. Their later success or failure in life may be attributed to her skills or shortcomings in mothering. However, when a woman grows old enough, roles are reversed and her children may be her major source of social support.

Beyond the family a woman's web of friendships frequently may develop through neighborhood gatherings, through work related to the involvement of children in schools, church, clubs, or other activities promoting the welfare of the young. Her friendships may develop through associations with the wives of the husband's occupational associates. While this is not to suggest that these are the only sources of her friendships, these probably are the most important ones for most older women. Though many women work outside the home little is found in the literature about interpersonal relationships formed in the workplace. Since women are rewarded for expressive behavior they may establish and maintain friendships with greater ease than men. Whatever the source of friendships originally, older women may find in later life that friends become a prime reservoir of emotional support.

Through the articles selected for this section on social bonds, we take a closer look at these three important areas: marriage, children and other kin, and friendships.

Given the crucial place of marriage in the life of a woman, its role as a source of satisfaction is vital. Do older marriages provide the happiness of the early years? Does custom simply hold the relationships together through habit without providing the joy once there? What is the effect of the husband's retirement on the marriage? When a marriage ends through divorce or widowhood, it must be one of the most drastic changes in the life of a woman. How can she restructure her life — no small undertaking for an older woman after spending more than half her life in a marriage relationship? Is remarriage a viable alternative? Chapters 14 and 15 examine the quality of older marriages (whether a continuation or a remarriage after widowhood). Chapter 16 measures the impact of retirement on the marriage, and Chapter 17 considers some of the changes that occur in life for a widow.

In Chapter 14, Nick Stinnett, Linda Carter, and James Montgomery examine the conflicting evidence on whether marital satisfaction increases or decreases with the years of marriage. With their own research, they try to analyze the relative satisfaction of latter years of marriage compared with earlier years, the sources of rewards or problems, and whether the views differ for hundreds of wives. Can married couples really live happily ever after — even after they are old?

Remarriage later in life may occur in the face of opposition by children, friends, and the community. In Chapter 15, Walter McKain explores the causes of opposition to such marriages, how the older man and woman became acquainted and decided upon marriage, and five crucial factors leading to success in late-life marriages.

When a husband retires, what is his wife's reaction to this event? Alfred Fengler (Chapter 16) suggests the attitude of the wife may be crucial in determining the success of a man's adjustment to the event and the happiness of the couple when the husband is home around the clock. The answer is not simple and the author classifies the wives by their orientation to the event as optimists, neutralists, and pessimists. For each retirement sentiment, the prospects for adjustment are evaluated.

Chapter 17 stresses that loneliness and isolation may affect more than 10 million widowed women — no longer wives after an adult lifetime of identity in that role. Because of a longer female life span and the custom of marrying men older than themselves, most married women will join the ranks of those who are "neither single nor married" and largely ignored by a community uncomfortable in their presence or unsure of quite how to help. Trained for dependence, they are now in a new situation which demands independence. Edward Wakin suggests some of the recent developments in society that offer support for widows.

What is the extent and nature of the social bonds tying the older woman to her grown children and other kin? While some years ago a few theorists thought the isolated nuclear unit was typical of families in the United States, such views are outdated. Older people are neither physically nor socially isolated from their children, and the family becomes a reserve for solace and support in time of need. Most older women are within a few minutes of their nearest children and communicate with their children frequently. While the frequency of contact is well established, questions might be raised about how meaningful the relationships are and whether such contact improves the morale of the older generation significantly. Relationships with grown children may be sources of gratification for all concerned, or the relationships may spring from a sense of duty with expectations for reciprocity and affection unrealized.

Chapter 18 examines the nature and strength of the ties between older parents and their grown children and other kin. Elizabeth Johnson and Barbara Bursk affirm that family involvement continues to provide affectional support for older men and women, about three-fourths of whom are living with or within 30 minutes of living children. That figure does not include the frequent use of telephones for communication between more distant parents and children. Continuity of shared interests and values contributes to the meaning of the relationship.

One might argue that given the centrality of marriage and the family for women, relationships outside that sphere might be less important for a woman than a man. On the other hand perhaps early socialization stressing affective ties provides a basis for forming relationships with a broad network of neighbors and friends in addition to the family. Since about one-fourth of women past 65 have no living children, the extent of friendship ties becomes an important research area. However as Chapter 19 demonstrates, the separation of "family" and "friends" is an artificial one and so most of the articles look at both. Nonetheless we are interested in the social bonds of friendship and have selected articles that, we think, provide important information about friendship — the relative importance of families and friends, the role of intimate friends and friendship ties formed in a variety of associational networks.

In Chapter 19 Greg Arling reviews the literature relative to family ties and friendship to determine their intricate relationship to morale and life satisfaction. He then presents the involved relationships that characterize his sample. He finds, for example, that an elderly widow's dependent relationships with family members may have different consequences for morale than the more reciprocal relations with her friends. Since much conventional wisdom is not supported by his findings, further research is clearly indicated.

Edward Powers and Gordon Bultena, in Chapter 20, examine "Sex Differences in Intimate Friendships of Old Age." Again, in contrast to the conventional view that women's friendship roles are more extensive and meaningful than men's, these data support some more carefully delineated conclusions. Among these they find most interesting: "In late life males have more frequent interaction" but ". . . diversity in *all* forms of social contact . . . contributes to female adaptability in late life." And "women are more likely to have an intimate friend in late life."

Their attention to the circumstances that influence the value and nature of friendships is a more sophisticated analysis than simply counting relationships and demonstrates that gerontological research is reaching a new level of maturity.

In summary, these articles demonstrate the complexity of analyzing friendship bonds. One striking conclusion, not surprising in itself but repeated continuously, emerges. Whether considering marriage, parent-child, or friendships, the quality of the original relationship persists into old age. Patterns of interaction established earlier — whether between a couple, parents and child, or friends — are not likely to change with the years. Loving relationships endure and the more problematic ones lead to unresolved difficulties later.

Chapter 14

OLDER PERSONS' PERCEPTIONS
OF THEIR MARRIAGES*

Nick Stinnett, Linda M. Carter, and James E. Montgomery

THE amount of knowledge obtained concerning the earlier stages of human development is much greater than that concerned with the area of gerontology. As a result, textbooks and courses in family life education devote very little space and time to marriage and family relationships in the later years (Troll, 1971).

As the number of older persons in the United States has increased from 9 million in 1940 to approximately 20 million in 1971 and as the number of older persons who are married and living with their spouses has increased from 6,906,000 in 1955 to 9,403,000 in 1970, there is a vital need for more research and education which will aid in the understanding of the older person's marriage and family relationships (U.S. Bureau of the Census, 1967, 1970a, 1970b). It is particularly important to obtain greater knowledge and understanding of marriage relationships during the later years since the older person may increasingly depend upon his mate to fulfill his basic emotional needs due to his gradually decreasing interaction with other institutions and with his children (Stinnett, Collins, and Montgomery, 1970). Such research could contribute to a greater awareness of the strengths and problems of marriage during the later years and could also be a positive contribution to the teaching of marriage and aging courses. Unfortunately, research concerned with the perceptions of older husbands and wives toward their marriage relationships and their present period of life is very limited.

The available review of literature concerning older persons' perceptions of their marriage relationships and present period of life suggests the following:

1. There is evidence that many older persons consider their marriage relationships to be as satisfactory as, if not more than, in previous years (Fried and Stern, 1948; Bossard and Boll, 1955; Lipman, 1961).

*From *Journal of Marriage and the Family:* 665-670, Nov. 1972. Copyrighted 1972 by the National Council on Family Relations. Reprinted by permission.

2. Evidence also exists from other studies that marriage satisfaction declines during the later years, particularly among lower socioeconomic class couples and among marriages in which a small amount of shared companionship and satisfaction existed in the earlier years (Townsend, 1957; Blood and Wolfe, 1960; Safilios-Rothschild, 1967).

3. Marriages perceived as satisfactory in the later years have usually been satisfactory from the beginning while those perceived as unsatisfactory have generally been regarded as such from the beginning (Fried and Stern, 1948).

4. *Love* is the area of greatest marital need satisfaction for both older husbands and wives, while *respect* is the area of least satisfaction for husbands and *communication* is the area of least satisfaction for wives (Stinnett, Collins, and Montgomery, 1970).

5. Housing arrangements, mental health, lack of social participation, physical health, and reduced income are reported to be common problems of the older person (Barron, 1961).

6. Marriage appears to contribute to morale and continued activity during the later years, and a high degree of marital need satisfaction is positively related to a high degree of morale (Neugarten, Havighurst, and Tobin, 1961; Goldfarb, 1968; Stinnett, Collins, and Montgomery, 1970).

Purposes

The general purpose of this study was to investigate the perceptions of older husbands and wives concerning marriage and their present period of life. The specific purposes were to:

1. Determine the perceptions of older husbands and wives concerning each of the following: (a) marital happiness, (b) whether own marriage has improved or worsened over time, (c) the happiest period of marriage, (d) whether most marriages improve or worsen over time, (e) most rewarding aspects of the present marriage relationship, (f) most troublesome aspects of the present marriage relationship, (g) most important characteristic of a successful marriage, (h) most important factor in achieving marital success, (i) major problems of the present period of life, and (j) the happiest period of life.

2. Determine if a significant difference exists in each of the above mentioned perceptions according to sex.

3. Determine if a significant difference exists in the morale scores of older husbands and wives according to each of the following perceptions: (a) marital happiness, (b) whether own marriage has improved or worsened over time, (c) the happiest period of life.

Procedure

Subjects

The names of the 408 older husbands and wives who participated in this study were obtained from the mailing lists of senior citizen centers in Oklahoma. The husbands and wives were requested to complete the questionnaires separately and not to compare answers. The data were obtained from February and March, 1969. The sample comprised 51 per cent males and 49 per cent females, whose ages ranged from 60 to 89 years with the greatest percentage, 36 per cent, being in the 65 to 69 age grouping. Ninety-six per cent of the sample was white. Approximately half of the subjects had lived for the major part of their lives in small towns under 25,000. The greatest proportion of the respondents (38 per cent) had less than a high school education while seven per cent had undertaken post-graduate study. The largest percentage of the subjects' occupations for the major part of their lives was clerical-sales (40 per cent) while farming constituted the smallest percentage (13 per cent).

Instrument

The questionnaire was composed of fixed alternative type questions and consisted of the following parts: (a) a general information sheet to obtain background data about the subjects, (b) questions relating to the respondents' perceptions of their marriage and their present period of life, and (c) the *Life Satisfaction Index-Z* which was used to measure the morale of the respondents.

The *Life Satisfaction Index-Z (LSIZ)*, developed by Neugarten, Havighurst, and Tobin (1961), and reported by Wylie and Twente (1968), was derived from the *Life Satisfaction Rating Scale* and has a reported reliability coefficient of .80.

Results

Percentage Description of Perceptions

A detailed percentage and frequency description concerning the older husbands' and wives' perceptions of marriage and the present

The Older Woman

period of life is presented in Table 14-I. A brief summary of these findings is as follows:

1. The greatest proportion of the respondents rated their marriages as *very happy* (45.4 per cent) or *happy* (49.5 per cent).

2. The majority of older husbands and wives reported that their marriage had become *better* over time (53.3 per cent).

3. The *present* time was reported to be the happiest period of marriage by most respondents (54.9 per cent).

4. Approximately 50 percent of the sample felt that most marriages become *better* over time.

5. The two most rewarding aspects of the present marriage relationship were most often reported by older husbands and wives as *companionship* (18.4 per cent) and *being able to express true feelings to each other* (17.8 per cent).

6. The two aspects of the present marriage relationship which were most often reported as being troublesome were *having different values and philosophies of life* (13.8 per cent) and *lack of mutual interests* (12.5 per cent).

7. The two most important characteristics of a successful marriage

Table 14-I

FREQUENCY AND PERCENTAGE DISTRIBUTION OF
OLDER PERSONS' PERCEPTIONS OF THEIR MARRIAGES
AND THE LATER YEARS OF LIFE*

Perceptions	No.	%
1. Own marital happiness		
Very happy	178	45.4
Happy	194	49.5
Unhappy	11	2.8
Undecided	9	2.3
2. Whether own marriage has improved or worsened over time		
Better	211	53.3
Worse	15	3.8
About the same	162	40.9
Undecided	8	2.0
3. Happiest period of own marriage		
Present time	206	54.9
Middle years	102	27.2
Young adult years	67	17.9
4. Whether most marriages become better or worse over time		
Better	183	47.2

Worse	25	6.4
About the same	112	28.9
Undecided	68	17.5
5. Most rewarding aspects of present marriage relationship		
Economic security	173	16.2
Having physical needs cared for	81	7.6
Standing in the community	75	7.0
Mutual expression of true feelings	190	17.8
Companionship	197	18.4
Being needed by mate	128	12.0
Affectionate relationship with mate	120	11.2
Sharing of common interests	99	9.3
6. Most troublesome aspects of present marriage relationship		
Lack of mutual interests	68	12.5
Inability to express mutually true feelings	47	8.6
Unsatisfactory affectional relationships	46	8.5
Differing values and life philosophies	75	13.8
Lack of companionship	20	3.7
Frequent disagreements	42	7.7
Other	46	8.5
Nothing troublesome	179	36.2
7. Most important characteristics of a successful marriage		
Respect	127	38.2
Personality growth	14	4.1
Emotional closeness	18	5.4
Sexual satisfaction	26	7.8
Sharing common interests	88	26.5
Effective expression of true feelings	44	13.2
Meeting physical needs	15	4.5
8. Most important factor in achieving marital success		
Being in love	86	48.6
Determination	21	11.9
Common interests	31	17.5
Compatibility of personalities	39	22.0
9. Major problems of present period of life		
Housing	122	27.5
Money	89	20.0
Use of leisure time	49	11.0
Poor health	94	21.2
Not feeling useful	44	9.9
Finding a job	13	2.9
Their marriage relationship	24	5.4
10. Happiest period of their lives		
Present time	190	50.3
Middle years	92	24.3
Young adult years	56	14.8
Teenage years	22	5.8
Childhood	18	4.8

*Items 5, 6, and 9 were multiple response items and therefore have total responses larger than the sample size.

were most often reported by the respondents as *respect* (38.2 per cent) and *sharing common interests* (26.5 per cent).

8. The most important factor in achieving marital success was most often reported as *being in love* (48.6 per cent).

9. The three most frequently mentioned major problems of the present period of life were *housing* (27.5 per cent), *poor health* (21.2 per cent), and *money* (20 per cent).

10. The *present time* was reported to be the happiest period of life by the greatest proportion of respondents (50.3 per cent).

Table 14-II

F SCORE REFLECTING DIFFERENCES IN MEAN MORALE SCORES
ACCORDING TO PERCEPTION CONCERNING MARRIAGE
AND THE LATER YEARS OF LIFE

Perception	$\overline{X}$	F score
1. Own marital happiness		
Very happy	9.35	
Happy	7.87	
Unhappy	4.45	14.34*
Undecided	6.89	
2. Whether own marriage has improved or worsened over time		
Better	9.02	
Worse	5.07	
Remained about the same	7.98	10.42*
Undecided	6.25	
3. Happiest period of life		
Present	9.56	
Middle years	7.42	
Young adult years	6.89	15.90*
Teenage years	6.27	
Childhood	7.17	

*=.001 level of significance.

Examination of Hypotheses

The *chi*-square test revealed that no significant differences existed in the various perceptions concerning marriage and the later years of life according to sex.

An analysis of variance was utilized to examine the null hypothesis that no significant relationship exists between morale of the older husbands and wives and selected perceptions concerning marriage and the later years of life. A more detailed description of the significant relationships is presented in Table 14-II. It was found that significant differences existed in morale scores according to each of the following:

(a) *Self rating of own marital happiness.* Those who rated their marriage as *very happy* received the highest mean morale score while those who rated their marriage as *unhappy* received the lowest mean morale score.

(b) *Perception of whether own marriage has improved or worsened over time.* Those who perceived their marriages as having become *better* over time received the highest mean morale score, while those who perceived their marriages as having become *worse* over time received the lowest mean morale score.

(c) *Perception of the happiest period of life.* Those who perceived the *present* as the happiest period of life received the most favorable mean morale score.

Discussion and Conclusion

The findings that the greatest proportion of the respondents rated their marriages as very happy or happy and that the majority of older husbands and wives reported that their marriages had become better over time are in sharp contrast with the prevalent image of marital satisfaction declining in the later years. These findings seem to be particularly related to Feldman's (1964) report that husbands and wives in the postparental stage indicated higher satisfaction with their marriages than did those in earlier stages and that this increase in satisfaction seemed to continue through the later years of marriage. The present findings are also consistent with the findings by other researchers that many older persons feel that their marriage relationship is happy and as satisfactory as, if not more than, in previous years (Fried and Stern, 1948; Tuckman and Lorge, 1953; Bossard and Boll, 1955; Lipman, 1961).

The finding that most of the respondents felt the present was the happiest period of marriage might be partially explained by the reports of Deutscher (1962, 1964) whose postparental couples indicated they were experiencing a new freedom in their marital interaction and a more satisfying form of interpersonal relationship. Perhaps with the children launched and the husband no longer employed, the older husband and wife have greater freedom to do what they desire, can go at their own pace, can spend more time together and enjoy each other's companionship more than in the past. It is also logical that through the years the older couple may have developed a greater degree of understanding, acceptance, and better communication patterns. This finding might also be partially explained by the study of Fried and Stern (1948) in which it was found that with age many couples seem to become better adjusted and tend to see themselves as less demanding, less temperamental, less egotistical, and less irritable. It is interesting that the present finding is consistent with another finding reported in this study that the present was reported to be the happiest period of life by most of the respondents.

Inasmuch as the middle years of marriage are so often portrayed as being characterized by conflict and dissatisfaction, it is of interest that this period was second in frequency of selection as the happiest period of married life and also second in frequency of selection as the happiest period of life in general. These findings appear related to the results of Hayes and Stinnett (1971) who found that the greatest proportion of middle-aged husbands and wives (51 per cent) perceived the middle years of marriage as the happiest.

The findings that *companionship* and *being able to express true feelings to each other* were most often chosen as the most rewarding aspects of the present marriage relationship are related to Lipman's research (1961) in which it was found that the expressive qualities such as companionship and understanding were seen by older couples as the most important things a couple could give each other in the later years of marriage. The present findings suggest that for many older husbands and wives these two qualities may be increasingly experienced in the later years of marriage. This could also be a partial explanation for the previously discussed findings that the majority of respondents perceived their marriage relationship as improving over time and that they perceived the present as the happiest period of marriage.

The findings that having different values and philosophies of life and lack of mutual interests were most often reported as the two aspects of the present marriage relationship which were most troublesome would seem to reflect personality incompatibility as a basic cause of marital problems among these couples. These findings are related to the report of Burgess and Wallin (1953) that compatibility of personalities was perceived by engaged couples as one of the most important factors conducive to marriage success.

That companionship was selected so infrequently as a troublesome aspect of the present marriage relationship is consistent with the previously discussed finding that companionship was selected most often as the most rewarding aspect of the marriage relationship. It is also noted that the largest proportion of respondents indicated that nothing is troublesome concerning their marriage.

The finding that respect was mentioned most frequently as the most important characteristic of a successful marriage is interesting in that this concept has not been stressed a great deal in the marriage and family literature. This finding is related to the report by Stinnett, Collins, and Montgomery (1970) that older husbands received their lowest subscore on the Marital Need Satisfaction Scale in the need category of respect, indicating that they believed this was an important need which had not been as satisfactorily fulfilled as they would have desired.

The finding that sharing common interests was selected second in frequency as the most important characteristic of a successful marriage coincides with Lipman's (1961) finding that sharing common interests helped in solidifying emotional bonds of older couples.

The finding that being in love was reported as being the most important factor in achieving marital success by almost half of the respondents is surprising in view of the commonly held belief that older persons value being in love less than do younger persons. This finding is particularly interesting in view of the fact that Feldman's research (1964) did indeed indicate older couples valued being in love less than did younger couples. Perhaps a more recent comparison of older persons and younger persons with respect to this perception would be fruitful.

That housing, poor health, and money were the most frequently mentioned problems of the present period of life is consistent with the findings of other studies (Barron, 1961). The finding that own marriage relationship was selected so infrequently as a problem of the present period of life is consistent with the previously mentioned findings that the majority of respondents have positive perceptions concerning their marriage relationships. This consistency suggests a certain validity concerning the findings of this study.

Consistent with the results of Stinnett, Collins, and Montgomery (1970) are the present findings that morale scores are significantly and positively related to the respondents' perceptions of: (a) their marriage as very happy or happy, and (b) their own marriage as becoming better over time. These results emphasize the importance of the older person's marriage relationship to his emotional well-being and are logical findings in that the husband and wife in the later years tend to depend more upon each other and less upon children and other institutions of society to fulfill their basic emotional needs. That morale was positively and significantly related to the respondents' positive perceptions concerning their marriages and the later years of life seems to be one indication of validity concerning the findings in that it suggests that those who gave positive reports concerning their marriages and the later years of life were being honest in their responses.

Perhaps the major conclusion which may be drawn from the results of this study is that the older husbands and wives in this sample expressed very favorable perceptions of their marriage relationships and present period of life. As a group, the respondents tended to perceive their marriage relationships as improving and increasing in satisfaction with the later stages of married life. These results suggest that progressive marital disenchantment over the life cycle may be a myth.

REFERENCES

Barron, Milton L.
1961 The Aging American. New York: Thomas Y. Crowell Company.
Blood, Robert O. and Donald M. Wolfe
1960 Husbands and Wives. New York: The Free Press.
Bossard, James H. and Eleanor S. Boll
1955 "Marital unhappiness in the life cycle." Marriage and Family Living 17:10-14.
Deutscher, Irwin
1962 "Socialization for postparental life." In Arnold Rose (ed.), Human Behavior and Social Process. Boston: Houghton-Mifflin.
1964 "The quality of postparental life." Journal of Marriage and the Family 26:52-60.
Feldman, Harold
1964 Development of the husband-wife relationship. Preliminary report Cornell Studies of Marital Development: Study of the Transition to Parenthood. Department of Child Development and Family Relationships. New York State College of Home Economics. Cornell University.
Fried, Edrita G. and Karl Stern
1948 "The situation of the aged within the family." American Journal of Orthopsychiatry 18:31-54.
Goldfarb, Alvin I.
1968 "Marital problems of older persons." In Salo Rosenbaum and Ian Alger (eds.), The Marriage Relationship. New York: Basic Books.
Hayes, Maggie P. and Nick Stinnett
1971 "Life satisfaction of middle-aged husbands and wives." Journal of Home Economics 63:669-674.
Lipman, Aaron
1961 "Role conceptions and morale of couples in retirement." Journal of Gerontology 16:267-271.
Neugarten, Bernice, Robert J. Havighurst, and Sheldon Tobin
1961 "The measurement of life satisfaction." Journal of Gerontology 16:134-143.

Rollins, Boyd C. and Harold Feldman
1970 "Marital satisfaction over the family life cycle." Journal of Marriage and the Family 32:20-28.
Safilios-Rothschild, C.
1967 "A comparison of power structure and marital satisfaction in urban Greek and French families." Journal of Marriage and the Family 29:345-352.
Stinnett, Nick, Janet Collins, and James E. Montgomery
1970 "Marital need satisfaction of older husbands and wives." Journal of Marriage and the Family 32:428-434.
Townsend, Peter
1957 The Family Life of Old People. London: Routledge and Kegan Paul.
Troll, Lillian E.
1971 "The family of later life: a decade review." Journal of Marriage and the Family 33:263-290.
Tuckman, Jacob and Irving Lorge
Retirement and the Industrial Worker. New York: Bureau of Publications, Teacher College, Columbia University.
U.S. Bureau of the Census
1967 Current Population Report. Population Estimates, Series P-25, No. 381. Washington, D.C.: Government Printing Office.
1970a Population Estimates and Projections. Series P-25, No. 448. Washington, D.C.: Government Printing Office.
1970b Statistical Abstract of the United States, 1970. 91st Edition. Washington, D.C.: Government Printing Office.
Wylie, Mary L. and Esther E. Twente
1968 Mobilization of Aging Resources for Community Service. National Institute of Mental Health, Grant No. MH 01472. The University of Kansas, Lawrence, Kansas.

Chapter 15

A NEW LOOK AT OLDER MARRIAGES*

WALTER C. MCKAIN

INSTITUTIONS once considered impregnable are being challenged in American society and the attack is coming from both ends of the age spectrum. Young people are raising questions about the aims of formal education, the value of work as an end in itself, sex codes, the judicial system, and the nation's international position. Older persons in preparing for the 1971 White House Conference on Aging were talking about guaranteed incomes, health insurance, the system of rewards, and the role of the family. Before social institutions begin to fall apart the ragged seams are often noticeable at those points in the life cycle where the wear and tear is greatest. Persons not caught up in the routine of earning a living and rearing a family must make uneasy decisions — that is, decisions for which society has provided no guidelines or guidelines that do not seem appropriate.

Remarriage and Other Options

One such issue is "Is remarriage an acceptable option for the older person who is widowed?" This has become an important question for three reasons. First, the number of persons who must make the decision has increased and will continue to grow. Second, the family which at one time offered an alternative solution is now in many cases either unable or unwilling to provide a home for the widowed parent. Third, it calls for the social acceptance of marriages late in life, a practice which heretofore has been generally unacceptable.

As in the case of all social issues the policy finally agreed upon will not be dictated by any one segment of society; it must receive a more general sanction. However, the growing number of widows and widowers adds to the importance of the issue and to the urgency of a solution. In 1970 there were over six million widows and a million

*From *The Family Coordinator*, 21:61-69, 1972. Copyrighted 1972 by the National Council on Family Relations. Reprinted by permission.

The research project was sponsored jointly by the National Institutes of Health, U.S. Public Health Service and the Storrs Agricultural Experiment Station at the University of Connecticut. Scientific Contribution No. 468.

and a half widowers over 65 in the United States. This represented a sixfold increase in the number of older widows and almost a fourfold increase in the number of older widowers since 1900. (U.S. Bureau of the Census 1971; U.S. Bureau of the Census 1963).

In general, these elderly widowed are in better health, their incomes are higher and more secure, and their mobility is greater than ever before. They have much to bring to the marriage partnership. The notion that older persons are no longer interested in or, if interested, no longer capable of sexual intercourse has been thoroughly discredited (Kinsey, 1948; Kinsey, 1963; Masters and Johnson, 1966). With more years to live and more resources at their disposal, older widows and widowers are demanding that the current opposition to remarriage be reconsidered.

Widowhood status has many disadvantages in a family-oriented society and these are especially severe for older widows and widowers. (Berardo, 1968; Lopata, 1971) Widowed persons ideally have four options available to them in the readjustment of their lives: (1) they can live alone, (2) they can move into some form of congregate living, (3) they can live with their children, or (4) they can remarry.

The last two options provide living arrangements in a family situation. The practice of living with adult children does not seem to fit a highly mobile and self-centered society. Riley and Foner conclude that "over time . . ., decreasing proportions of older people live in the same household with their children" and point out "Even when households are shared today the older person is, more often than not, himself the head of the house . . . ." (Riley and Foner, 1968; Shanas and Streib, 1965; and Burgess, 1957) The nuclear family, they indicate, has become two families — the young couple with or without children and the old couple without children. When death claims one spouse the remaining spouse cannot easily return to a family situation. His children are preoccupied with their own affairs, modern houses are too small, family functions have no need for the grandparent and indeed, the grandparent often does not want to find a place in the home of his child amid the confusion of his grandchildren. (Townsend, 1954; Albrecht, 1954)

Changes in life expectancy, in age at marriage, and in the age when the last child leaves home have meant that the children of many persons widowed late in life are themselves in the "empty nest" period, face-to-face with retirement. The youngest child no longer is in a position to postpone his marriage and look after a widowed parent.

The ethnic values of immigrant groups with strong family traditions in the past dictated that the elderly widow or widower live with one of the children. But these ethnic groups no longer migrate to the

United States in large numbers and their values have been diluted as their ranks have been thinned.

Opposition to Remarriage

Many widowed older persons who desire family life can find it in remarriage but not in the homes of their children. However, the decision to remarry must be made in the face of social disapproval. Society tends to discount remarriage late in life as a viable option. It is still not considered an appropriate solution for the elderly person who is widowed and who wants to live in a family. His friends, his children, and the community at large discourage his remarriage. He is accused of being immature, disrespectful and selfish and his motives are neither understood nor accepted. A barrier has been erected between what the widowed person wishes to do and what society expects of him. Cosneek reports that only 25 percent of the older widowed Jewish persons he studied would even consider remarriage. (Cosneek, 1970)

Children are especially likely to resist the remarriage of a parent. In some cases pecuniary self-interest lies behind a child's opposition to remarriage in that he is afraid such a move will reduce his inheritance. In addition, most children have never thought of their parents in the role of husband and wife. Instead, they have seen them only as mother or father — a self-sacrificing, asexual, and narrow role. The sudden role reversal in which they are asked to accept a new member of the family is beyond their comprehension and they begin to consider their parent as childish, perverse, and certainly not qualified to select a marriage partner. More important, where the tradition of filial responsibility persists, some children look upon a new mate for their widowed parent as evidence of their own failure to provide a home. In this case a feeling of guilt causes them to resist the marriage of their parent.

The public in general has not fully accepted the idea of marriage in the later years and believes that marriage is for young people and for the propagation of the species. Social sanctions have undoubtedly curtailed the number of such marriages and forced some older people to marry in secret, yet the barriers to remarriage are breaking down. An increasing number of older persons have been willing to risk public censure and their willingness will in time have the effect of changing public opinion. The coming generations of older persons may find remarriage an accepted, even an expected, social institution.

There is little statistical evidence upon which to resolve the issue of remarriage in the later years and to formulate a policy. Some argue that marriage is so personal a matter that it is futile to develop a general policy. Yet an implied policy exists and controls continue to be applied. The number of older men and women who actually live together without being legally married is perhaps not large but the number for whom remarriage has been ruled out by pressure from the family and community, though unknown, could be quite large.

Research on Remarriage of the Elderly: A Connecticut Study

Research on the remarriage of elderly widows and widowers is practically nonexistent. As with most social customs, remarriage late in life will only become institutionalized when and if more and more older persons remarry and discover it to be a satisfactory solution. Meanwhile it is important to know if these remarriages are likely to prove successful. Research was recently undertaken at the University of Connecticut to provide some answers. (McKain, 1969) The first published results suggest that older marriages are indeed generally successful and that factors related to success can be isolated.

The 100 couples included in the survey had been married for five years before the interviews took place. All the grooms were at least 65 years of age at the time of the marriage and all the brides were at least 60 years of age. Each of the brides and grooms had been widowed and each listed one of Connecticut's towns and cities as his place of residence.

An effort was made to get a random sample from a universe limited by prior marital status, age, and place of residence. Since the interviews were conducted after a lapse of five years there was attrition through death (77), migration (54), separation or divorce (8), and illness (11). In addition, nineteen couples refused to cooperate. Any bias resulting from deficiencies in the sampling procedures probably tended to reduce the number of unsuccessful marriages.

The couples became acquainted with each other in a variety of ways. In a surprising number of cases (9) they were already related by marriage. For example, a widower married his first wife's sister or a widow married the brother of her late husband. In a few instances the couple had been childhood sweethearts and had drifted apart and then been reunited late in life. Most couples (55) had known each other before either had been widowed. As a rule they had been neighbors, attended the same church, or met at an adult social function.

The widowers seldom waited more than a year or two before they remarried. Widows, on the other hand, frequently postponed their remarriage for several years, perhaps waiting until their youngest child left home. Undoubtedly the law of supply and demand influenced the differential waiting period for men and women but the urgency for men also involved their inexperience as a homemaker.

The patterns of assortative mating for the older couples were conservative; partly because of the age restrictions explicit in the sample. The grooms were usually older than the brides but not by very much. They came from similar backgrounds and income levels, possibly dictated by geographic propinquity. In almost all cases if there was a marked difference in education, income, or occupation it was in favor of the husband. The couples were almost always of the same religious persuasion and in those instances where different faiths had united, there was an absence of conflict before or after the marriage. Some of the social distinctions that seem so crucial in the younger years become blurred with age and are no longer important.

When the couple was seriously considering marriage, societal pressures began to mount and these were met in a variety of ways. Some of the restraints were direct, particularly those coming from adult children who were shocked and hurt that a parent would even consider remarriage. Friends and neighbors exerted a more subtle influence. Perhaps nothing was said but knowing glances, raised eyebrows, and periods of embarrassing silence more than told the story. Since many of the older widows and widowers had their own doubts and questions of guilt, the social pressures may have been partly imagined and greatly exaggerated.

A few prospective brides and grooms ignored public opinion and the complaints of their children. Others gave in. How many is not known but at least 25 percent of the sample confessed they almost decided not to remarry in the face of social pressures. Most of the couples who were interviewed bowed to public opinion at least to the extent of playing down the courtship, having a simple and sometimes a civil ceremony, and foregoing a honeymoon. (Hollingshead, 1952) The marriages were deliberately low key as if the bridal pair wished to hide the event. Courtship does more than enable the couple to become better acquainted and to determine whether their interests are compatible. It announces to the community that marriage is a distinct possibility and gives relatives and friends an opportunity to voice their approval or disapproval. If the courtship is kept secret because the couple anticipates public rejection, it no longer can perform one of its most important functions.

Yet despite the secrecy and shame involved, most of the marriages emerged as highly successful. Only six of the marriages appeared to be failures although 20 others, while mainly successful, still had minor problems to overcome. The criteria for success consisted of three independent measures. First was the respondent's own evaluation of the marriage. An independent appraisal was secured from the husband and the wife and a negative vote by either placed the marriage in the doubtful or unsuccessful category. Second, internal evidence from a series of questions on the decision making process was used to designate couples that were experiencing difficulties. Finally the interviewers closely observed the couple during the interviews, many of which lasted several hours. Outward signs of respect, consideration, affection, and pride together with obvious enjoyment of each other's company were evidences of success while any serious complaints led to an appraisal of unsatisfactory.

The high success rate is partly the result of the sampling procedure but success might have been expected for other reasons as well. Older persons bring one important ingredient to marriage which young people do not have — experience. Usually the older persons who remarried had had a successful first marriage. They were acquainted with the traits and patterns of behavior which are crucial for a happy marriage. They recognized these essential elements not only in their own marriage but in the marriages of their friends. The ability to scrutinize success and failure in a number of marriages and not be blinded by a romantic veil has improved the chances for marital success among older persons. A judicious ordering of priorities usually prevents the marriage that is unlikely to succeed and encourages the marriage that leads to happiness. Persons entering into marriage for the first time do not have insights. Young people not only lack personal experience, they seldom think of older persons in any role except that of father, mother, uncle, aunt, neighbor, or teacher. The once married person not only has had his own marriage to guide him in a subsequent marriage but in addition, he has had an opportunity to observe success and failure in the marriages around him.

The chances of success did not increase with the number of prior marriages, however. In fact there was some evidence that older persons who had been married twice or three times before were not as successful as those who had had but one previous marriage.

Since older widowed persons know what to look for in a marriage, the reasons they gave for flaunting public opinion and remarrying late in life carry added weight. Companionship was given as the major reason by nearly three-fourths of the men and by almost two-thirds of the women. The pleasure and satisfaction of having someone nearby, someone to talk to, someone to make plans with, and someone to care are included in companionship and not found in casual social contacts. But the desire for companionship is not self-centered. It includes the desire not only to be cherished by someone but to be useful to someone and to feel that another person's happiness was dependent on yours. The need to be needed does not fade in the later years.

Companionship also included love and affection and was the euphemism denoting sex. Very few older couples openly subscribed to the notion of romantic love but in a few cases it was apparent and in many more it was just beneath the surface. The notion that sexual enjoyment late in life is unbecoming or even obscene may have caused some of the older brides and grooms to deny its importance. The role of sex in the lives of the couples was not confined to making love. The husbands used remarriage as proof of their masculinity, the availability of sexual expression being as important to them as the sex act itself. Remarriage gave some of the men a sense of accomplishment. It enabled them to return to a role that had been rewarding to them for many years. The same was true for the widows who remarried. It gave them an opportunity to be useful by providing a home for someone who needed them and loved them.

There were other reasons for remarriage, some of them real, other rationalizations. The need to stretch retirement income was mentioned by several and some of the men claimed to be looking for a housekeeper or a cook. Widows wanted a home of their own or felt they should have a man around the house. Poor health is a constant threat in the declining years and some of the older widowed were lame, had poor vision or hearing, or needed a special diet. In a few instances either the husband or wife decided to remarry in order not to be a burden on the children. In general, widows and widowers who looked for a housekeeper, more income, or a nurse in the remarriage did not have as good a chance for happiness as those who based their marriage on companionship and love.

Young people may tend to marry mother and father substitutes, choosing consciously or unknowingly a mate who possesses the traits most admired in their parents, but the selection of a marriage partner in the retirement years is more often dictated by the older person's deceased spouse. The Connecticut research was not designed to measure the degree to which the second marriage partners resembled the first but this would be an hypothesis worth testing.

Success in Remarriage

Success in remarriage seems to be related to a number of factors. Although the number of cases in Connecticut is too small to generalize, some independent variables stood out and are worth noting. These can be summarized under five general headings.

Table 15-I

MARRIAGE SUCCESS OF OLDER COUPLES
BY SPECIFIED VARIABLES: CONNECTICUT 1969

	Successful	Unsuccessful	Total
1. Years between first meeting and marriage			
Fewer than 11 years	29	18	47
11 years or more	45	7	52
Total	74	25	99
$x^2 = 8.16$			
2. Number of courtship activities			
Less than 4	26	17	43
4-6	27	8	35
More than 6	21	1	22
Total	74	26	100
$x^2 = 9.47$			
3. Children of husband encouraged marriage			
Yes	45	11	56
No	9	6	15
Total	54	17 .	71
$x^2 = 12.20$			
4. Children of wife encouraged marriage			
Yes	47	12	59
No	7	5	12
Total	54	17	71
$x^2 = 11.92$			
5. Friends encouraged marriage			
Some	36	7	43
All other	35	19	54
Total	71	26	97
$x^2 = 4.59$			
6. Life Satisfaction Index of husband			
1-15	5	9	14
16-20	21	14	35
21-25	48	3	51
Total	74	26	100
$x^2 = 24.96$			

	Successful	Unsuccessful	Total
7. Life Satisfaction Index of wife			
1-15	3	15	18
16-20	14	7	21
21-25	57	4	61
Total	74	26	100

$$x^2 = 43.32$$

8. Former home ownership status and present residence			
One spouse owned house, now lived in it.	10	10	20
One spouse owned house, do not live in it.	16	3	19
Neither or both owned.	48	13	61
Total	74	26	100

$$x^2 = 7.71$$

9. Use of additional income by husband			
For luxuries	34	6	40
For necessities	30	19	49
Total	64	25	89

$$x^2 = 8.13$$

10. Use of additional income by wife			
For luxuries	35	8	43
For necessities	29	13	42
Total	64	21	85

$$x^2 = 4.30$$

11. Kept separate financial accounts			
Yes	19	18	37
No	54	8	62
Total	73	26	99

$$x^2 = 15.45$$

1. WIDOWS AND WIDOWERS WHO KNEW EACH OTHER WELL USUALLY HAD A SUCCESSFUL MARRIAGE. Many of the couples had become acquainted long before they were widowed and then remarried and nearly nine out of ten had a happy marriage. (Table 15-I, Item 1) Some of them had been neighbors and friends before their spouses died and had observed each other over the years, never thinking that the time would come when they would be marriage partners.

During the courtship period some couples discovered they had similar interests and participated in a variety of activities together. These activities included attending church together, having meals together with or without their adult children, participating in various forms of recreation or travel, and being members of the same clubs and organizations. If the couple shared fewer than four of these interests their chance of success was 60 percent. If they had four to six in common the success odds rose to over 75 percent and if they had more than six common interests the odds for a happy marriage jumped to over 95 percent. (Table 15-I, Item 2)

2. Remarriages which had the approval of friends and relatives had a greater chance for success than those which did not. The pressure against remarriage for widows and widowers may be lessening but it still exerts an influence. The older person must overcome a certain amount of resistance in most cases and tends to approach his remarriage cautiously. He doesn't want to risk the ridicule of the community and he begins to question the advisability of remarriage. It is at this point that he needs the reassurance of friends and the support of his children to overcome social pressures, real or imagined, that threaten his marriage. Eighty percent of the husbands and wives whose children encouraged the marriage had a successful remarriage. (Table 15-I, Items 3 and 4) An even higher success ratio was obtained when friends gave support to the marriage. (Table 15-I, Item 5)

As a rule, children who originally had opposed the marriage of their parent came out in favor of the marriage after they saw the happiness it brought. The reasons these children did not support the marriage and the factors that caused them to change their minds were not available in the Connecticut study. Additional research on this topic might provide information that would help children exert a positive influence before the marriage as well as after.

3. Widows and widowers who had been able to adjust satisfactorily to the role changes that accompany aging usually had a successful remarriage. When the last child leaves home the mother must rearrange her life. She has devoted much of her time to her children and now must find activities to fill the gap left by departing children. The older man has usually retired from gainful employment and his disengagement from the social system related to his occupation requires a major readjustment. A decline in health or in physical strength and perception also demands a major reassessment of objectives and daily activities. One of the most important of these, according to the Connecticut research, involves operating an automobile. When the older man or woman is forced to give up the license to drive more than the loss of convenient transportation is involved. The result is a significant loss in independence and a severe blow to pride and self-respect. Additional research is needed to demonstrate the importance that is attached to the operation of an automobile and the role changes that will be needed to absorb the loss of this activity.

Most of the couples who were remarried had adjusted to the various role changes which they encountered in old age. The Life Satisfaction Index developed by Neugarten, Havighurst, and Tobin was used as a measure of adjustment. Over one-half of the men and over three-fifths of the women had scores that exceeded 20 on a 25 point scale and only fourteen men and eighteen women had scores under fifteen. As might be expected there was a close correspondence between the Life Satisfaction Index scores and marital success since some of the same criteria were used in measuring happiness in marriage and the adjustment of individuals. (Table 15-I, Items 6 and 7) A needed research project would isolate the extent to which remarriage led to well-adjusted individuals and the extent to which successful remarriage was the result of well-adjusted individuals. Or perhaps there are important characteristics in individuals and their backgrounds that promote personal adjustment as well as a happy marriage.

4. WIDOWS AND WIDOWERS WHO OWNED A HOUSE BUT DID NOT LIVE IN IT AFTER REMARRIAGE TENDED TO HAVE SUCCESSFUL REMARRIAGES. Home ownership is a symbol of security representing much more than the monetary value of the property. Over the years it becomes a part of one's expanded personality. A home that is built or purchased by the husband and wife provides a bond between them and gives them status in the community. In the case of widows and widowers who have remarried the situation changes. Remarried widows may not like to live in a house that was furnished by the first wife. The home serves as a constant reminder of past associations connected with the earlier marriage. Similarly, widowers dislike to remarry and move into a house owned by the bride since home ownership tends to designate the head of the household.

Individuals who lived in the same house they had occupied before remarriage had a somewhat lower chance for a successful marriage than those who lived in a different house. (Table 15-I, Item 16) Couples had only a 50-50 chance for a successful marriage if only one of the spouses owned a house and the couple chose to live in it. It made little difference whether the bride or the groom owned the house. If the house was sold or otherwise disposed of and the couple lived elsewhere a successful marriage was almost always the result.

5. COUPLES WITH INSUFFICIENT INCOMES ARE LESS LIKELY TO HAVE A SUCCESSFUL MARRIAGE. The threat of dependency is a constant worry of older persons who live on a fixed income. A few remarried to help solve the problem of the declining dollar. Over half of the couples expressed concern over insufficient incomes. However, there appeared to be little relation between the extent of concern and the size of the combined incomes. Some persons with a relatively low income believed that it was adequate and others with a high income complained that it was insufficient. The use that was projected for hypothetical increments of additional income proved to be a more diagnostic vari-

able. Each remarried widow and widower was asked how he would spend an additional $1000 a year. If their replies included luxury items, their current incomes were deemed sufficient. If they mentioned only necessities, their current incomes were considered inadequate. Those who had sufficient money by this test tended to have successful marriages and those whose incomes were not adequate were less likely to have a happy marriage. (Table 15-I, Items 9 and 10)

Another income item closely related to marital success proved to be the keeping of separate financial accounts. Couples who spent their incomes jointly and set aside any capital they might have for emergencies and later for their children had a good chance for a successful remarriage. (Table 15-I, Item 11) Those who kept separate accounts and did not choose to pool their resources were less likely to have a happy marriage.

Even if older persons were encouraged to remarry the imbalance between widows and widowers would mean that many widows could not find a mate. (Bernard, 1956) Since most of these widows will not live with their children, they will not be living in a family situation. The idea of modifying the monogamous family to permit an older man to have more than one wife has been proposed but is not likely to be acceptable. (Kassel, 1966) More likely will be the development of living situations for older persons in which men and women can enrich each other's lives short of marriage. The housekeeping services and other assistance that women can give an older man are well known. The need that older women have for male companionship is readily apparent but not documented. Older widows tend to seek out male companionship in a variety of ways. To some extent their attendance at church and other social functions is related to this need. The male hairdresser, the handyman who keeps the house in repair, the garage mechanic, the doctor, the clergyman, the meter reader, the grocery clerk are all used by older women seeking male companionship. Experiments in congregate living are needed to demonstrate how older widows and widowers can receive the attention and companionship they seek from the other sex.

REFERENCES

Albrecht, Ruth E. Relationship of Old People with Their Children. *Journal of Marriage and the Family*, 1954, **16**, 32-35.

Berardo, Felix M. Widowhood Status in the United States: Perspective on a Neglected Aspect of the Family Life-Cycle. *The Family Coordinator*, 1968, **17**, 191-203.

Bernard, Jessie. *Remarriage*. New York: Dryden, 1956.

Burgess, Ernest W. The Older Generation and the Family. *The New Frontiers of*

Aging. (Wilma Donohue and Clark Tibbitts, Eds.) Ann Arbor: University of Michigan Press, 1957, 161.

Cosneek, Bernard J. Family Patterns of Older Widowed Jewish People. *The Family Coordinator*, 1970, **19**, 368-374.

Hollingshead, August B. Marital Status and Wedding Behavior. *Marriage and Family Living*, 1952, **14**, 308-311.

Kassel, Victor. Polygamy After 60. *Geriatrics*, 1966, **21**, 214-218.

Kinsey, Alfred C. *Sexual Behavior in the Human Male*. Philadelphia: Saunders Co., 1948.

Kinsey, Alfred C. *Sexual Behavior in the Human Female*. Philadelphia: Saunders Co., 1953.

Lopata, Helena Znaniecki. Widows as a Minority Group. *The Gerontologist*, 1971, **11**, No. 1, Part 2.

Masters, William H. and Virginia E. Johnson. *Human Sexual Response*. Boston: Little, Brown and Co., 1966.

McKain, Walter C. *Retirement Marriage*. Storrs, Connecticut: Storrs Agricultural Experiment Station, 1969.

Neugarten, Bernice, Robert Havighurst, and Sheldon S. Tobin. The Measurement of Life Satisfaction. *Journal of Gerontology*, 1961, **16**(2), 468-470.

Riley, Matilda White and Anne Foner. *Aging and Society*. New York: Russell Sage Foundation, 1968, 6.

Shanas, Ethel and Gordon F. Streib. *Social Structure and the Family*. Englewood Cliffs, New Jersey: Prentice-Hall, 1965.

Townsend, Peter. *Family Life of Old People*. London: Routledge and Kegan Paul, 1954.

U.S. Bureau of the Census. Marital Status and Family Status. *Current Population Reports, March* 1970, *Series* P-20, *No.* 212. Washington, D.C.: U.S. Government Printing Office, 1971, Table 1.

U.S. Bureau of the Census. Detailed Characteristics, U.S. Summary. *U.S. Census of Population* 1960, *Final Report PC* (1)-1D. Washington, D.C.: U.S. Government Printing Office, 1963, Table 177.

Chapter 16

ATTITUDINAL ORIENTATION OF WIVES TOWARD THEIR HUSBAND'S RETIREMENT*

ALFRED P. FENGLER

INTRODUCTION

ONE long-term trend that has been affecting increasing numbers of older workers is the advent of retirement. Between 1900 and 1968 the labor force participation rate among men 65 and over has decreased from 68.3% to 27.3% [1 (p. 164)]. Moreover, not only has this trend increased in the 1960s but more and more men are beginning to retire at even earlier ages than 65 [2 (p. 170)]. The result is that more men now, and an even greater proportion in the future, will spend some time in retirement.

Obviously, without adequate financial preparation the impact of retirement can be traumatic. About one quarter of the population over 65 years of age has incomes below the national poverty level [3]. Many people feel they cannot afford retirement if there is any alternative. However, beyond the financial loss is a psychological component which in some ways can be even more degrading. Kutner [4 (p. 81)] in examining the relationship between retirement and morale states:

> At best retirement seems to be a mixed blessing. Even for those who are economically prepared for retirement, the sudden acquisition of time, unoccupied, unfilled, available, creates problems. How to avoid a sense of uselessness, boredom, monotony? How to compensate for the loss of responsibility in one's life endeavors, to retain the prestige and status often tendered the older worker or executive, to find or acquire functional and satisfying substitutes for gainful employment to fill the vacuum created by retirement.

A recent study of retirement [5] argues that the harmful effects of retirement have been overestimated in the past. They found that the proportion of retired older persons who have feelings of uselessness

*From *International Journal of Aging and Human Development*, 6:139-152, 1975. Copyright 1975 by Baywood Publishing Company, Inc.

was less than a quarter of their sample. They also found that attitudes prior to retirement and distinctions between the first and later years of retirement were important in assessing morale. Other studies [6, 7, 8] have suggested that social class is an important variable in examining the adjustment men make to retirement.

What is missing in much of the literature on retirement is a consideration of the wife's reaction to this event. Kerckhoff [8 (p. 160)] asserts that "the literature on retirement has been concentrated almost exclusively on the reactions of the male retiree to the experience of leaving his work . . . . Previous investigators with rare exceptions have not collected data from and about members of the family other than the retiree himself." One exception is the study by Heyman and Jeffers [9] which explores the effects of health, age, occupation, activities and attitudes on the wife's reaction toward her husband's retirement. Further research on wives is perhaps lacking because retirement is considered an event that affects mostly the husband while the departure of children (the so-called empty nest) is more traumatic for the wife. Kerckhoff [8] found that the wife tended to be much less deeply involved than her husband in both expectations of and reactions to retirement. Because wives retained closer attachments to the family, Townsend [10] found that wives experience little of the disruptions and adjustments their husbands faced.

Nevertheless, although she personally may not be greatly affected by her husband's retirement, the success of his adjustment may greatly depend on her attitude toward his new role. H. R. Hall [11] in a study of executive retirement concludes that wives become of great value to their husbands in retirement. "She has more responsibility for his life, as it goes on, and, in part influences in some ways how and even whether it goes on. Over all more than ever in retirement time, the wife can make or break the home" [11 (p. 231)]. Donahue et al. [12 (p. 391)] report that the marriage relationship in retirement becomes so important that "harmony with the spouse" is "a condition sine qua non of positive adjustment."

Prior to retirement the husband had the support and recognition of society in his fulfillment of the role of breadwinner. Moreover, many of his activities (labor union, clubs) and friendships may have been directly related to his job. With the loss of his occupational role may come a decline in his own self respect. It is here that the wife's attitude may be important. Leslie [13 (p. 661)] feels that "if her conception of him remains that which she had before, then the husband may be able to hold on to his self concept in spite of lack of support for it from other people."

Finally, in spite of previous research, it seems probable that a sizeable number of wives may not look forward to their husbands' retirement and as a result it is highly likely that their husbands may be quite alienated. Wives who have established lifetime routines may not enjoy the prospect of a husband "underfoot" for twenty-four hours a day. Townsend [10] found that many wives preferred to have the home to themselves. "One said, 'There's nothing for them to do when they stop work in places like these. It's not as if there's a garden. As soon as they're down, they're gone . . . . I don't want him here'."

The purpose of this report is to explore the extent to which the wife feels she *has been* affected or *expects* to be affected by her husband's retirement. Furthermore, assuming that wives differ in their evaluation of this event, it will be useful to define which variables are associated with which evaluations. A brief discussion of the implications of this research for future investigations is included in the conclusion.

Procedure

The major information used in this report was drawn from a larger study concerned with changing marital relationships at various stages in the life cycle [14]. One phase investigated in this study was the impact of retirement on the marital relationship. Rather than employing questions which would structure the responses, an open-ended question was found to be most effective in tapping the range of attitudes felt toward retirement. The respondent was asked, with probes, "What effect do you think retirement will have (has had) on your relationship with your husband? That is, what do you think are the advantages or disadvantages as far as marriage is concerned?"

The population of interest consisted of women who were currently married and living with their husbands. In order to ensure a representative sample of ages and educational backgrounds a specific census tract in Madison, Wisconsin was used. Census data indicated that this tract maximized the range of age and educational backgrounds desirable for this study while still providing a high proportion of married couples. The median income of $6400 and education of 11.6 years was slightly below the median for families in the city as a whole while the median age of 30 is about five years older than the general population of this city.

The data were collected during the summer and fall of 1968. During this time the Wisconsin Survey Research Laboratory interviewed 174 wives. For this report a subsample of 73 women whose husbands were 50 years or older was used. This subsample was comprised of all white females ranging in age from 30 to 77 years with a median age of 56.

Their educational backgrounds varied widely from a third grade education to four years of graduate school. The median educational level is slightly below 12 years of schooling which is very close to the median of the entire census tract. The reason for selecting women whose husbands were 50 years of age or older was because it was felt that only around this age would reflections on retirement have some significance for the wives. Younger respondents' answers were too frequently given in terms of their present situation. Although this information could be useful, it was felt such an analysis would detract from those older adults who saw retirement as a present reality or a soon to be experienced reality.

As would be expected there was a varied range of responses to this open-ended question. Thus the following presentation is only meant to be suggestive of the kinds of classifications which could be used in a structured instrument.

Table 16-I

WIVES' RETIREMENT ORIENTATION:
BY HUSBANDS' AGE AND WORK SITUATION

	Retirement Sentiment			
Age and Work Situation	Optimists (29)	Neutralists (21)	Pessimists (23)	Total
Husband retired	33	28	39	100 (18)
Husband 60 and over but not retired	33	33	33	100 (18)
Husband 50-59 years old and not retired	46	27	27	100 (37)

In general three major groups of responses emerged from an analysis of the interviews. (Table 16-I) Although the respondents were encouraged to discuss both the advantages and the disadvantages of their husbands' impending retirement, most wives just evaluated it in either favorable or unfavorable terms, or saw no change. To identify each group we have labeled them the *Optimists,* the *Pessimists,* and the *Neutralists.* Even within these three broad classifications there is often wide variation. For example, Optimists might mildly welcome the event or be wildly enthusiastic. Pessimists ranged in attitude from mild displeasure and discomfort to outright dread. Others claimed their husbands would never retire. It should also be kept in mind that although other aspects accompanying retirement may also require significant adjustments (e.g., loss of income), the wives interviewed in this report were asked to comment only about the effect of their relationship to their husband.

Results

The Pessimists (32% of Sample)

There are two recurrent themes which represent the majority of responses voiced by the Pessimists. The first suggests a general concern that their husbands will find themselves with a surplus of time on their hands while the second theme reflects a fear that their husbands will be intruding into the wives' domestic domain. It is probable that both of these responses are interrelated since the wife who perceives her husband as lacking meaningful non-work activities can only conclude that he must compensate by invading her sphere of activity.

Wives concerned about post-retirement activity varied considerably in the emphasis they put on the husbands' failure to develop alternative interests. In some cases the wife seemed to share what she perceived would be her husband's problem. One wife noted that "the days will be longer and *we* will have to find some way to make it easier." A seventy-five year old wife of a retired assemblyline worker thought that retirement was just one more in a long line of activities which had been gradually relinquished over the life cycle and not adequately replaced with alternative interests. "We have too much time on our hands now and find too many things to disagree about. When we were younger and busier we got along much better." This woman did not find the disengagement process very satisfying.

Other wives were more likely to blame their husbands for the kinds of problems they envisioned for themselves and their spouses. One woman whose husband was an administrative assistant felt that retirement would be one more detrimental change for them. "He'll be home all the time. He has no interests. It might cause quite a bit of tension in our attitudes toward each other. He has changed so much already." Another woman replied succinctly: "He had no hobbies at all except to read and watch T.V. There'll be too much leisure time."

Other wives felt their husbands would never retire. One 77-year-old woman speaking of her 71-year-old husband, still an active carpenter, said: "He won't be satisfied unless he works. It would be pretty monotonous if he didn't. I'm afraid he wouldn't know what to do with himself. It might make for irritability perhaps but I know he'll work as long as he can pound a nail." Another woman felt that she would never have to "worry about it" because her husband would never retire. Another said it was "the worst thing in the world for a husband to retire." These women saw retirement to be avoided at all costs, and one can only wonder what consequences they feel would occur if their husbands were forced to retire. One wife of a 55-year-old laborer stated quite bluntly: "It won't work. He doesn't want to retire and will not retire; he will work as long as he can. My father retired and a month later he was dead. It's not good for a man not to work."

Most of the wives of this category described so far have stressed the detrimental effects that lack of work will have for their husbands. These women have not directed their replies to how their husbands' retirement will affect them as wives, homemakers, and in a few cases, mothers. Although not always directly stated it seems that many wives viewed their husbands' lack of alternative interests as creating a potential threat to their present style of life. One wife of a government worker stated: "I think if the husband doesn't have a hobby he gets bored — it's hard on the wife to have him around all the time. It's hard for me to work when there are people around. He talks a lot and wants me to listen." A frequent complaint was that they resented having "a man underfoot all the time." "He's liable to get on my nerves a little bit. I wish he would take up some hobbies."

Other wives were quite blunt in their concern that a retired husband would intrude on what was or had always been the wife's exclusive domestic domain. One wife had only one comment to make. "Just keep out of my kitchen." Another felt "he's a spoiler of plans for the kids — he sticks his nose in sometimes when they don't want his help." However, there is hope for many of these wives that an adjustment is possible. A wife of a presently retired former owner of a grocery store states: "It's a little complicated having him under your feet all the time when you want to clean but I wait until he's out of the house and then I get it all done."

These interviews seem to suggest that throughout most of their married lives there existed a natural division of labor. Work was the man's domain while hers was home and children. She accepted and even supported her husband in his desire to remain at work while simultaneously building her own distinctive life style around her home [10]. Their friends, their activities and their interests often developed apart from each other. Retirement however, would throw the husband into the home on a 24-hour basis. This could force adjustments to patterns which had changed little over 25 to 45 years of marriage. The husband becomes a stranger in his own home. He may demand more time and interest from his wife in whatever projects around the home he is involved in. This in turn may disrupt her schedule of household tasks and general family routine [15]. Moreover if he attempts to assist her with her household tasks he may do even more to disrupt her schedule. There is a certain thoroughness which the wife has followed for years; for the husband to adapt to her format may make for many irritating adjustments for both spouses. Furthermore, there is likely to be a clash of authority. The wife's position has traditionally carried with it some authority in the home. Meanwhile the retired husband has lost his earning power and occupational status and thus may try to compensate for this loss by asserting his dominance in the home.

> He expects to take on these tasks as an equal (or sometimes if he had a superordinate role in his occupation, unconsciously he expects to be a superior), but his wife has had no equal in the running of the house. Under the circumstances, either he meets rebuff with some damage to his self conception; or he starts a permanent conflict; or he threatens his wife's conception of herself; or they work out a new division of labor, usually gradually. [16 (p. 197)]

Cavan [17] describes the retired husband as "a bull in a china shop." He has internalized norms of competence and productivity and sometimes leadership. The expression of these norms has usually resided outside the family. With retirement he must not only readjust his self-conception of competence to a non-work role but if he seeks it in the family he may find himself trying to fill a role that is already well filled by his wife. Moreover, she in turn may find her husband inadept and perhaps threatening to her own self-image by intruding into her sphere of interest and authority. Rarely are inexperienced outsiders welcomed as new leaders.

The responses from the women in the Pessimist classification are consistent with the above explanations. Women are concerned that their husbands might often be "underfoot." Moreover even when a wife mentioned only the husband's lack of outside interests as a problem in *his* adjustment, it would be consistent to argue that she was thinking of her own situation as well. A husband without his own interests only increases the possibility that he may threaten and intrude upon his wife's style of living.

The Optimists (39% of Sample)

In contrast to the Pessimists, the Optimists saw no adjustment problems when their husbands retired and often saw retirement as a time for an exciting new life together. About one-quarter of the Optimists discussed retirement solely in terms of the husband's adjustment. One wife whose husband was retired felt that he "is more relaxed now. It gives him more time to work in his garden." Another commented that her husband "won't have to get up at six o'clock in the AM." In contrast to the Pessimists who were dreading retirement because their husbands seemed to lack outside interests, these wives perceived that their husbands' present hobbies would keep them busy and active in retirement. "I'm sure he will be busy with hobbies. He's a fishing enthusiast and we have a summer cottage." Another wife of a security policeman saw little difficulty since her husband worked at night and thus "putters around the house most of the day anyway." One enthusiastic wife of a local truck driver stated: "We've discussed retirement. The disadvantages would be that he'll be around the house more and he likes to eat all the time. But this can also be an advantage. He has so many varied interests and hobbies like hunting, fishing and going to our cottage, I don't think he'll be dull."

While some wives stressed their husbands' alternative interests and perhaps by implication the assurance that they would not interfere with their life styles, most Optimists were likely to stress the greater companionship that was likely to result. Comments like "more togetherness," "more understanding" and "an easier, calmer pace" were frequent responses. Some of the responses were uncomplicated and short. One 80-year-old woman said of her relationship: "I guess we seem to get closer and more dependent on each other." Another, the wife of a maintenance worker, said very simply: "I think it will be nice because he will be home with me."

Another group of wives, about half of the Optimists, often included references to "companionship" and "understanding" but in addition placed a heavy emphasis on shared active interests. They not only "had more time together" said one wife of a retired machinist but "they could *do* more together." They could share hobbies, visit children and grandchildren together, go shopping together and especially could travel together. Occasionally respondents would express concern for money or health but this is understandable since the kind of active life they were now living, or expecting to live, required much of both. One woman tempered her enthusiasm with the comment: "If you're retired you can go more places and enjoy life a little more. Now you have to be home in time for work. You'd be closer. You'd have a chance to do things together . . . . But perhaps there wouldn't be enough money to do any of these things." Another woman said "If our health is good maybe we can travel and do more things together." A wife of a fifty-year-old machine operator felt a couple would "have more freedom — to travel — to do some of the things together that you couldn't do when children are being raised." Nevertheless, she also commented that "you'd have to learn to get along without many things."

However, in spite of these doubts the tone of the replies was unmistakably positive and enthusiastic. Retirement would mean time to do things that one hadn't had time to do before. Life would be "enriched" through "spending more time in mutually shared interests and involvement." "We'll be able to do a lot of things we can't do now. We'll be able to go on trips without worrying about when we have to come back." A wife of a stockroom clerk enthusiastically and unconditionally asserted: "More time together! that's what we're both waiting for! more hobbies — we've just been waiting to do some of these things!"

In summary, the majority of Optimist wives look forward to retirement in order that they can spend more time together with their husbands. In some cases it's a very quiet feeling of growing together while in other instances there is a kind of enthusiastic fervor to participate actively in things postponed from earlier years. This orientation is much in keeping with the emphasis on the emerging companionship family in America [15]. These couples may either be expressing a consistent expressive marital orientation which they have held throughout their lives or rather this may be a reflection of a new "coming together" after they feel they have discharged their responsibilities to family and society.

The Neutralists (29% of Sample)

The neutralists were the least diversified of the three groups. Their statements were almost always very short and usually included such words as "no change" or "no difference" or "no disadvantages or advantages" or "same as always" and in some cases "no opinion" or "don't know." One woman refused to answer the question while another seemed to resent it. "I think that is a strange question. I have no idea if there will be a change or not. Right now I see no advantages or disadvantages. I don't like that question." There is a certain reluctance to speculate on this future event. One replied, "I don't know . . . . I just don't know." Another said, "There shouldn't be any change. I really can't tell — it's three years off." Another bluntly replied "I don't think of that time."

Lee Rainwater et al. [18] depict the working-class wife as being "psychologically passive." She does not feel she can command or direct events around her. She accepts things as given and rarely takes any initiative in exploring new things on her own. Lacking faith in personal efficacy she does not like to think about the future. The short statements, frequent disinclinations to comment about a future event, and the persistent "no change" response is characteristic of the wives in our sample. Change is frightening and mental activity arduous.

> She has little inclination or training to stand back at some distance from herself to reassess her situation in large terms . . . . She does not know how to estimate long range consequences of situations. By and large the working class woman is a person who wants to have things she can believe in with certainty, rather than have things she can think about. Thinking is associated in her mind with discomfort, and hence preferably avoided [18 (p. 66)].

Most of the women's husbands in the "Neutralists" classification could be considered working class. Most were semi-skilled maintenance men, truck drivers, or machine operatives. Of the three general orientations toward retirement the Neutralists represented a disproportionately large number of poorly educated husbands and wives.

Correlates of Retirement Orientations — Role Segregation, Kinship Interaction, Education and Age

One persistent theme which seemed to differentiate the Optimists from the Pessimists was the emphasis the wife placed on role segregation in the home. Pessimist wives perceived that the failure of their husbands to develop non-work interest would result in disturbances in their domestic routine and new demands on their time and energy. Optimist wives did not perceive retirement as a threat, and in most cases welcomed the opportunity to share more activities and interests with their husbands.

These role distinctions can be usefully explored by drawing on Elizabeth Bott's well-known analysis *Family and Social Networks* [19]. She argues that "the degree of segregation in the role relationship of husband and wife varies directly with the connectedness of the family's social network" [19 (p. 60)]. Since one of the main distinctions between the Pessimists and the Optimists was the wife's orientation toward recreational and domestic activities one would predict that a "close knit" network would be associated with the Pessimists and a "loose knit" network with the Optimists. By close knit Bott is referring to a high degree of interaction with friends, neighbors and relatives of the married couple. Many personal needs, emotional and domestic, can be shared with the larger network. Also, separate loyalties to spouse and kin may emerge [10]. On the other hand a loose knit network is associated with greater sharing in domestic tasks, more companionship, and overall a more intimate relationship between the spouses.

There is at least some suggestive evidence (given the limits of the sample size) that the retirement orientations that emerged in our interviews may be associated with the types of networks described by Bott. For example, 65% of the Pessimists but only 45% of the Optimists *agreed* that married couples should be willing to support their parents when necessary. On a behavioral item, 48% of the Pessimists but only 24% of the Optimists said they visited their children at least once a week.

Turning to the area of task segregation, some 26% of the Optimists as opposed to 41% of the Pessimist wives said they "always" or "usually" did the grocery shopping. Generally it was shared by both spouses equally. It is also possible that if other activities had been measured, one might find husbands selectively assuming full responsibility for tasks formerly carried out by the wife [20].

It could also be argued that Optimists not only are less interconnected with kin and more likely to share domestic chores but also tend to share more leisure interests and activities with each other. The Pessimists who are more involved in a close knit network have less need for communication and less need to share recreational activities. There was some evidence to suggest that Optimist wives were more likely to communicate about daily troubles with their husbands than Pessimist wives were. For example, only 39% of the Pessimists but 61% of the Optimist wives said they "always" or "usually" told their husbands when they had a bad day. Furthermore, although there was little difference in the proportion of wives who spent recreational time with their spouses, there was a difference in whether their activities were shared with others or done alone. Again, Pessimists were usually more likely to say they preferred to do things together with their husbands *in the company* of other friends or relatives. Many of the Pessimist wives also perceived the role of their spouse as that of *provider* and their own as that of *homemaker*. For example, only 7% of the Optimists but 39% of the Pessimists said the "provider" role comes first with their spouses these days. This is further evidence for the postulate that distinctive roles are associated with task-segregated activities. The husband's sphere of activity is outside the home while the wife's is inside the home. Since the wife perceives her husband fulfilling the provider role, should anything threaten his performance of that role he could lose status in her eyes [10 (p. 161)].

In addition, Bott recognized that social class seemed to be associated with different types of networks. The degree of network connectedness became the intermediate variable between social class and degree of role segregation. Our own data, although limited, do not indicate a close relationship between occupation and retirement orientation. However, a larger sample might make this distinction clearer. At most, our data indicate that there is some tendency among the younger and among the better educated wives to look with more favor on their husbands' retirement (see Table 16-I). For example, among wives whose husbands were still in their fifties, some 46% were characterized as Optimists and only 27% Pessimists. On the other hand only 33% of wives whose husbands had retired could be classified as Optimists while 39% could be classified as Pessimists.

The clearest distinction made by education was between the Neutralists and the other two orientations. Among the Neutralists only 48% of the wives had twelve or more years of education. This compares with 76% of the Optimists and 65% of the Pessimist wives who had twelve or more years of education. This description is consistent with the earlier discussion of the "psychologically passive" nature of the poor working class wife.

Conclusion

More than 70% of the middle age and elderly wives in this sample felt the husbands' retirement had brought or would bring some changes or adjustment in their marital relationship. Obviously this is only one dimension that may be affected by the retirement process. Nevertheless wives do vary in the degree of favorableness with which they anticipate this event, suggesting that retirement may entail some adjustments for them as well as for their husband. Since men were not included in this study it is impossible to support or question Kerckhoff's conclusions that wives are less deeply involved than their husbands in their reactions to or expectations of the retirement process. It is interesting to note in Kerckhoff's study that sizeable numbers of wives of both preretired and retired husbands were involved in the retirement process. For instance, a majority of wives of preretired husbands said they expected to do "more" and "fewer" things of interest after their husbands' retirement. It is possible to retain the significance of Kerckhoff's emphasis on sex distinctions while still accepting the conclusion that a sizeable number of women may be affected by their husband's retirement. On the other hand it remains to be seen exactly how important the wife's attitude is in the adjustment of the husband following retirement. Once again, interviewing a larger sample of pre- and post-retired *husbands* and wives would be necessary. Moreover it would be useful if such a sample could be investigated longitudinally.

It would seem that in the future the Pessimists may become fewer in number. With more educated cohorts entering the older age brackets and with greater ideological emphasis on role equality and companionship in marriage, the kinds of concerns expressed by the Pessimists with regard to task segregation may become a thing of the past. Kerckhoff [8] notes in his study that loose intergenerational ties and shared domestic tasks were associated with high morale.

However there is a possible dysfunction associated with the closer more intense companionate relations among husbands and wives. Townsend [10] indicates that the loss of a spouse was much more devastating for the husband than for the wife since he did not have a close network of surviving kin to provide alternative means of emotional support. Lowenthal and Haven [21] suggest that the loss of a confidant, whether spouse or some other, may have a deleterious effect on morale. Thompson and Streib [22] suggest that a family characterized by "togetherness" and involved in a loose knit social network runs the risk of "considerable desolation" when widowhood occurs.

REFERENCES

1. Riley, M. W., Johnson, M. and Foner, A. *Aging and Society*, Vol. 3. New York: Russell Sage Foundation, 1972.
2. Wolfbein, Seymour. *Work in American Society*. Glenview, Ill.: Scott, Foresman and Company, 1971.
3. U. S. Bureau of the Census, *Statistical Abstracts of the United States: 1972*. (93d edition) Washington, D. C., 1972.
4. Kutner, Bernard and Tanshel, David; Tago, Alice and Langner, Thomas. *Five Hundred Over Sixty*. New York: Russell Sage Foundation, 1956.
5. Streib, Gordon F. and Schneider, Clement J. *Retirement in American Society: Impact and Process*. Ithaca: Cornell University Press, 1971.
6. Loether, Herman J. *Problems of Aging: Sociological and Social Psychological Perspectives*. Belmont: Dickinson Publishing Company, Inc., 1967.
7. Friedmann, E. A. and Havighurst, R. J. *The Meaning of Work and Retirement*. Chicago: University of Chicago Press, 1954.
8. Kerckhoff, Alan C. "Husband-Wife Expectations and Reactions to Retirement" in

Social Aspects of Aging, Ida Simpson and John C. McKinney (eds.) Durham: Duke University Press, 1966.

9. Heyman, Dorothy K. and Jeffers, Frances C. "Wives and Retirement: A Pilot Study," *Journal of Gerontology,* Vol. 23, October 1968, 488-496.

10. Townsend, Peter. *The Family Life of Old People.* Pelican Books, 1963.

11. Hall, Harold R. *Some Observations on Executive Retirement.* Andover Press, Massachusetts, 1953.

12. Donahue, Wilma, Orbach, Harold L. and Pollak, Otto. "Retirement: The Emerging Social Pattern" in *Handbook of Social Gerontology: Societal Aspects of Aging,* Clark Tibbits (ed.). Chicago: University of Chicago Press, 1960.

13. Leslie, Gerald. *The Family in Social Context,* 2nd edition. New York: Oxford University Press, 1973.

14. Fengler, Alfred P. "The Effects of Age and Education on Marital Ideology." *Journal of Marriage and the Family,* Vol. 35, May 1973.

15. Burgess, Ernest, Locke, Harvey and Thomas, Mary M. *The Family: From Institution to Companionship,* 3rd edition. New York: American Book Company, 1963.

16. Rose, Arnold M. "Mental Health of Normal Older Persons," Vol. 3 in Arnold Rose and Warren Peterson (eds.), *Older People and the Social World.* Philadelphia: F. A. Davis Company, 1965.

17. Cavan, Ruth S. "The Couple in Old Age" in Ruth Cavan (ed.) *Marriage and Family in the Modern World.* New York: Thomas Y. Crowell, 1969.

18. Rainwater, Lee, Coleman, R. and Handel, G. *Workingman's Wife.* New York: Macfadden Books, 1959.

19. Bott, Elizabeth. *Family and Social Network.* London: Tavistock Publications, 1957.

20. Ballweg, John. "Resolution of Conjugal Role Adjustment after Retirement." *Journal of Marriage and the Family,* Vol. 29, May 1967, 277-281.

21. Lowenthal, M. F. and Haven, C. "Interaction and Adaptation: Intimacy as a Critical Variable." *American Sociological Review,* Vol. 33, February 1968, 20-30.

22. Thompson, W. E. and Streib, G. F. "Meaningful Activity in a Family Context" in *Aging and Leisure: A Research Perspective into the Meaningful Use of Time,* R. W. Kleemeir (ed.). New York: Oxford University Press, Inc., 1961.

Chapter 17

LIVING AS A WIDOW:
ONLY THE NAME'S THE SAME*

Edward Wakin

"THE funeral was over and suddenly I was all alone," said the grieving widow whose whole life had been wrapped up in being wife and mother. Her children were all grown up and gone. Now her husband. "No one to shop for, no one to talk to. The loneliness was so awful I thought I would go out of my mind."

Another widow, who had always worked, went back to her job one week after the funeral, making the same daily streetcar trip she had made with her husband. But that became too much of a painful reminder, leaving her upset, uncertain, afraid to look for a new job at her age — 50.

In the case of Mrs. J., she sat at home, depressed, listening to church music that she and her husband enjoyed together. One moment, she was determined to find a new home, the next morose and immobilized. Move or stay? She couldn't make up her mind.

Other widows can be encountered after adjustment and re-entry into the world around them. Such as Judge Lucille Buell who was sworn in last year (1974) as a Family Court judge in Westchester County (N.Y.) and who promptly cited her "broad experience in living" — "I was a wife, now I'm a widow. I am a mother [of two college students], a teacher, and a lawyer." Or Vivienne Thaul Wechter, a New York artist and teacher who remembers with warmth "a good marriage that developed over the years" and who adds: "I always try to have a full life. My advice is not to wallow in your widowhood."

From loneliness to fulfillment, from isolation to involvement, these women are members of a neglected minority — somewhere off in the wings of American society. They tend to be shunted aside, casualties of the worship of youth and of American discomfort with death, caught between the mythology of the swinging single and the frozen patterns of social life built on couples.

*From *U.S. Catholic*, 139-141, July 1975. Reprinted with permission from *U.S. Catholic*, published by Claretian Publication, 221 W. Madison St., Chicago, Ill. 60606.

151

More than 10 million women belong to this society of female bereavement, ultimately to be joined by the large majority of married women (given the longer life expectancy of women). Of all the widowed in America, 85 percent are women. They are neither single nor married, divorced nor separated. They are free — but for what?

Mostly, they are Americans looking for roles. Their search goes on without guidelines, with limited sympathy, and with little attention to their problems. As one expert has noted, widows are social pioneers looking for their place in American society.

As the life span increases, American women are becoming widows later in life and also spending more years as widows. In 1890, by the time her last child was married, the average woman was 55 years old and had been widowed for two years. By 1960, that average women was 47 when her last child married and was widowed at almost 64. In 1960, she faced an average of 15 years as a widow; but by 1970 an average of more than 18 years.

"The problem in American society — to the extent that a woman's identity is based on being a wife — is that the widow has no place to go," says Dr. Helena Zananiecki Lopata, a foremost expert on widowhood. "She can't be a widow, really, and she can't go back to being single. If she can't be a wife, can't be a widow, can't be single, her identity has to come from something else."

That search for identity, built on the ashes of a husband's death, strikes women unprepared, even when a long illness is involved. Widowhood is something that is not discussed, that is faced suddenly in the full force of grief, surrounded by well-meaning sons and daughters, relatives and friends. They are well-meaning but impatient. Concerned, but filled with misunderstanding and easy, often bad advice.

Widows have been largely left out of the vast American industry of professionalized advice-giving. Toddlers and teenagers get special attention, the just-married and the newly-divorced are recognized as special categories, and so are addicts, alcoholics, the unemployed, and the disabled. But not widows. They are expected to wipe their tears and get going. But how and where?

The fewer resources a woman had as a wife the less she is able to cope as a widow. The less money she has, the greater the effort it will take. The more empty the circle of her relatives and friends, the greater her isolation. The less education and the fewer the skills she has, the fewer her options are. The less flexible she has been as a wife, the more difficult her adjustment as a widow will be.

According to Dr. Lopata — who is professor of sociology and director of the Center for the Comparative Study of Social Roles at Loyola Unviersity of Chicago — the best advice for those wanting to help widows is to help them help themselves. "I recommend to everyone wanting to help widows that they help them become competent on their own and independent."

Belatedly, professionals in the fields of social science, counseling and mental health have begun to give more attention to the problems of widows. More churches and private agencies are beginning to offer special services. Through the efforts of all of these, more light has been thrown on what widows need and want, both from the practical and the psychological point of view.

Psychologically, widows are haunted by loneliness. It comes upon them after they reel under the impact of grief and as they struggle to find their place in the world — alone.

On the practical side, widows confront the legal, financial, and everyday problems commonly handled by husbands in a male-dominated society. They are called upon to perform actions and make decisions they have never faced before.

Finally, in finding their new place in society, they need a new sort of marriage — of attitude and frame of mind with information, know-how, and opportunity.

There are a number of services in existence to help widows. One is the Widows Consultation Center, in an office building in New York City's East 57th Street. Widow-to-Widow Programs are being started all over the country. And there is an organization called Naim, for widowed Catholic men and women, which has chapters in a number of dioceses. Other work is being done by Protestant churches and private agencies.

But these are only a beginning. Dr. Lopata points out that the "community ignores the widow," and she cites the "need for many more organizations focused on them." Father Edward Corcoran, national spiritual director of Naim, points out that the "widowed feel that the church has forgotten them."

In general, widows help widows better than anyone else does. This has been evident in the various programs that do exist, particularly the Widow-to-Widow Program developed under the auspices of the Laboratory of Community Psychiatry at Harvard University. Its director, Dr. Phyllis Rolfe Silverman, describes the many advantages a widow possesses as a caregiver: "As a teacher, as a role model, as a bridge person, she helps make order out of the chaos of grief and provides the widow direction in the role transition."

An experiment that was originated in the Dorchester section of

Boston from 1967 to 1971, the Widow-to-Widow Program located widows and then sent a widow to visit a widow. There was an immediate feeling that the visitor understood the problems, Dr. Silverman reports.

As one widow said of her widowed visitor: "It seemed as if nothing would be right again. I wanted to know how she managed. Looking at her now I couldn't believe she ever felt like I did." Another said: "When I first saw Mrs. M. I knew that there was hope for me. Here she was the same age as me, and she was able to think about helping others. . . ."

From sympathy and empathy, from a chance to talk to someone who shared the same experience, the widows then could move on to practical questions like legal assistance, social activities, or job-hunting. The idea was so successful that it is being picked up in more places than Dr. Silverman can keep track of. Widow-to-Widow Programs have been started from Newark to San Francisco, and early in 1974 Dr. Silverman went to Israel to help start such a program there.

Father Corcoran reports that chapters of Naim are springing up in a number of dioceses, from St. Petersburg, Florida, to Minneapolis. Naim is most active in Chicago, where it was founded. It is named after the town in which Christ restored to life the son of an anonymous widow. It shows the way for church-sponsored efforts to serve the widowed.

Chicago has 25 functioning Naim groups, whose membership ranges from 20 to 120 persons. There are monthly meetings, social gatherings, days of recollection, and talks by experts on the various problems facing the widowed. In such groups, the widowed find that their particular situation is receiving attention; and, more important still, they receive encouragement to draw on their own inner resources. The widowed, says Father Corcoran, do not want to be submerged in a Family Life program — as occurs in various dioceses — nor do they want to be lumped with "singles." "They are not seeking partners," he notes. "They have not lost a spouse through choice, but through death."

The death of her spouse often places the widow in a "crisis situation." At the Center in New York, the only professional service of its kind devoted exclusively to widows, the aim is clearly set forth: "Three out of every four wives in the United States eventually face widowhood. Despite this stark fact, no organized effort to help them meet their problems and build new lives for themselves existed until the Widows Consultation Center was established in 1970 as a nonprofit, non-sectarian agency."

The Center, whose constant backlog involves a month-long wait, receives a stream of inquiries from all over the country about a many-sided approach that is required in all programs for the widowed. Crisis intervention, in the form of counseling sessions and therapy, helps through the periods of depression that come immediately and often much later. Assistance in solving practical problems is provided by legal and financial experts. (In one example, a widow with $300,000 in the bank felt that she couldn't even afford a taxi.) The Center offers social opportunities along with various group activities. In a variant on the Widow-to-Widow Program, clients who have worked out their own difficulties get involved in helping others. One volunteer-client comes to the center every week and phones widows who are alone and suffering from isolation.

What Father Corcoran finds in his work with Naim is borne out by researchers: "Loneliness is the greatest problem." This was found true with seven out of ten widows in a check by the Widow-to-Widow Program. It was also borne out in a study of Chicago widows directed by Dr. Lopata: about half listed loneliness as their most serious difficulty, and another third ranked it as their second most serious difficulty.

The widows expressed this feeling in various ways: "I don't think anyone who hasn't experienced it can understand the void that is left after losing a companion of so many years — all the happy little things that come up and you think, 'Oh, I must share that' — and there isn't anyone there to share it with."

"You find even though there are people around, there is that great big void that's there. I don't think that the old saying, 'Time heals all wounds' is really true; because we were so close. I find that even being around friends and relatives you can be so lonesome in a crowd."

"It's very lonely. When the night comes, you wish someone would be there. We didn't do much but he used to just be there."

As expected, Dr. Lopata's research showed that the "more deeply the couple were involved" the more difficult the adjustment. But she adds a counsel that might not occur to a well-meaning relative or friend: the widow "must be allowed to grieve." Specialists use the term, "grief work," and it is the first step on the widow's way back.

Instead of encouraging the widow to forget her loss (impossible, anyhow), relatives and friends must allow her to work through her grief. She faces an emotional trial involving sorrow, guilt, loneliness, and fear. The experts recommend that a widow be encouraged to cry if she wishes, to talk of her late husband, and to describe how bad she feels.

Based on her own first-hand work, Dr. Silverman warns that it is a mistake to judge a widow's state of mind from the fact that her behavior may seem composed at the time of the funeral. For initially the widow is numb, and in handling duties connected with the funeral she is still acting as her husband's wife. "It is safe to say the real anguish and distress have not yet begun," Dr. Silverman says.

As the widow becomes aware of the finality of the loss, the fact that her husband is gone hits home. It can take her up to two years to accept this fact, and the process of grieving is necessary to her adjustment. If the process is avoided, Dr. Silverman says, it can create its own problems. But when faced it is a "prologue to the future."

Besides "grief work," Dr. Lopata cites four needs that all widows have: namely, companionship, solution of immediate problems, building of competence and self-confidence, and help in re-engagement in the world around them. It is in meeting these needs that relatives, friends, and agencies can aid widows in helping themselves.

Widows appreciate someone "just being there" as they learn to live alone. One widow spoke of "loneliness — nobody to talk to." Another spoke of coming home to an empty house: "It's a very lonely life — you have friends, you feel happy when you're with them, but you have to come home to an empty house." This need for companionship is complicated by the *ups* and *downs* of a widow's state of mind. Those close to her should have a special understanding and patience; they should stand by her, not avoid her.

Faced with her immediate problems, the widow is surrounded by advice — "too much of the wrong kind of advice," according to Dr. Lopata. Generally speaking, a widow should avoid making any important decisions during the first year of widowhood because the chance of making mistakes are great. Her outlook will change after she works through her grief and adjusts to being on her own.

Dr. Lopata is emphatic about a widow's doing her own decision-making: "No one should make decisions for her, unless absolutely necessary to avoid a serious disaster." Instead of advice that increases dependency, independence should be encouraged. Rather than off-the-cuff advice from the family on technical matters, widows need referral to experts: doctors, lawyers, bankers and accountants, and counselors. Here is where programs for widows perform valuable service.

Finally, widows need assistance in getting re-connected with society. "Keeping busy" is one frequent piece of advice that makes sense. In the beginning, activity is escape from loneliness; then it takes on meaning for its own sake. It plugs the widow into the life around her.

Unlike the young dropout, the widow usually does not drop out by choice. She is *forced* out by lack of skills and money, isolated by lack of transportation, handicapped by poor health, hamstrung by too much indifference and too little assistance.

As social pioneers, widows are forced to figure out their new roles in American society without guidelines and directions. Many of them — those endowed with money, education, skill, and, in particular, inner resources — stake out their new claims with scant assistance. They start up new lives on their own.

"The thing to stress," according to Dr. Silverman, "is that widows are not like delinquents. Most of them don't need clinics; they need contacts. They have the capacity to help each other and should do so, creating opportunities by themselves. They can use experts and specialists as collaborators, but what is most important is inner resources."

The goal is to stop being *widows* and to start being individuals — women who have lost a husband and learned to begin again on their own. Such as the widow who recalled how the Widow-to-Widow Program helped her get going:

"I looked around and I saw people worse off than me; they had no money or no family. One woman I know really died after her husband went. The way I was going that could happen to me; I wasn't sure that I wanted that to happen. Then I began to take stock. I was doing things I had never done before, going to meetings [of a widow group], driving people there. People were counting on me. I was needed. I was the one who was always so helpless and here I was helping someone else. I never thought I could change like that."

Then she expressed the life force that fills widows finding new roles in a society that has ignored them: "And I knew then that I had to go on living."

Chapter 18

RELATIONSHIPS BETWEEN THE ELDERLY AND THEIR ADULT CHILDREN*

Elizabeth S. Johnson and Barbara J. Bursk

THE goals of the research reported on in this paper were: (1) to explore the affective quality of relationships that elderly people have with their adult children from the perspective of both persons and (2) to understand the social, psychological, and environmental variables which influence the affective quality.

This study grew out of a concern with the way in which the family integrates its elderly members into a psychologically extended family structure. By psychologically extended family, we mean one in which there is supportive interaction between the generations but where the generations do not necessarily live within the same household. This process is clearly important for the individuals involved. Familial ties between elderly parents and their adult children cannot be regarded in isolation but are part of the total pattern of aging in our society. One aspect of this aging process involves the way that cultural norms, values, and roles affect the expectations of older people regarding their lives, which include relationships with adult children.

However, it is also true that in today's society there are no cultural guidelines, no specific norms, for behavior in the area of intergenerational relationships between elderly parents and their adult children. There is no socialization mechanism available for aiding elderly parents or adult children with their new roles at this life stage. Knowledge about the affective quality of existing relationships between adult children and elderly parents, as well as greater understanding of the factors which currently influence those intergenerational relationships, would facilitate the development of intervention strategies for use where improvement in intergenerational relationships is desirable.

An extensive literature review of factors related to the elderly parent-adult child relationship turned up only one empirical study of the affective quality of the relationship (Simos, 1973). No studies were identified in which both the elderly parent and an adult child(ren) were interviewed.

Overview of Family Relationships Between Elderly Parents and Adult Children

In contrast to the lack of societal guidelines for relationships between elderly parents and their adult children, Puner (1974) feels that the importance of family involvement with the elderly has not only *not* diminished but that the affectional and supportive functions of the family emerge as crucial integrative mechanisms for the elderly in American society. Troll's (1971) review of the literature led her to the conclusion that these family ties are the last social stronghold to which the elderly adhere.

Sussman and Burchinal's (1962a) assessment of the relationships between generations suggests that people as they age, become more involved with their families than with non-kin or other types of activities. They feel that the family's extended kin network is an extensive link between elderly parents and adult children and functions in indirect economic and social ways, such as the mutual exchange of services, gifts, advice, and financial assistance between the generations in as many as 93% of families.

In a second position paper, Sussman and Burchinal's (1962b) suggest that sociological and demographic changes in society have *not* changed the importance of family relations in the lives of the elderly, especially in times of illness, difficulty, or crisis, or on ceremonial occasions. They also suggest that emotional support by the adult children has replaced physical support and care of the elderly individual. Close intergenerational ties are based upon mutual affection, interdependence, and reciprocal giving. Puner (1974) suggests that the importance of the family is further demonstrated by the fact that the 10-12% of the aged who have no family or close relationships with kin are those individuals who constitute the caseloads of social agencies.

Satisfying relationships between the elderly and their children do not appear to be dependent on geographical proximity but are related to communication between parents and children. Both original research (Britton, Mather & Lansing, 1961; Shanas, Townsend, Wedderburn, Friis, Milhoj, & Strehouwer, 1968) and articles based on the research of others (Brody, 1970; Troll, 1971) have suggested that many of the elderly want to remain as independent as possible, preferring to live in their own homes, a choice which enables them to maintain their sense of autonomy. However, choices available often depend upon the social strata of the elderly; more choices are available for the elderly in the middle-class family (Smith, 1954).

Summaries of other people's research (Butler & Lewis, 1973; Puner, 1974) suggest that in the United States, 80% of all older people have living children and 75% of them live either in the same household or 30 minutes away. Kosa, Rachiele, and Schoomer (1960) found that one-third of all widowed, single, divorced, and separated males shared a home with their children, whereas half of all widowed, divorced, and separated females shared a home with their children.

Shanas (1960) found that the poorer the health of the older person, the more likely he/she was to be living in the same household with at least one child. Brody (1966) has reported on applicants to a geriatric institutional facility for whom the actual precipitating factor in the request for admission appeared to be only the last in a series involving the interpersonal relationship between the elderly person and his/her family. This factor tipped the balance so that the family (often also aging) could no longer sustain the elderly relative outside of an institution. Puner (1974) suggests that family relationships are more stable when separate households are maintained. As previously noted, separate households may depend on the health of the parent.

Brody (1970), Cottrell (1974) and Stern and Ross (1965) suggest that affect bonds with their children are very important for the aged. Hence, it is in the sphere of emotional and social gratification that the elderly parent derives much from his/her family relationships, even though the aged parents may be less integrated into the physical, day-to-day living pattern of their families.

Definition of Variables

On the basis of an extensive literature review completed by project staff (Ananis et al., 1976), four categories of variables appeared to have potential as correlates of the affectional quality of the relationship between the elderly parent and the adult child. These life areas were: health, living environment, finances, and attitude toward aging. Indicators were constructed for each of these four areas as well as for family relations. Questions included within an indicator were based on our informed (from the literature and experience) beliefs as to those aspects of the life area which had potential for influencing the affective quality of the relationship between elderly parent and adult child.

The family relations indicator included questions addressed to both the parent and the child about the openness of communication between them, their enjoyment of each other's company, their ability to count on each other, and an actual rating of the relationship.

The health indicator included questions about the parent's mobility outside of the home, the extent of medication usage, activity level, and rating of the parent's health.

The finances indicator included items about objective and subjective income adequacy, and problems between parent and child caused by finances.

The living environment indicator included questions about privacy, whether close friends live nearby, convenience to transportation, reason for moving to the present location, fearfulness in the home, and general attitude toward the surroundings.

The attitude indicator included questions about the parent's current happiness, the difficulty of his/her life, and general life satisfaction.

Our hypothesis was that a high over-all rating in each of these four life areas would contribute to a high over-all affective quality in the elderly parent-adult child relationship.

Sample Selection

Working under the direction of the first author, 18 (17 females, 1 male) second year social work graduate students each selected three elderly parent-adult child pairs to interview. The total number of elderly parent-adult child *pairs* in this nonprobability convenience sample was 54. The three elderly parents selected by each interviewer had to have at least one characteristic in common (e.g., ethnicity, religion, living situation, etc.). Attention was directed to insuring that a wide range of characteristics of the elderly parents were represented.

Given the importance of research in the area (Kaplan, 1975), and the desirability of obtaining a fairly large sample, it was preferable to use a nonprobability sample for this study than the much smaller probability sample which could have been obtained for the same time and cost effort. In addition, given the high refusal rate which was expected when the participation of two persons was required, it was not cost-effective to use a probability sample, in fact when nonresponse rates are high (28 individuals, evenly divided between parents and children, refused to participate in this survey), what was intended as a probability sample is more accurately considered a nonprobability sample.

The geographical area from which interviewees were drawn encompassed greater Boston and the surrounding suburbs. The sample was limited to white, noninstitutionalized elderly persons, aged 65 and

Table 18-I

CHARACTERISTICS OF THE ELDERLY PARENT SAMPLE
AND OF THE U. S. ELDERLY (65+) POPULATION

Characteristics		Sample	USA Population[a]
Age			
65-74		43%	62%
75+		57%	36%
Sex			
Female		81%	59%
Male		19%	41%
Marital status			
Male	widowed	30%	28%
	married	70%	72%
Female	widowed	81%	63%
	married	19%	37%
Housing location			
(metropolitan area)			
Central city		28%	53%
Suburbs		72%	47%
Employed status			
Employed		24%	14%
Not employed		76%	86%
Family income median			
Individual		$3060	$2397[b]
Couple		$8840	$5968[c]
Ethnicity			
Yankee		39%	
Jewish		26%	
Irish		22%	
Other		13%	
Religion			
Protestant		39%	
Catholic		35%	
Jewish		26%	
Living arrangements			
Alone		53%	
Spouse		26%	
2-generation		12%	
3-generation		4%	
Other		4%	

[a]Data obtained from *Developments in Aging 1973 and January - March, 1974:* A report to the Special Committee on Aging, U.S. Senate — pursuant to Senate Resolution 51, February 22, 1973.
[b]Median for elderly person living alone.
[c]Median for family headed by an elderly person.

over. The adult children were all 21 years old or older. Participants in the survey were not known to have sought therapeutic help around their parent-child relationship. The sample cannot be considered representative of the elderly population at large, nor can the relationship be viewed as typical of all elderly parent-adult child relationships. However, it is important to note that there are great difficulties in attempting to recruit two individuals, who do not necessarily live in the same household, for a study of this type.

The demographic characteristics of the elderly parents as compared with the national elderly population (where data were available) are presented in Table 18-I.

Our sample was older, more female, more suburban, and financially better off than the elderly population in the USA. The dominant white ethnic and religious groups of the area were well-represented. A majority of the elderly parents lived alone.

Instrument Design

The data collection instrument was a structured interview schedule which included both closed and open-ended questions. With a focus on the elderly parent, questions were developed in each of the following areas, general background information, family relationships, health, living environment, finances, and attitude toward aging. Emphasis was placed on certain practical considerations such as easily understood questions and amount of time to complete an interview, i.e., no more than an hour and a half. A second instrument, based on the pretested parent questionnaire, was constructed for use in interviewing the adult child.

Questionnaire Administration

Each potential participant was contacted by telephone or in person in order to arrange a mutually convenient time for the interview. Because the interview was conducted in the homes of the participants, the atmosphere was a positive, comfortable, and relaxed one. The interviewer asked the questions, interpreting unclear questions only when necessary. The elderly parent and the adult child were interviewed separately.

While receptivity to participation was an important factor in the inclusion of subjects for this study (resulting in restricted generalizability), one positive benefit was the good cooperation of the interviewees.

Each question was asked exactly as it was worded and the same order of the questions was maintained for all participants. Each interviewer was responsible for recording the participants' responses and for writing a profile of the relationship.

Data Analysis

As previously noted, indicators for each of the five areas, finances, health, attitude toward aging, living environment, and family relationships were constructed from selected questions in the interview schedule. Each question was subjectively evaluated for its association with the affective quality of the parent-child relationship. Responses were coded as to their assumed positive, in-between, or negative contribution to the affective quality of the relationship.

Analysis of the Data

The hypothesis that the four indicators selected, finances, health, attitude toward aging, and living environment, would be associated with the affective quality of the relationship between elderly parents and their adult children was explored by analysis of the data from the 108 questionnaires. The quantitative analyses included (1) correlations, (2) regression of the family relations indicator on the four life area indicators, and (3) regression of the single dependent variable, the parent's rating of the relationship with the interviewed child, on a selected variable from each of the four specified life areas. In addition to the quantitative data analyses, a more qualitative analysis was done of the profiles of the relationship pairs which were written by the interviewers.

While many correlations were carried out between the variables, those that were statistically significant (many more than would have been expected by chance), for the most part represent cross validation of variables. However, one interesting finding was the fairly high agreement ($r = .55$) between the responses of the elderly parents and adult children to the question, "how would you rate your relationship with your parent(child)?"

A multiple regression technique was used to identify the independent contributions of each of the four life area indicators to the affective quality of the family relationship indicator.

Using this multiple regression technique, the health and attitude toward aging indicators were statistically the most significant correlates of family relationships. The better the elderly parent's health (beta =, $p < .01$), the better the relationship between parent and child. Similarly, the better the elderly parent's attitude toward aging, the better the relationship between elderly parent and adult child (beta = 27, $p < .01$). The other two indicators, living environment and finances, were not statistically significantly related to the family relationship indicator. The amount of variance in the dependent variable, family relationships, accounted for by the four independent variable indicators was 25%.

A separate regression analysis was carried out using simply the parent's rating of the relationship with the interviewed child as the dependent variable. The independent variables (all based on parent responses) were the parent's perceived income adequacy, the parent's general attitude toward his/her housing, the parent's satisfaction with life, and the parent's rating of his/her health. In this case the only variable which was statistically significantly (beta = 24, $p < .05$) related to the parent's rating of the relationship with the interviewed child was the parent's perceived income adequacy. The more positively perceived was income adequacy, the more positively perceived was the parent-child relationship. The amount of variance in the parent's rating of the relationship which was accounted for by the independent variables (16%) was less than with the composite indicators.

From the profiles of the interviewed pairs we tried to delineate certain trends or themes within the four life areas which related to family relationships. These themes were:

(1) When parents and children shared similar values, and had a relationship based on mutual respect and trust, with realistic perceptions of the other, as seen by the interviewer, the pair seemed to give the quality of their relationship a higher rating. Less contact, with less shared values led to lower rating scores.

(2) In rating the quality of their relationships, the elderly person tended to rate the relationship with the interviewed child at least as high, often higher, than did the adult child. In only one instance did a child rate the relationship higher than the parent. When the interviewer perceived that there were difficulties in the parent-child relationship by rating it with a lower score, the child's rating score tended to coincide more with the interview's subjective rating than did the elderly parent's.

(3) A surprising majority of elderly parents were satisfied with their living environment, whether the living situation was dictated by circumstances of health, financial necessity, or their family's ability to accommodate them. When a move was involved, and the elderly

parent accepted the reason for their moving as valid, the elderly parent expressed satisfaction with his/her living environment. When the elderly parent had moved fairly recently, a loss of familiar friends was often mentioned.

(4) Felt financial security, not level of income, seemed of importance, but its impact was difficult for the interviewer to assess in terms of family relationships.

(5) Better quality relationships usually existed when the elderly parent was fairly engaged and kept busy in various activities. At the same time, these active elderly parents maintained regular contact with their children. This contact was felt to be warm and supportive. In general, the better perceived relationships were associated with parents who were in better health; not restricted in choice of daily activities; and independent.

(6) When health was more seriously impaired, and when the family relationship had already been perceived to be strained, the parental illness strained it more so.

Analysis of the data showed that the health and attitude toward aging indicators were statistically the most important correlates of the affective quality of the relationship between elderly parents and their adult children. The substantive importance of health as a factor in the affective quality of relationships between elderly parents and their adult children receives indirect support from the fact that health has consistently been viewed as a prime correlate of more general life satisfaction (Adams, 1971; Brand & Smith, 1974; Gubrium, 1970; Ryser & Sheldon, 1969; Spreitzer & Snyder, 1974). In addition, the analysis of the profiles completed *before* the statistical analysis had been carried out supported the results of the regression analysis using the life area indicators: health and attitude toward aging were perceived by the interviewers to be important correlates of the over-all affective quality of the family relationship.

Individuals in good health are not as likely to experience problems adjusting to old age. Elderly persons who are in poorer health not only experience general difficulties in adjusting to old age, but it appears that they may also experience problems in their relationships with their children. In addition, society's negative attitudes regarding the aging body may contribute to the diminished self-image that all elderly persons experience and which elderly persons in ill health may experience to an even greater degree. The resulting lowered self-esteem of the elderly person may result in increased family friction when these conditions are present.

This study also suggested the potential that parent's perceived income adequacy has as a possible source of family friction, at least from the parent's perspective.

However, it is important to note that when more complex indicators were used as both independent and dependent variables, i.e., when both the elderly parent's and the adult child's perceptions of their relationship, the parent's health, the parent's finances, the parent's attitude toward aging, and the parent's living situation were included in the regression analysis, the results were completely different than when less complex variables and only the parent's point of view were used. In fact, when other regression analyses were carried out using only single response independent and dependent variables rather than the composite indicators, there was a great deal of fluctuation in the results. When slight modifications were made in the variables included in the composite indicators, there were minor fluctuations in the beta weights but the health and attitude toward aging indicators remained statistically significant at the $p < .01$ level.

Implications

This study found a significant association between a positive elderly parent-adult child relationship and health and attitude toward aging factors associated with the elderly parent. Although replications using paired data from a larger sample of elderly parents and their adult children are needed in order to generalize the findings of this study to the greater elderly parent-adult child population, when the findings of other related research are considered, some preliminary implications about the results of the present study can be made.

While a better health-care delivery system for older persons (and people of all ages) stands by itself as a necessary national goal for our society, this study also suggests that good health for elderly people can be an important variable in how elderly parents and their adult children regard their relationship. This association between good health and good relationships indicates that intervention strategies for elderly who do experience poor health should not only be developed but should be considered essential given that poor health may exacerbate poor family relationships, and poor family relationships have implications for the institutionalization of the elderly parent as Brody (1966) suggests.

While improved preventative health care is a necessary societal goal for elderly (and all) persons, until this goal is realized, greater attention should be paid to intervention strategies which are aimed at ameliorating the relationship between poor health and a poor relationship between elderly parent and adult child. At present, poor health can increase the elderly parent's dependency on the adult child with an increase in resentment by the adult child (often caught between caring for his/her own children and caring for the elderly parent), and increasing frustration of the parent, with an over-all poorer relationship between parent and child as the result. To the extent that poor health is a factor in the elderly person's life, we as practitioners and as policy makers must try to find ways to alleviate the burden of the family through services which offer respite to the family and independence to the parent without resorting to institutionalization except as a last resort.

While elderly day-care centers and home-care corporations have begun to appear, their continued existence is often dependent on their ability to demonstrate that they cost less than institutional care.

The idea of respite care, whether for a few days per week, for a weekend, for vacations, or in an emergency, is an interesting concept (available in some other countries), and one which offers support to families who have an elderly member with health problems. Time away from the work and responsibility involved in the care of an aging parent who has health difficulties is often as much of a necessity for the adult child as it is for the parent with preschool children. The result of a convenient, socially sanctioned breather in the form of a respite care program might mean an increase in the family's ability to maintain the important relationship with the aging parent and also potentially reduce the incidence of institutionalization.

In addition, other supportive services for elderly persons such as convenient transportation to shops, medical, and other facilities, as well as home medical services should be developed for all elderly, not just for those who are in the extremely low income group. Services for elderly which take some of the burden away from their children may enhance better relationships between the generations and facilitate more involvement between elderly parents and adult children if and when more serious problems develop.

Finally, as both a cautionary note and as a possible intervention strategy, we feel that future studies should take into consideration the possible effects of the interview process on the relationships of the elderly parent and adult child (Rubin & Mitchell, 1976). The actual interview process could be the first step, for some of the participants, in thinking about the quality of their relationship. It is important that resources be made available to those interviewees who want assistance in discussing and/or dealing with their relationship, as a result of their thoughtful participation in the research.

REFERENCES

Ananis, R., Bursk, B., Flanzbaum, M., Gershman, L., Hartz, S., Isenberg, L., Karpinski, I., McPherson, D., Memolo, S., Motenko, A., Peck, E., Plaut, E., Reedy, J., Schley, H., Scobie, C., Streeter, S., Weiss, C., & Winer, B. *The quality of relationships between elderly parents and their adult children.* Master's thesis, Boston Univ., 1976.

Adams, D. L. Correlates of satisfaction among the elderly. *Gerontologist*, 1976, *11*, 64-68.

Brand, F. N., & Smith, R. Life adjustment and relocation of the elderly. *Journal of Gerontology*, 1974, *29*, 336-340.

Britton, J. H., Mather, W. G., & Lansing, A. K. Expectations for older persons in a rural community: living arrangements and family relationships. *Journal of Gerontology*, 1961, *16*, 156-162.

Brody, E. The aging family. *Gerontologist*, 1966, *6*, 201-206.

Brody, E. The etiquette of filial behavior. *Aging & Human Development*, 1970, *1*, 87-94.

Butler, R., & Lewis, M. *Aging and mental health.* Mosby, St. Louis, 1973.

Cottrell, F. *Aging and the aged.* William Brown, Co., Dubuque, IA, 1974.

Gubrium, J. F. Environmental effects on morale in old age and resources of health and solvency. *Gerontologist*, 1970, *10*, 294-297.

Kaplan, J. The family in aging (editorial). *Gerontologist*, 1975, *15*, 385.

Kosa, J., Rachiele, L. D., & Schoomer, C. Sharing the home with relatives. *Marriage & Family Living*, 1960, *22*, 129-131.

Puner, M. *To the good life: What we know about growing old.* Universe Books, New York, 1974.

Rubin, Z., & Mitchell, C. Couples research as couples counseling: Some unintended effects of studying close relationships. American Psychologist, 1976, *31*, 17-25.

Ryser, C., & Sheldon, A. Retirement and health. *Journal of the American Geriatrics Society*, 1969, *17*, 180-190.

Shanas, E. Family responsibility and the health of older people. *Journal of Gerontology*, 1960, *15*, 408-411.

Shanas, E. Townsend, P., Wedderburn, D., Friis, H., Milhoj, P., & Stehouwer, J. *Old people in three industrial societies.* Atherton Press, New York, 1968.

Simos, B. G. Adult children and their aging parents. *Social Work*, 1973, *18*, 78-85.

Smith, W. Family plans for later years. *Marriage & Family Living*, 1954, *16*, 36-40.

Spreitzer, E., & Snyder, E. E. Correlates of life satisfaction among the aged. *Journal of Gerontology*, 1974, *29*, 454-458.

Stern, B. M., & Ross, M. *You and your aging parents.* Harper & Row, New York, 1965.

Sussman, M. B., & Burchinal, L. Parental aid to married children: Implications for family functioning. *Marriage & Family Living*, 1962, *24*, 320-332. (a)

Sussman, M. B., & Burchinal, L. Kin family network: Unheralded structure in current conceptualizations of family functioning. *Marriage & Family Living*, 1962, *24*, 231-240. (b)

Troll, L. E. The family of later life: A decade review. *Marriage & Family Living*, 1971, *33*, 263-290.

Chapter 19

THE ELDERLY WIDOW AND HER FAMILY, NEIGHBORS, AND FRIENDS*

GREG ARLING

THE transition from middle to old age is marked by a change in social relationships. Important role changes occur in the family and with friends and neighbors. Widowhood and the residential mobility of adult children may severely diminish the content of the family role, while the death of peers and health and income problems may restrict involvement with friends and neighbors. Old age is accompanied by the prospect of increasing isolation.

To the extent that isolation is resisted and older people remain involved with family and friends, there is still the question of whether these forms of role involvement are meaningful or satisfying. Are there changes in the content of social roles which lessen their psychological importance?

In this paper I am concerned with the elderly widow and the problems she encounters in maintaining viable relationships with family, friends and neighbors. Does role involvement elevate morale or produce greater satisfaction with life? Is there a difference in the importance of family ties as compared to friendship and neighboring?

The Family

Widowhood is the event which constitutes the greatest change in the family status of older people. It may have deleterious consequences, not only because of the loss of a central role partner, but also because of the lack of cultural expectations regarding the proper role of the widow. The widow must realign her relationship with other family members in the absence of her spouse.

The number of widows living alone has increased dramatically over the last few decades — from 20 percent in 1940, to 50 percent in 1970 (Chevan and Korson, 1972). This trend is partly explained by the

---

rising proportion of elderly widows relative to younger widows with children. It is also consistent with the general trend for elderly persons to remain in their own households and avoid moving into the homes of their adult children (Wake and Sporakowski, 1972).

The family role of older people has been a subject of considerable debate. Parsons (1942) has proposed that the development of the nuclear family in modern industrial society has resulted in the atomization of conjugal units. This breakdown of the extended kinship structure is said to have left the aged forsaken by their adult children and other family members. Because the elderly widow is most likely to live alone, she is supposedly most subject to isolation.

However, most available evidence points to the fact that older people have a consistently high degree of contact with family members. Shanas (1968) found that over one-half of the elderly in her study saw family members the day before her interview, and many others had seen family members within the previous few days. Other research has supported her findings (Townsend, 1957; Adams, 1968; Pihlblad and McNamera, 1965; Bracey, 1966).

Contact with family also seems to be consistently strong throughout old age for married women, and widows in particular. The elderly female displays a closer relationship with her children (especially daughters) than the elderly male (Townsend, 1957; Adams, 1968; Shanas, 1968). Although the female has more contact and stronger emotional ties with her children, she is also more likely to be dependent upon them either emotionally or for material aid (Clark and Anderson, 1967; Rosow, 1967).

Despite the generally frequent contact with family members, especially children, the impact of family relationships upon morale is somewhat questionable. A number of studies have concluded that visits with family make little difference in the older person's feelings of loneliness or life satisfaction (Rosenberg, 1970; Pihlblad and McNamara, 1965; Blau, 1973). Brown (1960) reports that while two-thirds of the adult children in this study regularly visited with their aged parents, only one-fifth reported close affective ties. Kerkhoff (1966) discovered that elderly couples, who relied less upon their children and made fewer demands, were high in morale; and wives whose children lived close had lower morale than wives whose children lived far away.

Two reasons have been offered for the apparent lack of association or negative relationship between family contact and morale. First, elderly people and their children have contrasting interests and, thus, often do not make good companions. Generational differences in socialization and contrasting life-styles result in a dissimilar set of experiences. There can be substantial differences in their daily activities, friendship networks, norms and values (Hochschild, 1973).

The second difficulty, arising out of the relations between generations, is the dependency of the elderly person and the resultant reversal of roles that oftentimes takes place between parent and child. The inability of the aged widow to reciprocate for the services provided by the child can lower morale (Marris, 1956; Kent and Matson, 1972; Hochschild, 1973).

Middle-aged parents normally give more to their children than they receive, especially if the children are just beginning occupations or marriage (Hill, 1965; Adams, 1968). Upon reaching old age, the individual's family role is very often transformed, so that instead of being the provider, the older person is provided for, and instead of being the main source of authority in the family, the older person must acquiesce to adult children. In old age, the flow of assistance shifts and adult children begin to give more aid to their parents than they receive in return (Hill, 1965; Rosow, 1967). Even though contact with kin might not have declined, the functional importance of the older person within the family has decreased, and commensurately, the aged individual has lost the supportive role and taken on one of dependency (Brim, 1968; Martin, 1971). This is especially true for the older widow who has the lowest income of any segment of the elderly population (U.S. Senate Special Committee on Aging, 1971).

Friendship and Neighboring

Unlike family ties, which remain fairly consistent throughout old age, contact with friends and neighbors may be subject to variation. Because they are not formally prescribed like kinship roles, relations with friends and neighbors require a certain amount of initiative by the older person, and they frequently decline when conditions arise which make interaction difficult. Friendships may decrease with age, loss of income or physical incapacity (Shanas, 1962).

In middle age, friendship commonly develops around the work setting, through participation in voluntary organizations, or in the neighborhood. Middle-aged couples normally associate with other couples. With retirement, the basis for social ties with work associates will decline when there is no longer day-to-day interaction and the retiree loses contact with the concerns of the work setting (Hess, 1972). The widow faces an additional difficulty, for she may find it awkward to be with couples in the absence of her husband. If older people remain active in organizations, such as the church or service clubs, then friendships may be sustained in those settings; however, membership in voluntary organizations is most common among the middle class, and it tends to decline in old age when mobility is restricted. The neighborhood or the immediate residential environment is probably the best reservoir for potential friendships (Carp, 1966; Clark and Anderson, 1967; Rosenberg, 1970; Rosow, 1967).

Lopata (1973) stresses the importance of peer support in helping the widow adjust to her bereavement. Similarly, Blau (1961, 1973) contends that because widowhood is much more common in old age than in younger years, widows will find it easier to associate with other widows during old age.

Carp (1966), Hochschild (1973), Pihlblad and McNamara (1965), and Rosow (1967) found morale to be positively associated with involvement with friends. Whereas family ties are many times characterized by a dissimilarity of experience and an unequal exchange of aid, friends normally relate to each other through common interests, and generally are equal in their ability to exchange assistance. They thereby avoid the psychological consequences of emotional or material dependency.

The reciprocity of the friendship role is illustrated by an example from Hochschild's (1973) study of an apartment complex populated by elderly widows. Describing the relationship among the widows, Hochschild (1973:66-67) writes:

> All knew how to bake bread and can peaches, but no one knew how to fix faucets. They all knew about 'the old days' but few among them could explain what was going on with youth these days. They all had ailments but no one there could cure them. They all needed rides to the shopping center, but no one among them needed riders ... two neighbors might exchange corn bread for jam, but both knew how to make both corn bread *and* jam. If one neighbor made corn bread for five people in one day, one of the recipients would also make corn bread for the same people two weeks later.

Family Compared to Friends and Neighbors

Relationships with family, and with friends and neighbors, involve separate realms of activity which compliment each other, but which cannot ordinarily be substituted for each other. Those older people with strong family ties are just as likely to be integrated into a friendship network as those elderly who have no family or have infrequent contact with their relatives. In their studies of older persons living in apartment complexes, Rosow (1967) and Hochschild (1973) both discovered family and friendship to be separate dimensions of social involvement.

Generally, friendship and neighboring foster a kind of "belonging" based upon conviviality (Hochschild, 1973) and egalitarian norms (Hess, 1972). Both affection and material assistance are voluntarily offered and the relationship is bound by the mutual gratification that can be gained from the interaction.

Relationships with family members are regulated and sustained through formal kinship norms, and, in the instance of the adult child and elderly parent, emerge through long periods of association with prescribed roles. With the transition to old age, the conditions of the relationship may change as the child assumes full responsibility for himself as an adult, and the parent gradually loses self-sufficiency in old age. Their respective roles have switched with the aged parent coming to depend upon the adult child. The kinship norms and the emotional bonds still unite them. Their relationship can be personally meaningful, but also quite vulnerable. The elderly widow may be contemplative rather than convivial with her child (Hochschild, 1973), and she most likely will have to resolve the conflict between her own needs and obligations, and the needs and obligations of her child (Lopata, 1973). As dependency increases, the widow's emotional ties with family members become more problematic.

Reciprocity in social relationships has been a central concern of exchange theory (Homans, 1961; Blau, 1968). Homans, in particular, has assumed that individuals are motivated to seek personal gain within a relationship by maximizing the return of rewards through social exchange. Reciprocity becomes a kind of compromise, where a balance is reached, so that no party to the exchange gains too much advantage at the expense of the other(s). This conception of personal motivation — in which individuals seek to maximize personal gain — is inappropriate within the context of the dependency of the elderly widow. I am suggesting that reciprocity is essential to the widow not because she wishes to seek advantage, but instead, because she wants to *contribute* to the relationship. The elderly widow may receive material and emotional support far in excess of what she is able to return. To have a meaningful relationship she must have a degree of autonomy which ultimately results from her ability to reciprocate. Gouldner (1960) has stressed the compelling nature of the generalized norm of reciprocity.

PROCEDURE

The data base for this study consists of 409 questionnaires administered as household interviews to elderly widows in the Piedmont region of South Carolina in the fall of 1972 and the spring of 1973. The questionnaire was designed by Project P.L.E.A. (Piedmont Life Enrichment for the Aged), a social service agency of the South Carolina Commission on the Aged. The Project P.L.E.A. staff conducted a majority of the interviews and the rest were administered by a Sociological Research Methods Class at Clemson University. The study was devised primarily to assess the social service needs of the elderly, but the questionnaire also contained items covering social involvement, daily activities, and morale.

The respondents vary in age from 65 to 85. They reside in different-sized communities (from "50,000 and over" to "rural") throughout the Piedmont region. At the time of the study, their median income was between $100 and $150 per month. Seventy-five percent are white and 25 percent are black. Eighty-two percent live alone and the rest live in the household of a family member. None are institutionalized.

Their involvement with family, neighbors and friends is quite extensive. Eighty percent have at least one living child and 58 percent reside within an hour's drive of their children. Fifty-nine percent (including those living in the household of a child) see their children at least once a week. Sixty percent have five or more neighbors that they know well enough to visit. Only 5 percent know none of their neighbors. Sixty-nine percent visited with friends or neighbors during the week prior to the interview.

Operational Indices

The following items are used to measure family involvement, friendship and neighboring, and morale.

Family Involvement:

1. Do you have family members living within your household? (Yes, No)
2. How many living children do you have? (Number of children)
3. How many of your children live within one hour's drive from here (other than those that live with you)? (Number of children)
4. In general, how often do you see any of your children (other than

those that live with you)? (Number of times per month)
5. Do you have any relatives, such as nieces, nephews, in-laws, brothers, sisters or grandchildren that you see often? (Yes, No)

Friendship and Neighboring:

1. About how many of your neighbors do you know well enough to visit? (Number of neighbors)
2. Did you visit with a friend or neighbor during the past week? (Yes, No)
3. How many of your friends live in the neighborhood? (Number of friends) (Asked of only a subsample of 25 respondents.)

Morale:

1. Do you have as much contact as you would like with a person that you feel close to — somebody that you can trust and confide in? (Yes, No)
2. Do you find yourself feeling lonely quite often, sometimes or almost never? (Quite Often, Sometimes, Almost Never)
3. How often would you say that you worry about things? (Very Often, Fairly Often, Hardly Ever)
4. Do you sometimes feel unhappy because you think you are not useful? (Yes, No)
5. How much respect do older people receive in your community? (A lot of respect, Some respect, Not very much respect)

Analysis

Subsequent analysis will compare the way in which family ties, and friendship and neighboring, influence morale. From previous studies, I would expect friendship and neighboring to be positively associated with personal morale, while family ties would have little or no association with morale.

Next, I will determine if friendship-neighboring or family involvement are associated with the widow's participation in daily activities, and thus attempt to indirectly establish that friends and neighbors are a better source of companionship than family members. Finally, I will explore the possibility that the elderly widow's state of dependency influences the relationship between her contact with family members and her personal morale.

For the purposes of this analysis, no separation will be made between the black and white respondents. In previous reports from the same study (Arling, 1974; 1976), the author discovered that white widows had somewhat more frequent contact with children than black widows, while the black widows had more neighbors that they were able to visit. Moreover, no difference in morale emerged when black and white respondents were compared. At least within this sample, there are not significant differences between black and white respondents to justify separate analysis.

RESULTS

A Comparison of Family Ties, and Friendship and Neighboring as They Affect Morale

The initial step in the analysis is to determine the relationship between the various forms of involvement and the morale items. Table 19-I contains the correlation coefficients between family ties, friendship and neighboring, and morale.

Table 19-I

RELATIONSHIPS WITH FAMILY, FRIENDS AND NEIGHBORS, AND MORALE — CORRELATION COEFFICIENTS (PEARSON'S r)

Morale Items	Availability of Children	Contact With Children	Contact With Other Relatives	Neighbors Able to Visit	Contact With Friends	Friends in Neighborhood
Confidant	.11	.01	.09	.32*	.20*	.31*
Not lonely	.02	.02	.12*	.14*	.02	.24*
Not worry	.01	.06	.09	.09	.09	.11
Usefulness	.00	.00	.10	.16*	.07	.19*
Community respect	.00	.07	.08	.23*	.10	.25*

*Significant at the .01 level — t test.

The question regarding the availability of children measures the number of children that live within an hour's drive of the respondent. The contact with children variable indicates how often the respondents see their children, and includes only those respondents who have children living within an hour's drive. The variable measuring contact with other relatives includes all of the respondents.

The three neighboring and friendship questions cover how many neighbors the widow knows well enough to visit, whether she has visited with a friend or neighbor during the previous week, and how many friends she has living in the neighborhood. The latter question, pertaining to friends in the neighborhood, was asked of only a sub-sample; i.e. it was drawn disproportionately from rural areas, so the question is included primarily to supplement the other indices, even though its validity is questionable.

Table 19-I reveals that the family items are essentially unrelated to any of the indices of morale. Respondents with children living close-by have no higher morale than respondents who either have no living children or have none within an hour's drive. Similarily, the frequency of contact with children has no significant association with morale. The measures of involvement with children seem to be marginally associated with having someone in whom to trust and confide, but the correlation is not significant at the .01 level. If any one of the family items has an impact, it is the variable measuring contact with relatives other than children. Visiting with a sibling, grandchild, niece or nephew slightly reduces one's feelings of loneliness.

In contrast, the neighbor-friendship variables are significantly related to morale. Those elderly widows, who have a number of neighbors they can visit and many friends in the neighborhood, are most likely to have someone in whom to confide, are least likely to be lonely, feel generally most useful, and perceive the greatest community respect for elderly persons. Interestingly, although the number of neighbors and friends is significantly related to the morale items, the actual frequency of contact is *not* significantly related. Having a confidant is the only item that varies directly with the frequency of contact with neighbors and friends. It may not be the amount of interaction, *per se*, but rather the security of neighborhood involvement which elevates morale. Being able to rely upon neighbors and friends may be the essential factor, and the widow might not need to have daily contact with them.

Family Involvement and Morale Controlling for Friendship and Neighboring

Neither the availability of children, nor frequency of contact with children, seems to make a difference in any of the morale measures for the sample as a whole. However, these results were obtained without considering the varying degree of neighborhood and friendship involvement. Elderly widows with few neighbors and friends may experience high morale as a result of involvement with their children. By controlling for neighborhood involvement and friendship, one might find that those widows who are low in neighboring and friendship are able to substitute family ties, and therefore, experience higher morale.

When cross-tabulating the availability of children and the morale measures, with neighboring held constant, I found that none of the morale items were significantly associated with the measures of the availability of children. Some percentage differences were evident, but these could be attributed to random variation because of the relatively small number of cases within each cell when controlling for the neighboring variable. The percentage differences were not significant at the .01 level (*chi-square*) and they did not vary in a consistent direction; i.e., some of the associations were positive and some were negative.

Even among widows who had a low number of neighbors that they knew well enough to visit, the availability of children made little difference in their level of morale. Those widows with children nearby, or those living in the household of a family member, were no different in their level of morale than those with no children, or children living far away. They were not more likely to have someone in whom to confide, feel useful, or to perceive community respect for older people. They were just as likely to worry and feel lonely.

To extend the analysis, I examined the relationship between contact with children and the morale items when controlling for frequency of contacts with friends and neighbors. Again, contact with children did not elevate morale, even among those who had very little contact with friends and neighbors.[1] Regardless of their involvement with friends and neighbors, contact with children made virtually no difference in their level of morale.

Involvement with children does not seem to be an effective substitute or compensation for the lack of neighbors and friends. These findings support the conclusion that family and neighboring and friendship are separate domains of involvement. Further, it reinforces the observation that family relationships are quite problematic for these elderly widows.

---

[1]The tables displayed the association between family involvement and morale, with friendship and neighboring held constant, can be obtained from the author upon request.

Companionship and the Sharing of Activities

The fact that neighbors and friends make good companions, and are able to share experiences, has been offered as one explanation for the association between neighboring and friendship and morale. Family involvement is viewed as less meaningful because of differences in life-style and interests between the elderly widow and her adult children. The elderly parent and adult child do not ordinarily make good companions.

The research design did not include questions which measure whether activities were shared with either adult children, or neighbors and friends. However, it is possible to indirectly test the companionship hypothesis by determining the strength of association between these forms of involvement and the various activities.

Table 19-II presents the correlations between involvement with family and friends, and the indices of activity.[2]

Table 19-II

SOCIAL RELATIONSHIPS AND ACTIVITIES —
ZERO-ORDER CORRELATIONS (PEARSON'S r)

Dependent Variables	Availability of Children	Contact With Children	Contact With Other Relatives	Neighbors Able to Visit	Contact With Friends
Total Activities	.00	.01	.08	.19*	.33*
Television	.05	.05	.03	.05	.08
Radio	.04	.11	−.01	−.01	.09
Newspapers	.02	.05	.10	.08	.02
Books	.01	.06	.05	.09	.10
Walking	.01	.06	.12*	.15*	.34*
Attend Meetings	.00	.10	−.03	.21*	.21*
Hobby	.00	.00	−.03	.04	.14*
Shopping	.02	−.04	.05	.15*	.31*
Attend Religious Services	−.12*	−.06	.06	.24*	.32*
Social Events at Church	−.05	−.07	.09	.28*	.30*

*Significance at the .01 level — t test

[2]The respondents were asked whether they had participated in any of a number of daily activities during the past week prior to the interview. They gave either a "yes" or "no" response. For the *total activity* measure, the number of activities in which each respondent participated was summed and the respondent was given a total activity score; the higher the score, the greater the number of activities.

Generally, neighborhood involvement and contact with friends is more strongly associated with activity than any of the family variables. Respondents who have neighbors and friends with whom they visit, are more likely to take walks, go shopping, and attend organizational meetings, religious services, and social events at church. In contrast, the availability and frequency of contact with children and other relatives is not significantly related to daily activity. These findings tend to support the conclusion that friends and neighbors provide companionship and are able to share activities with the elderly widow.

Another possible conclusion can be drawn from these results. By virtue of their personalities or their physical capacities, those respondents who are involved with neighbors and friends *are also* disposed to be active in organizations, religious affairs, shopping etc. The association between neighboring-friendship and daily activities may be a consequence of factors such as the widow's health, income, and education, and not her companionship with neighbors and friends.

Previous research suggests that health (Clark and Anderson, 1967; Lowenthal and Boler, 1965; Talmar and Kutner, 1969), financial security (Kutner, 1956; Blau, 1961), and education (Lopata, 1974) are

Table 19-III

NEIGHBORING AND FRIENDSHIP, AND ACTIVITIES CONTROLLING
FOR PHYSICAL INCAPACITY, ECONOMIC DEPRIVATION,
AND EDUCATION — PARTIAL CORRELATIONS

	Neighbors Able to Visit		Contact With Friends and Neighbors	
Dependent Variables	Zero-Order r	Partial[a]	Zero-Order r	Partial
Total Activities	.19†	.11(n.s.)	.33†	.25
Taking a walk	.15†	.09(n.s.)	.34†	.29*
Attend meetings	.21†	.15‡	.21†	.15‡
Shopping	.15†	.01(n.s.)	.31†	.25*
Religious Services	.24†	.16‡	.32†	.24*
Social Events at Church	.28†	.22*	.30†	.24*

[a]Controlling for Physical Incapacity, Economic Deprivation, and Education
*Significant at the .001 level — F test
†Significant at the .01 level — F test
‡Significant at the .05 level — F test

related to both neighboring and friendship, *and* participation in activities. If so, the companionship of neighbors and friends may not in itself facilitate activities, but rather, the association would simply be a result of conditions such as health, financial security, and education, which lead the individual to both cultivate relationships and become involved in activities. The question becomes whether contact with neighbors and friends is related to activities independent of the effects of incapacity, deprivation, and education.

Table 19-III contains both the zero-order and the partial correlation between neighborhood and friendship involvement, and various activities, when incapacity,[3] deprivation,[4] and education[5] are introduced as control variables. While some of the relationships are no longer significant with control variables administered, for the most part, neighboring and friendship are independently related to the activity measures. Regardless of the level of incapacity, deprivation, or education, those respondents who know more of their neighbors or have frequent contact with their friends are more likely to engage in a greater number of total activities — especially religious events, organizational meetings, shopping, and going for walks.

Dependency and Role Reversal

A second explanation for the lack of association between family involvement and morale is the problem of dependency and resultant reversal of roles between parent and child. According to this viewpoint, interaction can serve two important functions. It can be a

---

[3]The incapacity scale was devised from the questions which follow: (1) Do you have difficulty getting about the house? (2) Do you have difficulty dressing and putting on shoes? (3) Do you have difficulty washing and bathing? (4) Do you have difficulty cutting your toenails? (5) Do you have difficulty going up and down stairs? The scale was constructed by weighting the answers as such: No difficulty = 1; Some difficulty = 2; Can't do at all = 3. The scores for each respondent were summed and the scale was constructed; the higher the total score, the greater the incapacity.

[4]The deprivation scale was constructed by weighting the following responses: (1) Unable to find transportation (Very often or often = 2; Occasionally, seldom, or never = 1); (2) Nutritional value of meals (None or only one of the basic food groups = 2; Two or more of the basic food groups = 1); (3) Housing (One or more basic household items in disrepair = 2; All basic household items in working order = 1); (4) Income (Less than $100/month = 2; Over $100/month = 1). A total score was obtained for each respondent by summing the weighted responses; the higher the score, the greater the economic deprivation.

[5]The education variable was coded as follows: 0-4 years = 5; 5-7 years = 4; 8 years = 3; 9-11 years = 2; 12 years or more = 1.

source of companionship or meaningful interpersonal involvement. It can also be a means of satisfying daily needs such as help around the house, transportation, financial assistance, etc. The substance of the relationship will depend upon the conditions which elicit companionship or aid. If contact occurs under circumstances of poverty or ill health, where the elderly widow is highly dependent, then the nature of the relationship will be much different than if she is healthy and financially secure. Under the former condition, the widow must rely upon her children to initiate interaction, while in the latter, the interaction can be structured by the widow herself, on her own terms. The latter holds at least the potential for reciprocity by which the widow can give, as well as receive, aid and companionship.

In order to test the dependency hypothesis, the relationship between family involvement and morale must be controlled for physical incapacity and economic deprivation. If dependency changes the nature of the interpersonal interaction, then family involvement should be negatively related to morale under conditions of ill health and poverty, and positively related when the respondents are healthy and financially secure. If health and economic status are suppressing the relationship, statistically significant results should emerge when controls are administered.

Table 19-IV

CHILDREN AVAILABLE AND MORALE, CONTROLLING FOR
PHYSICAL INCAPACITY AND DEPRIVATION (*GAMMA* STATISTICS)

Morale Items By	Physical Incapacity (control variable)		Economic Deprivation (control variable)	
Availability of Children	High	Low	High	Low
Confidant	.07	.22	.17	.25
	N=165	N=215	N=173	N=179
Not Feel Lonely	.08	.17	.15	.01
	N=174	N=222	N=180	N=187
Feel Useful	.13*	.17*	.07	.03
	N=168	N=216	N=174	N=182
Not Worry	.00	.08	.05	.00
	N=174	N=220	N=180	N=179
Community Respect	.07	.18*	.01	.08
	N=161	N=212	N=164	N=179

*Significant at the .05 level — *Chi-square*

The Older Woman

Table 19-IV contains the relationship between the availability of children and the morale items, controlling for physical incapacity and economic deprivation. The *gamma* statistics represent strength of association between the morale items and involvement with children variable, within the categories of high and low physical incapacity, and high and low economic deprivation. *Chi-square* is used to test for significance.[6]

The availability of children is only weakly associated with morale under varying conditions of incapacity and deprivation. Irrespective of state of health or financial security, having children nearby does little to raise morale. Three of the cross-tabulations are significant at the .05 level (*chi-square*), but the *gamma* statistics are quite low — indicating that the relationship is tenuous.

Table 19-V reveals similar results. Actual contact with children bears no significant relationship to morale, even when incapacity and

Table 19-V

CONTACT WITH CHILDREN AND MORALE,
CONTROLLING FOR PHYSICAL INCAPACITY AND
ECONOMIC DEPRIVATION (*GAMMA* STATISTICS)*

Morale Items By	Physical Incapacity (control variable)		Economic Deprivation (control variable)	
Contact With Child[a]	High	Low	High	Low
Confidant	.06	.09	.02	.22
	N=126	N=177	N=137	N=143
Not Feel Lonely	.08	.14	.18	.02
	N=133	N=182	N=142	N=149
Feel Useful	.22	.11	.03	.07
	N=129	N=179	N=139	N=145
Not Worry	.01	.01	.05	.06
	N=133	N=182	N=143	N=148
Community Respect	.12	.09	.02	.11
	N=122	N=174	N=130	N=142

[a]Includes only those respondents with living children.
*None of the *Gammas* are significant at the .05 level —*Chi-square*

[6]*Chi-square* was employed as a test of significance, rather than testing the significance of the *gamma*, because *chi-square* is a more commonly used test and is more easily interpreted.

deprivation are held constant. The *gamma* statistics indicate only a weak association between contact with children and morale among those widows with low physical incapacity, high physical incapacity, low economic deprivation, and high economic deprivation.

These findings must be taken with some qualification. In order to thoroughly test the impact of dependency, it is necessary to have respondents who differ widely in health and economic circumstances.

The widows in this study are predominately poor. Moreover, the widow's poverty compounds problems of health, because of inadequate diet, limited access to medical treatment, etc. For this reason, none of the widows may be sufficiently able to maintain independence, and their relationships with their children may reflect this fact. Family involvement has little impact upon morale for the sample as a whole.

Another problem with the analysis is that no index of the exchange of aid was incorporated into the research design. Consequently, the measure of dependency is based upon indirect inference — incapacity and/or deprivation in conjunction with level of family involvement. A direct measure of the flow of assistance is needed in order to get an adequate assessment of dependency.

DISCUSSION

From the above findings one may get the impression that family ties are incidental or even detrimental to the well-being of the elderly widow. That conclusion is unwarranted and misrepresents the argument the author is advancing.

There has been much concern in modern industrial society about the breakdown of the extended family, which supposedly leaves older people forsaken by their children and other relatives. Implicitly we assume that family contact, irrespective of its form or content, is emotionally satisfying to the elderly. Ironically, many of the research studies indicate a high degree of contact between older people and younger family members, especially adult children; yet, this contact is not directly associated with higher morale or greater personal satisfaction. The results that the author has reported from this study add to that body of evidence and suggest avenues for further research.

The adult child and aged parent may show concern for each other with frequent visits, phone conversations, or letter writing. They may be aware of each other's pleasures and sorrows. Their relationship, which has grown out of a lifetime of association and a prescribed kinship bond, may be characterized by love and devotion. Even though they are aware, and, in many instances deeply concerned about each other, they encounter difficulty truly *sharing* their experiences or empathizing with each other.

The adult child is ordinarily active and mobile, engaged in an occupation and the affairs of his own household, and has his own organizational and friendship network. The adult child typically experiences the involvement of middle age.

The aged parent is commonly more restricted in movement because of financial or health considerations, tends to be separated from the work setting, and normally participates in organizations or friendship groups which are composed largely of persons his or her own age.

When remembering the past or interpreting the events of the present, the adult child and aged parent will unavoidably have differing perspectives because they have been socialized in different generational age-cohorts and they are confronted with separate life-situations as a result of their respective stages in the life-cycle.

Certain intergenerational barriers are inevitable; however, conditions such as poverty and ill health may exacerbate the conflicts which arise in the relationship between aged parent and adult child. The older parent resists adopting the child-like role where he or she must come to depend upon younger family members for material assistance or emotional support. Typically, the aged parent, after experiencing a lifetime of increasing autonomy, must adjust to the loss of self-sufficiency in old age. This adjustment will not be easy; for the aged parent has usually been accustomed to serving as the figure of authority and provider of material assistance. The reversal of roles is particularly difficult in a society, such as our own, which emphasizes individualism and self-sufficiency (Clark and Anderson, 1967). Childhood is the only stage of the life-cycle in which the individual can appropriately assume the dependency role; and, in that situation, the child can anticipate increasing autonomy with advancing age. The older person must anticipate a further loss of autonomy as he or she ages.

The problem of dependency and the older person's relationship to family members must be investigated under various conditions. Consideration should be given to the economic and health characteristics of the older parent. Are healthy and financially secure older people more likely to have personally satisfying relationships with their children and other relatives? If they need assistance, is it forthcoming; and, if so, does the older person have something to offer in return?

In earlier stages of the life-cycle, what sort of ties did the aged person have with family members? How do both aged parent *and* others within the family view their relationship? To what extent are they bound together solely by prescribed kinship norms which engender forms of interaction that are superficial or ritualistic?

Finally, what importance can be attached to neighboring and friendship? What kind of assistance is exchanged between older people and their neighbors and friends? Under what circumstances are the elderly likely to maintain their friendships formed during the earlier years, or cultivate new friends in old age?

Bleckner (1965) notes that the filial crisis, and the resultant reversal of parent-child roles in old age, may have serious consequences for both adult child and elderly parent. Neither is prepared to accept the shift in roles; both find it difficult to relate to each other given their conflicting role prescriptions.

Avoiding the reversal of roles will necessitate maintaining the autonomy of the aged parent, through means such as providing income support or helping the parent cope with the loss of physical capacity, and enabling the child to respect the parent as an individual, with basic rights and freedoms, as well as personal needs. The continued autonomy of the parent and the respect of the child are interdependent conditions which are necessary for a satisfying interpersonal relationship.

REFERENCES

Adams, Bert N.
   1968 Kinship in an Urban Setting. Chicago: Markham.
Arling, Greg
   1974 "Social involvement and morale: A study of elderly widows." Unpublished doctoral dissertation. University of Illinois.
   1976 "Resistance to isolation among elderly widows." Aging and Human Development 7 (January):67-86.
Blau, Peter M.
   1968 "Interaction: Social exchange." Pp. 452-457 in D. L. Shils (Ed.), International Encyclopedia of the Social Sciences (Vol. 7). New York: Macmillan.
Blau, Zena
   1961 "Structural constraints on friendship in old age." American Sociological Review 26 (June):429-439.
   1973 Old Age in a Changing Society. New York: Franklin Watts.
Bleckner, Margot
   1965 "Social work and family relationships in later life with some thoughts on filial maturity." Pp. 46-61 in Ethel Shanas and Gordon F. Streib (Eds.). Social Structure and the Family: Generational Relations. Englewood Cliffs: Prentice Hall.

Bracey, H. E.
  1966 In Retirement: Pensioners in Great Britain and the United States. Baton
  Rouge: Louisiana State University Press.
Brim, Orville G.
  1968 "Adult socialization." Pp. 182-226 in John A. Clausen (Ed.), Socialization
  and Society. Boston: Little Brown.
Brown, Robert
  1960 "Family structure and social isolation of older persons." Journal of
  Gerontology 15 (April):170-174.
Carp, Frances M.
  1966 The Future of the Aged: Victoria Plaza and Its Residents. Austin, Texas:
  University of Texas Press.
Chevan, A., and J. H. Korson
  1972 "The widowed who live alone: An examination of social and demographic
  factors." Social Forces 51 (September):45-53.
Clark, Margaret, and Barbara Anderson
  1967 Culture and Aging. Springfield, Illinois: Charles C Thomas.
Gouldner, Alvin
  1960 "The norm of reciprocity: A preliminary statement." American
  Sociological Review 25 (April):161-178.
Hess, Beth
  1972 "Friendship." Pp. 357-396 in Matilda White Riley, Marilynn Johnson, and
  Anne Forner (Eds.), Aging and Society: A Sociology of Age Stratification (Vol.
  3). New York: Russell Sage Foundation.
Hill, Reuben
  1965 "Decisionmaking and the family life cycle." Pp. 113-139 in Ethel Shanas
  and Gordon F. Streib (Eds.), Social Structure and the Family: Generational
  Relations. Englewood Cliffs: Prentice-Hall.
Hochschild, Arlie Russell
  1973 The Unexpected Community. Englewood Cliffs: Prentice-Hall.
Homans, George C.
  1961 Social Behavior: Its Elementary Forms. New York: Harcourt, Brace and
  World.
Kent, Donald P., and Margaret B. Matson
  1972 "The impact of health on the aged family." The Family Coordinator 21
  (January):29-36.
Kutner, Bernard
  1962 "The social nature of aging." Gerontologist 2 (Spring):5-8.
Kutner, Bernard, David Fanshel, Alice M. Togo, and Thomas S. Langer
  1956 Five Hundred Over Sixty: A Community Survey of Aging. New York:
  Russell Sage Foundation.
Lopata, Helen Znaniecki
  1973 Widowhood in an American City. Cambridge, Massachusetts: Schenkman.
Lowenthal, Marjorie Fisk, and Deetje Boler
  1965 "Voluntary versus involuntary social withdrawal." Journal of Gerontology
  20 (July):363-371.
Marris, Peter
  1958 Widows and Their Families. London: Routledge and Kegan Paul.
Martin, J. David
  1971 "Power, dependence, and the complaints of the elderly: A social exchange
  perspective." Aging and Human Development 2 (May):109-112.

Parsons, Talcott
1942 "Age and sex in the social structure of the United States." American Sociological Review 7 (December):604-616.
Pihlblad, C. Terence, Robert McNamara
1965 "Social adjustment of elderly people in three small towns." In Arnold Rose and Warren Peterson (Eds.), Older People and Their Social World. Philadelphia: F. A. Davis.
Rosenberg, George S.
1970 The Worker Grows Old. San Francisco: Jossey-Bass.
Rosow, Irving
1967 Social Integration of the Aged. New York: Free Press.
Shanas, Ethel
1962 The Health of Older People: A Social Survey. Cambridge, Massachusetts: Harvard University Press.
Shanas, Ethel, Peter Townsend, Dorothy Wedderburn, Henning Friss, Paul Milhoj, and Jan Stehouwer
1968 Old People in Three Industrial Societies. New York: Atherton Press.
Tallmar, Margot, and Bernard Kutner
1969 "Disengagement and the stresses of aging." Journal of Gerontology 24 (January):70-75.
Townsend, Peter
1957 The Family Life of Old People. London: Routledge and Kegan Paul.
United States Senate, Special Committee on Aging
1971 Developments in Aging — 1970. Washington, D. C.: U. S. Government Printing Office.
Wake, Sandra Byford, and Michael J. Sporakowski
1972 "An intergenerational comparison of attitudes toward supporting aged parents." Journal of Marriage and the Family 34 (February):42-48.

Chapter 20

SEX DIFFERENCES IN INTIMATE FRIENDSHIPS OF OLD AGE*

EDWARD A. POWERS AND GORDON L. BULTENA

WILLIAMS and Loeb (1968) argue that the social sciences have progressed little in developing a scheme for analyzing and describing social life, largely because concern has been for either large-scale societal and institutional patterns or small group processes. They suggest, however, 'that we should begin mapping the social life space of individuals, paying attention to the number, intensity, and complexity (degree of homogeneity) of social contacts as determined by the age and sex of individuals. The rather extensive research on social relations, for the most part, has found these characteristics of social networks important in the analysis of interaction patterns. But investigations generally have utilized classroom or community samples of young and middle-aged adults. There have been few studies of the social life space of aged persons that have considered sexually-differentiated social ties in terms of number, intensity, and complexity. In this paper, one type of intense relationship — intimate friendships — is considered. We first assess the amount of social contact aged men and women have with different categories of interactants, and then examine the relative importance of intimate friends to the overall levels of social interaction. Finally, we explore the characteristics of persons involved in the late-life intimate ties that occur outside the immediate family.

Social relationships universally seem to be sexually differentiated. In both industrial and nonindustrial societies, male and female behavior is distinct. Men, for the most part, are more dominant and aggressive (see Babchuk and Bates, 1963; Bell and Boat, 1957; Blau, 1961; Booth and Hess, 1974; Campbell and Alexander, 1965; D'Andrade, 1966; Lowenthal and Haven, 1968; Naegele, 1958; Reiss, 1959; Rosenberg, 1970; Rosow, 1967, 1970; Sutcliffe and Grabbe, 1963; Williams, 1959). Although explanations for sexually-differentiated social behavior range from biological to sociocultural arguments, the social

*From *Journal of Marriage and the Family*, 38:739-746, 1976. Copyrighted 1976 by the National Council on Family Relations. Reprinted by permission.

190

behavioral sciences have emphasized the importance of differential socialization experiences.

From early childhood, American men learn patterns of behavior appropriate for their respective social networks. Through play, organized team sports, work, mass media, and war, men are taught the importance of cooperative behavior. The masculine sex role emphasizes aggressiveness and unemotional behavior: men are expected to *do* things, but are not expected to share intimate problems or anxieties. Male social participation, thus, is generally less affective or intense than that of women (Blau, 1973; Booth, 1972). Women, however, learn from experiences that emphasize expressive behavior. During early life, females are discouraged from participation in activities involving cooperative behavior. Even in sports, women tend to be channeled into individual efforts such as tennis, swimming or gymnastics. This relative isolation is furthered by the modern housewife role, since the American model of an autonomous and independent household unit demands a major portion of the time and energies of women (Chafetz, 1974). Women, nevertheless, form close friendships that usually are more diverse and affectively richer than those of men (Booth, 1972). The feminine sex role prescribes compassionate and expressive behavior, thereby freeing women to develop relationships in which they can more openly discuss intimate problems and needs.[1]

These sex differences in friendship patterns seem to extend into late life. Research on the social contacts of older persons (Arth, 1962; Blau, 1961; Booth, 1972; Booth and Hess, 1974; Lowenthal, Thurnher, and Chiriboga, 1975; Rosow, 1967) indicate that friendships are more extensive and meaningful for women. Whereas older men rely on wives for intimacy and experience greater social disruption with the loss of a spouse (Arth, 1962; Berardo, 1967; Blau, 1973), women more often turn to friends, usually of the same sex, for intimacy and affection.

Although aged men and women may differ in the frequency of social contacts, the maintenance of intimate friendships should be important to their adjustment. Late life has been viewed by many as a period of diminished social contact — a time of the constriction of the social world (Blau, 1961; Cumming and Henry, 1961; Lowenthal, 1964; Phillips, 1961; Rosow, 1967, 1970). During this period, intimate contacts may be a buffer counteracting decremental changes associated with increasing age. Whether it is argued that confidant rela-

---

[1]Yet male dominance occurs even in the same-sex friendships of females in that husbands have greater influence in initiating friendships and in determining who the best friends of the couple will be (Babchuk and Bates, 1963).

tionships reflect the capacity and need for intimacy (Blau, 1973; Lowenthal and Havan, 1968), or whether they serve as a substitute for lost social contacts (Rosow, 1970), the absence of close ties should be a factor in depression and low morale (Blau, 1973).[2] An intimate tie, then, may buffer the potential demoralization of widowhood, lessened social participation or retirement (Blau, 1973; Lowenthal and Haven, 1968).

Previous research, however, provides little insight into the intimate friendships of late life; that is, the personal, dyadic ties established outside the immediate family for postretirement-age individuals. Berardo (1967), Blau (1961), and Rosow (1967, 1970) have examined the status and structural elements of friendships in later life, but gave little attention to the intensity of relationships. Lowenthal *et al.*, (1975) and Arth (1962) investigated intimate friendships but only with preretirement-age samples. Booth and Hess (1974) and Booth (1972) considered sexually-differentiated close friendship with a sample that included both middle-aged and aged persons. Finally, Lowenthal and Haven (1968) and Palmore and Luikart (1972) were concerned with confidant relationships but included members of the immediate family as confidants. While studies have greatly extended knowledge of the social ties of adults, intimate friendships during late life remain relatively unexplored. Research has been limited to comparatively "young" samples, has given scant attention to the intimacy of relationships, or has included both immediate family and friends among intimate ties of late life.

In this paper these presumedly important social contacts are investigated. It was anticipated that women would have greater contact than men with various types of interactants, including intimate friends. Consistent with the literature on sexually-differentiated social networks, the social advantages and capacities for intimacy exhibited by adult women should exist in their late-life intimate friendships. Next, it was expected that factors associated with late-life intimate friendships would be different for men and women. Blau (1973) and Lowenthal and Haven (1968) have identified several factors that may be important for the formation and maintenance of intimate relationships in late life. Blau investigated "high friendships interaction" and Lowenthal and Haven considered confidants, most of whom were

---

[2]Contrary to the assumption of Blau (1973), the importance of intimate friends for personal adjustment in late life has not been based on research of intimate friendships. Rosow (1967) gave scant attention to the intensity of friendship contacts and Lowenthal and Haven (1968) included immediate family members as confidants. Thus, it may be that the greater morale exhibited by persons with confidants in Lowenthal's and Haven's work existed only for those whose confidants were immediate family (two-thirds of all confidants in their research were spouses or children).

spouses or children, whereas our study concerns intimate friends. Nevertheless, we followed their lead. Six factors, potentially important for the intimate friendship patterns of men and women, were tested: marital status, education, employment status, socioeconomic level, health and social involvement.

Finally, it was anticipated that there would be a high degree of homogeneity in the intimate friendships of both men and women. Despite the advanced ages of our sample, relationship homogeneity that characterizes adult friendships (Lowenthal *et al.*, 1975) should continue into late life.

METHODS

Noninstitutionalized persons, age 60 and older, were interviewed in a 1960 state-wide study in Iowa. Eleven years later, all respondents in five counties representative of the rural-urban distribution and economic levels of the state's population were restudied. Of a list of 269 potential respondents in the five counties, 235 persons were interviewed. Among the 34 eligible persons not interviewed, 16 had health problems that precluded participation, 12 were on vacation, and six refused to participate. The 87 percent completion rate exceeds most community surveys of aged populations. One respondent was not included in the analysis because she did not indicate if she had a confidant.

All respondents were age 70 or older, with 27 percent in their 80s, and 3 percent over 90. Most were women (70 percent), reflecting the unbalanced sex ratio that characterizes the aged. The low educational attainment of respondents, although striking, was anticipated. Consistent with national attainment levels of the aged, one-half had completed fewer than nine years of education, and nearly three-fourths had not completed high school. A majority of the respondents were reared in farm families (60 percent had a father who farmed) or in blue-collar families (24 percent). This occupational distribution also was consistent with national patterns of the aged. Only 11 percent had fathers who were in white-collar, business or professional occupations.

Interaction Patterns

Interaction scores were derived for each respondent based on the number of days they had face-to-face contact (daily, weekly, monthly, yearly) with a spouse, children and their families, intimate friends, and siblings. Regular contacts (*i.e.*, at least daily or weekly) with other relatives, friends, and neighbors also were recorded. Daily contact received a score of 365, weekly contact a score of 52, monthly contact 12, and yearly contact one. Calculation of the total number of yearly contacts with each interactant category permitted a mapping, of sorts, of the relational patterns of respondents. In addition to obtaining an interaction score within each interactant category, interaction scores with all persons were combined to obtain a total interaction score. This score ranged widely with a mean of 960.[3]

Intimate Friends

Intimate friendships were determined by responses to the following question, "Is there any person you feel particularly close to? We are thinking of someone you feel you can really depend on; in other words, someone who is closer to you than 'just' a friend." As in the work of Lowenthal *et al.* (1975), the intimate friend was someone with whom there was an element of reciprocity. Since the focus of this research was on social relationships outside the immediate family, respondents were not permitted to include a spouse or child as an intimate friend. Persons who listed an intimate friend(s) also were asked to provide their sex, age, and relational status.

Characteristics of Persons with Intimate Friends

Six factors identified by Lowenthal and Haven (1968) and Blau (1973) as important for intimate ties in late life were considered in our research: marital status, education, employment status, socioeconomic level, health, and social involvement. Marital status, education, and employment status were determined by standard questions. Health was measured by the number of major self-reported health problems. Socioeconomic level was measured by total family income. Social involvement was determined both by whether clubs and social groups were attended with some regularity, and by how frequently respondents got out of the house for visiting and shopping.

FINDINGS

Interaction Patterns

In considering the role of intimate friends in the social worlds of

---

[3]The few respondents with high interaction scores had jobs or businesses that placed them in regular contact with large numbers of persons.

the aged, it first was felt important to determine the prominence of intimate friends in the interaction profiles of men and women. Average interaction scores with various categories of interactants were computed and summed to provide a total interaction score.[4] Men had a significantly higher total interaction score (mean score = 1180) than did women (mean score = 864; see Table 20-I). This difference in overall interaction was a function of both the number of persons within the interactional network and the frequency of contact with interactants.[5] Although men had regular contact with a larger number of persons (average number of persons for men = 6.7; women = 6.0), one additional person within the interactional network of men would not have accounted for the difference in the total interaction scores of

Table 20-I

AVERAGE INTERACTION SCORES WITH CATEGORIES
OF INTERACTANTS BY SEX

	Men	Women	t-Score
	(N = 71)	(N = 163)	
Friends	265.0	115.7	2.8†
Neighbors	138.8	138.5	0.0
Children and their families	417.0	268.4	3.5†
Spouse	215.9	116.0	4.0†
Siblings	75.6	71.9	0.1
Intimate friends	44.9	109.5	3.0*
Other relatives	22.8	45.8	1.1
Total interaction score	1180.0	863.8	3.2*

*significant at .01 level
†significant at .001 level

---

[4]Social networks as measured by regular interaction scores do not reflect irregular or infrequent social contact. It is possible that the men in our sample may have largely limited interaction to members of the immediate family or to established friendships, while women spent a greater part of their time with more "superficial" contacts (*i.e.*, friends, neighbors, and distant relatives seen irregularly). We were unable to test this hypothesis, but there was nothing in the responses of our sample to suggest this conclusion.
[5]The residential propinquity of interactants affects interaction patterns with close relatives (Klatzky, 1972).

Table 20-II

CHARACTERISTICS OF PERSONS WITH INTIMATE FRIENDS BY SEX

| | Percentage With Intimate Friends | | |
	Total	Men	Women
	(N = 234)	(N = 71)	(N = 163)
Sex			
Men	41		
Women	59		
	X^2 = 5.80*		
Marital Status			
Widowed	60	62	60
Not married or divorced	63	a	69
Married	43	29	55
	X^2 = 6.97†	X^2 = 7.23†	X^2 = .96
Education			
8th grade or less	52	48	55
Some high school	56	36	62
Beyond high school	50	b	63
	X^2 = .37	X^2 = 2.19	X^2 = .88
Employed			
Yes	48	29	69
No	52	44	55
	X^2 = .14	X^2 = 1.11	X^2 = 1.17
Income			
Under $3,000	65	63	66
$3,000-$5,999	44	19	59
$6,000 or more	38	22	56
	X^2 = 11.63†	X^2 = 11.96†	X^2 = .87
One or more major health problems			
Yes	60	52	63
No	38	31	49
	X^2 = 7.87†	X^2 = 3.33	X^2 = 2.57
Attend organizations regularly			
Yes	56	44	61
No	49	38	55
	X^2 = .86	X^2 = .05	X^2 = .57
Frequency get out of house			
Daily	49	36	61
Less often	58	43	60
	X^2 = 1.74	X^2 = 1.23	X^2 = .02

aNot included in X^2 analysis because cell frequency was too small.
bCollapsed into above cell for X^2 analysis because cell frequency was too small.
*significant at .05 level.
†significant at .01 level.

men and women. As shown in Table 20-I, males also had more frequent contact with several categories of interactants — friends, spouses, and children and their families. In fact, male contact with their children and families was half again as high as female contact and their interaction with spouses and friends was twice as high. Higher male interaction scores with spouses were anticipated since twice as many men were still married, but there was no sex difference in the number who reported living children or friends.

Women had significantly higher contact with only one category of interactants — intimate friends. Aged females not only were more likely to report intimate friends (see Table 20-II), but they also had more frequent contact with these persons. Intimate friends, in fact, contributed nearly as much to the total interaction scores of women as did spouses.

Thus, older men, as a group, regularly interacted with a greater number of persons and had more frequent contact with several categories of interactants. Intimate friends, however, seem to be a relatively small part of their social worlds, at least in regard to the frequency of contact. Close friends were important for aged women, however, and made nearly as great a quantitative contribution to their overall social contacts as did spouses.

Persons with Intimate Friends

It has been suggested that older women have greater social advantages and capacities for intimacy (Blau, 1973; Lowenthal and Haven, 1968). Our findings only partly support this argument. It was men, not women, who had higher interaction scores and who regularly interacted with a greater number of persons. But it was women who were more likely to have intimate friends. Two-fifths of the men and three-fifths of the women reported at least one close friend outside the family (see Table 20-II).

That older women are more likely to establish intimate ties outside marriage was further suggested by information obtained about past intimate friendships. We asked respondents about friendships that had ended because of death, mobility, or gradual deterioration over the years. Men were more likely to have never had an intimate friend. Two fifths of the men (42 percent) and one-third of the women (30 percent) did not currently have a close friend and had never lost one.

Aged men also were less likely to replace a relationship that had been terminated. One-half of the men (52 percent) and nearly three-fourths of the women (71 percent) who had lost a close friend currently were involved in another intimate friendship.

We found important sex differences in the characteristics of persons who had formed intimate friendships. The current circumstances and decremental changes experienced by women seem to have little effect on whether or not they had an intimate friend. As demonstrated in Table 20-II, whether or not aged women had intimate friends was not materially altered by marital status, community involvement, income, health, or employment status. The intimate friendship patterns of men, however, more often reflected their life situations. Men who were widowed and who had low incomes were more likely to report an intimate friend. Although differences were not statistically significant, retired men and those in poor health also seemed to be more likely to have close friends in late life. Evidently, aged men turn to intimate ties outside marriage upon experiencing the loss of basic personal resources.

Homogeneity of Intimate Friendships

The final question considered was the homogeneity of late life intimate friendships. We examined affinity, age, and sexual similarity. Consistent with patterns observed at earlier stages of the life cycle (Lowenthal *et al.*, 1975), late life intimate friendships tended to be homogeneous. First, approximately one-third of the close friends of both men and women were relatives (*e.g.*, brothers, cousins). Second, a majority of the intimate friends of both men and women were within a few years of age of the respondents. Given the advanced ages of respondents (70 to 95 years of age), it was anticipated that very few would have friends much older than they. Indeed, only one individual reported an intimate friend ten years his senior. A number of the friends, however, were a good deal younger. Two-fifths of the intimate friends of men and one-fourth of those of women were at least 16 years younger. For some, the observed age difference was likely to be important. One-third of all friends were under 60 years of age, whereas all respondents were at least 70. Thus, contrary to the pattern of general friendships, there were a sizable number of the intimate

However, there was no reason to assume sexual differentiation in the propinquity of various categories of interactants.

friends of both men and women who were significantly younger.

Third, there was considerable sexual homogeneity between respondents and intimate friends. Less than one-tenth of the friendships of women and one-third of those of men were cross-sex. Given their relative infrequency, the characteristics of cross-sex relationships were of interest. Their number, of course, was small, and the findings must be considered tentative. The data suggest, nevertheless, that there is age and kinship homogeneity in both cross-sex and same-sex intimate relationships. The only observed difference between same-sex and cross-sex relationships was in the marital situation of respondents. Eight of the ten men and six of the nine women with cross-sex friends were widowed, and two of the five remaining individuals had never married. This is not to say, however, that all widowed persons form cross-sex relationships. A large number of the widowed reported having no intimate friends. Of those who did, only 12 percent of the women and one-half (56 percent) of the men [were] involved in cross-sex relationships.

Table 20-III

INTIMATE FRIENDSHIPS BY SEX

	Total	Men	Women	*Chi* Square
For existing friendships (N = 159)		Percentage		
Related to Respondent	33	29	35	$X^2 = 0.01$
Age Relative to Respondent				
11 + years older	—	—	1	
Within 10 years	60	50	62	$X^2 = 1.1$
11 - 15 years younger	11	9	12	
16 + years younger	29	41	25	
Cross-sex Relationship	14	29	9	$X^2 = 0.22$

CONCLUSIONS

In the plethora of research on adult social networks, surprisingly little attention has been paid to late life intimate friendships. Previous work on social participation suggests that the social ties of aged men and women are distinct, and that these contacts may perform important functions for personal adaptations to the status transitions associated with aging. In our research on intimate ties outside the family we were concerned with two issues: the relative prominence of close friends in the social world of older men and women and the nature of these friendship ties. Four major conclusions emerge from the data.

In late life males have more frequent social interaction. Prevailing stereotypes suggest that older women are more active in groups and organizations and spend a great deal of time with family, friends, and neighbors. Men, on the other hand, are supposed to retreat to workshops, solitary leisure pursuits, or rocking chairs. Our findings do not support these images. Males had higher average interaction scores reflecting not only contact with a larger number of persons, but also more frequent contact with these persons. Unfortunately, the data do not permit determination of whether the social contacts of respondents were a continuation of earlier patterns or were substitutions for lost contacts. This is an important question for future research. But whatever the explanation, the higher levels of social contact for males that has been observed in middle age, at least for contacts that demand little affection, also seem to exist in late life.

Older men have more frequent social contacts than do women, but the social networks of men basically are limited to three types of persons — friends, children and their families, and spouses. These interactants account for three-fourths of all regular social contacts of older men. While women have less frequent overall social contacts, their interaction is distributed over a wider range of interactants.

The higher death rates of older men and the association between increasing age and male suicide have been of long-standing concern. Lowenthal and Haven (1968) and Blau (1973) suggest that greater female versatility in the choice of the objects of intimate relationships may partly explain greater female adaptability for survival. Our data reveal that in late life women not only have a greater variety of intense relationships — spouse, children, and intimate friends — but also more equitably distribute their social contacts across all interactant categories. There is some suggestion that non-intense social contact — visiting neighbors, telephone visits, and the number of neighbors — is related to life satisfaction (Edwards and Klemmack, 1973). Perhaps it is diversity in *all* forms of social contact, not just in intimate relationships, that contributes to female adaptability in late life.

Women are more likely to have an intimate friend in late life. Women more often turn outside the family for emotional support. If they lose close friends, they usually establish new relationships. It may be that for men intimate ties in late life are related to the loss of certain basic resources — a spouse, income, job and health.

Apparently, the social networks of aged men do not extend much beyond the immediate family and friends. Males were not likely to have intimate friendships for social and emotional support in late life except when they had experienced the loss of other resources. Perhaps Arth's (1962) observation that older men jokingly suggest that their only close friends are their wives may have revealed something important about the late life social ties for men. Women, however, have a number of intimate ties. The death of family or friends may not be any less difficult for older women, but they are more likely to have a greater range of social contacts and alternative intimate ties to which to turn.

There were many men and women who had never formed close ties outside the immediate family. Two-fifths of the men and one-third of the women in the sample indicated they did not currently have, and had not lost, a close friend. This, of course, is inconsistent with a frequent theme in the social science literature which suggests that interpersonal intimacy is important for personal well-being, and that a basic human need is to feel connected to others and to be involved with them (see Coutts, 1973; Jourard, 1964; Dahms, 1972). Yet the precise relationship between social interaction styles and life satisfaction in old age is unclear.[6] In the concern to measure the frequency and importance of social contacts, it may well be that social scientists have forgotten that a number of aged individuals do not have intimate ties and such persons do not always experience low morale (Lowenthal and Haven, 1968).

Although the motivation for late life friendships may differ, there is little sexual differentiation in the homogeneity of the intimate ties.

The findings above suggest that the social worlds of aged men and women are distinct in many ways. Men have more frequent social contact but limit their interaction to family and friends. Men are less likely than women to have intimate friends and are less likely to replace lost friends. Women have a diverse social world and many have intimate ties outside the immediate family. It is somewhat ironic that the last years of men's lives should be so precarious in a society that has been largely oriented toward the privileged position of men.

---

[6]The evidence bearing on this question is inconclusive. While some have found social interaction to be positively related to life satisfaction (Riley and Foner, 1968; Maddox, 1963; Bultena and Oyler, 1971), others have found no relationship between these variables (Lemon, Bengston, and Peterson, 1969; Smith and Lipman, 1972; Edwards and Klemmack, 1973). In fact, Conner, Powers, and Bultena (1975) found no relationship between life satisfaction and the social interaction of older persons when measuring social contact in terms of frequency, scope and exclusivity, age grading, or content.

REFERENCES

Arth, Malcom
  1962 "American culture and the phenomenon of friendship in the aged." Pp.
  529-534 in Clark Tibbitts and Wilma Donahue (Eds.), Social and Psychological
  Aspects of Aging. New York: Columbia University Press.
Babchuk, Nicholas, and Alan Bates
  1963 "The primary relations of middle class couples: A study in male
  dominance." American Sociological Review 28 (June): 377-384.
Bell, Wendall, and Marian Boat
  1957 "Urban neighborhoods and informal social relations." American Journal
  of Sociology 62 (January): 391-398.
Berardo, Felix
  1967 "Social adaptation to widowhood among a rural-urban aged population."
  Washington Agricultural Experiment Station, Bulletin 689. Pullman:
  Washington State University.
Blau, Zena
  1961 "Structural constraints on friendships in old age." American Sociological
  Review 26 (June): 429-439.
  1973 Old Age in a Changing Society. New York: New Viewpoints.
Booth, Alan
  1972 "Sex and social participation." American Sociological Review 37 (April):
  183-192.
Booth, Alan, and Elaine Hess
  1974 "Cross-sex friendship." Journal of Marriage and the Family 36 (February):
  38-47.
Bultena, Gordon and Robert Oyler
  1971 "Effects of health on disengagement and morale." Aging and Human
  Development 2 (May): 142-148.
Campbell, Ernest, and C. Norman Alexander
  1965 "Structural effects and interpersonal relationships." American Journal of
  Sociology 71 (November): 284-289.
Chafetz, Janet
  1974 Masculine/Feminine or Human? Itasca, Illinois: F. E. Peacock Publishers,
  Inc.
Conner, Karen, Edward Powers, and Gordon Bultena
  1975 "Correlates of distributed and focused interaction styles of the aged." Paper
  presented at the Gerontological Society Meetings, Louisville, Kentucky, October.
Coutts, R. L.
  1973 Love and Intimacy. San Ramon, California: Consensus Press.
Cumming, Elaine, and William Henry
  1961 Growing Old. New York: Basic Books, Inc.
D'Andrade, Roy
  1966 "Sex differences and cultural institutions." Pp. 174-214 in Eleanor Maccoby
  (Ed.), The Development of Sex Differences. California; Stanford University
  Press.
Dahms, Alan
  1972 Emotional Intimacy. Boulder, Colorado: Pruett Publishing Co.
Edwards, John and David Klemmack
  1973 "Correlates of life satisfaction: A re-examination." Journal of Gerontology

28 (October): 497-502.

Jourard, Sidney
1964 The Transparent Self. Princeton: Van Nostrand.

Klatzky, Sheila
1972 "Patterns of contact with relatives." Washington, D. C.: American Sociological Association.

Lemon, B., V. Bengston, and J. Peterson
1969 "Activity types and life satisfaction in a retirement community: An exploration of the activity theory of aging." Paper presented at the 18th International Congress of Gerontology, Washington, July.

Lowenthal, Marjorie
1964 "Social isolation and mental illness in old age." American Sociological Review 29 (February): 54-70.

Lowenthal, Marjorie, and Clayton Haven
1968 "Interaction and adaptation: Intimacy as a critical variable." American Sociological Review 33 (February): 20-30.

Lowenthal, Marjorie, Majda Thurnher, and David Chiriboga
1975 Four Stages of Life. San Francisco: Jossey-Bass.

Maddox, George L.
1963 "Activity and morale: A longitudinal study of selected elderly subjects." Social Forces 42 (December): 195-204.

Naegele, Kaspur
1958 "Friendship and acquaintances: An exploration of some social distinction." Harvard Educational Review 28 (Summer): 232-252.

Palmore, Erdman, and Clark Luikart
1972 "Health and social factors related to life satisfaction." Journal of Health and Social Behavior 13 (March): 68-80.

Phillips, Bernard
1961 "Role change, subjective age and adjustment: A correlational analysis." Journal of Gerontology 16 (October): 347-375.

Reiss, Albert, Jr.
1959 "Rural-urban and status differences in interpersonal contacts." American Journal of Sociology 65 (September): 182-195.

Riley, Matilda, and Anne Foner
1968 Aging and Society: An Inventory of Research Findings (Vol. 2). New York: Russell Sage Foundation.

Rosenberg, George
1970 The Worker Grows Old. San Francisco: Jossey-Bass., Inc.

Rosow, Irving
1970 "Old people: Their friends and neighbors." American Behavioral Scientist 14 (September/October): 59-69.
1967 Social Integration of the Aged. New York: Free Press of Glencoe.

Smith, Kenneth J., and Aaron Lipman
1972 "Constraint and life satisfaction." Journal of Gerontology 27 (February): 77-82.

Sutcliffe, J. P., and B. C. Grabbe
1963 "Incidence and degrees of friendship in urban and rural areas." Social Forces 42 (October): 60-67.

Williams, R.
1959 "Friendship and social values in a suburban community: An explanatory

study." Pacific Sociological Review 2 (Spring): 3-10.

Williams, Richard, and Martin Loeb
    1968 "The adult's social life space and successful aging: Some suggestions for a
    conceptual framework." Pp. 379-381 in Bernice Neugarten (Ed.), Middle Age and
    Aging. Chicago: The University of Chicago Press.

Part V

Women and Society's Institutions

INTRODUCTION

One of the major movements of the last twenty years has been an assault by women on some of the institutions of society: education, politics, economics and the work force, and religion. However, this activity, for the most part, has not filtered down to the older woman. Her previous socialization and limited education have prevented her participation at the same levels as younger women. Most women who are older at this point in time — the decade of the seventies — seem neither to be equipped for nor to desire leadership roles in most of the major institutions. For the most part older women are not comfortable with the changes. We will consider the involvement of the older woman with each of these major institutions in turn.

Getting an education meant a few years in a small school for most of the older women of today. If the family could find limited money for education, it usually was spent on the males in the family who were expected to earn a living. Females worked outside the home only before marriage in some properly feminine occupation such as teaching, which in the early part of the century did not require a college education.

Although the education she received in her childhood was sufficient for the time, it was far less than younger people have today. She applauds her children and grandchildren at each graduation from high school and beyond, but less often does today's older woman return to school. Later cohorts will probably find educational programs a pleasant retirement activity. This is a safe prediction, for in the early 1970s the Census Bureau reported that 424,000 "older women," i.e. 35 years of age and older, were enrolled in colleges and universities. This age group would be considered young or middle-aged in most situations, but they are "older women" in comparison with the traditional college student.

When a mother of 93 and a daughter of 70 enrolled in the University of Wisconsin's "Live In and Learn Program," they found that younger students accepted them well (Chapter 21). Living in the dormitory in adjoining rooms, the pair found education a source of challenge and pleasure. Such programs may someday offer interesting educational opportunities to large numbers of older people.

While politics is crowded with older men even in the highest offices of the nation, in the main older women have not run for office — and probably would not have been elected if they had. Leadership has been assumed to be a masculine virtue, and some have suggested that women are too emotional for cool-headed decisions. Perhaps older women with their traditional orientation believe politics is not a "ladylike" endeavor, or perhaps their limited participation in most political affairs leads them to feel ill equipped for activities beyond voting. They do have very high participation in voting behavior, but Chapters 22-24 suggest other possible areas of involvement for older women in the political arena.

Even politically active women seem to overlook the potential contribution of older women. Myrna Lewis and Robert Butler (Chapter 22) deplore this state of affairs, for they maintain that older women have much to contribute to the struggle for equality of the sexes. The authors see older women as having the potential for being the most liberated women of all — free of many of the demands of younger women. They detail a long list of what older women can teach the young. Someday old women with money, brains, and political strength may provide the leadership for change.

One older woman whose vibrant presence electrifies the air as she charges around demonstrating gray power shows that even the activities of one older person can lead to change. Of course, Maggie Kuhn has attracted people of all ages to her aggressive banner as the Gray Panthers speak up for their rights and protest prevailing conditions. In Chapter 23, Maggie Kuhn demands public awareness of what older people can contribute to society through experience, skills, and resources.

Rosemary Redmond, a lawyer and a Project Director of the Older Americans Legal Action Center in Dallas, Texas, examines (Chapter 24) a number of legal issues affecting the older woman, from low retirement benefits for women (including a clear explanation of why they are low) to higher health insurance rates than men of the same age would pay. A discussion of exploitation and neglect of the older woman follows; Redmond reminds us that con men and sometimes even close friends and family members prey on the naive older woman to deprive her of her limited financial resources or to physically abuse her. Redmond suggests that legal counseling must become the right of every old person.

If income were tied to conditions twenty years ago and expenditures to today's zooming prices, it might be hard to balance the budget.

However, suppose income were one-half or one-fourth of what it was twenty years ago — and the prices were still today's? Poverty, not just a tight budget, would be the result.

No wonder so many older women are poor. Even if the husband were lucky enough to have a pension or Social Security, family income was slashed when he retired, and in many cases the income was cut again with the death of the husband.

The extent of poverty, the increase in employment status of many older women, prospects for retirement income, and many other factors related to the financial well-being of older women are discussed in detail in Chapters 25 and 26. Surprisingly, although traditionally a woman's home life has been emphasized, it was not at all difficult to find articles in the areas of economics and the work-force; the difficulty was in limiting the articles to these quality discussions presented here.

This section on economics and work includes two not-too-optimistic articles about the prospects for adequate income in the later years of the older woman's life. A tremendous increase in the labor force participation among women 55 and older has occurred in the last twenty-five years; however, some improvements in private and public pension plans since 1970 have allowed a slight decrease in the participation of women 65 and over.

Merton Bernstein forecasts (Chapter 25) the economic outlook for older women: "cloudy and colder" with a future not much brighter than the present. He discusses retirement income needs of women, Social Security and its benefits, and the need for pension reform if older women are to have adequate incomes in retirement. He predicts that over one-fourth will remain poor.

Testifying before the House Select Committee on Aging, Tish Sommers presents a femininist critique of Social Security (Chapter 26). Why are older women poor? Sex-labeling of jobs, discrimination, lack of credit for labor in the home, paying Social Security twice but collecting once, and more than a half-dozen other reasons that she cites contribute to poverty. A number of helpful suggestions follow to implement the needed changes. Her final advice to older women is to turn the ballot box into political clout.

In many churches on Sunday morning, the worshippers present the spectacle of a sea of gray hair. Since the older generation seems to be more religious than younger cohorts and women outlive men, these gray-haired people tend to be women. This is one social institution where the participation of women has been normative. Given this fact, one might assume it would be easy to find appropriate articles dealing with older women and religion; yet, this was not the case. We found it difficult to locate suitable articles in any source — sociological, gerontological, or religious.

Two articles are included on religion as a social institution. Letitia and Jon Alston provide the reader (Chapter 27) with an analysis of the place of religion in the life of the older woman, contrasting her experiences with both younger women and older men. The authors analyze data from over 700 women 65 years and over and find that half of them attend church more than three times a month — a behavioral testimony to the importance of religion to older women. Marital status, presence of children, health status, and working status of the women also influence religiosity — perhaps in unanticipated ways. For example, employed women over 50 seem more likely to be weekly church attenders than those not working! All in all, the authors present a rare examination of a vital aspect of life for older women.

Don Blazer and Erdman Palmore (Chapter 28) compare the same individuals at different ages to determine both religious activity and religious attitudes. Their evidence suggests women are more religious than men in both activities and attitudes. Patterns of change in religious activity and stability in religious attitudes show little variation by sex. The latter changed little as the sample aged; participation, however, declined for both men and women as age-related disabilities increased.

Chapter 21

MOTHER AND DAUGHTER
BACK IN SCHOOL*

MRS. Zelda Stanke, 70, and her mother, Mrs. Mollie Fritz, 93, believe there's a place for the grandmother image on campus.

Both are part of the University of Wisconsin-Whitewater's "Live In and Learn Program," which enables senior citizens to live in the dorms while auditing courses or taking them for credit.

Mrs. Stanke, a widow, enrolled in the program in the fall of 1974. She enjoyed it so much, she convinced her mother to enroll with her last year.

The two women live in adjoining rooms in Wells Hall. "We have a code system of knocks on the wall to signal if Mother needs anything," says Mrs. Stanke.

She recalled that when she and her husband, a former Methodist pastor, were nearing age 70, "We agreed that something could happen to either one, so we decided the one who was left should find something interesting and challenging."

"After his death, I heard about this program. I got myself over here to the orientation and felt it was just the thing. I find the students a delight. They are very friendly and warm and understanding."

Mrs. Stanke adds, "We haven't felt any students have resented us, although we haven't tried to boss things. I think in general students have accepted us well. They tell us our contribution far outweighs anything else."

Mrs. Stanke said one of her most prized possessions is a certificate of appreciation from Whitewater Chancellor James Connor for being a pioneer in the "Live In and Learn Program."

While she and her mother have gotten along well with other students, she concedes: "Their way of life is different. But maybe they're pioneering new ways, too."

Mrs. Stanke believes the elderly "must just accept the challenge and get out and do something different. A goal like that keeps us looking forward and not in the past. The young, middle-aged and senior

*From *Aging*, 6:266-7, Dec.-Jan. 1976-7.

citizens have a right to go out after things beautiful. It gives zest and sparkle to living."

Mrs. Stanke and her mother drive to the campus on Mondays from their home in Belleville 40 miles away and return there Thursday when their classes for the week are completed.

The two are auditing courses, rather than taking them for credit and, consequently, they pay no tuition under the UW-program which provides courses free for auditors 62 and older.

Participants in Live-In and Learn pay $75 a month for a dormitory room and $17.61 a week for meals. If they prefer, preparation of meals in their rooms is permitted.

During her first semester, Mrs. Stanke took courses in psychology, ecology and man, art metal and jewelry, and estates and trusts. Last fall she took additional courses in psychology and retirement and another in social issues.

Mrs. Fritz has taken a course on the psychology of retirement and an English course that included poetry and play reading. She has written poetry all her life and took the course to have some of her poems evaluated. When she brought them to class for her instructor to critique, he said, "Mrs. Fritz, you're improving with age." She hopes eventually to be able to compile a booklet of her poetry.

Mrs. Stanke says that her mother was delighted at being asked to serve as hostess for a session of her retirement course last year. She responded by preparing Christmas cookies and serving them to her classmates.

Live-In and Learn, designed as an alternative to retirement living, has been slow in gaining popularity at UW-Whitewater. Four students enrolled for the fall 1974 semester. Last fall, Mrs. Stanke and Mrs. Fritz were the only two participating in the program, although there were about 100 senior citizens auditing classes and living at home. Any Wisconsin resident over the age of 62 can audit classes at any school in the State university system free.

Asked her opinion on why the program has not attracted more people, Mrs. Stanke notes, "I think the hesitancy of people to leave their home environment has contributed to its lack of success so far.

"But if people could just see this. This is a great alternative to passive retirement. It costs less here than you would pay to stay home and maintain your house."

She conceded, however, that "you must have good health and energy to come. We both have that. I inherited that from my mother.

Chapter 22

WHY IS WOMEN'S LIB
IGNORING OLD WOMEN?*

Myrna I. Lewis and Robert N. Butler

THERE are eleven million women in this country who are sixty-five years of age and older. Yet they are being ignored by the women's liberation movement. Neither the truly oppressed condition of old women nor their potential political and economic strength is firing the otherwise active imagination of the women's movement. The issues of women's liberation have been the issues of the young and middle-aged — day-care centers, abortion reform, educational discrimination, etc. Obviously these are not the most immediate problems for old women who have been discriminated against all their lives and as a result are frequently poverty-stricken, socially isolated, and culturally obsolete. The newly formed National Women's Political Caucus which first met in Washington, D. C., in July 1971 formed a policy council which included no women members over sixty-five years of age. Interestingly only one member was under thirty-five years and the younger women immediately rallied to protest discrimination against youth. But there was no such protest from old women.

Why is a socially sensitive movement like women's liberation neglecting its older "sisters," leaving them to fend for themselves? Why aren't old women raising vehement protestations? The answer to such questions require a look at a newly defined but very familiar prejudice called "ageism." Ageism can be described as a process of systematic stereotyping of and discrimination against people because they are old, just as racism and sexism accomplish this with skin color and gender. Old people are categorized as senile, rigid in thought and manner, old-fashioned in morality and skills. Ageism allows all of us to see old people as "different" from those of us who are younger. We subtly cease to identify with them as humans and thus we can feel more comfortable about their frequently severe social and economic plight. We can avoid the notion that our productivity-minded society

*From *International Journal of Aging and Human Development*, 3:223-231, 1972. Copyright 1972 by Baywood Publishing Company, Inc.

really has no use for the nonproducers — in this case, those who have reached retirement age. There is an added factor in ageism: unlike the racists and sexists who never need fear becoming black or female, ageists are all too aware that if they live long enough they will end up being "old" and thus the object of their own prejudice. Ageism is a thinly disguised attempt to avoid the personal reality of human aging and death. The traditional buffers of religious beliefs are in a process of challenge and change. No general ethical or philosophical system has yet evolved to deal with human life and death as a whole. The individual fills the frightening vacuum with a self-protective prejudice, and old people are the victims. As is often the case with prejudice, the victims tend to believe the negative definition of themselves. Old people in this country are still silently accepting the treatment meted out to them. They have not yet reached the point of moral outrage and outcry but there are increasing glimmers of demand for "senior power."

For females, ageism has a special bitterness, combined as it is with the cultural denigration of the female. Little girls quickly are taught that in this society it will be much tougher to be an old woman than an old man. Fairy tales set the mood with depictions of old hags, evil crones, scary old witches, and nasty biddies of all sorts. In real life, unmarried aunts are scorned as "old maids." Even beloved grandma becomes a family nuisance as she outlives grandpa and experiences and expresses the emotional and physical facts of aging. The message comes across early in life that a woman is valuable in order to bear children and raise them, and perhaps to nurse father in his dotage, but after that it's clearly downhill all the way. Therefore it is no surprise that women's liberation is currently experiencing a blind spot with respect to age since ageism is a national habit which has yet to be challenged by even the old themselves.

Old Women and Women's Lib Need Each Other

Our contention is that older women not only need the liberation movement but that they have the potential to add significantly to the strength and viability of the struggle for women. Consider for a moment that older women are growing rapidly in total numbers and in proportion to the rest of the population. Old men and women now represent 10 percent of the population. With medical breakthroughs in cancer and heart disease they could make up 25 percent by the turn of the century. The elderly have a far higher rate of voter registration (90 percent) and actual voter participation (two-thirds of those registered do vote regularly) than any other age group. Added to this is the fact that there are numbers of women who have inherited enormous wealth from their departed husbands — wealth which might become a resource for the women's movement if older women were encouraged to join. If this combination of voting strength and wealth were found in any other group, politicians would be trampling each other in the rush to gain their favor and support. But no one has yet been able to grasp the notion that old women can be anything but "old" and "women," not even elderly women themselves.

The Low Visibility of the Elderly Woman

One of the traditions of the American social system is to keep its "undesirables" out of sight. For years we knew little about the poor or the blacks until they were "discovered" with great alarm. Even today such elementary information as an accurate census count of Chicanos, Indians, and black males is not available. In the case of the elderly and specifically the elderly women, facts are gathered but they lie hidden in government reports and scholarly papers. A White House Conference on Aging comes along every ten years to dust them off, but then it's back to the shelf. Newspapers and magazines rarely see the condition of individual old people as news unless they are doing something extraordinary. Elderly women must be truly exceptional to be noticed — Helena Rubenstein at ninety-three running a business empire, Grandma Moses painting primitive art, Martha Graham still dancing at seventy-six, Helen Hayes performing superbly at seventy or Lil Hardin dying at the piano at seventy-one while playing a jazz tribute to Louis Armstrong. To be anything less than remarkable is to be invisible.

Profile of the Elderly Woman

What is the life of an average older woman like? In general being an old woman means living alone, on a low or poverty-level income, often in substandard housing with inadequate medical care and little chance of employment to supplement resources.

Financial Status

A small proportion of older women are well off financially and some few have inherited enormous wealth. At the other end of the spectrum are those women who have been poor all their lives and who can expect greater poverty in old age. But in between these two groups are a multitude of women who lived comfortably throughout their lives and first experienced poverty after they became old — they are the "newly poor." Poverty is not reserved for women alone since old men too are often in dire financial condition. Yet whenever poverty is found, it is generally more profound and of greater consequence for women. In 1968 according to the official poverty index of $1,749.00 yearly per person sixty-five and over (surely a stringent estimation of living needs), 4.8 million of the nation's 20 million elderly men and women lived on or below the poverty line. While representing 10 percent of the population, the elderly make up 20 percent of America's poor. By a more realistic definition of poverty, 7 million aged live in extreme privation. And one-half or 10 million live on less than $75.00 a week or $10.00 per day. It is a common misconception that Social Security and Medicare adequately provide for the elderly. In 1967 the average Social Security benefits for a retired man were $95.00 a month while women averaged $72.00. The average retirement benefits of women workers were 76 percent of the average amount for men. Nonwhite women averaged only $56.00 monthly. Medicare covers about 45 percent of health needs, so available income must go not only for food and shelter but also for health expenses. Little is left for clothing, recreation, travel, or anything beyond bare survival items.

Even women with sufficient income have problems because many of them do not know how to handle money for their own benefit. It is here particularly that societal patterns of passivity and accedence to masculine financial management shows itself. Women tend to turn their money over to men to manage — bank representatives, guardians, lawyers, male children, etc. Those who do take care of their own often are ill-prepared and unable to make sound decisions. A study of business and professional women found that they were good savers but suffered badly from inflation because of the way they invested. These were women who were well above average in income, job level, education, and years of experience but they knew little about investments or how to increase capital. Money management was a passive activity in which they preferred the false security of savings, cash, and annuities over a sounder investment program which required an understanding of economics and finance. This seems to be typical of most older women and women in general.

Employment Opportunities

One million older women work to make ends meet and keep themselves active. Many had never worked before and are employed in dead-end unskilled jobs. Others may have worked previously but earned less money than men all along the life cycle. Both situations result in lower Social Security and private retirement benefits and, combined with a longer life span for women, produce a lower income which must be stretched over a longer number of years.

Employers are reluctant to hire older women because of the stereotyped attitude that older women are not adaptable to today's jobs and technology — old women are seen as cantankerous, sexually unattractive, overly emotional, and unreliable because of health problems — yet studies indicate that they make exceptionally good employees, with lower turnover, higher productivity, and less absenteeism than men or younger women. The government itself is one of the worst offenders on employment. For example, in 1969 the Department of Health, Education and Welfare decided to close the door on any woman over thirty-five years as potential appointees for high-level jobs in the Department. Later this was changed to age fifty. But it remains an insult, considering the numbers of men in government and politics who are not only over fifty but many well into their eighties.

The Social Security system discriminates against older women in a number of ways. We have mentioned that women earn less, and therefore receive fewer benefits. Many jobs held by women have only recently been covered under Social Security — agriculture, hotel and restaurant work, hospital jobs, and domestic work (the latter is still frequently uncovered). Much work done by women has earned them nothing — primarily work as housewives and mothers. A widow receives only 82.5 percent of her husband's benefits even though she has worked all her life as a full-time household employee in her home. If a man and woman are married, they may receive less Social Security than if they were not married, thus some old couples live together without marrying in order to obtain the benefits they both have earned. The Social Security "means test," which limits the amount of income which can be earned, is especially hard on women since they live longer and use up their resources. Many are reduced to bootleg work to hide their income from the government because they need to survive. Finally, Social Security is a regressive tax with a base rate of $7,500.00; therefore, women pay more proportionately than men because of their lower incomes.

Marital and Family Status

Of the 11 million women, age sixty-five and above, over 6 million are widows and an additional 1.2 million are divorced or single. Thus, 65 percent of all older women are on their own, an ironic fact when one remembers that older women, more than any younger group, were raised from childhood to consider themselves dependent on men. Most of them married early, had little education or career preparation, functioned totally as housewives for forty to fifty years and then, *shock!* Their job descriptions, already diminished when their children grew up, vanish completely with the death of their husbands. They are left both unemployed and familyless at a point when they are least able to adjust.

Why so many widows? Women are outliving men everywhere in the world where they no longer perform physical labor and where maternal mortality is reduced. In the United States more boy babies are born than girls, but girls begin to outnumber them at age 18 and by the time they reach age 65 there are 139 females per 100 males in the 65 and above age group. This increases to 156 females at age 75. The difference in life expectancy seems to be a rather recent and poorly understood occurrence. In 1920 men could expect to live 53.6 years and women, 54.6 — only one year difference. But by 1970 a seven-year spread was evident, with a life expectancy for men of 67.5 years and women, 74.9 years. Women are given the dubious privilege of living longer than men, after years of financial and psychological dependency — ill-prepared to survive on their own, much less to use their added years with enjoyment and fulfillment.

Old men have tremendous advantage over old women when it comes to marriage. Because they tend to marry younger women who will outlive them, they are much less likely to be widowed. More than that, they can count on a fairly healthy spouse to nurse them as they age. Should their wife die prematurely, they have more options for remarriage. At age sixty-five when men number 8 million, the 11 million women already outnumber them by 3 million and the odds "improve" as men grow older. In remarrying, men can bypass their own age group altogether and marry women from sixty-five all the way down to girls in their twenties and teens. We can readily see what is happening to older women in all of this. Their chances for remarriage are small. Only 16,000 find a second husband each year and the rest must resign themselves to being alone or scrambling for the remaining unattached men. It is socially frowned upon for an older woman to date or marry a man much younger than herself, a blatant form of discrimination when men are freely allowed this option.

This leads to the question of what older women do about sex. There are problems other than just the unavailability of older men. Many younger people assume old women have no sexual interests whatsoever. They are the neuters of our culture who have mysteriously metamorphosized from desirable young sex objects, to mature, sexually "interesting" women, and finally, at about age fifty, they descend in steady decline to sexual oblivion. This is the way society sees it. But this is not the way a lot of old women see it. They don't understand why older men can be considered "sexy" but never older women. They are angered that old men can attract younger women and be commended for their prowess, whereas older women are seen as "depraved" or "grasping for lost youth" when they show an interest in sex at all, let alone, younger men. Biologically, the cards are stacked heavily in favor of women. A woman in reasonably good health can expect to respond to and enjoy sex in her seventies and eighties, and even nineties if she has maintained a frame of mind which encourages this. Orgasms are possible, but as with younger women, they are not essential to the total enjoyment of sex. The situation is necessarily more precarious for the older man. He cannot simply relax and enjoy sex with the same ease, since "performance" is a more crucial factor.

Yet in spite of their capacities, older women have limited sexual outlets. They have been trained and locked in by the culture to accept the idea that they are no longer desirable sexual partners and that only younger women have sexual prerogatives. We are all familiar with the origins of this idea — namely, that women are sexy as long as they are young and pretty and able to enhance a man's feelings of status and power. What would happen if women had equal access to status and power on their own? Presumably, they might suddenly appear much sexier and attractive, whatever their ages. At the very least older women should demand to be recognized for their true sexual interests and capacities. It is in their interest to insist that something be done about increasing the male life-expectancy as well as allowing women the same sexual and companionship possibilities now enjoyed by males.

Living Arrangements

Thirty-four percent of elderly women live alone, 18 percent live with husbands, 39 percent with relatives, 4 percent with nonrelatives, and only 5 percent in institutions. Many women never lived alone until old age. It is estimated that up to 60 percent live in substandard housing. Although two-thirds of all elderly own their own homes which were purchased forty or fifty years previously, many cannot afford to maintain them. Rising inflation, cost of utilities, taxes (for example, an average 30 percent increase from 1963-69), combined with a fixed income, leaves old people, and more often old women, unable to meet expenses — they scrape by, cutting corners on food and all other needs. Moreover, homes are often located in deteriorating sections of town as are the cheaper rental locations. Old women, white and nonwhite, are easy victims for robbery, burglary, purse-snatching, and even rape. Determined to remain in their homes, they will deny themselves food, medical care, and safety before they will move to unfamiliar surroundings.

Health

Old women can't count on the medical profession. Few doctors are interested in them. A familiar medical school term for an old woman is "crock," and their physical and emotional discomforts are often characterized as "postmenopausal syndromes" until they live too long for this to be an even faintly reasonable diagnosis. After that they are assigned the category of "senility," which is an excuse for no treatment at all since senility is not seen as disease-based. Doctors complain about being harassed by their elderly female patients and claim that they are merely lonely and seeking attention. Yet old age brings realistic health problems which deserve careful diagnosis and treatment. Eighty-six percent of all older people have some kind of chronic health condition and both depression and hypochondriasis commonly accompany these many physical ailments. Perhaps one step toward assuring better medical care would be the presence of many more female doctors who could, if able to overcome their own ageism, identify more readily with the physical and emotional problems of old women. Another possibility is a geriatric subspecialty just for the problems of older women. Again old women must demand the kind of care they want.

Old Women Are Their Own Worst Critics

The phenomenon of self-hatred is found in most groups of people who are the victims of discrimination. If enough people tell you something bad about yourself for a long enough time, you end up believing it. Thus old women typically discredit themselves in both obvious and subtle ways. For example, Gloria Swanson, age seventy-two with a successful film career of fifty-eight years, admits that men are favored as actors over women in old age. Yet she insists she has no use for women's liberation: "No no no. I want a man to know more. . . . Physically I want him stronger, mentally I want him stronger." Simone de Beauvoir, in an allegedly autobiographical work called *The Age of Discretion,* writes of a woman, age sixty, who is brilliant, a leading intellectual, possessing acute sensibility and social purpose, but who is revealed to herself as deluded by her success, dependent on men, mean in spirit, and afraid of growing old. On another level, a representative of the Department of Labor's Women's Bureau said many older women have a "Uriah Heep attitude" about employment, feeling they must appear obsequious and obedient because they have little else of value to offer an employer.

There are women who profit from and exploit the insecurities of their contemporaries. Helena Rubenstein, one of the world's wealthiest self-made women, is a fascinating example of a female who maintained her power and influence until age ninety-two, but made her millions off the cravings of women to stave off their inevitable aging. Older women rushed to buy her products to delay their banishment to "neuter land," the realm of women who are no longer youthfully pretty.

Emotional Adjustment Problems

A pervasive theme in the efforts of old women to find a satisfying life is the preference for male company and the downgrading of female companionship. Many cannot see themselves as fulfilled unless they have a husband or at least some male to whom they can devote themselves, and this becomes more difficult as the male population thins out. Some women compensate with an overbearing idolization of a son or grandson. Others make sad, futile efforts to appear young and thus recapture the lost sex-rights of their youth and middle age. The top-heavy ratio of women to men encourages an already culturally established pattern of competition with fellow females for the few remaining men. The mother-in-law syndrome is another way women may express their disdain toward their own sex (their daughter-in-laws) as well as the envy an older woman feels toward a young woman's youthfulness. The harsh experience of women during the aging process makes it understandable why they may see the young as rivals, not only for the attention of males but also for the very economic resources necessary for their survival in old age.

Some elderly women turn to religion in a passionately excessive manner which seems less of a spiritual search and more of a way of filling the void of their former family. If a man is not available, then perhaps a masculine God-figure can give some sense of comfort and meaningfulness. Religion can serve as a cover-up for terribly lonely women who have no relevant human beings in their lives.

The club and charity set is another example of the manner in which older women attempt to find usefulness. Club and charity organizations reveal an effort to extend mothering to the whole world of orphans, the sick, poor, blind, and halt. Yet noble as this sentiment appears, it quickly is evident in many cases that the real purpose is to fill empty time and lend a sense of importance rather than to get down to the serious task of relieving suffering. Women's clubs and charities are notorious for endless meetings, complicated organizational bickerings, and very little in the way of solid service. Women in general are naive about social and political problems, having left that up to men for so many years. They are too dilettante to become expert because they were conditioned to the lesser role and thus they congregate together aimlessly to fill up their lives.

What's Good About Being an Old Woman?
Implications for the Women's Lib Movement

We have detailed some of the difficulties of old women. But there is more. Old women have much to teach the young and middle-aged about the double whammy of sex and age discrimination as well as pointing to future possibilities for all ages.

What, then, is good about being an old woman? They have the potential for being the most liberated group of women in terms of personal expression. In addition, with increasing good health and longevity, they don't have to fight the conflicts between mothering versus careers which plague younger women. They can function as the only adult females who are truly free of the demands of child responsibility and in many cases marital responsibilities. Old women, of course, want the life expectancy of males raised more nearly approximate to their own, but widowhood or lack of males need not carry the stigmata of failure. The idea of dependency on a male is deeply ingrained but old women may be responsive to challenges of this tired stereotype. Many women were forced into marriage by cultural and family pressures and might have been happier as single career or professional women. Educational programs should be designed especially for them to explore late-life careers. Other older women are homosexuals who have been hiding as "heteras" for a lifetime and might be willing to "come out" if the climate were favorable. Numbers of others could have satisfied heterosexual companionship and maternal needs without marriage or children and still can. They could challenge the sex-age prejudice and obtain the options now reserved for men. We might, for example, be surprised at the number of secret liaisons between young males and older females which could surface if they became socially acceptable.

Older women by example could give younger women confidence to resist the beautiful face and body trap, with the knowledge that a rich life can await them as they age. Women of all ages may begin to refuse to be discarded and to demand recognition as humans. Young women and even the middle-aged are floundering for viable female models to follow. A considerable number of old women have forged unique positions for themselves in terms of identity, personal achievement, and even financial and political power but they need to be located and made visible.

Another unique asset of age is that most older women have adjusted in some way to the idea of personal death. It is characteristic to the elderly to fear death much less than the young. They may attain a certain degree of extra objectivity from this vantage point. There is a possibility for a greater sense of moral commitment and flexibility beyond their own egos. Old people are often thought of as conservative but in truth they are inclined to be dovish on war and liberal of political and social issues. In terms of flexibility this is the generation which indeed has, as Nikita Khrushchev so aptly put it, gone "from the outhouse to outer space" in one lifetime.

Politically, the older woman is in a most advantageous position and it is likely to improve. With a voting strength of eleven million, two-thirds of whom are registered voters, most of whom vote regularly, they represent a major and fast-growing constituency which already could elect their own congresswoman in those states where they reside in high proportions. They have the available time and energy to lobby, campaign, and promote candidates since 90 percent are retired from active employment. There is reason to suppose that women candidates for the presidency and supreme court may come from this age group since older people often fill these positions.

In spite of widespread poverty for many women, there are tremendous sums of money in the hands of widows and female heirs. It is time that women took up their own financial management, instead of entrusting it to surrogate husbands. Women of wealth could exert much greater influence in economic, social, and artistic spheres if they used the resources they already have. They could provide backing for the women's liberation movement and specifically for their own age group problems.

Many elderly women have lived out their last years as characterized by Edna St. Vincent Millay: "Life must go on — I forget just why." But there is a sturdy and hopefully growing group of old women who are undaunted and look to life with enthusiasm. Old women will not accept their bleak lot forever because they have the brains, money, and voting strength to do something about it. An eighty-three-year-old former suffragette who recently became excited by the women's liberation movement states, "I don't want to leave the world without being a part of this."

Chapter 23

GRASS-ROOTS GRAY POWER*

Maggie Kuhn

I AM convinced that the Life Cycle Project is absolutely on target. It comes to the churches and to society at the existential moment. When we consider the increasing numbers of people over 65 in America, and in America's future, it is very important that there be new public awareness of what the elders can contribute to our society. We also need an aroused public awareness of the forces and institutional policies which demean and diminish old people — while denying us the rich resources, experience, and accumulated skills that the elders can feed into the political processes of our time.

Through the process of consciousness-raising, old people can update our remembrance in terms of what we know and what we can do in the present human situation. We have been so completely brainwashed by society that we devalue experience and consider it no longer useful. During consciousness-raising remembrance, we see, after all, that what we have learned through the years has continued usefulness today, that there is a continuum of human experience. It is an important way to move toward relating our personal lives and our personal experience and competence to the public political sphere of life.

Consciousness-raising among groups of us oldsters is basic to our own image and self-esteem. It is also basic to societal change and redirection. A technological society is basically wasteful — wasteful of people and wasteful of human resources. We have always been a prodigal society, plundering the land, exploiting the people and moving on, motivated by a quick financial return and a high productive yield.

Consciousness-raising is also an important element in building the new supportive caring community — essential to maintaining life at any age, but absolutely essential to selfhood in old age. Many of us feel lonely and lost because we are bereft of children or spouses or because we have been arbitrarily retired and deprived of the community of work which had been a supportive element in our lives for

---

*From *Prime Time*, 2:4-6, 1974.

so long. The new community we have to build together will provide opportunity to interact with each other and to create a quality of life which has in it a measure of power — or effectiveness.

The consciousness-raising envisioned in the proposal moves in the direction of new corporate power. The individual old person has been socially, economically, and politically isolated in our culture. We need a sense of oneness — of the commonality of certain kinds of human experience which are characteristic of all of us who attain a great age. (The larger goal of consciousness-raising is, of course, self-determination — which is affirmed as the basic goal of the proposal.) We give lip service to being a democratic society, but by and large our lives are governed, managed, and manipulated by forces beyond our control. This is true for all except the relatively few people who control *our* lives and the political processes governing production and profits. But in old age the suppression, oppression, and lack of power become aggravated and extreme. The self-determination which we seek cannot be achieved unless the people affected by decisions are involved in making, enforcing, and monitoring them.

The institutions set up to deal with the whole question of dependency generally do not really deal with it — except in demeaning, demoralizing, and dehumanizing ways. The people who are dependent because of age, infirmity, mental retardation, or some other kind of handicap are not helped. They are made even more subject to the manipulation and controlling power of others by the services that are provided. This is particularly true in old age. Take, for instance, the so-called Golden Age Clubs which I call glorified playpens. It is assumed that old people are like children and that what we really need, in order to feel contented and cared for, is a place to play. And of course, like children, we must be protected from physical danger. We are thus isolated from the mainstream of life, not only by playing instead of working and producing and contributing, but by the fact that we are not given even a shred of choice of "games." Golden Age Clubs run by mayors' offices funded by governors' commissions on the aging are run by well-meaning professionals who are not old and who seldom consult their clients as to what they need or want. Shuffleboard courts are provided for our Golden Age in the city of St. Petersburg, for example.

It is assumed that those who run the services know what we need and want without asking us. A vital element in our self-determination will be to gain a place at the table where decisions are made. To achieve this requires that we have some understanding of our own power as persons, that we find our goals, and that we realize what we have to contribute. All of these understandings about ourselves, at a highly personal level, can be most quickly surfaced and articulated in the group setting which the consciousness-raising methodology provides.

I see the relationship of consciousness-raising and alternate life styles as part of the same effort to reform society and to turn it around. Old people have been acculturated by our technological society to devalue their human characteristics, to consider old age as a plague — to be denied or hidden. The fact that it is so traumatic for many old people to admit their age is an indication of the way we have been conditioned to hate our true selves, to reject our own bodies and the passage of time — yet time affects us all. And the elders' revolution, contrary to other revolutions, has a universal effect! All of us are aging and all of us, if we survive, will be old some day. Therefore, if we join old people to fight the system that denies the value of age, if we can open up new life styles that enable us to function with power and authority and influence, then we are working for the survival of society as a whole.

Consciousness-raising opens up new options. It is a way of identifying and encouraging the emergence of new leadership, and of equipping people who haven't had leadership roles even in the work that they did in former years. Through consciousness-raising they can achieve a new awareness of what they have to offer in the resolution of problems, and how they can interact with each other to accomplish important social change.

Any new life style that we attempt to demonstrate and live out should, of course, challenge the present economic structures which have not served human needs and have tended to depersonalize and diminish human values. Our present system dealing with old people has extremely limited options. We have devised the nursing home and the retirement community. We have experimented in very incomplete ways with various kinds of communal living. The profit system has created false values and has plunged us into efforts which deprive us of participation in the main stream. So I think of consciousness-raising as catalyzing the motivation to work for the larger public good. I see it also as a means of personal liberation and social liberation for old people. In order to be liberated from the second childhood myth (of playpen and shuffleboard) we must have a consciousness of our own powers and the validity of our accumulated wisdom and skills.

Consciousness-raising also helps us to deal with our own physical infirmities and our private fears — even the terror of physical infirmities that cripple or incapacitate. And our fear of death. I think we are not so much afraid of death as the final closure of life; what we fear is the extraordinary medical manipulation that may extend our lives so that we become vegetables — non-persons. Through consciousness-raising we can affirm our power to maintain control over our lives, even at its closure. And in the supportive community which we can help to build through the consciousness-raising groups, we will be creating a kind of power base that will enable us to confront medical technology and to affirm our right to die in dignity and triumph.

I think consciousness-raising also provides a new kind of awareness in the professional person working with older people. We need to confront these well-meaning professionals with their own fear of age and death and dying. Only when they come to grips with their own psychological mechanisms and needs can they be helpful with ours. Consciousness-raising might help some professional workers face up to the fact that to enable powerless elderly people to become self-determining, contributing members of society requires a new kind of skill. The people who can help us most effectively are those who know how to organize, energize, encourage others to function. This is a very different professional role than that of the average director of recreation services, of telephone reassurance services, of meals on wheels, or even of homes for the aging. So we need new standards for personnel and new standards for performance on the job — as well as a new interactive role between the professionals and politicos who run institutions and programs vis-à-vis the participants in the programs.

Consciousness-raising should also prepare us to function as effective members of boards, committees, and agencies that provide the services. If we really take seriously the goal of self-determination, what is required is that old people residents of an old people's home or retirement village, for example, ought to have the controlling vote on the board. They should be determining the policy that prevails in the program, and should be monitoring the performance of the staff in providing the kinds of services that they need and desire.

Another aspect of consciousness-raising concerns the basic issue of human sexuality. The fact that we are sexual beings until the very end of life is seldom appreciated by the church. Indeed, a kind of monastic, medieval, mortification of the flesh still prevails. Many old people have been so conditioned by this evasion of sex that we have strange and distorted views of the relationship that ought to obtain between men and women. The fact that we are male and female is so influential in determining who we are and how we perform and how we relate to others! Indeed, it is the material of life itself and to deny it in old age is to deny life itself. I would hope that the new life style program could begin to raise the question about the sex life of older men and women. Now if men and women need each other to be fully human, and need to interact and relate to each other for their own self-esteem and self-identity, then we have to be compassionate and wise in creating, for old people and young people together, new life styles that make it possible for old people to have some kind of sexual expression. I think the church has a long way to go to educate its younger members, particularly the people of middle years. The children of my peers, for example, are horrified, antagonistic, and bitter when their mothers or fathers seek to remarry.

A final point about consciousness-raising would be to help The Elders to return to society as contributing members. We must recognize that the goal of old age is to be continuing, maturing, and developing adults reaching out to others until the very end of life. Young people, by helping to "recycle" their elders, will be expanding the horizons of their own later years.

Chapter 24

LEGAL ISSUES INVOLVING
THE OLDER WOMAN

ROSEMARY REDMOND

AMERICAN society is becoming more and more familiar with the special legal problems of older citizens. These problems include discrimination in employment, reduction of employment benefits, high costs for health insurance, and the social and legal difficulties encountered in the financial exploitation, neglect, and physical abuse of older persons.

Within the aging community, the lack of quality legal services available to this group of citizens has an especially serious effect upon women. During the four-year operation of the Older Americans Legal Action Center in Dallas, Texas, roughly 68 percent of the client services rendered for eligible participants over the age of 60 was received by women.

Problems of Employment:
Discrimination and Reduced Benefits

Because women in our society tend to live longer than men, a typical client is either retired or has never engaged in employment outside the home, lives alone, and is either divorced or widowed. Her primary concern is to make very reduced retirement benefits cover the expenses of daily living. Inequities and gaps in the Social Security system's treatment of women have been increasingly recognized as women's roles in society have changed.

Women were originally viewed as wives and homemakers economically dependent on their husbands. In 1940 only 17 percent of married women participated in the labor force. Now the number of married women in the labor force is expected to exceed 50 percent. Increased participation of women in the labor force does not, however, aid the number of older women who are now retired and are securing Social Security protection through their husbands' credits in the Social Security system.

Two factors lead to lower retirement benefits for women. The av-

228

erage monthly benefit for male retirees in June of 1976 was $229.00, compared to $182.00 for female retirees. This discrepancy occurred in spite of the fact that benefit formulas are weighted in favor of lower-paid workers. Lower benefits occurred because women have formerly been concentrated in low-paying occupations with median earnings equalling only about 60 percent of men's median earnings. This figure has remained constant over the past twenty years. In addition, women's working lives are broken up by the responsibility of rearing children; dropping out of the labor force for intermittent periods of time deprives women of continuous earning records. The Justice Department claims that the Social Security system is unable to cope with the employment pattern of the majority of women who are neither full-time homemakers nor full-time employees.

A third factor affecting women's coverage under the Social Security system is the rising divorce rate. According to the Census Bureau, one in every three marriages of women between 26 and 40 years of age is terminated by divorce. Yet women are not entitled to benefits based on their former husbands' earning records unless they have been married twenty years (ten years, effective January, 1979). Homemakers entering the work-force after divorce have less time to build up their own earnings credits.

Retirement benefits and our society's ability to deal with these discrepancies are the crucial issues affecting women who are over the age of 62 and are eligible for Social Security or for private retirement programs. The lack of sufficient retirement income in these later years affects every area of an elderly woman's life. Her lower retirement income may affect her nutrition, the quality of medical care that she is able to afford, her ability to afford adequate private health insurance, and her ability to obtain legal assistance; it may leave her a victim of financial exploitation and physical abuse.

The Social Security system, giving benefits to the elderly at age 62 or age 65, was intended to be a supplement to various retirement programs available to American workers. However, since the majority of women who are now reaching retirement age have never worked or have rarely worked in the employment sector, this meager Social Security income plus a small benefit from Supplemental Security Income may constitute their entire subsistence.

Obviously if work in the home were covered, gaps in earning credits and the dependence of the homemaker on the status worker spouse would be eliminated. Currently homemakers who become disabled in the home are not covered, and the family of a deceased homemaker receives no benefits under the Social Security system.

Legislation offered by Congresswoman Barbara Jordan of Texas would eliminate most spouse and survivor benefits in favor of giving earned credits for homemaker service, with such credits based on the average wages currently paid for services performed. The definition of homemaker in the Jordan plan is broad enough to apply to someone who keeps house (not for pay), is between 19 and 65 years of age, is not entitled to a monthly Social Security benefit, and is not employed for more than 135 hours a month. A single person living alone could qualify under this program.

Removing the dependent status of women is still a controversial issue. In a nation where one in three marriages ends in divorce, there is much ambivalence about whether an individual or family focus is desirable. The tension between concepts is simply an earnings replacement program versus one which would provide basic protection against disability, loss of homemaker and mother in the home, and poverty and old age; these problems must be dealt with, for they will not go away. Legal advocacy groups for older women will not let us forget the meager subsistence retirement of these women who have contributed so greatly to rearing future generations.

The Problem of Discriminatory Health Insurance Rates

Inequities in retirement benefits for many women are further compounded by higher costs for health insurance through the use of sex classification and actuarial tables. These rates are used to justify higher costs for insurance to women. These elaborate tables document medical services rendered in the past to both men and women and are used to predict what a company is likely to have to pay for medical care. For example, the tables show that women visit their doctors more than men — according to a 1975 study, 9.7 times per year, as opposed to 4.3 for men.

If a woman in good health purchases a health insurance policy from a major insurance company and a man in good health, of the same age, purchases the same policy, the woman generally pays about $40.00 more per year for the same health coverage. Such discrepancies are unfair because many of the medical expenses incurred by younger women are related to reproduction and should be borne more evenly by the women of that age group or by the male half of society that shares the benefits.

In effect, the older woman is statistically made a part of this stereotyped group of women for insurance purposes and must bear higher insurance costs as a result. Each year, one out of six persons enters the hospital, staying eight days on the average and spending about $2,000.00. Older women past age 65 may be eligible for Medicare, but that particular health insurance pays only 80 percent of the high cost of medical services. Since these expenses can be financially depleting, additional private health insurance, calculated under the actuarial tables, is a necessity — at least until national health insurance is enacted, a development which even optimistic observers place years in the future.

Problems of Personal and Social Life: Financial Exploitation, Neglect, and Physical Abuse

The generally lower retirement benefits and statistically more expensive health insurance point, then, to the larger problem of lack of access to mainstream society for the older American woman. Because of this dilemma, she may be more vulnerable to problems of financial exploitation by various tricksters who have fraudulent schemes to sell. Although her mental faculties may be excellent, she may not be adept at recognizing these encounters as illegal and potentially harmful to her income and savings.

The Legal Protective Services for Adults Component of the Older Americans Legal Action Center investigates cases of financial exploitation involving older persons. Since 1976, roughly 78 percent of the clients in this category have been women. Since women tend to live longer than men, many older women live alone in the family home as widows. These women are prey to home repair fraud, sales of worthless insurance policies, get-rich-quick schemes, and a vast number of con games limited only by the ingenuity of the thieves involved.

Often clients advise us that they are currently living at a much lower standard of existence than in younger days when they were supported by the earning power of a husband and family. To the victim, dishonest schemes may appear to be ways of increasing her meager resources. She may invest in any number of dishonest enterprises, often sacrificing her entire life savings for a "can't lose investment." The banking industry is especially concerned with depositors who withdraw large sums of money and clients who sign blank checks, expecting the current amount of the purchase to be filled in correctly.

In an effort to pay bills with a minimum of physical effort, such persons may place another trusted individual on their bank accounts. The bank account of Mary Jones, for instance, might add the name of

Jane Doe as a second depositor so that Jane Doe can use her added mobility to pay the first party's debts. The bank account would read "Mary Jones or Jane Doe," and therefore, even though Jane Doe does not contribute any money to the account of Mrs. Jones, Ms. Doe can withdraw all of the money at her option. The "or" account is an excellent device for married couples to share the responsibility of the community property of marriage. However, the "or" account may not work as well for Mary Jones, a disabled widow who needs assistance in paying her monthly financial responsibilities. In case after case at the Older Americans Legal Action Center, the intent of the client, Mary Jones, is abused in a legal manner when the second signee of the account, Jane Doe, removes all of the assets of the account and leaves Mrs. Jones penniless.

In such a case very little can be done legally to force Jane Doe to reimburse the account since technically she had full access to the total amount deposited. Newer and more restrictive legislation is needed by the banking industry to protect the assets of these older persons who are in need of honest and responsible persons to assist them in financial management.

The fear of trusting outsiders may encourage an older individual to become more and more reclusive. The news of financial exploitation by a neighbor's family or friends can lead to paranoia, which results in extreme cases of self-neglect. Our Legal Protective Services for Adults Unit has investigated a number of cases involving self-neglect to the point of complete disregard for everyday functions of eating, sleeping, and bathroom needs. Such a reclusive or paranoid individual may, additionally, be physically abused by the family members with whom she lives. Such cases are very similar to child abuse, but current laws do not protect the aged individual since she is over the age of 18 and legally a competent adult.

It is certainly an advantage to be considered legally competent until proven otherwise. Such legal assumptions are the foundation of our constitutional right to freedom of movement. A problem occurs, however, when an aged person is either severely neglected or abused and is unable or unwilling to consent to society's intervention.

The conflict between an individual's right to the assumption of legal competency and society's interest in protecting neglected and abused aged persons has been resolved by some states through the passage of legal protective services legislation designed to allow assistance to persons who are abused and neglected within the statutory definition. Generally, such laws allow for the removal of individuals aged 60 or over from living situations that place the individual in immediate danger of loss of life. Oklahoma, Tennessee, Florida, and California have enacted such laws. California in particular has seen a raging battle between civil libertarians, who feel such laws encourage gestapo tactics, and social services personnel, who look upon such laws as absolutely necessary for the protection of nonconsenting abused or neglected persons.

The Legal Protective Services for Adults Unit of the Older Americans Legal Action Center in Dallas has investigated over 100 cases of abuse and neglect during its three years of operation. Since the majority of these cases involve elderly women, prevention as well as protective services legislation will be needed to prevent adult abuse.

With increased life expectancy of women, it is conceivable that more and more aged individuals will continue to be part of the average household. Skills must be taught to families to assure the older individual of a dignified and safe environment with the family. In several instances, our Legal Protective Services for Adults Unit learned that the abusing child, who continually beats Mother black and blue and then alleges she fell out of bed, was himself an abused child of that particular mother. This cyclical effect of abuse points to the need for continual utilization of available social services skills by these families.

Older persons can themselves prevent such abuse and neglect by encouraging an ever-widening array of friends and acquaintances of all age groups. Such stimulation helps prevent the paranoia that may cause the older person to distrust loved ones.

Legal services to assist in matters of abuse, financial exploitation, and neglect, as well as services to plan and assist in a financially rewarding retirement, will be more available in coming years. It is the responsibility of the legal profession to assist the elderly with high quality and relevant legal services. The American Bar Association through its use of prepaid legal services and legal services projects, specifically designed for older individuals of limited means, has been a leader in offering such assistance. The National Senior Citizen Law Center in Los Angeles and in Washington, D.C., carefully monitors legal protective services for adults laws in the various states and offers specific legal assistance through class action suits to prevent an imbalance between the right to individual liberty and the right for the protection of society against exploitation, neglect, and abuse. These concerned programs for the elderly point to a future in which legal counseling will be recognized as a right for every individual of any age or economic circumstance.

Chapter 25

FORECAST OF WOMEN'S RETIREMENT INCOME: CLOUDY AND COLDER; 25 PERCENT CHANCE OF POVERTY*

MERTON C. BERNSTEIN

$\mathbf{A}$LMOST one quarter of old people are poor; a majority are women. The older they are, the poorer they are and the greater the proportion of women. This baleful situation results from these realities: Most wives outlive their husbands; married women often depend upon their husbands' incomes; Social Security benefits for widows are low, and private pensions generally do not provide for widows' benefits. The future may be better, but probably not much.

In 1973, Social Security paid almost $50 billion in benefits. Divided among more than 29 million recipients (19 million over 65), the average annual benefits were modest — $1,977 on the average for retired workers and, even lower, $1,872, for widows. Newly eligible beneficiaries fared only slightly better, reflecting the somewhat higher earnings of more recent retirees. Obviously, Social Security benefits unaided will not prevent poverty, let alone sustain preretirement standards of living. While many elderly own their own homes with small mortgages or none, their other savings generally are extremely modest. A minority qualify for private pensions that in the main do not pay benefits to widows.

Meanwhile, retirement age comes earlier, with strong pressures to lower normal retirement age below 65. The consequences of such a trend is to shorten periods of earnings and to lengthen periods of dependence on income substitution programs. Earlier retirement without commensurate deductions in benefits makes such programs more expensive and thus less able to improve benefit amounts or liberalize conditions of eligibility. These developments are specially portentous for women who generally earn lower wages and salaries than men and live longer.

What women need from retirement programs are higher benefits

---

*Reprinted from *Industrial Gerontology*, *1(2)*:1-13, Spring 1974. ©The National Council on the Aging, Inc., Washington, D.C.

from Social Security and assured eligibility and widows' benefits from private pension plans. Social Security has made steady improvements, while private pensions remain unreliable for men and seriously inadequate for women.

Retirement Income Needs of Women

Throughout this century, large numbers of nonwhite women have worked for pay. Only during the past three decades have substantial groups of older white women begun to do so. Now about half of all women work at paid jobs.

Single, Divorced and Widowed Women

Clearly, single women who work need an income substitute as much as men do when they retire. As lower income workers, they need a higher percentage of earned income replacement than do men. Divorced women frequently do not receive alimony, and their retirement needs are at least the same as single women; the interruptions in work occasioned by family duties will, on the average, prevent their attaining equal Social Security benefits. Widowed women at work may be better or worse off, depending on whether they have young children at home. The children probably would receive Social Security survivor benefits, but they also make full-time work difficult. Single, divorced and widowed women make up somewhat more than a third of working women (U.S. Bureau of the Census, 1972).

Married Women: Two-thirds of Working Women

The major new development in work patterns in the past two decades is that an ever-larger proportion of married women work. In 1971, of the 32 million women at work, almost two-thirds were married. And here are the amazing figures: Among married couples, *there are more husband-wife families in which both husband and wife work than those in which only the husband works* (U.S. Bureau of the Census, 1972). Over 25, age is not a significant factor in this pattern. Throughout the age group 25-54, about half the married couples had both husband and wife earners. In contrast, such families in which only the husband worked varied from 47.4 percent for those 25-34 to 24.8 percent for those 45-54 (the remaining percentages are accounted for by families in which the husband and a family member other than the wife works). Among blacks, the proportion of husband-wife worker families is even higher.

Income in Husband-wife Families

So, in about half the husband-wife families, the living standard of the family depends on not only the husband's but the wife's income. One study several years ago reported that the median income of husband-wife families exceeded that of husband-only-worker families. For the almost 39 million husband-wife families, the median income was $5,313 in 1958. In the 11 million families in which both the husband and wife worked, median income was $6,214, considerably above the $4,983 median income of families in which the wife did not work. Forty percent of the families with working wives had incomes of $7,000 or more, compared with 24 percent of those with non-working wives (U.S. Department of Labor, 1960).

The day is past when we could regard women as working for pin money. Their earnings make a significant difference in their families' standard of living — at every age before retirement. It follows that such income requires substantial replacement when work for pay ceases because of age or infirmity. And as contributors to their husbands' ability to earn money, they deserve, as well as need, wives' and widows' benefits.

Let us explore in more detail how they fare under Social Security and private pension plans.

Social Security

Enacted in 1935, Social Security at first provided benefits only for retired workers. Benefits varied according to the amounts individual workers paid in Social Security taxes. (Since its beginning, employees and employers have paid equal payroll taxes based on the individual's creditable earning — originally $3,000 a year, $13,000 a year in 1974. Most economists regard the employer-paid tax as part of the wage bill which, in effect, comes initially from the employee. Who ultimately bears the cost is a matter of controversy.)

Equity Versus Adequacy

Even before the first benefit payments came due in 1939, Congress changed the program's design. Instead of the principle of "equity" (individual benefits that vary in proportion to one's contributions),

Congress provided dependent and survivor benefits based on a concept of "adequacy" to social needs. Put another way, social insurance means that, compared with their contributions, some groups will obtain proportionally more from the system and some less. Meeting pressing social needs justifies the disproportion — so children obtain benefits when orphaned, although childless families thereby "get less."

But before making too much of this point, it must be understood that each generation of beneficiaries gets more from the system than its contributions would purchase, which happens because the system transfers funds from the currently employed to retirees and survivors. Indeed, some obtain benefits for which they contributed not a cent — for example, the many million already retired when Medicare went into operation.

Wives, Husbands and Dependency

In 1937, when only a small proportion of white married women worked for pay, wives were regarded as "dependent" upon their husbands' income. Hence, the Social Security Act provided that when a man retired he would be entitled to a benefit based on his earnings (the primary benefit) *and* the couple also would receive a wife's benefit equal to half of the retiree's. Also, on the husband's death, the wife qualified for a widow's benefit (now 100 percent of the husband-retiree's). However, women's spouses received the spouse and widower's benefits only if they *demonstrate* dependence by showing that half their support came from their wives. Last year, a Federal court held such unequal treatment illegal and ordered Social Security payments to a young widower with children. Such patent discriminations (eliminated in Sweden, for example) probably will be changed by legislation before long if the courts don't do it first.

Women's Benefits

But a major complaint of some groups is that women do not obtain a proper recompense under Social Security for their paid work, in that they can obtain as much or more from the system without working, simply by drawing the spouse's benefit. In fact, most women receiving benefits draw on their own account (83 percent) rather than as wives. (They can choose whichever is more advantageous; on becoming widows, they can choose again.)

Two factors are involved:

- The benefit formula pays more, proportionally, to low-wage earners because of the generally sound notion that a greater portion of low wages goes to essentials (a principle that often does not operate fully in two-income families).
- The benefit formula is applied to the life-time average of credited earnings. Thus, although women generally command lower pay than men and work less steadily, the benefit resulting from their own wage history usually surpasses their portion of the spouses' benefit (50 percent of the primary benefit).

Some assert that the growing disparity between the average pay received by men and women will alter this pattern. But it has developed in the face of more rapid pay increases for men, possibly due to the greater number of years women now work. Hopefully, the Civil Rights Act ban on employment discrimination will reduce, if not eliminate, differences in pay and opportunity.

Low Wages and A Regressive Tax

Despite this seemingly reassuring description, other factors tend to victimize women. Without cavil, the Social Security tax is regressive, indeed doubly regressive: Not only is it uniform for all income groups to which it applies; it does apply only to the lower end of the income scale. Hence, as low earners, women are specially victimized by the tax regressivity. Some argue that the weighted benefit formula offsets the regressive nature of the tax. That is questionable, because non-whites (typically relegated to low-wage jobs) have shorter lives, and unmarried family heads (which many black women are) will never enjoy the spouse's benefit, which the families of upper-income white males will. Moreover, the family maxima on benefits are proportionally more generous to upper-income earners.

Hopefully, the regressivity problem — which also bears heavily on both nonwhite and white male low-wage earners — will be alleviated to some degree by the exemption of some amount of low pay from the payroll tax, with the difference made up by general revenue obtained at relatively progressive rates. While this problem now is receiving more attention, there is no assurance that this remedy will be adopted.

Working Wives and Homemakers

The chief complaint of groups concerned with sex discrimination is that married couples, where both partners work, pay disproportionately large taxes and (perforce) obtain disproportionately small benefits. This stems from the fact that some women receive a spouse's benefit with no or (more frequently) small payroll tax payments. Even where a woman takes her own benefit, the argument goes, her work and taxes produce only the *difference* between the spouse's benefit (to which she is entitled without work) and her own. Some even insist that working women are paying for nonworking wives' benefits.

To make such criticism valid, it would be necessary to reverse the basic concept of Social Security that, although benefits are "earned" by contributions, the benefits need not — indeed, should not — be proportional to contributions (taxes).

Paid Work Narrows Limit

Moreover, some (including this author) would contend that a definition limiting work to paid employment is too narrow. On the contrary, child rearing and homemaking frequently are as hard, as constructive as work for money — and often more so. Whatever their comparative merits, these nonpaid tasks will continue to be performed by many women for substantial periods of their lives. Such nonearning periods lower life-time earning averages and, therefore, lower the average of earnings on which Social Security benefits are based.

One solution proposed would credit nonpaid homemaking as if it were a paid job for Social Security purposes (Bell, 1973), a proposal I heartily espouse (Bernstein, 1973). But the "solution" entails problems of its own. What value should be assigned to such work? It could be uniform, recognizing that, although there are many variations, practicality necessitates an arbitrarily assigned value. It might be varied according to the number of children — but, then, some would insist that the children's ages should be a factor (but neither numbers nor age indicate how much work such children generate). Many, probably most, women who work for pay also perform substantial household duties. How should their work at home be credited? Time spent provides no sure measure because of varying degrees of efficiency. Again, some arbitrary amount may have to be set. And what of men who wash dishes, market, baby sit, take children on outings, drive the kids to school and dance lessons and help entertain their wives' working associates?

Probably more perplexing is how to pay for such credits. To tap public funds would constitute a discrimination between homemaking and "working" wives. However, there are precedents for this: For example, millions of people without Social Security eligibility were blanketed into Medicare at its inception, and the cost was borne by general revenues. If such benefits could be earned by *"hausmen,"* men and women would be freer to assume their roles with greater attention to their tastes, capabilities, and opportunities. I doubt that the American public and Congress are ready to treat any men as housewives, but the courts may be. To limit such credits to those willing to pay would exclude families with low incomes, a thoroughly undesirable result.

Congress has yet to address itself seriously to giving credits for housework. But, in 1973, Representative Bella Abzug (D., N.Y.) led a group of six House members in introducing H.R. 252 which would confer credit for housework to a person residing with someone who works; cost of the coverage would come from general revenues. This year, Representatives Barbara Jordan (D., Texas) and Martha Griffiths (D., Mich.) introduced H.R. 12645 to achieve this goal. It would provide three methods of computing contributions for homeworkers and grant a tax credit favoring all low-income earners.

Under existing law, families with the same earned income may earn substantially different benefits. As former Social Security Commissioner Robert Ball pointed out last summer, a couple with the man earning $9,000 will receive more than a couple where the husband earns $6,000 and the wife $3,000 (lifetime yearly averages). In the first situation, the entire $9,000 produces both a full primary benefit *and* a spouse's benefit (50 percent of the primary benefit). With the couple earning $6,000 and $3,000, however, the wife cannot draw both her own and the spouse's benefit.

Husbands/Wives Combine Accounts

To equalize treatment, it is proposed to allow husbands and wives to combine their accounts. A House Ways and Means proposal to achieve that goal would have a comparatively low cost and so is eminently practical. The equalization of treatment recognizes that equal family incomes require equal substitutes and (I would add) that both spouses participate to some degree in producing all the family earnings.

The National Women's Lobby objects to the "mythology" that makes men the heads of households and casts all others as dependents; it proposes that all be treated as "individuals" under Social Security, apparently meaning elimination of the spouse's benefit. If applied suddenly, it would leave women who chose or had no choice but to work in the home without a benefit to meet the greater need of a couple. With the passage of time, the formula "every person for him and herself" may fit the general pattern where all persons work most of their adult lives. Until that occurs, the spouse's benefit seems necessary.

If the spouse's benefit were eliminated, the resources "saved" would be available to raise primary benefits, recognizing the contention that an equal percentage of all lost income should be replaced — a policy wholly at odds with the notion that larger families need a greater replacement of lost income. A more expensive variation would treat all individuals alike *and* pay spouse's and dependent's benefits on the husband's and the wife's account. The argument in support is: The Social Security benefit constitutes only a partial substitute for lost income. When families are concerned, a larger portion of lost earnings must be provided because more persons (spouse and children) depend upon it. Such dependency occurs whether the lost earnings were of the husband-father or wife-mother. However, such an approach would pay larger benefits to a two-worker family than to a one-worker family with the same income.

Without doubt, there are clear sex discriminations in the law, primarily in the treatment of husbands and widowers, obviously undervaluing women's work. They are in the process of extinction, in all likelihood, and should be.

I earnestly suggest that all of us concerned about the living standards of women concentrate on the clear shortcomings of Social Security: inadequate benefits in all categories and the classification of homemaking and child rearing as nonwork.

Private Pensions

Social Security now covers most of the paid work force except Federal employees. Other than for disability, benefit eligibility is readily achieved despite interruptions in work and long stints of part-time or part-year employment. Private pensions have proliferated to supplement the low level of benefits.

Sparse Coverage

Unfortunately, private pensions cover less than half the private work force; coverage for women is sparse; only a minority of those covered will achieve benefits; benefits for spouses are almost unknown, and few widows qualify for survivor benefits.

Pension plan coverage is concentrated among higher-paying jobs, while the bulk of women gain employment in poorer-paying positions. Benefit eligibility generally requires full-time, long-term, uninterrupted employment — typically 10 or 15 years at a minimum. Most women are excluded, in effect, as workers, as wives, and as widows. Even in pension-covered areas, women generally have shorter service. One study reports that twice as many men as women had private pension coverage on their longest private-sector job (Kolodrubetz, 1971).

Conditions for Eligibility Onerous

Both men and women hold many jobs throughout a working lifetime. Most pension plans (about three fourths) provide that an employee who leaves a position after 10, 15 or 20 years of service will qualify for benefits at retirement age. Such provisions are called vesting. Although in widespread use, they afford little protection in practice, because the great bulk of people separating from jobs cannot satisfy their requirements.

An extensive study by the U.S. Senate Labor and Public Welfare Committee (1972) showed that under plans requiring *more* than 10 years for vesting, 92 percent of all separating from such jobs left with no pension eligibility. For 10-year vesting plans, the comparable figure was 73 percent. Given past employment patterns, a larger proportion of women employees were among the losers than men. A glance at job tenure data explains why. (See Tables 25-I and 25-II.)

Table 25-I

MEDIAN YEARS ON CURRENT JOB

Age	Men	Women
30-34	3.9	1.8
35-39	5.8	2.6
40-44	8.4	3.2
45-49	10.2	4.4
50-54	12.6	6.2
55-59	14.7	8.2
60-64	15.1	9.4

Source: "Job Tenure," MONTHLY LABOR REVIEW, September 1969, pp. 18-19.

Table 25-II

MEDIAN YEARS — SELECTED OCCUPATIONS

| | Men by Age | | Women by Age | |
| | | 45 | | 45 |
Selected Occupations	25-44	and over	25-44	and over
Manufacturing:				
Durable Goods	4.5	14.3	2.4	8.3
Nondurable Goods	5.3	15.4	2.8	9.1
Wholesale and Retail Trade	3.3	8.8	1.5	4.9
Operatives and Kindred Workers	3.8	12.8	2.1	7.7
Public Administration	5.0	12.1	2.7	8.1

Source: "Job Tenure," MONTHLY LABOR REVIEW, September 1969, pp. 18-19.

Similar disparities occur where only pension-covered jobs are involved. It can readily be seen that a 10-year vesting requirement would yield nothing to the women below the median — those most likely to be separated from their jobs.

The reduction of sex-based job discrimination and a wider range of paid work for women may narrow these differences in time. But newly opened job opportunities also mean that women are only beginning to build up pension credits on better-paying jobs formerly closed to them. Where seniority governs layoff, they will be the first to be separated. Recent job gains are all too readily cancelled by unanticipated occurrences, such as the energy crisis (real or bogus, it has prompted hundreds of thousands of job separations). Women more often than men work part-time and/or part-year; pension plans generally are geared to full-time employment.

These barriers to benefit eligibility mean that the great majority of employed women will not earn a private pension retirement income substitute in whatever their current jobs are. Men face the same problem, but for women the hurdles are more numerous and higher.

Widows' Benefits are Rare

"The day he died, the pension checks stopped coming," one elderly woman recently wrote to me. Her husband had worked 50 years for one company (he started at age 15) and had received retirement benefits for only 13 months when he died.

Few plans assure widows a pension. Hence, even when the retiree does win benefits, his family is usually cut off when he dies. According to one government estimate, only two percent of widows collect private pension benefits.

Ostensibly, many plans provide for some kind of "joint-and-survivor" election under which, prior to retirement, the employee may choose to take a lower benefit during his lifetime so that his survivor (if any) may receive a benefit after his death. In addition to the two percent figure, other evidence indicates that the option seldom is exercised. Faced with such a difficult choice, most men apparently opt for the larger benefit during their lifetime. Even under one state public employee plan (where one might expect a high percentage of elections), survivors constituted only one of seven benefit recipients. In contrast, among recipients of Social Security, where no option is exercised, survivors account for one of every two beneficiaries.

As with Social Security, pensions should provide for both the retiree and survivors who shared earned income (and, as with spouses, so often enabled the employed family member to work to the extent that he did).

Pension Reform Legislation

As I write, both houses of Congress have passed pension "reform" bills. Regrettably, they promise little improvement over the patterns described.

The measures do not deal effectively with spotty coverage for the bulk of the employed. Those few employed who have income to spare and lack pension coverage would receive favorable tax treatment for savings held in retirement accounts. An obvious aid to upper-income groups, this provision will not begin to spread coverage to those most in need of it.

On the crucial issue of vesting, the Senate-passed bill would require vesting of 25 percent of pension credits after five years of service, growing by five percent increments to 50 percent after 10 years, then by 10 percent a year for 100 percent vesting after 15 years. The bulk of job separations takes place before 10 years on a job are achieved. Given the modest benefits of most plans, the amounts salvaged would also be modest. A typical blue-collar plan would yield a benefit of $6.25 a month ($75 a year) to someone achieving vesting after five years.

The House bill is weaker yet. It gives employers the choice of three formulas: That of the Senate bill, 10 year vesting, or the "rule of 45" under which 50 percent vesting occurs when age and credited service (no less than five years) add up to 45. Naturally, employers will choose the least expensive, least protective measure. The vesting provisions could be meaningless. For example, maintaining a young work force under a "rule of 45" arrangement could easily result in the avoidance of vesting. That device only complicates an unpromising hiring scene for the older worker.

Both measures would not become effective until 1976 at the earliest (new plans which tend to be small must comply from the outset). For existing union-negotiated plans, the effective date can be delayed until 1981. Between 1976 and 1980, the benefit formulae would be phased in, so that in 1976 the meager five-year benefit already described could be halved — *i.e.*, $3.12 1/2 would be payable for a month ($37.50 a year). As if that were not gradual enough, plans covering multi-employer groups could apply for additional delays.

On widows' benefits, the bills require only that all plans must offer the ineffectual joint-and-survivor option. A really protective provision, tentatively adopted by the Ways and Means, was dropped. It would have provided that both the retiree and the spouse would have to agree to waiving a survivor benefit.

Forecast is Cloudy

The outlook for meaningful pension reform is cloudy, at best. In the unlikely event that further legislation on the subject would be forthcoming (another 10 years is an optimistic guess), the fruits of such change would be slow to ripen — as the description of the current measure demonstrates. As in any tax-related field, the gravy flows to the well-to-do and the gruel, at best, to the many.

In contrast, Social Security already contains a cost-of-living escalator provision. Whatever improvements Congress makes can become effective in a matter of months or a year at most.

No effective lobby exists to back pension reform. In contrast, organized labor and some retiree groups do work effectively for Social Security improvements.

Women have barely gotten into the legislative game. Until they do, their interests will be underrepresented, and they will experience many chilly days in retirement.

REFERENCES

Bell, Carolyn Shaw. Testimony in Hearings "On the Economic Problems of Women" before the Joint Economic Committee, Congress of the United States, 93rd Congress, 1st Session, 1973.

Bernstein, Merton C. "Rehabilitating Workmen's Compensation," SOCIAL SECURITY: POLICY FOR THE SEVENTIES, Booth, Ed., 1973.

Kolodrubetz, Walter W. "Characteristics of Workers with Pension Coverage on Longest Jobs," SOCIAL SECURITY BULLETIN, 36(11): 8, 1971.

U.S. Bureau of the Census. 1972 STATISTICAL ABSTRACT OF THE UNITED STATES, Washington, D.C., 1972.

U.S. Department of Labor. 1960 HANDBOOK ON WOMEN VOTERS, Women's Bureau Bulletin No. 275, 1960.

U.S. Senate Committee on Labor and Public Welfare. INTERIM REPORT OF ACTIVITIES OF THE PRIVATE WELFARE AND PENSION PLAN STUDY, 1971, Senate Report 364, 92nd Congress, 2nd Session, 1972.

Chapter 26

SOCIAL SECURITY:
A WOMAN'S VIEWPOINT*

Tish Sommers

BACK in the early thirties, the streets in San Francisco where I lived were jammed with marchers for old age pensions. Townsend clubs had headquarters in every town of any size in California. In 1934, the muckraking journalist Upton Sinclair was campaigning vigorously for governor, calling for a $50-a-month pension as part of his EPIC program (End Poverty in California). Mass rallies attracted thousands of elderly persons who had drifted west to California as to Mecca.

Along with all that senior activism came the pension hucksters, who demanded more than the going wage for any retired person. Nobody ran for any office without curring the favor of the organized elders, and any coalition without them did not get very far. Since the government wasn't doing anything for senior citizens, they were busy doing something for themselves. They were making noise.

At last the squeaky wheels got a squirt of grease at least — the Social Security Act of 1935. The act was a string of compromises, a minimum attempt to solve the crisis of the aged in the United States, which was far behind other industrial countries. Most of all, that legislation served its purpose of blunting the political thrust of the populist Townsend movement and militant senior activism. Seniors were demanding comprehensive health insurance among other things, but compromisers insisted that this would come later. How much later was not dreamed of.

TIMES ARE CHANGING

Rugged individualism was presumed to be an American tenet of faith. Every *man* should be able to take care of *his* family. The success of the system has rested upon the contributory insurance premise that

---

*Testimony given to members of the House Select Committee on Aging, September 11, 1975. Reprinted from *Industrial Gerontology*, 2(4):266-279, Fall 1975. ©The National Council on the Aging, Inc., Washington, D.C.

247

a *man* earns *his* pension himself, we are told. Even after numerous changes, i.e., the 1939 amendments which added dependents' allowances and the concept of society's responsibility to even things out on the basis of need, the insurance language and mythology remains. The Social Security Administration (SSA) has always insisted that, without it, the American people would never accept a pension system.

Now how about women? When the system was introduced we were supposed to be homemakers, with our earnings of very secondary importance to the family income. But we've come a long way since 1935, both in terms of the economy and our own heads. Forty-three percent of women 16 to 64 work; 38 percent of the work force is female (1970 figures). Nine out of 10 women will work at some time in their lives.

Nowadays, it would be more precise to say, "Woman, breadwinner-homemaker." Women still do the lion's share of raising children and keeping house, as well as voluntary community service, but they're also putting in their time in the marketplace.

The American family, too, is changing, as has been widely noted by sociologists and the media. The divorce rate was doubled just between 1960 and 1973. A fourth of the divorces filed are after more than 15 years of marriage. The national trend in divorce legislation is toward no-fault dissolution and, without fault, spousal support becomes limited or just fades away. It is *expected* that both parties will be self-supporting. Of heads of household, 15 million or 22 percent were women in 1972. That's a 46 percent increase in one decade. The older we become, of course, the more likely we are to be alone. Only 66.5 percent of women 55-64 are still living with husbands, which leaves a third of us on our own.

Nor can we omit the impact of the women's liberation movement upon the changing scene. Self-sufficiency is a canon, based upon sad experience with dependency. The struggle to break through traditional job barriers is fueled by poverty, low pay and dull work in occupations formerly and, to a large extent, still relegated to women.

Discrimination Against Men?

Is the Social Security system equal for men and women? Ask any liberal lawyer whether there is sex discrimination in the Social Security law, and you will be told, yes, it discriminates against men, because women are assumed to be dependents and receive benefits automatically, which are difficult for men to obtain.

This was the essence of the recent Weisenfeld case,[1] in which the Supreme Court last March struck down a gender-based distinction on survivor benefits. Widowers now can receive benefits on the same basis as widows. The American Civil Liberties Union, which fought the case as part of its "women's rights program," argued that benefits to widowers, without having to prove dependency, give the same value to *her* work as his. Benefits to a woman after she is dead, of course, are meager compensation. However, egalitarian lawyers, mostly men, are quick to see inequities when it is a question of extending some protection provided for women to males but less sharp in observing the fundamental inequalities which remain. In fact, to see the Social Security system as discriminatory toward men is to view the law, as Anatole France described it, in its majestic impartiality that prohibits the rich and poor alike from sleeping under bridges.

Nevertheless, the Weisenfeld decision was a very significant one. Justice Brennan's opinion spoke of "archaic" generalizations not tolerated under the Constitution, which assume a man supports the family and women's earnings are not vital to its support. That decision practically mandated Congress to take a new look at Social Security law. Since Congress is still overwhelmingly male, it behooves women to get some input in there while we can. With this in mind, here is a feminist viewpoint.

A FEMINIST CRITIQUE OF SOCIAL SECURITY

Since the purpose of Social Security, interpreted broadly, is to provide security in old age or disablement, how well does it serve women? Like any program, it must be judged by its results. Or in equal opportunity parlance, what is the impact of this, our key retirement plan, on the economic welfare of a *majority* of our citizens? I emphasize majority, because women comprise 59 percent of persons over 65 and almost two-thirds of those over 75. So we're talking about most of us.

According to Martha Griffiths (former Democratic representative from Michigan), "Fourteen percent of aged women, compared to one percent of aged men, have no income. Among persons age 65 or over who have income, the median annual income of men is over $3,750 (little enough) while that of women is $1,900. Forty-two percent of women, versus 19 percent of men, received less than $120 a month in

---

[1] See Schuchat. "Report of the Sixth Advisory Council on Social Security," *Industrial Gerontology*, 2(2):167-171, Spring 1975.

Social Security in 1972."

Benefit levels are much higher for retired male workers than female. Men are more than three times as likely as women to be entitled to the minimum. Of the 4.3 million, or 22 percent of the elderly who live in poverty, over two-thirds are women, mostly widows. Even these figures underestimate the true situation, because the statistics defining poverty are based on the needs of younger persons.

Why are we so poor? Let's analyze the reasons:

Sex Discrimination in Employment Begets Sex Discrimination in Retirement

The exclusion from "man-paying" jobs continues to haunt us into our old age. In 1971 the median annual earnings of women were $2,986, just 40 percent of the men's median earnings of $7,388, and it is on earnings that the benefit formula is based. Since women typically earn low wages, they also receive low benefits as retirees or disabled workers. So, after a lifetime of hard work at low-paying, often exploitive jobs, a woman retires at 65 to receive the minimum payment. "That's all there is — after I've worked all my life?" she asks.

Women are Punished for Motherhood

The long periods women are out of the job market for child rearing show up later in reduced benefits. If staying home and taking care of children is so important to the fabric of American society that we are denied child-care centers for that reason, wouldn't you think that we would be entitled to retirement benefits like other workers for doing that job? On the contrary, the *benefit formula* averages out earnings, so that every year out for child raising is counted as a zero, thus reducing the average earnings. Though the five lowest years are not included, given the child-care situation in this country and the presumed responsibility of women for young children, this method of computing benefits has a decidedly negative impact for mothers.

According to an SSA document (Mallan, 1974), if women had the same work lives as men (that is, if they didn't take time out for motherhood), only 11 percent, as opposed to 24 percent, would receive minimum benefits, and twice as many would receive the highest. Motherhood and apple pie may be sacred in America; neither provides security in later life.

As long as women have more years of zero earnings than men, even the total elimination of wage and job discrimination would leave benefits lower for women. In the same article, Mallan states: "The Social Security program lacks any provision to give credit for — or even to disregard — child-rearing years in computing women's benefits." So now you have two factors, each compounding the other — low earnings and time out for child rearing, or zero earning years. Here comes another.

If You Can't Support Yourself, You'll Have to Take Less for Life

This is better known as actuarial reduction. If you are entitled to benefits, not as a dependent but as a worker, you may elect to take them at 62 BUT the monthly payment will be reduced by actuarial tables to the equivalent on a lifetime basis of what you would receive if you waited until 65. In 1970, half the women workers and only a third of the men claimed benefits at age 62. Seventy percent of women did not hold out until they were 65.

Though some had other sources of income, the many who did not condemned themselves to an even smaller benefit than they were entitled to.

Why would they do that? For many there was no choice; older women, especially those without a job, have a terrible time finding one. In times like these, the only jobs available to them are really exploitive — physically and emotionally draining jobs of baby sitting, live-in domestic work, homemaker and chore services for the elderly — all at low pay scales — or part-time work, such as in department stores, which take advantage of older women to avoid paying fringe benefits.

Employment figures for women show a sharp drop when we reach our fifties, though you would expect them to rise because the children are grown. In 1972, the labor force participation rate for women aged 45-54 was 53.9 percent. At ages 55 to 64 it dropped to 42.1 percent. Yet these are crucial years for collecting those Social Security quarters. Since 1972, as we all know, jobs have not been easy to come by. What do you do when you find yourself unable to find a job that pays enough to live on, or one that you can physically cope with? In many cases, such women opt for early retirement.

There you have a one-two-three combined package — a circular pattern of discrimination with a compounding impact. When we work, we are either paid less or confined to lower paying jobs, which is the same thing. Our wages are low, so our benefits are low. Then we are out of the job market for child rearing, with those zero years averaged into our lifetime earnings.

Just before retirement time, we hit rampant job discrimination because employers, mostly men, prefer the women around them to be young, part of their own aging hang-ups. So we give up and take early retirement, thereby condemning ourselves to lifelong poverty. Yet, from a strictly legal point of view, all of this is perfectly equal.

Pay Twice — Collect Once

All wage earners pay into Social Security at the same rate, regardless of the family situation. But benefits go to individuals and their dependents. When more than one person works in the family, retirement income may be no greater than if only the presumed breadwinner paid into the system. The employed wife receives no benefit for *her* payroll tax contribution.

A recent article in *Family Circle* (Harris, 1975) played up the fact that the woman who works may not receive any more than the woman who stays home and doesn't "work." (Though why washing 689,000 socks and two million dishes and packing 9,000 lunches isn't considered work, I wouldn't know.) This facet of the law performs a D & C (as we say in the movement): Divide and conquer. It pits employed women against those who work at home. The NOW legislative office received over 100 letters from that one article, urging action to correct this inequity.

And the inequity is a real one. For example, a retired couple in which only the husband had worked, averaging $9,000 a year, would receive $531.80 a month — his benefit plus an additional 50 percent for his dependent wife. Another couple, averaging the same income of $9,000 (his $6,000, hers $3,000), would receive a smaller benefit; their monthly benefits would be only $444.50.

In more than a million cases, the elderly wife who has been employed receives more as her husband's dependent, getting nothing extra for her taxes. In the so-called dual entitlement classification, more than 99.9 percent are female. "I paid all those taxes, but don't get anything for it? I might as well have stayed home!"

No Credit For Labor in the Home

According to the California Commission on Women, a recent study estimates that more than 28 million nonsalaried wives and mothers perform about $340 billion worth of services each year, as housekeeper, decorator, cleaning woman, bookkeeper, cook, dietitian, nurse, gardener, chauffeur, shopper, seamstress and psychologist.

That list, of course, is far from complete. If a homemaker drew a paycheck, her annual earnings would be well over $12,000. If she weren't a wife, how many men could afford her? Yet her services, extolled to the skies annually on Mother's Day, don't even rate a Social Security card. The largest body of workers, still uncovered by what purports to be a universal retirement system, are homemakers.

But she is covered, says the SSA. That's why dependency benefits were added in 1939. Let's examine that.

Pitfalls of Homemaker Dependency

In the first place, a homemaker has no coverage for disability. So what happens if she has an accident? The home is a dangerous place, we are told by insurance companies. If someone has to be hired to replace her services, there is exactly the same impact on family income as though a wage earner lost a salary. And income replacement is the presumed function of disability insurance.

Further, if the concept of having earned one's retirement benefits is important to wage earners, it is equally important to homemakers. There is the question of independence. Curious, isn't it, that independence, so highly regarded for men, is not deemed necessary for us? Earned benefits versus handouts is the great strength of Social Security, we are told. But not for women working in the home.

There are other pitfalls. If benefits follow the breadwinner, what happens when a dependent homemaker is divorced, which is happening in epidemic proportions these days? We can now receive benefits if we were married 20 years. But if a homemaker is divorced by her husband after 19 years, she loses all rights to Social Security as his dependent, even though her labor at home made possible her husband's labor at work. One more year and she would have squeezed under the wire. If marriage as a partnership is recognized at 20 years, it could only be one-twentieth less so after 19 years.

I was married 23 years, but I happened to be older than my husband (it's not that rare, just hidden). I will not be eligible until *he* reaches 65, and suppose he elects to postpone retirement? I would have to wait still longer. And it is not just retirement income I lose. What about Medicare?

An absurd example of dependency pitfalls was recently reported in the newspapers. A 73-year-old widow, after 40 years of marriage, lost her benefits because her dead husband had not been properly divorced from his first wife. In 1974, there were 119 widows who lost benefits in this way. I recently received a letter from one such woman, who was desperate but couldn't even let her children know of her plight, because she didn't want them to suffer the disgrace of illegitimacy. The law, in its majestic impartiality, just doesn't take such things into account.

The Widow's Gap

When the youngest child reaches 18, the widow's benefits cease until she reaches 60, or is *totally* disabled. Yet the homemaker-widow at 50 faces severe job handicaps because of her age, sex and lack of "recent job experience." She is ineligible for Aid for Families with Dependent Children (AFDC) or medical benefits and, in some states, even general assistance. Her plight is exploited by those seeking cheap labor.

The Weisenfeld case touched on this question. According to that decision, the law was written on the premise that a mother should have a choice of staying at home while there were young children; once they are grown, it is presumed that savings or the grown children will support her.

The decision demands a new look at the realities of modern life. What savings? How many grown children support their mothers?

What do they do, these widows who fall in the gap? Some of them write to us. "I was 54 years old this past Christmas Day," says a woman widowed since 1971. "My husband earned the family income and I remained home to raise three sons and take care of my husband's parents and my mother. As of right now, I receive survivor's Social Security but next year my son turns 18. How do I eat and what if I get sick?"

Anyone who wonders why more people don't care for their aged relatives in their homes should ponder what happens to some of those who do.

The Displaced Homemaker . . . a New Category of Disadvantaged Persons

There are today 2.2 million women who have fulfilled a role lauded by society and now find themselves "displaced" in their middle years . . . widowed, divorced or separated. Too old to find jobs and too young for Social Security, they are victims of changing family roles, "liberalized" divorce laws and the fact that, when men remarry, they often choose younger brides. Unlike other workers, displaced homemakers have no cushions to soften their sudden loss of support — no unemployment insurance, no emergency job programs, no union benefits. Their situation harks back to the pre-thirties sink-or-swim conditions.

At what age do women become eligible for senior citizens' programs, Medicare and Social Security? Usually at that magic figure, 65, that Bismarck picked as the age *men* could retire from the work force. However, homemakers often face mandatory retirement much earlier, complete with the trauma of feeling useless and "over the hill." Suicides peak for women in the middle years, while they go up sharply for men after 65.

In other words, the displaced homemaker is a discarded segment of our population, outside all the social protection from sudden hardships won through collective effort — unemployment insurance, workers' compensation, even AFDC and Supplemental Security Income (SSI).

The Impact of Inflation is a Further Squeeze on Skimpy Dollars

Each inflationary year inflicts another cut in the real income of those already on the borderline of survival. A widow who outlives the breadwinner for many years experiences the cumulative effect of that inflation. Hard money paid in usually ends up as a minimum Social Security payment to the widow. For older widows, the new cost-of-living raises come too late.

Take the case of Elsie DeFratus of St. Petersburg, Florida, age 80. As rent and utilities went up along with the cost of transportation to pick up her $97 Social Security check, her food allowance went down to less than 65 cents a day. By the end of the month, it had run out. She told a friend, "I don't see anything but down." Her Social Security check arrived the same day she died.

Inflation hits all of us, but not equally. The poor are the ones who suffer, and old women are more often poor.

The Regressive Nature of the Payroll Tax Falls Heaviest on the Lowest Paid, Most of Whom are Women

This is part of the price we pay for limiting Social Security to payroll deductions. This tax has increased 800 percent during the last 20 years — more than 10 times the rise in the cost of living. Since December 1970, the maximum payroll tax has increased by 120 percent. Though masked by insurance terminology, this "contribution" is the biggest tax bite that most working women pay. Those earning salaries over $32,000 pay less than two percent of their income on Social Security taxes; those earning under $10,000 pay almost six percent.

Sexism Institutionalized

Now add up all these points, and what do you have? A classic syndrome of institutionalized sexism. Social Security, as it now stands, is highly discriminatory against women — not in an abstract, "equal under the law," sense but in the far more real test of how well it keeps the wolf from the door. There, it serves us very poorly.

The underlying culprit is what Justice Brennan termed an "archaic" presumption: Man the breadwinner, woman the homemaker-dependent. Benefits calculated on earnings rates, motherhood penalized by averaging earnings, no benefits for homemakers, dependents' benefits tied to the breadwinner, actuarial deductions, regressive tax rates — all these and more.

Just as Social Security helps to extend institutionalized racism for blacks into old age, thereby almost certainly mandating poverty for all but a small number, so, too, it reinforces the economic impact of sexism, punishing women for the roles society most approves.

In the long run, it condemns a very large number of us to abject poverty. In no time of life is the payoff of woman's traditional role more clearly revealed than in old age. No wonder we feminists are beginning to reach a whole new segment of the population who never before understood what the "woman-libbers" were talking about!

WHERE DO WE GO FROM HERE?
NEW PATCHES FOR GAPING HOLES

Having made this scathing attack on Social Security, I will now beat a hasty retreat. For heaven's sakes, let's not get rid of Social Security until we have something better! Because that's *all* we have. And most of those who are ready to chuck the whole works and substitute some type of cash payment based upon a strict means test are thinking of providing *less* money, not more. The Administration made that clear in January, proposing to cut down cost-of-living increases for persons on Social Security, to chop the poor off Food Stamp rolls and to add charges for Medicare.

Our Social Security blanket is a patchwork quilt, seemingly made under the influence of LSD: The squares are all out of kilter. If there was once a consistent design, so many new swatches have been added that now the pattern is lopsided. The whole thing is too small to keep us covered; it has lost its resiliency to stretch over our growing frame. If one inequity is patched, another is created. However, we have a hard winter coming up, so let's keep on mending until a new blanket is woven.

Suggested Changes

Here are some suggested patches (in shocking pink): On point one — the impact of low wages on retirement income — any legislation to increase the minimum payment would be of help, since the minimum is what so many of us receive. Since old women are at the bottom of the heap, major attention should be placed at raising the system from the bottom.

Punishment of women for motherhood, point two, could be lessened by providing credits for this socially important service to the nation. At the very least, child-rearing years — however many there are — could be excluded while averaging out benefit levels. This could, of course, apply to men as well as to women.

On point three, actuarial reductions, the problem is addressed in such proposed legislation as Rosenthal's (D., N.Y.) sweeping reform bill, HR 5149. Perhaps more specific measures might be introduced, such as elimination of the actuarial reduction for those who receive minimum benefits, those who have been out of the job market for a prescribed period or persons with partial disability. In other words, if you *can't* work, you must have a liveable income.

On the fourth point — pay twice, collect once — several bills have been introduced into the 94th Congress which would combine earnings of spouses.[2] HR 775 (Murphy, D., N.Y.) for example, would provide payment of benefits to married couples based on combined earnings records where higher, if both live in the same household. Payment would be computed by combining average monthly wages as if those were the wage of an individual and multiplying by 75 percent.

Abzug's (D., N.Y.) HR 4357 would also permit the payment of benefits to a married couple on its combined earnings record. (Other House bills on this subject are 156, 901, 1948, 2529, 4357 and 4501). Working women feel strongly on this issue; they undoubtedly will exert pressure for attention to this inequity.

---

[2]For a review of legislation in the 93rd Congress, see Jane Bloom, "Congress Seeks to Equalize Treatment of Women," *Industrial Gerontology*, *1(2)*, Spring 1974.

Credits for Home Labor

The fifth point, credits for labor in the home, was an idea pioneered by former representative Martha Griffiths, One piece of legislation in the current Congress is the Jordan (D., Tex.) and Burke (D., Calif.) bill, HR 3009, which provides benefits for homemakers based on a self-employment concept. Three options for computing the amount to be paid are offered. While such a law would serve to establish the principle of homemaking as labor like any other, it would offer protection only to a limited number of families who could afford to pay double taxes without double income.

A more far-reaching bill, called the Fraser Plan,[3] is scheduled for introduction soon. It views marriage as a partnership, with credits going to both partners on an optional basis, similar to a joint income tax return.

Numerous bills have been introduced to compensate for the pitfalls of homemaker dependency. The arbitrary 20-year rule for divorced women to qualify for wife's or widow's benefits would be reduced to five in an Abzug bill, HR 159. Another pitfall, that of seniors living together to prevent benefit losses, has been a favorite television topic this season, and a number of legislators have responded. Among projected bills which would provide that remarriage would not cut benefits are Hecker's (R., Mass.) HR 3006, Young's (R., Fla.) HR 5284 and Koch's (D., N.Y.) 580 (also 6305 and 5149).

Simultaneous benefits would be permitted under Holtzman's (D., N.Y.) HR 3242, providing the individuals may receive simultaneously old age or disability *and* widow's benefits. Solarz's (D., N.Y.) HR 5492 is similar, providing 100 percent of the larger and 50 percent of the smaller of the two. Mink (D., Hawaii) seeks benefits for the women whose marriages are found invalid. Her bill, HR 4918, would make such women eligible.

The widow's gap is tackled in HR 5149, which would (among other things) provide for payment of widow's or widower's benefits at age 50 regardless of disability and without actuarial reduction. Quillen's (R., Tenn.) HR 1983 is limited to this one issue. Perkins' (D., Ky.) HR 818, specifying "woman" and reducing the age to 45 for a widow's benefit, is probably not constitutional in view of the Weisenfeld case. (Other bills on this subject are 63105 and 5149.)

---

[3]This legislation, "Equity in Social Security for Individuals and Families," will be introduced by Donald Fraser (D., Minn.) by the end of 1975.

The Displaced Homemakers

For those who don't currently fit within the Social Security system — the displaced homemakers — we have been working for special legislation, spearheaded by the Alliance for Displaced Homemakers and the NOW Task Force on Older Women. Yvonne Burke's (D., Calif.) HR 10272 tackles that problem, and a Senate version has been introduced.[4] These bills would provide multipurpose service programs and training to help such persons move from dependency to self-sufficiency, laying the basis for bringing displaced homemakers under unemployment compensation programs.

To insure that such programs would not be ill-prepared, a California bill would set up a demonstration center in the state, involving displaced homemakers in its preparations. A key facet of the California program would be job creation, based on the principle that a homemaker's job skills and life experiences can be recycled into socially useful jobs which she can help develop.

The movement is spreading into other states. The remarkable response to "displaced homemaker" legislation, both on the state and national levels, indicates that we have struck a nerve. The California bill received broad bipartisan support, and final passage is expected momentarily.[5] From one TV appearance alone, hundreds of letters poured in. The common theme: "At last, something for us . . . a candle of hope!"

THE NEW SECURITY BLANKET

As we patch up the old Social Security system, we should all be hard at work devising something better; the issue of income maintenance, particularly in old age, needs a whole new look.

We could start by questioning some very basic assumptions. Is the insurance principle outdated? Rugged individualism does not take into account social forces outside the control of the individual, like changes in the value of money, changing family structure or automation, the latter of which pushes the unskilled and semiskilled out of the labor market. Also, rugged individualism has meaning only to a

---

[4]S2541 was introduced by Senator Tunney (D., Calif.) on October 21, with 13 cosponsors.
[5]This legislation (SB 825), cleared the two houses of the California legislature by a nearly unanimous vote. Governor Brown signed the bill on September 25, 1975.

minority of citizens: White males. The rest of us can't afford that luxury. We need to survive when we grow old, and we are barely making it.

While social change has been moving at a gallop, social policy has followed at a crawl. Forty years after the introduction of Social Security is high time to review that "archaic assumption" that man is the breadwinner, and woman is the homemaker.

Retirement and Age

Let's look again at the concept of retirement. Should it necessarily be age related? Over the years, an idea that started as "can retire" has become "must retire," so that even the Age Discrimination in Employment Act (ADEA) covers only those between 40 and 64. At 65, we suddenly lose our right to work. Retirement must be redefined as a *choice*, with alternative work opportunities provided for those ready for a change of life style.

Why not new versions of Vista and the Peace Corps, as well as the types of alternative service now open to military personnel? Many older persons, including displaced homemakers, would like the opportunity for socially useful service if it provided income maintenance. Why not the "senior status" of U.S. judges over 70 for *all*, permitting continuation of work on a reduced basis?

Volunteerism should be neither age- nor sex-related. We should *all* be encouraged to pitch in to improve the quality of life and to bring about needed changes. Instead of volunteer work only as something to do when you can't get a job or are forced to retire, better that those who need to work get paid for what they are doing as volunteers.

Creating New Jobs

Which brings us back to job creation. The bold pattern of our new blanket should make the development of new ways to work a central theme. In the Alliance for Displaced Homemakers, we have been brainstorming new jobs, all of which fit into national projections but which won't be accessible to us unless we work for them politically. We welcome such legislation as HR 50, Hawkins' (D., Calif.) Equal Opportunity and Full Employment Act, and will try to ensure that it includes the job needs of women of all ages. The best way to cut down on the number of persons on any pension system is to provide adequate, varied employment opportunities.

Finally, as the Social Security blanket of the future is woven, here are a few principles for all legislators to keep in mind:

- Each person needs security in his/her own right. Enough of dependency pitfalls!
- Our generation is not expendable in the march forward toward equality and better things. When devising remedies, the impact on us must be considered as well as on those coming along behind.
- Social Security, income maintenance, health and welfare services, job opportunity and retraining are all interrelated issues and must be tackled in a coordinated way.
- Fourth, though service programs are nice, adequate income to provide for ourselves is far better and, in the long run, far less expensive to the community or the nation. A minimum goal should be to bring everyone up at least to the poverty line.

Like the original Social Security Act, these goals must be fought for. They will not come to us merely because they are just or because there are righteous lawmakers.

Prognosticator Jeanne Dixon foresees the streets filled again as in the sixties, this time not with young people but with elders. If she's right, and I hope she is, older women will be in the front ranks. With our Post Menopausal Zest (or PMZ, as Margaret Mead calls it), we will become a force to be reckoned with.

Once our own self-concept becomes strong and positive and we move into action, we can confront ageism with the same vigor that young women attack sexism, giving us extraordinary new energy — energy that will turn traditional ballot box support into potent political clout.

REFERENCES

Harris, Janet. "How Social Security Cheats Working Women," FAMILY CIRCLE, July 1975.
Mallan, Lucy B. "Women Born in the Early 1900's: Employment, Earnings, and Benefit Levels," SOCIAL SECURITY BULLETIN, March 1974, pp. 1-25.

Chapter 27

RELIGION AND THE OLDER WOMAN*

LETITIA T. ALSTON AND JON P. ALSTON

INTRODUCTION

Religious Behavior and the Life Cycle

THIS paper is concerned with the question of whether or not life-cycle stages influence religious behavior. We focus on selected status and age variables that may be associated with frequency of church attendance among women over fifty.

From the point of view of the individual, religion is one of the more enduring institutions. There are Sunday schools for children, youth groups for teenagers and adolescents, and numerous church-related events and services for adults, most of which are age and life-cycle related. In addition to Sunday services, many churches offer programs for single adults, young marrieds, parents of pre-schoolers, and older couples. These church programs are oriented in terms of specific age groups, reflecting the general societal belief that age-group differences exist and that the church should be both willing and able to cater to the age-specific needs of persons in all stages of their life cycles.

It is also assumed that people continue to have religious interests throughout their lives, although the relationship between age and religious activity is the subject of continuing controversy, both in social gerontology and in the sociology of religion. Unfortunately, there is as yet little consensus on the specific nature of the relationships among age, life-cycle changes, and religious feeling and behavior. Do women, for example, increase their religious activities after children are born and then reduce their activities when children

[1] A preliminary edition of this study was delivered during the annual meeting of the Southwestern Sociological Association, Houston, Texas, 1978. We wish to thank the Department of Political Science, Texas A&M University, and the Inter-University Consortium for Political and Social Research for making the data used in this paper available to us. The Mini-Grant Program and the College of Liberal Arts at Texas A&M University provided computer support. The authors bear all responsibility for the analyses presented here.

262

are no longer living at home? On the other hand, it is also possible that women increase their religious activities in later age stages as a replacement for child-rearing activities. In addition, there is little information on whether or not women decrease their religious activities when they are both married and working full-time.

Such questions acknowledge that a person has more than one age-specific social status at a time. Although life-cycle stages are usually age-related (e.g. being over sixty-five years old is usually associated with retirement), age and life cycle are not always in complete synchronization. A woman aged fifty-five may be single or married, may have children or not, and may work or not.

We noted earlier that there is little agreement as to the exact relationship between age and religious behavior. A cohort analysis of survey data on church attendance during the period 1939-1969 (Wingrove and Alston, 1974) indicated that, while different age groups in America did exhibit variations in the extent of church attendance, there were also consistent variations by birth cohorts. All cohorts decreased their attendance levels after 1965; the cohort born 1894-1904 showed consistently higher church attendance levels than younger cohorts.

In other words, in addition to the aging process itself, specific cohort membership and general societal environment are important factors in accounting for age differences. Historical events, or generational changes, can produce attitudinal and behavioral differences in specific age strate that may complement or even contradict the effects of aging (Riley, 1973; Mannheim, 1968).

For example, while most people who are now over the age of 50 must deal with the idea of retirement as did older persons a generation ago, the earlier preretirement cohort differed from the current one in terms of health, mother tongue, educational levels, and general life expectations. In addition, the person retiring today faces a different economic climate, involving in part more extensive pension plans and a society geared more to leisure than in the past. As a consequence, today's retiree appears to be more willing to retire than yesterday's.

Life course changes also have different effects on individual behavior depending upon the specific social characteristics of the persons involved, such as income and social class levels, sex, education, and regional identification. For example, Lopata (1973) found that the impact of widowhood on women differed according to educational level. The more highly educated the woman, the more she was likely to experience a short period of disorganization at her husband's death. Nevertheless, because of her greater access to social and economic resources, the more highly educated woman was able to adjust more satisfactorily to this life-course change.

Gender and Church Attendance

While contradictory evidence exists on the relationship between age and religious participation, very consistent evidence exists regarding the relationship between gender and religious participation: women display higher levels of church attendance than men at all ages (see O'Reilly, 1957; Webber, 1954; Lazerwitz, 1961; Lenski, 1961; Fichter, 1952; Bultena, 1949; Blazer and Palmore, 1976; Glock et al., 1967; Orbach, 1961; Moberg, 1965; Moberg and Gray, 1977; Harris, 1974; Duncan and Duncan, 1978:144-45) regardless of religious affiliation or country (Alston, 1972). There is also evidence that women are more likely than men to express traditional religious beliefs (e.g. Keeley, 1976; Fagan and Breed, 1970; Campbell and Fukuyama, 1970) as well as more likely to maintain that religion is an important element in their lives (cf. Glock et al., 1967).

A review of some of the explanations for these consistent sex differences in religious attitudes and behavior indicates the existence of two general categories of explanation. One category focuses on the assumed psychological differences between men and women. For example, the greater emphasis on submissiveness and expressiveness in female socialization means that the emotional and authoritarian aspects of religion are more likely to appeal to women than to men (Garai and Scheinfeld, 1968).

The second category of explanation hinges on the subordinate or secondary position that women hold in society relative to men. This deprivation-compensation model suggests that religion functions, in part, as compensation for frustration. Glock et al. (1967), analyzing a sample of Episcopalian parishioners, found that the elderly and women (particularly women with incomplete families or with lower educational levels and no other important organizational memberships) were the most active members. Their interpretation of these findings was that the church offers alternative rewards to those deprived of status gratification in the secular world (Glock et al., 1967:205).

Campbell and Fukuyama (1970), utilizing a large sample of Church of Christ members, found that socially deprived groups such as women, older people, and the poor were more likely to express traditional beliefs, although religious participation was more strongly related to privilege. Complementary to these findings is Luckman's report that European working women — presumably more like men in their status opportunities and life styles than nonworking women — are found to be less religious than nonworking women (1967:30).

Perhaps because of the consistency of the findings on religious behavior among women, few researchers have chosen to focus exclusively on the patterns of religious behavior among women. Older women have constituted a particularly neglected group in research dealing with life course changes, and even in Lopata's (1973) now classic study of widowhood, religion played a relatively minor role in the analysis. Given the general lack of research on the topic we intend to look at the church attendance patterns of women at various stages in the life cycle and to compare them with attendance patterns for men at similar stages. Our emphasis will be on the older woman.

Data

The data presented below are derived from six national annual surveys of the American population during the years 1972 through 1977 and conducted during March of each year in order to avoid seasonal variations. They form part of the General Social Survey National Data Program for the Social Sciences, conducted by the National Opinion Research Center. These surveys are based upon sampling techniques that result in data that are representative of the American, noninstitutionalized, adult population.[2] Each annual survey contained a number of similar questions, and when the six surveys are combined, the data set contains over eight thousand respondents, 700 of whom are females over sixty-five years of age (see Table 27-I).

The question of age versus generational effect is an important one. Unfortunately, the data presented below do not allow us to address it directly. Our data are cross-sectional in nature, dealing, in other words, with different age groupings at a single point in time. Ideal data would be longitudinal data, derived from the same persons studied repeatedly over a period of time. The differences we discuss may be the product of (1) the aging process and changes across individual life courses, (2) the different historical experiences of the different birth cohorts represented here, or (3) a combination of both.[3]

---

[2]See Davis et al. (1977). These surveys were sponsored by the National Science Foundation project GS 31082X, conducted by the National Opinion Research Center and distributed by the Roper Public Opinion Research Center.
[3]See Maddox, 1976;21-30 for a summary of the age, period and cohort problem.

FINDINGS

Church Attendance

The first variable we consider is church attendance. We define church attendance patterns in terms of four frequency categories: less than once a year (low), several times a year (yearly), once to three times a month (monthly), and nearly once a week or more (weekly).

Frequency of attendance is one of the more sensitive measures of the behavioral dimension of religiosity. Most religious groups define church service attendance as a religious duty; for most Americans, being religious is partly reflected by faithful church attendance. Attendance shows, if not one's religious feelings, at least one's loyalty to the religious institution. In fact, people who "feel" their religion also are generally those who take part in religious activities and services. While attendance and commitment are not completely comparable, we will assume that attending church services frequently is evidence of one type of religious commitment.

It can be seen in Table 27-I that women are more frequent church-goers than are men.[4] This male-female difference is a constant found in all surveys of church behavior, whether the respondents are French (Alston, 1973b and 1975), British, or American (Argyle and Beit-Hallahmi, 1975:72; Alston, 1972). Table 27-I also indicates a high level of religious activity among older females. Among females sixty-five years old and over, half attend church services more than three times a month. This is certainly an indication of high levels of religious activity among females. Moreover, age is an influential variable for both sexes: in this sample, both older males and older females attend religious services more frequently than those who are younger.

A plateau seems to be achieved at age 50; while there is a slight increase in church attendance frequency between the 50-64 and the 65+ age categories, the difference is not statistically significant. Thus, the current population of older persons does attend church at significantly higher levels than the younger segments of the population, and

---

[4]Whenever appropriate, we based our data interpretations on two statistical tests, chi square and gamma. Our sub-samples are large enough so that, generally, differences of eight-to-ten and over percentage points are statistically significant at the .05 level and beyond. The gamma statistic is presented to indicate the strength of the relationship between the independent variable and church attendance. All gamma values are computed using the four church attendance categories presented in Table 27-I.

Table 27-I

CHURCH ATTENDANCE PATTERNS BY AGE AND SEX[1]
(In Percentages)

Age	Sex[2]	*Frequency of Church Attendance*				Total N (%=100)
		Low	Yearly	Monthly	Weekly	
20-29	Female	24%	29	18	29	1108
	Male	28%	36	16	20	994
30-49	Female	17%	25	17	41	1751
	Male	23%	32	14	31	1439
50-64	Female	14%	22	15	49	1118
	Male	21%	28	15	36	970
65 +	Female	17%	18	13	52	780
	Male	25%	23	14	38	674
Total	Female	18%	24	16	42	4757
Total	Males	24%	30	15	31	4077

[1]The question was: "How often do you attend religious services?"
[2]Statistical association between age and frequency of church attendance, as measured by Gamma: Females = .18; Males = .13. The differences in church attendance between the sexes for each age group is statistically significant (Chi Square) at the .05 level and beyond. The total male-female difference in church attendance is statistically significant (P = .001 ; Gamma: .19).

this tendency is especially pronounced for women.

Marital Status

One variable that might logically influence church attendance is marital status. Marriage is an important event in the life cycle, as is the loss of a spouse. Marriage increases the number of social roles a woman occupies, among which are the roles of wife, daughter-in-law, mother, and housekeeper. Loss of a spouse, on the other hand, means the loss of at least one role and often a decrease in income, making the continuation of some activities financially difficult. Since many church-related activities are couple and/or family oriented, one expects marital status to have some effect on church attendance patterns, especially among older women who no longer have children at home and for whom "not married" most often means being widowed.

Table 27-II indicates that marriage is associated with higher church attendance levels for both women and men.[5] It is not at the older ages that marriage is most influential, however. It is for those persons aged thirty to forty-four that marriage appears to have the greatest impact on church attendance. This is the age during which people are most likely to have school-age children. A more detailed analysis not reported here indicated that marital status differences in attendance in this age group were largely the product of the "divorced" category. While there is little difference in the church attendance patterns of widowed and married persons — especially women — the divorced are far less likely to be frequent attenders.

Several interpretations are possible. It is possible that frequent church attenders are less likely to believe in divorce. Attendance is therefore less affected by marital status than marital status is protected by the beliefs reflected in high attendance. It is also possible that the established religions, with their emphasis on stable family life and on family-centered activities, offer less emotional or social support to the divorced woman (Moberg and Gray, 1977).

For older women, the "not married" category is dominated by widows. The data indicate that, for these women, absence of a spouse is not associated with lower attendance levels, suggesting that these women neither disengage from religious participation when they no longer have a partner nor increase their participation to compensate for this loss.

Marital status appears to have a greater impact on men than on women. For persons over 30, there are greater differences between married and unmarried men than between married and unmarried women. The divorced men, who make up the majority of unmarried men in the thirty to forty-four age category, are even less likely to be frequent church attenders than are divorced women in the same age category. In addition, loss of a spouse seems to mean lower levels of church attendance for men than would be predicted from

---

[5]Table 27-II presents only the proportion of those attending religious services three times a week or more. Presentation of the distributions of all four attendance categories would take too much space when we control for more than age and sex in terms of the attendance variable. However, the two statistics presented were computed on the basis of all attendance categories.

Table 27-II

PROPORTION OF WOMEN WHO ATTEND CHURCH FREQUENTLY[1]
BY AGE, MARITAL STATUS, WORK STATUS, AND HEALTH

Age	Sex	Marital Status		Work Status		Health	
		Married	Not Married[2]	Working	Not Working[3]	Excellent or Good	Fair or Poor
20-29	Female	32	26	28	30	31	23
	Male	22	18	20	21	20	16*
30-49	Female	44	31	42	41	43	34
	Male	33	18	31	33*	33	20*
50-64	Female	49	50	54	46	53	44
	Male	37	29	36	36	36	34
65 +	Female	57	50	57*	52	56	49
	Male	41	30	44	37	41	35
Total	Female	46%	39	45	42	46	38
Total	Male	33%	24	33	32	32	26

*N less than 100
[1]Defined as attendance three times a month or more.
[2]Includes the widowed, divorced, separated, and those who have never married.
[3]Includes both the retired and the never worked.

age alone (Table 27-I).[6]

Work Status

It is possible that frequency of attendance is influenced by a woman's work status. First, married women have traditionally been expected to be housewives first and income producers second. That is, a woman's first duty, if financially possible, has been to her family rather than to an occupational career. This suggests the possibility that working women who are also married may be less traditional than married, nonworking women and that this non-traditional attitude may be expressed in lower interest in religious activities as well.

Secondly, time limitations must be considered. If a woman works, she has less time to devote to other roles, including her religious ones. If time is limited, then a married working woman might be faced with the necessity of giving up extra-familial roles in order to be a "good" housewife/mother. Thus, a married woman who also works may be less likely to attend religious services either because she has too little time or because she is less traditional (i.e. family oriented) than a woman whose major statuses are wife and mother.

A generalization from the findings of Glock et al. (1967) leads us to the same conclusion. Working women presumably enjoy more of the economic and status rewards that society deem important than those received by nonworking women. If church activity functions as an alternative source of rewards for the relatively deprived, working women should show lower attendance levels than nonworking women.

In order to achieve subsamples of sufficient size for reliable analysis, work status was dichotomized into working and nonworking. The latter includes those respondents who have worked but are now retired as well as those who have never worked.

Table 27-II indicates that, in general, there is little association between work status and frequency of church attendance when age is

---

[6]The importance of marital status at the active child-rearing stage of the life cycle (30-44) prompted us to investigate the influence of the presence of children on church attendance. For most couples, marriage also means children, and it has been argued that church attendance is heavily influenced by the presence or absence of children. It is assumed that parents feel responsible for the religious and moral education of their children, and as they involve their children in church programs they usually become more religiously active themselves. Preliminary analysis indicated that among women of all ages the presence of children did not significantly alter attendance patterns. Inasmuch as very few older persons reported living with children, these data are not presented.

introduced as a control. Work status is significantly related to attendance only for women aged fifty to sixty-four. Those who are working are *more* likely to be weekly attenders than those who are retired or keeping house. Thus, working does not force a woman to give up this role outside the home. If anything, work increases attendance, at least for those women fifty to sixty-four years of age.

Perceptions of Health

Health can, obviously, be an important influence on church attendance under a number of conditions. Incidences of chronic illness increase with age, and physical mobility can decrease significantly at advanced ages. There are older persons who may want to attend church services but cannot do so because of illness or disability.

In an analysis not shown here, work status and perception of health were controlled simultaneously. Although the subsamples tended to be too small for consistently reliable analysis for all cells, the data indicated that much of the difference in attendance patterns for working and nonworking women aged fifty to sixty-four disappeared when contols were introduced for perception of health. When women perceived their health as excellent or good, working and non-working women attended church in similar proportions. It was only among women who perceived their health as poor that work status influenced church attendance. For these women, not working was associated with lower attendance levels.

If attendance is defined as one measure of religiosity, then the increasing availability of work outside the home for married women should not be blamed for increasing secularization or the decline in religious interest. Working women are as likely or more likely to attend church services frequently than are women who are not employed.

Our measure of health status is a subjective one and measures morale in part. Survey respondents were asked to evaluate their health. Thus our measure relates to perceptions of health rather than to an objective definition of physical conditions. There is some correspondence between subjective perception of health and actual health status, although the extent of correspondence is being debated. Regardless of whether or not a person's physical state is good, a person may "feel" physically bad if he or she is despondent because of other problems, whether economic, dietary, social, or familial.

Age and perception of good health are of course strongly related.

Using the four younger-to-older age categories, the proportions of the female respondents who said their health was "excellent" or "good" were 84, 77 and 47 percent, respectively. For males, the corresponding percentages were 89, 83, 65, and 54. The other answer category denoted a negative ("fair" and "poor") perceptions of one's health. The gamma values of these distributions for females and males were .44 and .49, respectively.

We find in Table 27-II that a positive perception of health is associated with church attendance. Women who feel that their health is excellent or good are statistically more likely to be active church goers regardless of age. Among males, on the other hand, health is a significant variable only for those sixty-five and over. For both sexes, however, age is the more important variable.

STRENGTH OF RELIGIOUS IDENTITY

Church attendance is only one measure of religiosity. Another indicator of religious feeling is the strength of identification with one's religion. Respondents in our surveys were asked their religious preference (Catholic, Protestant, Jewish, etc.); those who state a religious

Table 27-III

RELIGIOUS INTENSITY BY AGE AND SEX[1]
(IN PERCENTAGES)

Age	Strong Religious Intensity		Low Religious Intensity		Total N (% = 100)	
	Female	Male	Female	Male	Female	Male
20-29	32%	27%	68	73	663	526
30-49	43%	35%	57	65	1092	814
50-64	53%	34%	47	66	713	574
65 +	65%	45%	35	55	527	424
Total	47%	35%	53	65	2995	2338

Gamma values measuring the strength of the association between age and religious identification: Females: −33; Males: −17.

[1]The question was: "Would you call yourself a strong (Protestant, Catholic, or Jew) or a not very strong (religious preference)?" The answer categories were: strong, not very strong, and somewhat strong. We collapsed these categories into the dichotomy of strong vs. the second and third answers.

preference were then asked to rate the strength of their religious preference or identity. As Table 27-III indicates, 47 percent of females and 35 percent of males said the strength of their religious preference was "strong."

Table 27-III indicates that there is an overall male-female difference in religious identification, and this difference is greatest among those fifty years old and over. Among those in their twenties, males and females are almost equal in the proportions saying their religious identity is "strong," and the small difference is not statistically significant. Thus, females in America are not "naturally" more religious than males, since sizable sex differences are found only among those thirty years old and over, and these differences occur most strongly between males and females fifty to sixty-four years old. The increase in religious identification with age is, in fact twice as strong for females as for males, based on the gamma values for the respective distributions.

Unfortunately, we cannot be certain that women and men become more religious as they age, although Table 27-III suggests this. It may well be that those who are over sixty-five years old now also strongly identified with their religion when young, although there have been only slight changes among the American population in recent years in terms of their perceived levels of religious intensity. During 1965, almost half (47%) of Americans said their religious faith was "very strong"; the corresponding figure for the mid-seventies was 42 percent (Alston, 1973b).

Research done on political behavior suggests yet another possibility. Duration of membership seems to increase feelings of identification. When Campbell et al. (1960) controlled for length of party membership, they found that those persons with longer membership histories saw their attachment to the party as stronger, whatever their ages. With respect to religion, age may have an indirect effect on identification in that older age groups have had the opportunity to acquire a longer membership and activity history. Since, as we have seen, females are more likely to be frequent church attenders than males throughout the life cycle, older women might be more likely to develop stronger feelings of identification with their religion because of their prolonged association with this institution.

Table 27-IV indicates the relationship between perceived strength of one's religious preference and frequency of church attendance. As would be expected, these data indicate that there exists a strong relationship between the two variables for all age groups. For both sexes, roughly two-thirds of those characterized by strong religious identification attend church services frequently regardless of age. Age, in itself, has little effect upon attendance at religious services when religious identification is strong. Sex differences are also reduced when religious identification is held constant. That is, males who state that their religious identification is strong are as likely to be frequent church attenders as females.

Table 27-IV

PROPORTION OF AMERICANS WHO ATTEND CHURCH
THREE TIMES A MONTH OR MORE BY AGE, SEX,
AND RELIGIOUS INTENSITY

	Religious Intensity			
	Strong		Not Strong	
Age	Females	Males	Females	Males
20-29	71	61	13	8
30-49	68	70	18	16
50-64	73	74	24	15
65 +	67	65	29	19
Total	70%	68	19	14

Among persons less intensely identified with religion, age is more closely associated with higher levels of church attendance. In fact, those over sixty-five who perceive themselves as less religious are twice as likely to attend church services frequently than those in their twenties, even though their attendance levels fall far below those of the strongly identified. This suggests that duration of membership may not be the only factor at work and that, contrary to such authors as Boyd and Oakes (1969:226-7), the church does fulfill some social and/or psychological function for older people, especially for older women — even among those not strongly identified with their religion.

SUMMARY AND CONCLUSIONS

Our data indicate that today's older woman is far more likely to be a frequent church attender than her male counterpart or today's younger woman. Furthermore, the effects of variables such as marital status, presence or absence of children, and work status on the attendance patterns of women are less than might be expected. Age is a more important variable for predicting the church attendance levels of women today than their involvement in other roles.[7]

The data also indicate that the age of thirty is a significant watershed. At this point, the proportion of women who are frequent attenders shows a greater inter-stratum increase than is shown at any other age interval. The women in the twenty to twenty-nine cohort were born after World War Two — a period of great change for women — and reached maturity in a social setting that increasingly offered the work role as a legitimate one for women. In addition to changes in acceptable role careers for women, younger women have faced a different pacing of life-cycle roles. As Glick (1955, 1977) has pointed out, median ages at various stages of the family life-cycle have been gradually decreasing. For example there was a two-year interval between marriage of the last child and death of spouse for women born in 1890. For women born in 1950, this interval is expected to be on the order of 14 years. Theoretically, this has freed younger women to take advantage of the widening scope of acceptable roles. For young women today, there is also a greater probability of becoming a female head of house or a working mother than was the case for their mothers, and certainly for their grandmothers.

Thus, younger and older segments of the female population confront different timing sequences in life-cycle patterns and, at least theoretically, different role definitions of femaleness as a result of social and economic changes since 1940. While it is logical that these changes might have some impact on church attendance, the data indicate that the attendance patterns of younger women are no more affected by their participation in work than they are for older women. These younger women may simply be reflecting the increasing secularization of society in general. Stark (1968) and others have also pinpointed World War Two as a watershed in the secularization of religious beliefs, and if Meddin (1975), Strommen (1972), Riley (1973), and others are correct, it is the younger groups who change first and most rapidly. Some of the age differences in our data no doubt reflect these generational differences.

---

[7] A four-way analysis of variance using sex, age, presence/absence of children, and work status was computed using the SPSS ANOVA technique with the regression option. For the main effects, only work status had an F-value that was not statistically significant. When religious intensity is introduced into an ANOVA model, it becomes the most significant variable. This suggests that the importance of age as a predictor of church attendance is mediated by the effect of the respondents' level of strength of religious feeling, which in turn is positively associated with being female and being older.

We feel that the data also indicate that the changes inherent in the aging process may have important effects on religious participation. The very regularity of the attendance differences at the older ages suggests age-strata rather than generational differences. The argument for the importance of aging is supported by the events of the 1950s and 1960s. All age cohorts participated in the religious "revival" of the 1950s by increasing their attendance frequencies, and all decreased their attendance levels after 1960 (Wingrove and Alston, 1974); even so, the different age cohorts maintained their relative positions on attendance.

A progressive change with age is also suggested by the data on religious identification. Table 27-III indicated that women are more likely to express a strong religious identification than men and that older women are most likely to express a strong identification. The findings on political party membership already cited suggest that there may, indeed, be a strengthening of religious ties.as one ages, encouraged by the duration of the membership.

Our data also indicate that women are more religiously active than men at all ages and that the more frequent attendance of women is highly correlated with their greater identification with their religious affiliation. Similarly, the usual sex differences in church attendance are greatly reduced when men also express a strong religious identification.

REFERENCES

Alston, Jon P.

1972 "Social Variables Associated with Church Attendance, 1965 and 1969: Evidence from National Polls." Journal for the Scientific Study of Religion 10 (Fall):233-6.

1973a "Comparison of French and American Church Attendance Patterns." Journal for the Scientific Study of Religion 12 (September):453-5.

1973b "Perceived Strength of Religious Beliefs." Journal of the Scientific Study of Religion 12 (March):109-11.

1975 "A Cross Cultural Comparison of Church Attendance Patterns in the United States and France." International Journal of Comparative Sociology 16 (Sept.-Dec.):268-80.

Argyle, Michael and Benjamin Beit-Hallahmi.

1975 The Social Psychology of Religion. London: Routledge and Kegan Paul.

Bahr, Howard M.

1970 "Aging and Religious Disaffiliation." Social Forces 49 (September):60-71.

Blau, Zena.

1973 Old Age in a Changing Society. New York: New Viewpoints.

Blazer, Dan and Erdman Palmore.
1976 "Religion and Aging in a Longitudinal Panel." The Gerontologist 16, part 1 (February):82-5.

Boyd, Rosamonde R. and Charles G. Oakes (eds.).
1969 Foundations of Practical Gerontology. Columbia, S.C.: The University of South Carolina Press.

Campbell, Angus, Philip E. Converse, Warren E. Miller, and Donald E. Stokes.
1960 The American Voter. New York: John Wiley and Sons.

Campbell, Thomas C. and Yoshio Fukuyama.
1970 The Fragmented Layman: An Empirical Study of Lay Attitudes. Philadelphia, Boston: Pilgrim Press.

Crittenden, John.
1962 "Aging and Party Affiliation." Public Opinion Quarterly 26 (Winter):648-57.

Davis, James A., Thom W. Smith, and C. Bruce Stephenson.
1977 Cumulative Codebook for the 1972-1977 General Social Surveys. Chicago: National Opinion Research Center.

Davis, Jerome.
1936 "The Social Action Pattern of the Protestant Religious Leader." American Sociological Review 1 (February):105-14.

Duncan, Beverly and Otis Dudley Duncan.
1978 Sex Typing and Social Roles. A Research Report. New York: Academic Press.

Fagan, Joen and George Breed.
1970 "A Good, Short Measure of Religious Dogmatism." Psychological Reports 26 (April):533-4.

Fichter, Joseph H.
1952 "The Profile of Catholic Religious Life." American Journal of Sociology 58 (September):145-50.

Garai, J. E. and A. Scheinfeld.
1968 "Sex Differences in Mental and Behavioral Traits." Genetic Psychology Monographs 77:169-299.

Glick, Paul C.
1955 "The Life-Cycle of the Family." Marriage and Family Living. 17 (February):3-9.

1977 "Updating the Life Cycle of the Family." Journal of Marriage and the Family 39 (February):5-13.

Glock, Charles Y. and Rodney Stark.
1965 Religion and Society in Tension. Chicago: Rand McNally and Company.

Glock, Charles Y., Benjamin B. Ringer, and Earl R. Babbie.
1967 To Comfort and To Challenge. Berkeley and Los Angeles: University of California Press.

Gray, Robert M. and David O. Moberg.
1977 The Church and the Older Person. Grand Rapids, Michigan: William B. Eerdmans Publishing Company.

Harris, Louis and Associates.
1975 The Myth and Reality of Aging in America. Washington, D.C.: National Council on the Aging.

Keeley, Benjamin J.
1976 "Generations in Tension: Intergenerational Differences and Continuities in

Religion and Religion Related Behavior." Review of Religious Research 17 (Spring):221-31.

Lenski, Gerhard E.
1963 The Religious Factor, Rev. ed. Garden City, N.Y.: Doubleday.

Lopata, Henena Z.
1973 Widowhood in an American City. Cambridge, Mass.: Schenkman Publishing Company, Inc.

Luckman, Thomas.
1967 The Invisible Religion. London: Collier-Macmillan Ltd.

Maddox, George and James Wiley.
1976 "Scope, Concepts and Methods in the Study of Aging." Pp. 21-30 in Robert Binstock and Ethel Shanas (eds.), Handbook of Aging and the Social Sciences. New York: Van Nostrand, Runhold Co.

Meddin, Jay.
1975 "Generations and Aging: A Longitudinal Study." Journal of Aging and Human Development 6(2):85-101.

Moreland, K. J.
1964 Millways of Kent. New Haven, Conn.: College and University Press.

Orbach, Harold L.
1961 "Aging and Religion: Church Attendance in the Detroit Metropolitan Area." Geriatrics 16 (October):530-40.

Riley, Matilda White.
1973 "Aging and Cohort Succession: Interpretations and Misinterpretations." Public Opinion Quarterly 37 (Spring):35-49.

Riley, Matilda White, Marilyn Johnson and Anne Foner.
1968 Aging and Society. Volume 3: An Inventory of Research Findings. New York: Russell Sage Foundation.

Stark, Rodney.
1968 "Age and Faith: A Changing Outlook or an Old Process?" Sociological Analysis 29 (Spring):1-10.

Strommen, Merton P., Milo L. Brekke, Ralph C. Underwager, and Arthur L. Johnson.
1972 A Study of Generations. Minneapolis: Augsburger.

Wingrove, C. Ray and Jon P. Alston.
1974 "Cohort Analysis and Church Attendance, 1939-1969." Social Forces 53 (December):324-31.

Chapter 28

RELIGION AND AGING IN A LONGITUDINAL PANEL*

DAN BLAZER AND ERDMAN PALMORE

RELIGION is thought to become increasingly important with the onset of late life and the inevitable approach of death. For instance, a conversation was overheard between two children. The first asked, "Why is Grandma spending so much time reading the Bible these days?" "I guess she is cramming for final exams," the second replies. This exemplifies the stereotyped view that the primary concern of the elderly in our society is religion and preparation for death. Mathiasen (1955) has asserted that religion is "the key to a happy life in old age. A sense of the all-encompassing love of God is the basic emotional security and firm spiritual foundation for people who face the end of life."

Investigators who have studied religious activity and attitudes of the elderly have been limited to cross-sectional analysis (Havighurst, 1953; Orbach, 1961) with the exception of two limited longitudinal studies (Streib, 1965; Wingrove, 1971). The general impression from the existing literature is that church attendance is generally at a high level among men and women in their 60s, but it becomes less regular in advanced old age (Riley & Foner, 1968). On the other hand, Orbach (1961) found no consistent age trends in church attendance when he controlled for other related factors. Private religious activities (devotional practices) have been shown to be greater in older age categories in one denomination (Fukuyama, 1961), and, again in cross-sectional analysis, such activities as Bible reading and prayer are reported in a greater percentage of the elderly than in younger age groups (Erskine, 1965). One study indicates that these private activities increase with advancing age (Cavan, Burgess, Havighurst, & Goldhamer, 1949). There have been no longitudinal studies over an extended period of time to substantiate these conclusions. The cross-sectional differences

*Copyright 1976 by the Gerontological Society. Reprinted by permission. From *The Gerontologist*, *16*:82-85, 1976.

This study was supported by grant HD-00668, NICHD, USPHS, and by grant 5-T01-MH 13112-03, NIMH, USPHS. Computer programming was done by Jennifer Buzun.

by age groups may be due to waning religious activities in younger cohorts, rather than increasing activities with older age.

The general hypothesis that church-going and religious interests are significantly correlated with old age adjustment is stated by many authors (Barron, 1958; Mathiasen, 1955; Moberg, 1970). Edwards and Klemmach (1973), Scott (1955), Shanas (1962), and Spreitzer and Snyder (1974) have shown a significant correlation between life satisfaction and church attendance and church related activities. On the other hand, Havighurst and Albrecht (1953) found little relationship between professed attitudes toward religion and personal adjustment.

The Duke Longitudinal Study of Aging provides the first opportunity to examine the amount and patterns of decline or increase in religious activities and attitudes over time. The purpose of this paper is to analyze these patterns and to examine the correlates of religion with happiness, usefulness, personal adjustment, and longevity.

Longitudinal Study of Aging

The data examined in this study were collected as a part of the first longitudinal study of aging at Duke University (Palmore, 1970, 1974). The original sample was composed of 272 volunteers from the Durham area. The age range was 60 to 94 years with a median age of 70.8, at the first round of interviews (1955-1959). The sample contained both white and black, male and female participants in proportions that approximated the race and sex distribution of the community from which the sample was drawn (67% white and 33% black; 48% male and 52% female). Socioeconomic class was determined on the basis of manual (45%) versus nonmanual occupations (55%). Survivors have been followed for nine rounds of examinations over the past 20 years. Ninety percent were Protestant and 94% said they were church members. This is a somewhat higher proportion than the 78% of all persons in the United States over age 50 who reported that they are members of a church (Erskine, 1964).

The Chicago Inventory of Activities and Attitudes was administered in each of the nine rounds to date (Burgess, Cavan, & Havighurst, 1948). The religion subscale of the Activity Inventory, which includes measures of church attendance, listening to church services on radio and TV, and reading the Bible and/or devotional books, was used as an indicator of religious activity at a given point in time. Data was coded on a 0-10 scale (10 indicating the highest level of religious activity). The religion subscale of the Attitude Inventory, which is based on agreement or disagreement with such statements as "religion is a great comfort," and "religion is the most important thing to me," was used as a rating of positive religious attitudes at a given point in time and was coded on a 0-6 scale (6 indicating the most positive religious attitude).

The "happiness" and "usefulness" subscales of the Attitude Inventory were examined for correlations with the religion subscales. The Cavan Adjustment Scale, a rating of social and emotional adjustment by the interviewing social worker, was used as a measure of personal adjustment (Cavan et al., 1949). A longevity quotient was also tabulated for each panelist, which controls for the effects of age, race, and sex (Palmore, 1974). The LQ is the observed number of years survived after initial examination, divided by the actuarilly expected number of years to be survived after examination based on the person's age, sex, and race. For those who were still living (about one-fifth of the panel), an estimate was made of how many years they will have lived since initial testing by adding the present number of years survived since initial testing to the expected number of years now remaining according to actuarial tables.

Religious activity and religious attitude were then correlated with happiness, usefulness, personal adjustment, and longevity. Controls were also introduced for sex, age, and occupation. These correlations were computed for both Round 1 and Round 7 to see if the relationships changed as the panel aged.

Some questions that were asked only in Round 1 were also analyzed. These included questions concerning religious activity at age 12, amount and type of prayer life, frequency of church attendance, frequency of listening to religious programs on radio and TV, and frequency of Bible and devotional reading.

Frequency

Religious activities were relatively frequent in this sample compared to national samples of persons over 65. For example, 61% of our sample reported in Round 1 that they attended church at least once a week compared to only 37% of a national sample (*Catholic Digest*, 1953). In addition, 59% listened to religious programs on radio or TV at least once a week, and 79% read the Bible or a devotional book at least once a week. Also, 43% reported that they prayed at a regular time during the day and 31% said that they "prayed continuously during the day," whereas only 3% said they did not pray at all.

Background Factors

The women were significantly more religious than men in activities (about .7 higher on the religious activity subscale, t-test significant at .02 level), and in attitudes (about .3 higher on the religious attitudes subscale, t-test significant at .05 level). This supports the general finding that women tend to be more religious than men (Orbach, 1961; Riley & Foner, 1968).

Persons from nonmanual occupations also tended to be more active in religion than those from manual occupations. The nonmanual group had a mean religious activity score of 7.2 compared to 6.1 for the manual group (t-test significant at .01 level). The mean religious attitude score for nonmanual group was 5.7 compared to 5.1 for the manual group (t-test significant at the .001 level).

However, church attendance at age 12 had no significant relationship to present church attendance. This is contrary to the idea that childhood training determines religious practices for the rest of life. Substantial proportions of those who attended church regularly as a child now attend rarely. There was a general decline in church attendance from age 12; 80% attended once a week or more at age 12 compared to 61% at Round 1.

Change

In order to analyze change over time in religious activities and attitudes, we plotted the differences in mean scores between each round and the initial round for the survivors to that round. Thus, these differences represent true longitudinal changes and cannot be attributed to attrition in the sample, because each comparison between the initial and later round is based on the scores of the same persons in the initial and later round. These analyses were also controlled for sex, socioeconomic status, and age. Religious activity did show a gradual but definite decrease over time. This decrease from Round 1 was significant at the .02 level in Rounds 3, 5, 6, 7, 8, and 9. The decrease became steadily greater after Round 5 (about 10 years after Round 1). Religious activity among females remained significantly higher than that for males over time but declined in a similar manner. There was a greater decrease in religious activities among persons from nonmanual occupations than those from manual occupations, perhaps because those from nonmanual occupations started from a higher level of religious activity. There was also more decline among those over age 70 at Round 1, probably because of a greater decline in health, vision, and hearing.

In contrast, average religious attitudes remained quite stable over time, with almost identical levels at the early and the last rounds.

There was a slight, but temporary, increase in positive religious attitudes during the middle rounds (1964-1968). When separated by age, sex, and manual versus nonmanual, no significant variation from this stable pattern was noted. Thus it appears that, when measured longitudinally, religious activities tend to gradually decline in late old age, but religious attitudes and satisfactions tend to remain fairly level, neither increasing nor decreasing substantially.

Correlates

Because our earlier analysis of longevity (Palmore, 1971) had found significant correlations between total activity and the longevity quotient (r = .15) as well as between total attitudes and the longevity quotient (r = .26), we expected that there would be substantial correlations of religious activities and attitudes with the longevity quotient. These expectations were contradicted by the data. There was almost no correlation between religious activities and the longevity quotient (r = -.01), nor between religious attitudes and longevity (r = -.06). Thus, in this sample, religion was clearly unrelated to a longer life.

On the other hand, many of the correlations of religious attitudes and activities with happiness, feelings of usefulness, and personal adjustment were significant (.01 level) and moderately strong, as expected. Religious attitudes were not significantly related to happiness, but they were significantly related to feelings of usefulness (r = .16),[1] especially among those from manual occupations (r = .24). Religious attitudes also had a small correlation with adjustment (r = .13) which reached significance among those from nonmanual occupations (r = .24).

Religious activities generally had even stronger relationships to happiness, usefulness, and adjustment. Religious activities were significantly related to happiness (r = .16), especially among men (r = .26), and persons over the age 70 at Round 1 (r = .25). Religious activities were most strongly related to feelings of usefulness (r = .25), especially among those from manual occupations (r = .34), and those over age 70 (r = .32). Similarly, religious activities were significantly related to personal adjustment (r = .16), especially among those from manual occupations (r = .33) and among males (r = .28). These stronger correlations between religious activities and various measures of adjustment, compared to religious attitudes and adjustment, sug-

---

[1] All the correlations in this section come from Round 1. Correlations for Round 7 were similar unless noted otherwise.

gest that religious behavior was more important than attitudes in influencing adjustment.

The fact that these correlations were generally higher among the older persons is similar to the fact that the correlations tended to increase between Rounds 1 and 7. These facts support the theory that religion tends to become increasingly important in the adjustment of older persons as they age, despite the decline in religious activities such as church attendance.

Importance of Religion

In this "Bible Belt" community, most of the elderly studied reported relatively high levels of religious activity and positive attitudes toward religion. Women and persons from nonmanual occupations tended to be more religious in activity and attitudes. There was a general shift from more church attendance in childhood to less in old age. Part of this shift may reflect the general shift toward less church attendance in our society over the past half century.

Longitudinal analysis over 18 years showed that positive religious attitudes remained stable despite a general decline in religious activities. This supports the cross-sectional findings of decline in religious activities in old age but contradicts the theory of increasing interest in religion among aging persons.

There was no correlation of religious activity or attitude with longevity, but they were correlated with happiness, feelings of usefulness, and personal adjustment, especially among men, those from manual occupations, and those over 70. It was also observed that these correlations tended to increase over time. The greater correlations at older ages and in later rounds support the theory that religion becomes increasingly important for personal adjustment in the later years.

The stronger correlations between religious *activities* and various measures of adjustment, compared to the correlations between religious *attitudes* and adjustment, suggest that religious *behavior* was more important than attitudes. When interpreting these results several cautions should be borne in mind: the sample was composed of volunteers from a limited area, those who respond positively on one item tend to respond positively on others, correlation does not prove causation, etc. Nevertheless, limited as they are, these findings do support the theory that, despite declines in religious activities, religion plays a significant and increasingly important role in the personal adjustment of many older persons. One implication would be that churches need to give special attention to their elderly members in order to compensate for their generally declining religious activities and to maximize the benefits of their religious experience.

REFERENCES

Barron, M. L. The role of religion and religious institutions in creating the milieu of older people. In D. Scudder (Ed.), *Organized religion and the older person.* Univ. of Florida Press, Gainesville, 1958.

Burgess, E. W., Cavan, R. S., & Havighurst, R. J. *Your attitudes and activities.* Science Research Associates, Chicago, 1948.

Catholic Digest. How important religion is to Americans. 1953, *17*, 7-12.

Cavan, R. S., Burgess, E. W., Havighurst, R. J., & Goldhamer, H. *Personal adjustment in old age.* Science Research Associates, Chicago, 1949.

Edwards, J. N., & Klemmach, D. L. Correlates of life satisfaction: A reexamination. *Journal of Gerontology*, 1973, *28*, 497-502.

Erskine, H. G. The polls. *Public Opinion Quarterly*, 1964, *29*, 679; 1965, *29*, 154.

Fukuyama, Y. The major dimensions of church membership. *Review of Religious Research*, 1961, *2*, 154-161.

Havighurst, R. J., & Albrecht, R. *Older people.* Longmans, New York, 1953.

Mathiasen, G. The role of religion in the lives of older people. *New York State Governor's Conference on Problems of the Aging.* New York, 1955.

Moberg, D. O. Religion in the later years. In A. M. Hoffman (Ed.), *The daily needs and interests of older people.* Charles C Thomas, Springfield, 1970.

Orbach, H. L. Age and religion: A study of church attendance in the Detroit Metropolitan area. *Geriatrics*, 1961, *16*, 530-540.

Palmore, E. *Normal aging.* Duke Univ. Press, Durham, 1970.

Palmore, E. The relative importance of social factors in predicting longevity. In E. Palmore & F. Jeffers (Eds.), *Prediction of life-span*, Heath, Lexington, 1971.

Palmore, E. *Normal aging.* II. Duke Univ. Press, Durham, 1974.

Riley, M. W., & Foner, A. *Aging and society.* Russell Sage Foundation, New York, 1968.

Scott, F. G. Factors in the personal adjustment of institutionalized and noninstitutionalized aged. *American Sociologist Review*, 1955, *20*, 538-540.

Shanas, E. The personal adjustment of recipients of old age assistance. In R. M. Gray & D. O. Moberg (eds.), *The church and the older person.* Erdmans, Grand Rapids, 1962.

Spreitzer, E., & Snyder, E. E. Correlates of life satisfaction among the aged. *Journal of Gerontology*, 1974, *29*, 454-458.

Streib, G. *Longitudinal study of retirement.* Final Report of the Social Security Administration, 1965.

Wingrove, C. R., & Alston, J. P. Age, aging and church attendance. *Gerontologist*, 1971, *11*, 356-358.

Part VI

Alternative Life Styles

INTRODUCTION

Throughout the book we have been bothered by the fact that over and over we slip into the trap of writing (and thinking) about the Older Woman as though all older women are alike. From time to time we have reminded the reader (and ourselves) that this is not true, but we slip back into the semantic trap. We have only three chapters in this section, each portraying a different life-style; we have barely scratched the surface. There is no chapter on the rich old woman who lives in luxury class hotels around the world. There is no chapter on shopping bag ladies. There is no chapter on the older women who live in the Sun Cities of America. There is no chapter on old women who live on the farm. As we noted earlier, we have not included chapters that portray the rich ethnic and racial differences that exist. Myriads of life-styles are not included. We hope, however, that this section serves as a kind of corrective for our readers, reminding them that, while there are commonalities in the problems and life circumstances of many older women that justifies our speaking of them in groups, it would take an encyclopedia to do justice to the differences in older women in America today.

Elsewhere in the book we have portrayed the older woman in a family setting. The chapters in this section concentrate on the older woman who is alone: living in federally subsidized housing, in an SRO (single room occupancy hotel), and finally (as it is finally for many older women) living in a nursing home.

Arlie Hochschild shared much of the life of those she writes about in "Communal Life-Styles for the Old" (Chapter 29). This insider's view gives a special acuity to the observations she makes. The life-style she describes is, we suspect, more widespread than is usually recognized. Providing much social support, it allows older women to maintain their independence for a longer period than would be possible in single dwelling units in age-integrated housing.

The life patterns and self-sufficiency of older women living in single room occupancy hotels is examined in detail by Maureen Lally et al. (Chapter 30). These women, portrayed as having life-styles based on mobility, extreme individualism, and independence, exemplify yet another variation of living patterns. Probably affecting a relatively small number of older women, it nonetheless reminds us that some older women have achieved independent life-styles that serve their needs.

Finally, we have an article written by a perceptive nurse, Aloyse Hahn, from the perspective of her grandmother (Chapter 31). Attempting to slip into the mind of an older woman confined to a nursing home, she shares with us the frustrations and feelings that must crowd her life space. It's tough to be old!

Chapter 29

COMMUNAL LIFE-STYLES FOR THE OLD*

Arlie Russell Hochschild

THE forty-three residents of Merrill Court (a small apartment building near the shore of San Francisco Bay), thirty-seven of them women, mainly conservative, fundamentalist widows from the Midwest and Southwest, do not seem likely candidates for "communal living" and "alternatives to the nuclear family." Nonetheless, their community has numerous communal aspects. Without their "old-agers commune" these 60-, 70-, and 80-year-olds would more than likely be experiencing the disengagement from life that most students of aging have considered biologically based and therefore inevitable.

The aged individual often has fewer and fewer ties to the outside world, and those which he or she does retain are characterized by less emotional investment than in younger years. This case study, however, presents evidence that disengagement may be situational — that how an individual ages depends largely on his social milieu — and that socially isolated older people may disengage, but that older people supported by a community of appropriate peers do not.

Rural Ways in Urban Settings

Merrill Court is a strange mixture of old and new, of a vanishing Oakie culture and a new blue-collar life-style, of rural ways in urban settings, of small-town community in mass society, of people oriented toward the young in an age-separated subculture. These internal immigrants to the working-class neighborhoods of West Coast cities and suburbs perceive their new environment through rural and small-town eyes. One woman who had gone shopping at a department store observed "all those lovely dresses, all stacked like cordwood." A favorite saying when one was about to retire was, "Guess I'll go to bed with the chickens tonight." They would give directions to the new hamburger joint or hobby shop by describing its relationship to a

---

*Published by permission of Transaction, Inc., from *Society*, 10(5):50-57. Copyright © 1974 by Transaction, Inc.

small stream or big tree. What remained of the old custom of a funeral wake took place at a new funeral parlor with neon signs and
printed notices.

The communal life that developed in Merrill Court may have had
nothing to do with rural ways in an urban setting. Had the widows
stayed on the farms and in the small towns they came from, they
might have been active in community life there. Those who had been
involved in community life before remained active and, with the
exception of a few, those who previously had not, became active.

For whatever reason, the widows built themselves an order out of
ambiguity, a set of obligations to the outside and to one another
where few had existed before. It is possible to relax in old age, to
consider one's social debts paid, and to feel that constraints that do
not weigh on the far side of the grave should not weigh on the near
side either. But in Merrill Court, the watchfulness of social life, the
Protestant stress on industry, thrift, and activity added up to an ethos
of keeping one's "boots on," not simply as individuals but as a community.

Forming the Community

"There wasn't nothin' before we got the coffee machine. I mean we
didn't share nothin' before Mrs. Bitford's daughter brought over the
machine and we sort of had our first occasion, you might say."

There were about six people at the first gathering around the coffee
machine in the recreation room. As people came downstairs from
their apartments to fetch their mail, they looked into the recreation
room, found a cluster of people sitting down drinking coffee, and
some joined in. A few weeks later the recreation director "joined in"
for the morning coffee and, as she tells it, the community had its start
at this point.

Half a year later Merrill Court was a beehive of activity: meetings of
a service club; bowling; morning workshop; Bible-study classes twice
a week; other classes with frequently changing subjects; monthly
birthday parties; holiday parties; and visits to four nearby nursing
homes. Members donated cakes, pies, and soft drinks to bring to the
nursing home, and a five-piece band, including a washtub bass,
played for the "old folks" there. The band also entertained at a nearby
recreation center for a group of Vietnam veterans. During afternoon
band practice, the women sewed and embroidered pillow cases,
aprons, and yarn dolls. They made wastebaskets out of discarded
paper towel rolls, wove rugs from strips of old Wonder Bread

wrappers, and Easter hats out of old Clorox bottles, all to be sold at the annual bazaar. They made placemats to be used at the nursing home, totebags to be donated to "our boys in Vietnam," Christmas cards to be cut out for the Hillcrest Junior Women's Club, rag dolls to be sent to the orphanage, place cards to be written out for the bowling-league banquet, recipes to be written out for the recipe book that was to go on sale next month, and thank you and condolence cards.

Social Patterns

The social arrangements that took root early in the history of Merrill Court later assumed a life of their own. They were designed, as if on purpose, to assure an "ongoing" community. If we were to visually diagram the community, it would look like a social circle on which there are centripedal and centrifugal pressures. The formal role system, centered in the circle, pulled people toward it by giving them work and rewards, and this process went on mainly "downstairs," in the recreation room. At the same time, informal loyalty networks fluctuated toward and away from the circle. They became clear mainly "upstairs" where the apartments were located. Relatives and outsiders pulled the individual away from the circle downstairs and network upstairs, although they were occasionally pulled inside both.

Downstairs

Both work and play were somebody's responsibility to organize. The Merrill Court Service Club, to which most of the residents and a half-dozen nonresidents belonged, set up committees and chairmanships that split the jobs many ways. There was a group of permanent elected officials: the president, vice-president, treasurer, secretary and birthday chairman, in addition to the recreation director. Each activity also had a chairman, and each chairman was in charge of a group of volunteers. Some officers were rotated during the year. Only four club members did not chair some activity between 1965 and 1968; and at any time about a third were in charge of something.

Friendship Networks

Shadowing the formal circle was an informal network of friendships that formed over a cup of coffee in the upstairs apartments. The physical appearance of the apartments told something about the network. Inside, each apartment had a living room, kitchen, bedroom, and porch. The apartments were unfurnished when the women moved in and as one remarked, "We fixed 'em up just the way we wanted. I got this new lamp over to Sears, and my daughter and I bought these new scatter rugs. Felt just like a new bride."

For the most part, the apartments were furnished in a remarkably similar way. Many had American flag stickers outside their doors. Inside, each had a large couch with a floral design, which sometimes doubled as a hide-a-bed where a grandchild might sleep for a weekend. Often a chair, a clock, or a picture came from the old home and provided a material link to the past. Most had large stuffed chairs, bowls of homemade artificial flowers, a Bible, and porcelain knick-knacks neatly arranged on a table. (When the group was invited to my own apartment for tea, one woman suggested sympathetically that we "had not quite moved in yet" because the apartment seemed bare by comparison.) By the window were potted plants, often grown from a neighbor's slip. A plant might be identified as "Abbie's ivy" or "Ernestine's African violet."

Photographs, usually out of date, of pink-cheeked children and grandchildren decorated the walls. Less frequently there was a photo of a deceased husband and less frequently still, a photo of a parent. On the living-room table or nearby there was usually a photograph album containing pictures of relatives and pictures of the woman herself on a recent visit "back East." Many of the photographs in the album were arranged in the same way. Pictures of children came first and, of those, children with the most children appeared first, and childless children at the end.

The refrigerator almost always told a social story. One contained homemade butter made by the cousin of a woman on the second floor; berry jam made by the woman three doors down; corn bought downstairs in the recreation room, brought in by someone's son who worked in a corn-canning factory; homemade Swedish rolls to be given to a daughter when she came to visit; two dozen eggs to be used in cooking, most of which would be given away; as well as bread and fruit, more than enough for one person. Most of the women had once cooked for large families, and Emma, who raised eight children back in Oklahoma, habitually baked about eight times as much corn bread as she could eat. She made the rounds of apartments on her floor distributing the extra bread. The others who also cooked in quantities reciprocated, also gratuitously, with other kinds of food. It was an informal division of labor, although no one thought of it that way.

Most neighbors were also friends, and friendships, as well as information about them, were mainly confined to each floor. All but four had their *best* friends on the same floor and only a few had a next-best friend on another floor. The more one had friends outside the building, the more one had friends on other floors within the building. The wider one's social radius outside the building, the wider it was inside the building as well.

Neighboring

Apart from the gratification of friendship, neighboring did a number of things for the community. It was a way of relaying information or misinformation about others. Often the information relayed upstairs influenced social arrangements downstairs. For example, according to one widow:

> the Bitfords had a tiff with Irma upstairs here, and a lot of tales went around. They weren't true, not a one, about Irma, but then people didn't come downstairs as much. Mattie used to come down, and Marie and Mr. Ball and they don't so much now, only once and again, because of Irma being there. All on account of that tiff.

Often people seated themselves downstairs as they were situated upstairs, neighbor and friend next to neighbor and friend, and a disagreement upstairs filtered downstairs. For example, when opinion was divided and feelings ran high on the issue of whether to store the club's $900 in a cigar box under the treasurer's bed or in the bank, the gossip, formerly confined to upstairs, invaded the public arena downstairs.

Relaying information this way meant that without directly asking, people knew a lot about one another. It was safe to assume that what you did was known about by at least one network of neighbors and their friends. Even the one social isolate on the third floor, Velma, was known about, and her comings and goings were talked about and judged. Talk about other people was a means of social control and it operated, as it does elsewhere, through parables; what was told of another was a message to one's self.

Not all social control was verbal. Since all apartment living rooms faced out on a common walkway that led to a central elevator, each tenant could be seen coming and going; and by how he or she was dressed, one could accurately guess his or her activities. Since each resident knew the visiting habits of her neighbors, anything unusual was immediately spotted. One day when I was knocking on the door of a resident, her neighbor came out:

I don't know where she is, it couldn't be the doctor's, she goes to the doctor's on Tuesdays; it couldn't be shopping, she shopped yesterday with her daughter. I don't think she's downstairs, she says she's worked enough today. Maybe she's visiting Abbie. They neighbor a lot. Try the second floor.

Neighboring is also a way to detect sickness or death. As Ernestine related, "This morning I look to see if Judson's curtains were open. That's how we do on this floor when we get up we open our curtains just a bit, so others walking by outside know that everything's all right. And if the curtains aren't drawn by mid-morning, we knock to see." Mattie perpetually refused to open her curtains in the morning and kept them close to the wall by placing potted plants against them so that "a man won't get in." This excluded her from the checking-up system and disconcerted the other residents.

The widows in good health took it upon themselves to care for one or two in poor health. Delia saw after Grandma Goodman who was not well enough to go down and get her mail and shop, and Ernestine helped Little Floyd and Mrs. Blackwell who could not see well enough to cook their own meals. Irma took care of Mr. Cooper and she called his son when Mr. Cooper "took sick." Even those who had not adopted someone to help often looked after a neighbor's potted plants while they were visiting kin, lent kitchen utensils, and took phone messages. One woman wrote letters for those who "wrote a poor hand."

Some of the caretaking was reciprocal, but most was not. Three people helped take care of Little Floyd, but since he was blind he could do little in return. Delia fixed his meals, Ernestine laundered his clothes, and Irma shopped for his food. When Little Floyd died fairly suddenly, he was missed perhaps more than others who died during those three years, especially by his caretakers. Ernestine remarked sadly, "I liked helping out the poor old fella. He would appreciate the tiniest thing. And never a complaint."

Sometimes people paid one another for favors. For example, Freda took in sewing for a small sum. When she was paid for lining a coat, she normally mentioned the purpose for which the money would be spent (for example, bus fare for a visit to relatives in Montana), perhaps to reduce the commercial aspect of the exchange. Delia was paid by the Housing Authority for cleaning and cooking for Grandma Goodman, a disabled woman on her floor; and as she repeatedly mentioned to Grandma Goodman, she spent the money on high-school class rings for her three grandchildren. In one case, the

Housing Authority paid a granddaughter for helping her grandmother with housework. In another case, a disabled woman paid for
domestic help from her Social Security checks.

The "Poor-Dear" Hierarchy

Within the formal social circle there was a status hierarchy based on
the distribution of honor, particularly through holding offices in the
service club. Additionally, there was a parallel informal status hierarchy based on the distribution of luck. "Luck" as the residents defined it is not entirely luck. Health and life expectancy, for example,
are often considered "luck," but an upper-class person can expect to
live ten years longer than a lower-class person. The widows of Merrill
Court, however, were drawn from the same social class and they saw
the differences among themselves as matters of luck.

She who had good health won honor. She who lost the fewest loved
ones through death won honor, and she who was close to her children
won honor. Those who fell short of any of these criteria were often
referred to as "poor dears."

The "poor-dear" system operated like a set of valves through which
a sense of superiority ran in only one direction. Someone who was a
"poor dear" in the eyes of another seldom called that other person a
"poor dear" in return. Rather, the "poor dear" would turn to
someone less fortunate, perhaps to buttress a sense of her own
achieved or ascribed superiority. Thus, the hierarchy honored residents at the top and pitied "poor dears" at the bottom, creating a
number of informally recognized status distinctions among those
who, in the eyes of the outside society, were social equals.

The distinctions made by residents of Merrill Court are only part of
a larger old-age status hierarchy based on things other than luck. At
the monthly meetings of the countywide Senior Citizens Forum, to
which Merrill Court sent two representatives, the term *poor dear* often
arose with reference to old people. It was "we senior citizens who are
politically involved versus those "poor dears" who are active in recreation." Those active in recreation, however, did not accept a subordinate position relative to the politically active. On the other hand,
they did not refer to the political activists as "poor dears." Within the
politically active group there were those who espoused general causes,
such as getting out an antipollution bill, and those who espoused
causes related only to old age such as raising Social Security benefits
or improving medical benefits. Those in politics and recreation referred to the passive card players and newspaper readers as "poor

dears." Uninvolved old people in good health referred to those in poor health as "poor dears," and those in poor health but living in independent housing referred to those in nursing homes as "poor dears." Within the nursing home there was a distinction between those who were ambulatory and those who were not. Among those who were not ambulatory, there was a distinction between those who could enjoy food and those who could not. Almost everyone, it seemed, had a "poor dear."

At Merrill Court, the main distinction was between people like themselves and people in nursing homes. Returning from one of the monthly trips to a nearby nursing home, one resident commented:

> There was an old woman in a wheelchair there with a dolly in her arms. I leaned over to look at the dolly. I didn't touch it, well, maybe I just brushed it. She snatched it away, and said, "Don't take my dolly." They're pathetic, some of them, the poor dears.

Even within the building, those who were in poor health, were alienated from their children, or were aging rapidly were considered "poor dears." It was lucky to be young and unlucky to be old. There was more than a twenty-year age span between the youngest and oldest in the community. When one of the younger women, Delia, age 69, was drinking coffee with Grandma Goodman, age 79, they compared ages. Grandma Goodman dwelt on the subject and finished the conversation by citing the case of Mrs. Blackwell, who was 89 and still in reasonably good health. Another remarked about her seventieth birthday:

> I just couldn't imagine myself being 70. Seventy is old! That's what Daisy said, too. She's 80 you know. It was her seventieth that got her. No one likes to be put aside, you know. Laid away. Put on the shelf you might say. No sir.

She had an ailment that prevented her from bowling or lifting her flower pots, but she compared her health to that of Daisy, and found her own health a source of luck.

Old people compare themselves not to the young but to other old people. Often the residents referred to the aged back in Oklahoma, Texas, and Arkansas with pity in their voices:

> Back in Oklahoma, why they toss the old people away like old shoes. My old friends was all livin' together in one part of town and they hardly budged the whole day. Just sat out on their porch and chewed the fat. Sometimes they didn't even do that. Mostly they didn't have no nice housing, and nothin' social was goin' on. People here don't know what luck they've fallen into.

They also compared their lot to that of other older people in the area. As one resident said:

Some of my friends live in La Casa [another housing project]. I suppose because they have to, you know. And I tried to get them to come bowling with me, but they wouldn't have a thing to do with it. "Those senior citizens, that's old-folks stuff." Wouldn't have a thing to do with it. I tried to tell them we was pretty spry, but they wouldn't listen. They just go their own way. They don't think we have fun.

On the whole, the widows disassociated themselves from the status of "old person," and accepted its "minority" characteristics. The "poor dears" in the nursing home were often referred to as childlike: "They are easily hurt, you know. They get upset at the slightest thing and they like things to be the way they've always been. Just like kids." Occasionally, a widow would talk about Merrill Court itself in this vein, presumably excluding herself: "We're just like a bunch of kids here sometimes. All the sparring that goes on, even with church folk. And people get so hurt, so touchy. You'd think we were babies sometimes."

If the widows accepted the stereotypes of old age, they did not add the "poor dear" when referring to themselves. But younger outsiders did. To the junior employees in the Recreation and Parks Department, the young doctors who treated them at the county hospital, the middle-aged welfare workers, and the young bank tellers, the residents of Merrill Court, and the old people like them, were "poor dears."

Perhaps in old age there is a premium on finishing life off with the feeling of being a "have." But during old age, one also occupies a low social position. The way old look for luck differences among themselves reflects the pattern found at the bottom of other social, racial, and gender hierarchies. To find oneself lucky within an ill-fated category is to gain the semblance of high status when society withholds it from others in the category. The way old people feel above and condescend to other old people may be linked to the fact that the young feel above and condescend to them. The luck hierarchy does not stop with the old.

The Sibling Bond

There were rivalries and differences in Merrill Court, but neither alienation nor isolation. A club member who stayed up in her apartment during club meetings more often did it out of spite than indifference. More obvious were the many small, quiet favors, keeping an eye out for a friend and sharing a good laugh.

There was something special about this community, not so much because it was an old-age subculture, but because the subculture was founded on a particular kind of relationship — the sibling bond. Most residents of Merrill Court are social siblings. The custom of exchanging cups of coffee, lunches, potted plants, and curtain checking suggest reciprocity. Upstairs, one widow usually visited as much as she was visited. On deciding who visits whom, they often remarked. "Well, I came over last time. You come over this time." They traded, in even measure, slips from house plants, kitchen utensils, and food of all sorts. They watched one another's apartments when someone was away on a visit, and they called and took calls for one another.

There are hints of the parent-child bond in this system, but protectors picked their dependents voluntarily and resented taking care of people they did not volunteer to help. For example, one protector of "Little Floyd" complained about a crippled club member, a nonresident:

> It wasn't considerate of Rose to expect us to take care of her. She can't climb in and out of the bus very well and she walks so slow. The rest of us wanted to see the museum. It's not nice to say, but I didn't want to miss the museum waiting for her to walk with us. Why doesn't her son take her on trips?

The widows were not only equals among themselves, they also were remarkably similar. They all wanted more or less the same things and could give more or less the same things. They all wanted to *receive* Mother's Day cards. No one in the building *sent* Mother's Day cards. And what they did was to compare Mother's Day cards. Although there was some division of labor, there was little difference in labor performed. All knew how to bake bread and can peaches, but no one knew how to fix faucets. They all knew about "the old days" but few among them could explain what was going on with youth these days. They all had ailments but no one there could cure them. They all needed rides to the shopping center, but no one among them needed riders.

Their similar functions meant that when they did exchange services, it was usually the same kind of services they themselves could perform. For example, two neighbors might exchange corn bread for jam, but both knew how to make both corn bread and jam. If one neighbor made corn bread for five people in one day, one of the recipients would also make corn bread for the same people two weeks later. Each specialized within a specialization, and over the long run the widows made and exchanged the same goods.

Hence the "side by sideness," the "in the same boat" quality of their relations. They noticed the same things about the world and their eyes caught the same items in a department store. They noticed the same features in the urban landscape — the pastor's home, the Baptist church, the nursing homes, the funeral parlors, the places that used to be. They did not notice, as an adolescent might, the gas stations and hamburger joints.

As a result, they were good listeners for each other. It was common for someone to walk into the recreation room and launch into the details of the latest episode of a mid-afternoon television drama ("It seems that the baby is not by artificial insemination but really Frank's child, and the doctor is trying to convince her to tell . . ."). The speaker could safely assume that her listeners also knew the details. Since they shared many experiences, a physical ailment, a death, a description of the past, an "old-age joke" could be explained, understood, and enjoyed. They talked together about their children much as their children, together, talked about them. Each shared with social siblings one side of the prototypical parent-child bond.

This similarity opened up the possibility of comparison and rivalry, as the "poor-dear" hierarchy suggests. Whether the widows cooperated in collecting money for flowers, or competed for prestigious offices in the service club, bowling trophies, or front seats in the bus, their functions were similar, their status roughly equal, and their relations in the best and worst sense, "profane."

Not all groups of old people form this sibling bond. Although we might expect subcultures to arise in nursing homes, certain hospital wards, or convalescent hospitals, the likes of Merrill Court are rare. It is not enough to put fairly healthy, socially similar old people together. There is clearly something different between institutions and public housing apartments. Perhaps what counts is the kind of relationships that institutions foster. The resident of an institution is "a patient." Like a child, he has his meals served to him, his water glass filled, his bed made, his blinds adjusted by the "mother-nurse." He cannot return the service. Although he often shares a room or a floor with "brother" patients, both siblings have a nonreciprocal relationship to attendants or nurses. Even the research on the institutionalized focuses on the relation between patient and attendant, not between patient and patient. If there is a strong parent-child bond, it may overwhelm any potential sibling solidarity. If the old in institutions meet as equals, it is not as independent equals. The patient's relation to other patients is like the relation between *real*, young siblings, which may exaggerate rather than forestall narcissistic withdrawal.

The widows of Merrill Court took care of themselves, fixed their own meals, paid their own rent, shopped for their own food, and made their own beds; and they did these things for others. Their sisterhood rests on adult autonomy. This is what people at Merrill Court have and people in institutions do not.

The Sibling Bond and Age Stratification

The sibling bond is delicate and emerges only when conditions are ripe. Rapid currents of social change lead to age stratification, which, in turn, ripens conditions for the sibling bond. Tied to his fellows by sibling bonds, an individual is cemented side by side into an age stratum with which he shares the same rewards, wants, abilities, and failings.

French sociologist Emile Durkheim, in his book *The Division of Labor*, describes two forms of social solidarity. In organic solidarity there is a division of labor, complementary dependence, and difference among people. In mechanical solidarity there is no division of labor, self-sufficiency, and similarity among people. Modern American society as a whole is based on organic solidarity, not only in the economic but in the social, emotional, and intellectual spheres as well.

Different age strata within the general society, however, are more bound by mechanical solidarity. This is important both for the individual and the society. Although division of labor, complementary dependence, and differences among people describe society's network of relations as a whole, they do not adequately describe relations among particular individuals. An individual's complementary dependence may be with people he does not know or meet — such as the person who grows and cans the food he eats, or lays the bricks for his house. And in his most intimate relations, an individual may also have complementary relations (either equal or unequal) with his spouse and children. But in between the most and least intimate bonds is a range of which there are many sibling relationships that form the basis of mechanical solidarity.

In fact, many everyday relations are with people similar and equal to oneself. Relations between colleague and colleague, student and student, friend and friend, relations within a wives' group or "the guys at the bar," the teenage gang or army buddies are often forms of the sibling bond. These ties are often back-up relations, social insurance policies for the times when the complementary bonds of parent and child, husband and wife, student and teacher, boyfriend and girlfriend fail, falter, or normally change.

From an individual's viewpoint, some periods of life, such as adolescence and old age, are better for forming sibling bonds than are other periods. Both just before starting a family and after raising one, before entering the economy and after leaving it, an individual is open to and needs these back-up relationships. It is these stages that are problematic, and it is these stages that, with longer education and earlier retirement, now last longer.

From society's point of view, the sibling bond allows more flexibility in relations between generations by forging solidarity within generations and divisions between them. This divides society into age layers that are relatively independent of one another, so that changes in one age layer need not be retarded by conditions in another. The institution that has bound the generations together — the family — is in this respect on the decline. As it declines, the sibling bond emerges, filling in and enhancing social flexibility, especially in those social strata where social change is most pronounced. The resulting social flexibility does not guarantee "good" changes and continuity is partly sacrificed to fads and a cult of newness. But whether desirable or not, this flexibility is partly due to and partly causes the growing importance of the sibling bond.

The times are ripe for the sibling bond, and for old-age communities such as Merrill Court. In the social life of old people the problem is not the sibling bond versus the parent-child bond. Rather, the question is how the one bond complements the other. The sisterhood at Merrill Court is no substitute for love of children and contact with them; but it offers a full, meaningful life independent of them.

The Minority Group Almost Everyone Joins

Isolation is not randomly distributed across the class hierarchy; there is more of it at the bottom. It is commonly said that old age is a leveler, that it affects the rich in the same way it affects the poor. It does not. The rich fare better in old age even as they fared better in youth. The poorer you are, the shorter your life expectancy, the poorer your health and health care, the lower your morale generally, the more likely you are to "feel" old regardless of your actual age, the less likely you are to join clubs or associations, the less active you are and the more isolated even from children. Irving Rosow's study of 1,200 people over 62 living in Cleveland found that roughly 40 percent of the working class but only 16 percent of the middle class had fewer than four good friends. Another study of 6,000 white working-class men and women showed that of those over 65 with incomes under $3,000, a full third did not visit with or speak to a friend or neighbor during the preceding week. The rock-bottom poor are isolated, but they are not the only ones.

The isolation of old people is linked to other problems. The old are poor and poverty itself is a problem. The old are unemployed and unemployment, in this society, is itself a problem. The old lack community and the lack of community is itself a problem. There is some connection between these three elements. Removed from the economy, the old have been cast out of the social networks that revolve around work. Lacking work, they are pushed down the social ladder. Being poor, they have fewer social ties. Poverty reinforces isolation. To eliminate enforced isolation, we have to eliminate poverty, for the two go together. The social life of Merrill Court residents, who had modest but not desperately low incomes, is an exception to the general link between social class and isolation.

Even if every old person were in a Merrill Court, the problem of old age would not be solved. But, allowing every old person the possibility of such an arrangement could be part of the solution. The basic problem far exceeds the limits of tinkering with housing arrangements. It is not enough to try to foster friendships among the old. Even to do that, it is not enough to set up bingo tables in the lobbies of decrepit hotels or to hand out name cards to the sitters on park benches. This would simply put a better face on poverty, a cheerful face on old age as it now is, at not much social cost.

Merrill Court is not set in any island of ideal social conditions; it is essentially an adjustment to bad social conditions. For the lives of old people to change fundamentally, those *conditions* must change. In the meantime, Merrill Court is a start. It is a good example of what can be done to reduce isolation. I do not know if similar communities would have emerged in larger apartment houses or housing tracts rather than in a small apartment house, with the married rather than the widowed, with rich rather than poor residents, with people having a little in common rather than a lot, with the very old person rather than the younger old person. Only trying will tell.

Merrill Court may be a forecast of what is to come. A survey of 105 University of California students in 1968 suggested that few parents of these students and few of the students themselves expect to be living with their families when they are old. Nearly seven out of ten (69 percent) reported that "under no circumstances" would they want their aged parents to live with them, and only three percent expected to be living with their own children when they are old. A full 28 percent expected to be living with *other* old people, and an additional 12 percent expected to be "living alone or with other old people."

Future communities of old people may be more middle class and more oriented toward leisure. Less than ten percent of the students expected to be working when they passed sixty-five. A great many expected to be "enjoying life," by which they meant studying, meditating, practicing hobbies, playing at sports, and traveling.

But some things about future communities may be the same. As I have suggested throughout this chapter, communal solidarity can renew the social contact the old have with life. For old roles that are gone, new ones are available. If the world watches them less for being old, they watch one another more. Lacking responsibilities to the young, the old take on responsibilities toward one another. Moreover, in a society that raises an eyebrow at those who do not "act their age," the subculture encourages the old to dance, to sing, to flirt, and to joke. They talk frankly about death in a way less common between the old and young. They show one another how to be, and trade solutions to problems they have not faced before.

Old age is the minority group almost everyone joins. But it is a forgotten minority group from which many old people dissociate themselves. A community such as Merrill Court counters this disaffiliation. In the wake of the declining family, it fosters a "we" feeling, and a nascent "old-age consciousness." In the long run, this may be the most important contribution an old-age community makes.

Chapter 30

OLDER WOMEN IN SINGLE ROOM OCCUPANT (SRO) HOTELS: A SEATTLE PROFILE*

MAUREEN LALLY, EILEEN BLACK, MARTHA THORNOCK,
AND J. DAVID HAWKINS

IN recent years a number of social programs have been mounted on behalf of the aged, yet subpopulations of older adults can be found whose needs are little understood and whose access to delivery systems remains minimal. One such group is older women who live in downtown hotels in urban communities.

Historically, studies of low-income urban residents who live downtown have focused on skid road residents (Bahr, 1970). Until recently, the impression lingered that low-income people who reside in urban centers are downwardly mobile, often emotionally disturbed and "disaffiliated" (Bahr, 1976; Stephens, 1976). Recently, investigators have begun to recognize that a number of elderly people who reside downtown must be distinguished from what is primarily a younger "skid road" population. Several studies have investigated the characteristics of some of these older people, known as SRO (single room occupancy) hotel elderly (Ehrlich, 1971; Erickson & Eckert, 1977; Shapiro, 1976; Stephens, 1976).

Research indicates that older men are found in greater numbers in SRO environments than older women, and studies of SRO elderly have generally based conclusions on predominately male populations (Ehrlich, 1976; Erickson & Eckert, 1977; Stephens, 1976). Recently investigators have suggested that SRO elderly women may represent a distinct subgroup, psychologically and socially distinct from their male counterparts, and worthy of greater research attention (Stephens, 1976).

Available information on SRO elderly women is somewhat contradictory. Stephens (1976) studied residents of one SRO hotel and found subjects of both sexes to have a high need for privacy and independence, to relate in a superficial and utilitarian way with others and to

*Copyright 1979 by the Gerontological Society. Reprinted by permission. From *The Gerontologist, 19(1)*:67-73, 1979.

isolate themselves from, and be resistant to, close social contacts. Stephens interpreted the avoidance of ties as a primary coping skill in an environment with high potential for deviance. In contrast to Stephens, Shapiro's study of nine SRO hotels (1971) found that black SRO elderly women were leaders in an interdependent social environment, forming the matriarchal center of intricate mutual aid networks with more dependent, often alcoholic males. Bahr's (1970) study of "disaffiliated" women living downtown suggested two distinct subgroups: (1) women reduced to the life-style because of old age, illness, or poverty; (2) women whose whole life has been characterized by interpersonal failures — broken marriages, alcoholism, and the like. In spite of these differences, researchers have agreed that SRO elderly of both sexes are generally suspicious of social service agencies and underutilize the services for which they are eligible.

The present study was undertaken to further assess the characteristics and needs of SRO elderly women in urban communities in light of the apparent contradiction in existing descriptions of this population. The purpose was to obtain information on the backgrounds of these women, the processes by which they became inner-city residents, and how they manage their lives and cope with their environments. A goal of the research was to discover whether these women, because of their life-style, have needs which are not being adequately addressed by traditional aged-serving social agencies; and if so, to learn how services and programs might be tailored to be more useful and acceptable to them.

The Setting and the Residents

Data were collected by three female investigators through observation and informal open-ended interviews with 16 older women living in 10 hotels in downtown Seattle. Hotels were selected based on pre-study visits to determine the presence of elderly women residents, management cooperation, and suitability of the hotels as SRO sites using the criteria of previous authors:

(1) furnished rooms with or without any self-contained bathroom;
(2) usually without kitchens;
(3) management services provided (i.e., desk, managers, linens, housekeeping);
(4) at least half of the occupants permanent residents;
(5) hotel neither Federally subsidized nor licensed for institutional care;
(6) hotel located in a commercial area (Ehrlich, 1976).

Approximately 30 hotels in downtown Seattle fit these criteria. Twelve of these were found to have elderly women residents. Access was denied to two; the remaining 10 were used as sites for the study.

Prior to approaching potential subjects, the three investigators spent several weeks in hotel lobbies and coffee shops as observers. During this time data were collected on hotel routines and environments, as well as on activities of potential subjects. This initial period also allowed the women to become somewhat familiar with the investigators, which facilitated subsequent requests for interviews. This was an important consideration, because the literature suggested SRO elderly would be wary of strangers. The initial observation period also included contacts with informants such as hotel managers, desk persons, maids, and staff of social service agencies serving the downtown population.

After the period of observation, contact with women was made in three ways: (1) introduction by informants; (2) direct approach to women in their rooms without introduction, and (3) chance meetings in hotel lobbies and coffee shops. Statements by informants in the hotels and the community suggest no reason to believe that the women studied were atypical of white older female residents of the 10 hotels studied or of Seattle SRO elderly white women generally. However, the sample of women was not randomly drawn and we cannot guarantee its representativeness. At best, it represents Seattle's *white* elderly SRO women.

Women were interviewed in their rooms or in secluded areas of the hotel lobby. The interview was open-ended and nondirective. However, all three investigators consistently covered the following content areas during interviews:

(1) biographical background, including the woman's childhood family, socioeconomic status, and relationships with parents and siblings;
(2) adult biography, including living arrangements, marriages, employment, and family ties;
(3) circumstances of move to downtown hotel, and history of downtown living;
(4) current life situation, including how time is spent, routines, social contacts, stresses, concerns, and contacts with social agencies.

The 16 women interviewed ranged in age from 55 to 91 years. Fifteen were white and one was black. Six women were on Social Security, three received small pension checks, three were on SSI (Supplemental Security Income), two were on public assistance, and two were employed full-time.

Work Histories and Identification with Fathers

The women came from a variety of socioeconomic backgrounds with family patterns that exhibited few consistent characteristics. Interestingly, however, in describing their childhoods the women showed strong identification with, and preference for, their fathers. Mothers were repeatedly described in negative or neutral terms: "sick;" "too young to raise me;" "not demonstrative." Fathers were consistently portrayed more positively: "my father was the best provider a man could be;" "I took after my father more than my mother." A close identification and strong affect for fathers has not been previously documented for SRO women; neither has the antipathy towards mothers. Childhood experiences may have had a strong influence in the personality development of these women and should be further explored. It is possible that some of the traits of SRO residents reported in the literature and discussed later in this study, such as strong verbalized norms of independence, can be traced back to early family relationships and socialization experiences.

Another important, and perhaps related, finding is the work experience of the women. Fourteen (87%) of the Seattle women had been in paid employment most of their adult lives, holding a variety of jobs over the years. Interestingly, 1/2 of the subjects had spent a considerable portion of their work careers in traditionally male dominated occupations including work as longshoremen, truck drivers and electricians. Two had been school teachers.

Erickson and Eckert (1977) found nearly 1/2 of the middle-class hotel dwellers in San Diego had held clerical jobs, while the skid road and working-class groups, had more mobile and unstable work histories. Stephens (1976) found the Detroit population to have had episodic and marginal work situations with very few having "formal" careers. In the Seattle sample, five of the women had been members of unions whose membership was largely male. These women ventured into occupational areas where women were rarely found long before the current concern with sex-role stereotyping. It is interesting to speculate whether their fathers' influence affected their career choices, especially in light of Hennig and Jardim's (1977) study of 25 women managers which emphasized the influence of father on choice of occupation. An alternative hypothesis worthy of further investigation is that these Seattle women entered male-dominated trades during World War II while men were off fighting and continued in these fields after the war.

National demographic data on the educational level of the population 65 and over indicates that 50% have not completed eight years of elementary education and 8% have graduated from college. In Erickson and Eckert's San Diego population, the average education was 10.5 years for the group studied (1977). The Seattle women reported a significantly higher educational level than the national average. Ten of the sixteen (62%) had completed high school, seven reported some college education, and two had completed college and had teaching careers.

History of Downtown Living

Five (31%) of the women had lived in downtown hotels all their adult lives. Eleven (69%) moved downtown after a major life change including widowhood, divorce, or retirement. Hotel hopping was common. Generally, the women portrayed their residence in SRO hotels as a purposeful *choice* made for the inherent advantages rather than as a last resort. While a few spoke of how their lives would be different if they could afford to live elsewhere, they were quick to describe the merits of their current situations. Seven (43%) of the women said they chose to live in downtown hotels because of convenience factors including proximity to department stores, and availability to maid service. Four also noted an economic advantage of lower rent than for a comparable size apartment. The women also mentioned factors such as privacy and independence afforded by hotel living, as well as the security provided by hotel staff.

When asked what they thought about downtown living and residence in a hotel, the Seattle women volunteered twice as many positive comments as negative comments. There was no consistency in descriptions of what the women did not like about living in a hotel. Individuals expressed concerns about rents being too high, noise caused by other tenants, dishonest or unfriendly management, presence of racial minorities in the area, and drunk/deviant behavior. Only three mentioned fear of crime or violence. The low reporting of undesirable environmental aspects of SRO living contrasts with results of prior SRO studies. In hotels studied by Erickson and Eckert (1977), Shipiro (1971), and Stephens (1976), environmental factors such as crime, threat of fires, and physical violence were frequently identified as stressful by SRO residents. One possible interpretation of this failure to volunteer greater concern about environmental factors is that not identifying such concerns is a way of coping with tenuous downtown conditions. However, the fact that Seattle women did volunteer concerns about other issues such as money suggests that they did not deny all unpleasant aspects of their situations and may actually not have felt as personally threatened by crime or violence as other SRO populations. This may reflect a comparative freedom of the Seattle downtown area from advanced stages of urban decay found in larger and older cities.

Relationships with Others

Notably, these women had few significant relationships with others. Although 11 of the 16 had been married at one time, all but one lived alone at present. All but two of the 11 women who had been married had living adult children. However, no subject described a close ongoing relationship with her adult children. Most had little or no contact with their children; comments from those who had contacts indicated that relationships were strained.

The majority of subjects volunteered comments which indicated that being on one's own, independent, and self-sufficient were extremely important values to them. Two specifically described themselves as "independent" and others made comments that reflected self-sufficiency: "I've always resented and I still do resent anyone telling me to do something. I figure I'm smart enough to see if something needs to be done and I'll do it myself;" "I would like to have a nice apartment but I can't afford it so why get yourself shook up. That way I am not dependent on my family anyway. I'm independent ... I've always been and I hope I always am."

Whether these assertions of independence were rationalizations for solitary lives or associated with a series of conscious life choices, the women had clearly developed an ideology of independence which organized, oriented, and justified their current living pattern both to themselves and others. The women had developed daily routines consistent with this ideology. Most subjects spent considerable time alone in their rooms, reading, listening to the radio, watching television, or doing housekeeping, laundry, etc. Devoid of decorations, their rooms were furnished with hotel furniture plus personal items of a very functional nature — hair brushes, cooking utensils, books and magazines. A few of the women cooked and ate almost all meals alone in their rooms. The rest both ate alone in their rooms and alone at nearby restaurants, most frequently at downtown cafeterias. Despite their solitary lives, only five subjects made any direct or indirect admission of loneliness.

Although subjects had periodic functional contacts with hotel staff members, they rarely interacted with other hotel residents. Replicating Stephens' findings (1976), the Seattle women viewed their rooms as private places and visiting or entertaining in rooms was not common. The women consistently claimed to neither be friends with or even know other women in their hotels. Those who volunteered the reason for this lack of contact most frequently indicated it was because they considered the other women to be socially inferior: "This is not the class of people I would go with." However, three of the subjects did have longstanding friendships with men who lived in their hotels or whom they had met in previous hotels and with whom they maintained contact.

Personally Experienced Problems

Almost all subjects expressed a strong worry about not having enough money to live on, yet spoke optimistically about their life situations: "I've had my ups and downs but God's been good to me;" "I have fun all the time, darling. I promised myself as long as I'm alive I'm going to live."

Although all but two of the subjects were ambulatory, 14 (87%) reported or were observed to have one or more significant health problems. These included, in order of frequency, hearing problems, nervous disorders, skin problems, and arthritis. Three had been hospitalized for mental illness at some time in their lives, and two of these appeared to be still disturbed.

In spite of having obvious health problems as well as near-poverty-level incomes, almost 1/2 of the subjects reported no present contact with any type of social or health agency. Only 1/3 reported being under regular medical care. Only three had contact with a public assistance agency. All three volunteered negative comments and unpleasant experiences with social workers from the assistance agency: "I didn't get much sleep last night. She (worker) disturbed me and I couldn't get to sleep 'till after 3 a.m. She told me I couldn't stay here, that I couldn't take care of myself. She says I should move." Other negative comments were related to the fear that social workers would force the women to move into nursing homes — an onerous possibility to these women.

Both Shapiro (1971) and Stephens (1976) characterized SRO populations as socially deviant. Erickson and Eckert (1977) found that nearly 1/2 of the SRO population they studied had been in jail, and also found a high percentage of ex-mental patients in the study population. The sample of Seattle women studied did not display the extent of social deviance described in other studies. As noted above, three had experienced hospitalization for mental disorders. However, none manifested indications of other deviance, such as heavy drinking or criminal activities.

Hotel Employees

Interestingly, hotel employees were extremely knowledgeable about individual social and personal traits of these older women. They were generally sympathetic to the needs of older tenants, especially to more frail women, and were frequently involved in providing extra attention or special favors for them including rent reductions, delivering meals to rooms, and the like. Discussion with the hotel managers revealed a shared perceived dilemma regarding the conflict between trying to cover inflating costs by raising rents and the impact such rent increases would have on these elderly women.

Discussion and Implications

Seattle SRO women are a population of contrasts. They express concern over their economic situations and at the same time voice optimism about the future. They are better educated than average for their age cohort, but live in near poverty in low-income neighborhoods. Almost all are currently experiencing serious health problems, yet they assert their independence and desire to be on their own. They boast of solitary independent lives, yet a few admit loneliness. They claim to have chosen SRO residence, but admit that their hotels and neighborhoods are populated by types with whom they prefer not to associate.

Through all these contrasts one theme repeats: the claim of self-sufficiency and independence. These assertions of independence and self-sufficiency can be understood as an ideology or belief system which allows these women to continue to perceive themselves as purposeful, choice-making individuals in control of their own destinies. Whether or not this self-perception is "objectively" accurate, it is essential that we recognize that it is a central element of the normative system shared by all these women. It is a fundamental building block of their self-concepts.

Accompanying this belief system is an objective life-style. Perhaps the most important characteristic of this life-style is the restrictive nature of the social networks of these women. The social contacts of most of these women are limited primarily to interactions with hotel staff and proprietors of the downtown businesses the women frequent. MacElveen (1974) has characterized "restricted" networks: "isolated persons who are strongly bonded with no one or only a few people who are sometimes fairly isolated also." She has noted that, like these SRO women, individuals with restricted networks characteristically value independence believing that they are responsible for solving their own problems. Such individuals typically give and receive little support and help from others.

According to social network theorists, an important characteristic of restrictive networks is that they are easily exhausted by prolonged or multiple crises because they do not provide a "cushion" of potential support which a more extensive social network can provide. Startling evidence has been uncovered by Berkman (1977) of the impact of social network on mortality and morbidity. In a study of mortality of 7,000 adult residents of Alameda County, California, over a 10-year period, she found that people with fewest social contacts had the highest mortality rates from all causes. The extent of social contacts predicted mortality rates *independent of* self-reported health, socioeconomic status, life satisfaction, or preventative health behavior. Apparently a restricted network increases vulnerability to both disease and mortality. The high prevalence of health problems among Seattle SRO women may be directly related to their social isolation.

The strong value placed on independence, privacy, and autonomy exhibited by the Seattle women, coupled with their apparently limited social networks, suggests they may be both more statistically susceptible to illness and more vulnerable to the physical and emotional consequences of illness and other stresses than older individuals rooted in more extensive interpersonal networks. Recalling that 14 (87%) of the sample had one or more serious medical conditions at the time of the study, we begin to wonder how long many of these women will be able to retain their life downtown if their present health deteriorates or if they are subject to additional health problems of other stresses. It appears that many of these women may need outside support from social service and health agencies at some point.

We are confronted with a dilemma. These SRO women have adopted a life-style which is likely to be associated with social and health problems and even early death. Yet they have developed a belief system which provides them with a sense of meaning and purpose in their present lives. They have maintained self-esteem and personal dignity by maintaining an ideology of independence and self-sufficiency. They claim to be satisfied with their lives and with their restricted networks. Ironically, the very ideology of independence, which allows these women to maintain a sense of self-worth while living in isolation and poverty in the inner-city surrounded by strangers of different cultural, ethnic, and economic backgrounds, may contribute to their being vulnerable when confronted with health problems or similar crises because it perpetuates their isolation from social supports.

They are reticent to enter dependent relationships with "helpers" which they perceive could compromise their self-concepts. They either lack contact with or underutilize existing social services which they distrust because they believe representatives of these agencies have power to deny them the life-style of their choosing. The fear is based to some extent on experience. Two subjects had been forced against their will to move from their hotels into nursing homes; both have since returned to the hotel, one claiming to have left the nursing home "against doctor's orders." Word of such incidents spread quickly among SRO elderly. The aversion to social workers means that these women, while eligible for certain financial and service supports, will likely not be approachable or accessible to outreach delivered in the traditional manner by social service workers.

Faced with this dilemma and the apparent need, what approach should be taken in the delivery of social and health services to these women? Should the ideology of independence be respected and these women left as an underserved population to cope with their problems as best they can? Should social service providers ignore the belief system which allows these women a sense of personal dignity and force them into living situations and arrangements which might lead to receipt of better social and health services and perhaps to more expansive network connections? Can and should people be forced into such connections "for their own good?" Or can services be tailored to respect the ideology and belief system of the population? These are difficult questions with no easy solutions, but they must not be ignored.

While social network theory has alerted us to the special problems of this population, it may, as well, provide direction toward reasonable solution of these problems. There may be ways to provide needed services to these women in a manner which will not negatively impact their self-concepts.

One promising approach to service delivery may be to understand and utilize the existing contacts these women have to develop informal helping networks which could provide professionals with additional resources and indirect access to the population through gatekeepers.

Prior studies suggest central figures in the social network, even when restricted, may already function as sources of support and can be utilized in extending social and health services. Dumont (1967) discusses bartenders as primary caregivers in the tavern culture. Feldman (1971) describes utilizing indigenous Alaskans as public welfare aides to help provide services to their communities. Collins and Pancoast (1976) advocate strategies to uncover and support such indigenous resources in the existing social networks as a promising approach to social and health service delivery.

It appears that several people already in routine contact with SRO women could provide a useful link between SRO women and social services. Hotel managers and staff, druggists, waitresses, and grocery-store checkers are all people with high contact present in the environment who could possibly be mobilized. As noted earlier, hotel staffs are in an especially important central position in these women's networks. They are well aware of the special problems of their tenants, and many appear genuinely concerned with assisting the elderly SRO women. As noted earlier, several hotel personnel provide informal care and assistance to tenants when in need, checking on them when ill, bringing food to their rooms, straightening, and even cooking a cup of soup when needed.

Perhaps the support of such people in key positions can be further mobilized. Rewards (money, community gratitude or acknowledgement, etc.) will need to be offered to potential helpers, and it will be important to determine what services are realistic to expect from these people.

One obvious possibility would be for social service agencies to provide information and education to hotel management and staff regarding the services available for older women living in their hotels. Hotel managers and staff already supportive of SRO residents and trusted by them could function to some extent as outreach workers for social services, suggesting appropriate services to tenants for which they were eligible. It might be possible, with appropriate resources and training, to involve some hotel personnel as direct conduits for services and financial assistance. Serving as gatekeepers for services to the population could be advantageous both to hotel personnel and their tenants. Obtaining adequate resources for tenants could help ensure that rent bills would be paid, that hotel residents would encounter fewer disruptive health emergencies and that chronic health needs would be met with adequate services. Ultimately this approach might enable the elderly women to stay in the hotels rather than facing the prospects of rapid deterioration and the dreaded move to a nursing home.

There are other approaches which would not necessarily change the restricted network style of these women but enhance the coping skills and style in which they wish to live. For example, instead of moving SRO women into high-rise senior communities, the possibility of providing rent subsidies to help maintain their current autonomy within their environment could be explored. A program of direct cash payments or food vouchers usable in neighborhood restaurants could also be established in addition to the usual low-cost meals at senior citizen centers which this population rarely attends. Rather than insisting on group involvement with this population, one-to-one instruction in individual techniques of coping and stress reduction could be offered. Examples could include various conventional relaxation techniques, biofeedback, or meditation exercises. Finally, we would suggest that instead of extensive traditional needs-assessment surveys used to plan for this population, research on this population be carried out in a low-keyed, nondirective, and nonthreatening manner, informally in hotels or restaurants and other frequented settings in order to allow subjects the greatest latitude to define who they are and what needs they face in their environment.

We hope this paper will do more than draw attention to the necessity for more research about this unique and little-known population. We hope it will encourage those involved in planning and service delivery to inner-city residents to consider the culture of independent SRO women and to develop service approaches which complement rather than depreciate their chosen life-styles and self-concepts.

REFERENCES

Bahr, H. M. *Disaffiliated man: Essays and bibliography on skid row, vagrancy and outsiders.* Univ. Toronto Press, Toronto, 1970.

Bahr, H. M., & Garrett, G. R. *Women alone.* Health & Co., Washington, 1976.

Berkman, L. F. *Social networks, host resistance and mortality: A follow-up study of Alameda County residents.* School of Public Health, Dept. of Epidemiology, Univ. California, (dissertation), Berkeley, 1977.

Collins, A., & Pancoast, D. *Natural helping networks: A strategy for prevention.* NASW Publ., Washington, 1976.

Dumont, M. Tavern culture: The sustenance of homeless men, *American Journal of Orthopsychiatry*, 1967, *37*, 938-945.

Ehrlich, P. A study: Characteristics and needs of the St. Louis downtown SRO elderly, In *The Invisible Elderly.* The National Council on the Aging, Inc., St. Louis, May 1976.

Ehrlich, P. *Housing Committee Report*, unpubl. paper, 1976.

Erickson, R., & Eckert, K. The elderly poor in downtown San Diego hotels, *Gerontolo-*

gist, 1977, *17,* Part 1, 440-446.

Feldman, F. L. Reaching rural Alaskan Natives through human service aides, *Welfare in Review,* 1971, *9,* 9-14.

Hennig, M., & Jardim, A. *The managerial woman.* Anchor Press, New York, 1977.

MacElveen, P. M. Social networks, in *Clinical Practice in Psychosocial Nursing.* Appleton-Century Co., New York, 1974.

Shapiro, J. *Communications of the alone, working with single room occupants in the city.* Association Press, New York, 1971.

Stephens, J. *Loners, lovers, and losers: Elderly tenants in a slum hotel.* Univ. Washington Press, Seattle, 1976.

Chapter 31

IT'S TOUGH TO BE OLD*

ALOYSE HAHN

I AM 94 years old. Six years ago, my family put me in a nursing home, but I don't know why. I hear them say, "No one home . . . everyone works . . . unsafe to be alone," but I do not understand. Of course, I accepted their decision — I came here — but I cry inside every day. Each time they come to visit me, I beseech them to take me home.

My life is a moment to moment proposition; for me there may be no tomorrow. All I want is to die in my own bed at home — not in a world of strangers. I want to hold my daughter's hand and be surrounded by those people and things I love. And when I can no longer see, or hear, or touch — when my time has come — I want to know that my family will protect me — will use me right — will lovingly dress my body and lay it to rest.

How can I trust these strangers? What if I should die with no one here? Will they wrap me in that mummy sheet and haul my body onto that steel cart? I've seen others die here; I've seen the actions and heard the sounds that accompany such a happening. I'm afraid.

My mind slips rapidly and I know this, but I cannot prevent it. What I remember best are things that happened in the past, only they seem to be really happening now. To me there is no past, present, or future; the 1960s or the 1900s are equally current with me. I look for my own mother. Or my babies are small and need care. "Confused, disoriented," the nurses say, not knowing the inner workings of my mind.

Actually, I'm well aware of most situations but, with things flashing through my mind the way they do, I'm likely to speak of my school days in the same breath as I talk about the noise of traffic outside my window. I know it's confusing to others, but I can't help it. I cry out in desperation, "What's happening to me!" I wish the nurses wouldn't write me off as "not in touch." I wish they wouldn't discuss me as if I couldn't hear or didn't realize what's going on. I wish they wouldn't take my responses for granted.

*From American Journal of Nursing, 70(8):1698-99, Aug. 1970. ©1970. Reproduced with permission.

But there's one nurse who is such a joy — she gently touches me and smiles at me when I look questioningly at her. She tries to explain what is happening and, though I don't always understand, I feel comforted and safe because I know she means me no harm. Sometimes she puts her arm around me or pats my shoulder just to let me know that everything's all right. She never fails to hold my hand for a few seconds after she puts me to bed and she always says, "Goodnight, sleep tight."

Another thing she's so good about is when I have an accident with my bowels or urine. I get so upset because I don't always know when I need to go to the bathroom. Sometimes I'm so mortified that I tell the nurses, "It wasn't me — must have been someone else who soiled my bed." But this nurse always tells me it's all right, manages a little smile, and helps me put on dry clothes. Not like the others who shake their fingers at me and shame me for this. Sometimes they even let me lie or sit in it for punishment.

Many times I can't eat my food. Most of the time I'm just not hungry, but sometimes I can't chew the food and sometimes I daydream and forget it is there. The nurse I like always sits with me for a few minutes and coaxes me. And if she hasn't time to sit very long, well, she comes back sometimes to feed me a forkful, sometimes to talk to me, sometimes to show me what to eat next. Some of the others, though, try to put a knife between my lips and teeth so I'll open my mouth. Others just leave the tray there for about 15 minutes and say, "Well, she won't eat anyway."

But I can't chew raw carrots and celery or cabbage, and sometimes the meat is burned and dried. I don't like it when the food is all jumbled together; it makes me sick to look at it. Often they spill the coffee and milk so I only have a couple of mouthfuls left to drink. Have you ever tried to eat dry pancakes for supper? If only I could explain why I can't eat.

Some days I am more tired than others and need to lie on my bed for an hour or so to rest. I don't always sleep — sometimes I just lie there awake — but most of the nurses don't like it. I don't think they understand that the days from seven in the morning to eight at night are often too long for me. I wonder if those who make me sit up all day will be half as energetic when they are 94.

I used to have a whole house of my own but now my world has shrunk to this little area of my bed and chair. Most nurses are respectful of my area, treating the few things I have left with care. But others are like some bold children who visited in my home once and pawed through my drawers and broke my antique vase. Some of the people here remind me of the neighborhood bullies who thought the world was theirs for the taking and knocked down anyone in their way.

And another thing that is devastating is to have my room changed. Time and time again I see a friend hauled off to a new eight by six area in a strange room. And sometimes it happens to me: suddenly, without warning a caravan of nurses and aides will appear and begin taking clothes from my closet in preparation for the move. All of us dread this happening.

I need to know, when I get out of my bed in the morning, that I can get back into that same bed at night. Some days I'm so afraid I won't be able to that I resist getting up. And sometimes I refuse to go for a walk in the hall because it may be a ruse to move me into another room. If I have to move again, I think it will break my heart.

I've had a hard life — never much money or many clothes or possessions. I'm not extravagant. I have known depression days and times of hunger, and I have patched the patches on my clothes. Is it any wonder that I like to have a small piece of bread or cracker in my purse just in case there is no food tomorrow or in case I get hungry tonight? There's no pantry or ice box I can go to. Sometimes an aide brings a cup of juice or milk. But nothing to eat. "It makes crumbs," she says. Or, "Well, you should have eaten your supper. Then you wouldn't be hungry."

I often say, "I want to die." But I don't really want to die. What I'm actually saying is that I just desperately want relief from some painful situation at the moment. I cling tenaciously to the scraps of my life. I fear the unknown. I'm very frail.

Sometimes I look deep into the eyes of a nurse and ask, "How would you like to be me?" I can remember back to my youth when I never gave a thought to growing old, and I think these youngsters who are nurses are doing today what I did then: they are hiding — from thoughts of old age. They don't really want to look at me — to know me — because in me they would see themselves as they will be some day and they don't want to do that.

Some day you'll be just like me, I want to say to them when I'm feeling bitter. Will you remember then another little old lady a long time ago who said, "How would you like to be me?"

It's tough to get old. I know that sometimes I'm stubborn. And I know that my very slowness in thinking, pondering, and taking time to be sure before I do anything exasperates others. But I have lived more days and seen and done more things than anyone around me — that makes my values a little different. Now I need security and understanding and hope. I need respect, too, but most of all I need love.

Part VII

Looking Ahead: Old Tomorrow

INTRODUCTION

In the century ahead, what will the world be like for the aged? Two gerontologists take educated guesses on different ways of answering that question. Chapter 32 evaluates the status of the aged relative to that of younger people in the future, and Chapter 33 predicts the health, wealth, and education of the aged in two possibly differing worlds of the future.

Erdman Palmore questions (Chapter 32) whether the *relative* status of the aged in education, occupation, income, and health will increase or decrease with the years. Using hard data such as Census and National Center for Health statistics, Palmore compared different time periods in the 1960s and 1970s as a basis for projections of later conditions. The outcome provides a generally optimistic assessment of the future, especially for improvements in the relative incomes of aged women.

Bernice Neugarten considers (Chapter 33) contrasting views about the kind of world it will be in 2025 — with widely different positions for the aged in the two worlds. If problems of over-population, pollution, inflation, etc., doom us to failure, the aged may be disadvantaged or even expendable. In a world of "equilibrium," the treatment of the elderly may symbolize society's most humane achievements. All in all, our forecasters of the future predict a better world for those old tomorrow!

Chapter 32

THE FUTURE STATUS OF THE AGED*

Erdman Palmore

Writers on the future of aging usually agree that the next generation of older persons will be healthier, will have more income, higher status occupations, and more education than the present generation (Neugarten, 1975). However, little attention has been devoted to the future status of the aged *relative* to that of younger persons. There is considerable evidence that the health, income, occupations, and education of younger age groups are also rising. Therefore, it is possible that despite small absolute gains in these areas, the aged will not keep up with younger age groups and will suffer relative losses when compared with the gains of younger groups. Indeed, we have demonstrated that this is exactly what happened between 1940 and 1968 in the areas of income, employment, education, and residential density (Palmore & Whittington, 1971). Furthermore, we have shown that the relative status of the aged generally tends to decline with modernization, although the decline appears to taper off in the most modernized societies (Palmore & Manton, 1974). The question this paper attempts to answer is whether the relative status of the USA aged in health, income, occupation, and education is likely to increase or decrease during the rest of this century.

This question has relevance for several theoretical controversies in gerontology and sociology. Does the relative status of the aged continue to decline in modernized societies (Cowgill & Holmes, 1972)? Is age stratification becoming more or less important in the USA (Riley, Johnson, & Foner, 1972)? Are the aged becoming more or less like a disadvantaged minority group (Palmore & Whittington, 1971)? The question also has practical relevance for policy planning and for the future outlook of the present middleaged generation.

Health

There are several factors affecting the relative health of the aged

---

which could have opposing effects. First, the aged as a group are becoming older. Between 1960 and 1970, the group over 75 grew at a rate three times as great as the group aged 65 through 74 (34% vs. 13%; Brotman, no date). Since older age is associated with increasing rates of illness and disability, the increasing age of the older population would be expected to increase illness and disability rates. This could be called the aging factor.

A second factor, changing cohorts, should have the opposite effect. As cohorts born since the turn of the century replace those born earlier, the average health of the aged should improve because of the better nutrition, health care, and general living standards enjoyed by the later cohorts during their formative and early adult years.

A third factor is the presumed improvement in medical care for the aged. The start of Medicare and Medicaid probably improved health care for older people during the last decade. However, the effects of this improved health care on the actual health of the aged have been unknown and debatable. It is usually assumed that better health care brings better health. However, some fear that this is not true for the aged in the USA. They suggest that better health care and longevity among the aged may result in *more* senility and physical disability among the aged population.

Fortunately, we can now measure the net effect of these factors on the relative health status of the aged since 1961, because in that year the National Center for Health Statistics began publishing periodic statistics on the prevalence of diseases and impairments by age groups (National Center for Health Statistics, 1963-1975). These statistics are based on the National Health Interview Survey (NHIS) which involves a probability sample of the entire civilian, noninstitutionalized population of the USA. The statistics are adjusted by age, sex, and race in order to closely resemble the age, sex, and race composition of the total USA population. They are recognized as the most representative, unbiased, and accurate estimates of general health in the USA. They do not include those in institutions, but this leaves out only 1% of those under 65 and 4% or 5% of those over 65.

The NHIS has five indicators of general illness or disability.

(1) LIMITATION OF ACTIVITY DUE TO CHRONIC CONDITIONS. This includes limitations in major activity (such as work, housework, or going to school) and limitations in other activities (such as athletics, clubs, and hobbies).

(2) LIMITATION OF MOBILITY DUE TO CHRONIC CONDITIONS. This includes three categories of mobility limitation: confined to the house, cannot get around alone, and has trouble getting around

alone.

(3) RESTRICTED ACTIVITY DAYS (PER PERSON). These are days in which a person cuts down on his usual activities for the whole of that day on account of an illness or an injury. This covers the range from substantial reduction to complete inactivity for the entire day and includes all bed days.

(4) BED-DISABILITY DAYS (PER PERSON). These are days in which a person stays in bed for all or most of the day because of a specific illness or injury. All hospital days for inpatients are considered to be days of bed disability even if the patient was not actually in bed at the hospital.

(5) ACUTE CONDITIONS (PER PERSON). These are conditions which have lasted less than 3 months and which have involved either medical attention or restricted activity. All conditions classified as chronic because of their long-term effects are excluded from this category regardless of onset.

These measures are the only indicators of general illness and disability available from the NHIS over the period since 1961, but together they present a fairly comprehensive picture of trends in relative health status. For each indicator we plotted the ratio of the measure for those over age 65 to the measure for those under 65, for each year in which data were available. These ratios have the advantage of controlling for fluctuations in the over-all levels of the measure (due to epidemics, other unusual conditions, or changes in survey methods) as well as indicating how the health of the aged compares to that of others.

The top two indicators, limitation of mobility and limitation of activity, show clear declines during this period, which indicates improving health among the aged compared to the non-aged. Two other indicators, bed disability days and acute conditions, show small declines, while restricted activity days show no consistent trend. It seems clear that the relative health status of the aged is certainly not getting worse and in some respects it appears to be improving.

Therefore, it appears that the improved medical care for the aged and the changing cohorts among the aged are canceling out the effects of the aged population growing older, so that the relative health status of the aged is improving at least in some respects.

Income

Our previous study (Palmore & Whittington, 1971) showed that the income gap between persons over 65 and those under 65 widened steadily between 1950 and 1967. Even though the absolute levels of income among the aged went up, they did not keep up with the faster rate of increase among those under 65. On the other hand, Schultz (1972, 1975) has projected income and asset data for the aged to the year 1990 and concludes that their economic welfare will show a substantial improvement. But will this improvement keep up with the over-all improvement among those under 65?

One basis for answering this question is to plot the recent trend in the income ratio of the aged to the non-aged and assume that, other things being equal, this trend will continue for the rest of this century. The ratios of the mean money income for those over 65 compared to those under 65 have increased substantially since 1967 for both men and women. The men's ratio went up from .466 to .521 and the women's ratio went up from .563 to .634. If we project this increase to the year 2000, the aged men would have about 73% as much income as non-aged men, and aged women would have about 90% as much income as non-aged women (whether this is a reasonable projection is discussed below).

Another basis for answering the question is to observe the recent trend in frequency of poverty among the aged compared to the non-aged (Current Population Reports, 1975). In 1967 there were over twice as many of the aged below the official USA poverty ("low-income") levels compared to the total population (29.5% compared to 14.2%). But by 1974, the proportion of the aged in poverty had been cut in half so that their proportion was only 4 percentage points higher than that of the total population (15.7% compared to 11.6%). Apparently the increased Social Security benefits, the new Supplemental Security Income, and other programs for the aged have succeeded in reducing poverty among the aged to levels approaching those of the total population.

Thus, it is clear that around 1967 there was a turn-around in the declining income status of the aged so that their relative income has substantially increased since then. *If* this trend continues for the rest of the century, poverty among the aged will be at about the same level as among the rest of the population, and the average older person will have about 73 to 90% as much income as the average younger person.

The big question is whether these trends will continue. The spread of pension plans will tend to increase income of the aged. Social Security benefits and other government pension programs will probably continue to rise because they now have provisions to automatically increase benefits as the cost of living increases. In addition to increasing pensions, Social Security benefits and other government programs, the main forces behind the aged's increasing income are their rising occupation and education levels. Higher occupations and more education mean more and better pensions, Social Security benefits, savings, and earnings. Therefore, if occupations and education continue to rise relative to those of younger persons, then the relative income of the aged also should continue to rise. We now turn to estimates of the future occupation and education levels of the aged.

Occupation

In our previous analysis (Palmore & Whittington, 1971), we found that one of the few dimensions in which the aged had gains relative to younger persons was their occupation distribution. There was an over-all increase of four percentage points in the occupation Similarity Index between 1940 and 1965.

The Similarity Index (SI) is the best single indicator of the relative similarity or equality of two groups on any noncontinuous variable such as occupation. It may be described in several ways. In its application to the similarity between the occupation distributions of the aged and non-aged, it is the proportion of the aged and non-aged occupation percentage distributions which overlap each other. Or, it is the proportion of the aged who are similar to the same proportion of the non-aged in their occupations. It can be thought of as the percentage of complete similarity, because 100 would mean that there is complete identity between the two percentage distributions, and 50 would mean that 50% of the inferior group would have to move upward to equal the higher group. The SI is simple to calculate: the percentage of the aged in a category is compared to the percentage of the non-aged in that category, and the lesser of the two percentages in each category are summed. Algebraically, it may be stated as $\sum_{i=1}^{N} (a \bullet X_i + b \bullet Y_i)$

where X = percentage of one group in i category, Y_i = percentage of the other group in the i category; $a = 1$ when $X < Y$; $a = 0$ when $X > Y$; $b = 1$ when $Y < X$; and $b = 0$ when $Y > X$ (Palmore & Manton, 1974).

The difficulty with comparing the occupations of the aged and non-aged at present is that the majority of the aged no longer have any occupations. However, we can estimate the *future* similarity of the aged and middle-aged by comparing the occupations of the present middle-aged generation (ages 45-64) with those of the present young adults (ages 25-44), because in 20 years the present middle-aged will constitute most of the future aged[1] and the present young adults will be the future middle-aged. Assuming little shift in relative occupation distributions of these two generations, the comparison of present middle-aged with young adults gives us an estimate of what the occupational similarity between the aged and middle-aged will be 20 years from now. (The expected 1970 to 1990 upward shift in occupations of the present young adults will probably be about the same as the 1950 to 1970 shift of the 1950 young adults used in the trend comparison below.)

We used the 1970 USA Census data on the 11 major occupation categories to compute the SI (separately by sex) for those 45-64 compared to those 25-44 who were employed. The results showed that men had an occupation SI of 92 and women had an occupation SI of 91. This means that in 1990 about 92 and 91% of the aged men and women, respectively, will have had occupations similar to those of the middle-aged men and women. Or to put it the other way, 8 or 9% of the aged men and women will have had lower occupations than 8 or 9% of the middle-aged.

Then, in order to establish the trends, we did the same calculations for the year 1950 to get an estimate of the occupation SI for the 1970 aged and middle-aged. This resulted in an occupation SI of 89 for the men and 87 for the women. Thus, between 1970 and 1990 the occupation SI for the aged and middle-aged should rise by about three or four points. The effects on the SI of differential mortality by occupation should be about the same for the two time periods. This gives us one basis for predicting a continued rise in relative income for the aged. We now turn to an examination of the fourth dimension, educational status, to see if it is also rising.

Education

Our previous study found that despite increasing average educational levels among the aged, they did not keep up with younger people, and between 1940 and 1969 the education SI of those over 65, compared to those aged 16 through 64, steadily decreased from 77 to

---

[1]In year 2000, 90% of those over age 65 will be under age 85 (Administration on Aging, 1975).

63 for a loss of 14 points. However, the *rate* of increase in completed education among younger people (which accounts for the decrease in the aged/non-aged SI) appears to have slowed, so that the similarity in educational levels between the aged and non-aged may "bottom-out" and actually increase in the future.

Fortunately for our purposes, the over-all distribution of cohorts over age 25, by years of education completed, changes little over a 20-year period. Therefore, we can estimate the 1994 education SI for the future aged and middle-aged by computing the 1974 education SI for the present middle-aged (45-64) and young adults (25-44). Using USA Census data on completed years of education by age groups, this SI turns out to be 80 for men and 83 for women (Current Population Reports, 1975). This means that in 1994, about 80% of aged men and 83% of aged women will have educations similar to the same percentages of middle-aged men and women (the effects of differential mortality by education would be to increase the education SI by 1994).

When we compute the 1974 education SI for the present aged and middle-aged, we find that they are substantially lower: 72 for men and 73 for women. Thus, over the next 20 years the education SI for the aged compared to middle aged should rise by about eight to ten points. This gives us a second basis for predicting a continued rise in relative income for the aged.

Forces Behind Rising Status

This evidence that the relative status of the aged in health, income, occupation, and education is rising and probably will continue to rise for the rest of this century contradicts the theories that the status of the aged continues to decline in modernized societies, that age stratification is becoming more important in the USA, and that the aged are becoming more like a disadvantaged minority group. On the contrary, it supports the opposite theories that in the most modernized societies such as the USA the relative status of the aged "bottoms-out" and begins to rise; that we are moving in the direction of an "age-irrelevant society" as far as the socioeconomic status of the aged are concerned, and that the aged are losing some of their minority group characteristics.

One basic force behind this change from declining status to rising status for the aged is the slowing in rates of change for the younger cohorts. The dramatic rate of improvement in health and longevity achieved in the first half of this century has decreased. Increases in purchasing power of income has leveled off. The massive shifts from rural to urban occupations and from lower status to higher status occupations have been reduced. Educational attainment has begun to level off. All of these diminished rates of change have the effect of reducing the discrepancies between older and younger generations so that the future older generation will not lag so far behind the younger. As a result, the status of the aged relative to younger people begins to rise.

Another force has been the increase in both government and private programs to improve the health, income, occupations, and education of the aged. Continuation or expansion of these programs are probably required for the continued rise in status of the aged. Thus, these findings should not be interpreted as justification for diminishing the public and private programs which have contributed to the aged's rising status. On the contrary, this evidence could be interpreted as demonstrating the beneficial effects of these programs and justifying their continuation and expansion.

Summary

The question this paper attempts to answer is whether the status of the aged, relative to that of younger groups, is likely to increase or decrease in the areas of health, income, occupation, and education. Using data from the National Health Interview Survey since 1961, it was found that two of the five indicators showed clear improvements in the relative health status of the aged, two other indicators showed small improvements, and the fifth remained fairly level. Using USA Census data on mean incomes by age since 1967, it was found that the relative incomes of both older men and older women have substantially increased. Also, the proportion of the aged in poverty has declined at a faster rate than in the general population. Using USA Census data to compute occupation Similarity Indexes for the aged compared to the middle-aged in 1970 and estimating these indexes for 1990, it was concluded that the relative occupational status of the aged should rise by about three or four points by 1990. Similar estimates were made for the education Similarity Index of the aged compared to the middle-aged in 1974 and 1994, and it was concluded that the relative educational status should rise by about eight to ten points by 1994. These rises in the relative status of the aged were interpreted as being caused by both the slowing rates of change among younger persons in these areas and by the increased public and private programs to improve the health, income, occupations, and education of the aged. This evidence indicates that present programs for the aged are having beneficial effects and can be used to justify the continuation or expansion of such programs. It also contradicts the theories that the status of the aged continues to decline in modern societies, that age stratification is becoming more important, and that the aged are becoming more like a disadvantaged minority group.

REFERENCES

Administration on Aging. Estimates of the size and characteristics of the older population in 1974 and projections to the year 2000. Statistical Memo No. 31, DHEW, Washington, 1975.

Brotman, H. The older population revisited. *Facts and Figures on Older Americans, 2,* Administration on Aging, DHEW, Washington, no date.

Cowgill, D., & Holmes, L. (Eds.), *Aging and modernization.* Appleton-Century-Crofts, New York, 1972.

Current Population Reports. Money income and poverty status of families and persons in the U.S.: 1974. Series P-60, No. 99. USGPO, Washington, 1975.

National Center for Health Statistics. Data from the National Health Survey, Series 10. USGPO, Washington, 1963-1975.

Neugarten, B. (Ed.) Aging in the year 2000: A look at the future. *Gerontologist,* 1975, *15,* 1:2, 1-40.

Palmore, E., & Manton, K. Modernization and status of the aged: International correlations. *Journal of Gerontology,* 1974, *29,* 205-210.

Palmore, E., & Whittington, F. Trends in the relative status of the aged. *Social Forces,* 1971, *50,* 84-91.

Riley, M., Johnson, M., & Foner, A. *Aging and society, Vol. 8: A sociology of age stratification.* Russell Sage Foundation, New York, 1972.

Schultz, J., Comparative simulation analysis of Social Security systems. *Annals of Economic & Social Measurement,* 1972, *1,* 109-127.

Schultz, J. *The search for retirement income adequacy.* Brandeis Univ. Press, Waltham, MA, 1975.

Chapter 33

THE AGED IN THE YEAR 2025*

BERNICE L. NEUGARTEN

ALL through history men and women have con-
templated the future and have made various forms of predictions.
There have been at least three types of professional futurists: first,
visionaries and utopians; second, science fiction writers; and third,
scientists who identify their work as "futures research."

For the most part it has been science fiction writers who have been
concerned with the future of aging and the aged, although there are a
few exceptions among scientists. A few biologists have begun to make
predictions about solving the secrets of the aging cell and extending
the human life span, and now a few social scientists have begun to
look at the changing numbers of old and young in the population at
the fact that ours is an aging society, and at some of the social,
economic, political, and ethical implications.[1]

What Kind of World Will It Be in 2025?

A wide range of predictions regarding the future of the world have
been put before the public in the past few years, some of them optimistic, others pessimistic.

Some futurists are saying that man will solve the problems of over-
population, food and energy shortages, inflation, environmental pollution, and the threat of nuclear distruction, and that he will do so
largely by the continued growth of science and technology. Other

---

*From Aging in America's Future: A Symposium. Nov. 1975, pp. 10-21.
[1]A group of faculty and graduate students at the University of Chicago have been trying
to forecast demographic and social developments, to anticipate the problems of aging
and the aging society that lie ahead, and then to decide what types of new research are
needed for formulating social and governmental policies that will be future-oriented.
This paper draws liberally from a prior publication, "Aging in the Year 2000: A Look
at the Future," The Gerontologist, Vol. 15, February 1975, Pt. 2, Bernice L. Neugarten,
editor; and from a group of papers prepared for a conference held in May 1975 on
"Social Policy, Social Ethics, and the Aging Society," whose proceedings will appear
soon in book form, edited by Bernice L. Neugarten and Robert J. Havighurst.

futurists are saying that, because of the very growth of science and technology, the problems are now so vast that man's efforts are doomed to failure. In the latter view, as for instance, in Robert Heilbroner's *The Human Prospect*, there will be a few decades in which economic and political crises will escalate, and social disorganization will follow; then, a period of about 50 years in which there will be various forms of social and political transformations, including genuine economic decline; and then, about a century from now, a more stable form of civilization based on small communities, agricultural economies, and very slow rates of social change. In short, if man survives, he will — in the course of a century or so — move from the industrialized to a deindustrialized society. We are, therefore, headed toward a new version of the Dark Ages.

A less grim prospect is held by others, such as my colleague, Professor Robert Havighurst, who has begun to talk about an "equilibrium" society in which the size and then the age distribution of the American population will stabilize. The economic growth rate will decline and be close to zero by the year 2000. There will be new sources of energy, with coal, atomic fusion, and solar energy replacing petroleum. Pollution will be partially controlled, although it will still present dangers. The large proportion of the world's energy and food output now being consumed by the United States will be substantially reduced. While the picture will be different in various parts of the world, especially in the so-called underdeveloped nations, overall it will be a world of dynamic equilibrium, not growing, not diminishing; and in societies like the United States there will be a reasonable level of material comfort. The tasks for the more affluent nations will be, first, to achieve a stable equilibrium of population and production; and, second, to cooperate with poorer nations in helping them achieve similar goals.

The position of the aged would be very different in these two future worlds. In the first scenario, there would be increasing alienation, conflict between age groups as well as between other groups, and the old would be greatly disadvantaged, even expendable. In the second scenario, the social system would continue to become more equitable as interdependence of all groups and all nations becomes more inescapable. Older persons would get their fair share of whatever goods would be produced, for on the one hand their labor would be more needed than now, and on the other hand, the presence of many frail elderly would come increasingly to symbolize man's most humane achievements. Along the latter lines, we are being told, for instance, that values will change from competition to cooperation; that the dominant ethic will change from an exploitative to a self-realization ethic,. both for individuals and nations; that either a "humanistic capitalism" or a "humanistic socialism" will be one step on the way to the Ethical State and the Moral Society.

Whether these views are visionary or not, it is certain that the society in which people grow old will be very different in the year 2025 and that all aspects of life will be affected.

How Many Older Persons Will There Be?

Whatever the uncertainties in other areas, the numbers of older people can be relatively safely projected for the next 50 years, because the projections depend on death rates and not on birth rates. Everybody who will be old by the year 2025 is already 15 years old or older. But will he live a great deal longer than his predecessors?

Two general strategies for lengthening life are being pursued by biomedical and biological researchers: the first is the continuing effort to conquer diseases; the other, to alter the intrinsic biological processes presumed to underlie aging — that is, to discover the genetic and biochemical secrets of aging, then to slow the biological clock that is presumably operating. This second approach is directed at *rate control* rather than disease control. Thus far all the increases in longevity have been due to disease control.

Are there likely to be dramatic discoveries with regard to rate control that will lead to a mushrooming in the numbers of older persons by the year 2025? A group of us at the University of Chicago have been making inquiries of leading biological researchers, and while there are a few notable exceptions, on the whole their responses add up to this: By the year 2000, biologists will probably *understand* the aging process, but there is not likely to be any treatment or magic elixir to prolong life that will be widely available, let alone widely used. By the year 2025, the situation may be different, for 50 years is a very long period of time for making predictions with regard to scientific discoveries. It would appear, nevertheless, that even by 2025, the increases in longevity are likely to continue to accrue from gains in disease control. Even if there were a so-called biological breakthrough, the wide-scale human testing that would be required of any drug or anti-aging treatment would not have had time to establish clear-cut results with regard to both efficacy and safety.

But even without any new basic biological discoveries and without any sudden jump in the length of the human life span, the numbers of aged will increase dramatically.

IF DEATH RATES STAY APPROXIMATELY THE SAME: At present there are slightly under 22 million persons aged 65+ in United States. The Census Bureau estimates that by the year 2000 the total will be about 28 million; and by the year 2025 it will be over 42 million. (These projections are based on very slight declines in death rates until 2000, then no declines). Under this conservative estimate, the number of old will be almost doubled by 2025.

Roughly two out of three of the old are aged 75+, a group that can be called the "old-old." While the proportion of this group will go up and down a bit, it will remain about one-third of the aged population.

Older women outnumber older men, and unless we discover why this is so and how the lives of men can be prolonged — a series of discoveries not likely to occur in only 50 years — the disparity is not likely to disappear. Thus by 2025 our aged population will be even more heavily weighted toward women, and toward widowed women.

IF DEATH RATES DECLINE: Suppose we take a different set of assumptions: namely, that mortality rates will decline as a result of increasing medical knowledge, improved health practices, and improved health-care delivery. Suppose, for instance, that they are reduced by 2 percent per year for all persons aged 20+, with these reductions cumulative from year to year. (This projection may be overly optimistic. It may depend upon such practices as reduced cigarette smoking, reduced consumption of foods that now increase the likelihood of heart disease, reduced atmospheric pollution, and improved health services. Or it may depend upon factors that we do not yet know about, especially since the latest drops in deaths from heart disease do not seem to be the result of the factors just mentioned — not, at least, according to the National Center for Health Statistics. In any case, this projection does not seem altogether unreasonable in light of the latest data that show that life expectancy has increased more in the three years 1969-1971 than at any time in the past two decades.)

Under this set of assumptions, in the year 2000 the number of old will be about 35.5 million (instead of 28); the number of old-old will be about 18 million (instead of 12) and will be closer to 1 out of 2 of the aged population instead of 1 out of 3. For the year 2025, it is clear that the numbers would be far beyond those we have mentioned and with an even greater piling up of persons at advanced old age.

This 2 percent drop in death rates would add about 3 to 5 years of life expectancy by the year 2000 *for persons who reach 65;* and it might add about 5 to 8 years by the year 2025. (Today a man who reaches 65 can expect to live to 78.5; a woman, to 82.5. Add to these averages another average of 5 to 8 extra years, and we would have enormous numbers of persons living into their 90s and very large numbers of centenarians.)

What Proportion of the Population Will Be Old?

The *proportions* of older people will depend, of course, upon the total size of the population and, in turn, upon birth rates. Because the latter have been so unstable, the Census Bureau now publishes 6 different sets of projections, each based on a different birth rate. One of these projections leads to zero population growth as early as 2027, only a few years beyond our target date of 2025. If zero population growth does occur by then, the American population will be about 254 million in total, an increase of about a fourth, but the number of old, as we have already said, will have doubled.

What is meant by an aging society can be seen also by another comparison: At present, for every person 65+ in the society, there are about 4 young persons — that is, children and adolescents under age 20. But in 2025, if zero population growth has been achieved, for every person 65+ there will be only 1.5 young persons.

It may be difficult to keep these figures in mind, but it is worth commenting that the numbers game has been played with a great many errors. The mass media have been making startlingly inaccurate statements. We should take as science fiction the headlines that say that by the year 2000 there will be 25 percent or 33 percent of the population who will be old. That cannot happen unless women suddenly stop having babies altogether.

At present the old constitute about 10 percent of the population. In 2000, if birth rates remain low, even as low as the zero population growth rate, the old will constitute no more than about 12 percent. And in 2025, under the same conditions, they will constitute around 16 percent.

What Will Be the Health Status of Older People?

Given the assumptions that life expectancy will continue to increase, and that the increase will come from continuingly improved disease control, it follows by definition that older persons will have improved health in the future.

The realities are in fact more complex. The relations of various forms of morbidity to mortality are not well understood, nor the relations of mortality at younger ages to mortality rates at later ages. There are various definitions of health and various indices used for measuring it. Levels of education and socioeconomic status are related both to morbidity and to mortality, and so on. Suffice it to say that for the short-run future, we can presume better levels of health for older persons because poverty has been diminishing over the life-cycles of successive cohorts of persons, because educational levels have been rising, and because more effective forms of public health and health care have had their effects — all this for persons who are presently middle-aged and who will be the old of the year 2000.

If, in the longer run, the same general conditions continue to prevail so that the persons who are presently young will continue to have these benefits, then they too will be relatively healthier when they reach their own old age. But here we are, of course, on shakier ground, just as we will be throughout the remainder of this paper, for it is harder to predict the new combinations of public health measures, air and water pollution, expenditures to be made in health care delivery, and so on, for the period after 2000.

All this says little, furthermore, regarding the period of disability that can be expected to occur for most people in the very last phase of life. For the moment, we have little basis for predicting that this period will become shorter — either by the year 2000 or by the year 2025. It would be ideal if a person could maintain physical and psychological vigor through his eighth or ninth decade, then die quickly without a long period of terminal illness. An example is Picasso, who reputedly maintained his full physical, mental, and creative abilities to the day before his death. But the prospect may be the opposite: that with increasing age, people will have a drawn-out period of physical and psychological debility, with medical services that can keep them alive, but keep them neither healthy nor happy. This is, indeed, the spectre that haunts most of us when we think of our own old age; and it is the spectre that haunts medical and social planners when they think of the aging society.

Income and Work

The economic situation of the old in United States has improved dramatically in the past 2 decades, just as it has in other industrialized societies. (Very generally speaking, the economic status of the old has depended upon the level of industrialization in a given country more than upon one or another political ideology.) At present it is a minority of the old in this country who are poor (not that this minority does not constitute an important problem). The range of incomes and other economic assets is wider for old people, of course, than for young, and there are many older people who are rich.

Economic status is a complex topic. A person's economic status in old age depends, not only on the level of technology, but on many other factors: his earlier work pattern, his savings pattern, public and private pension systems, and most important, the political and ethical questions that underlie the formation of public policy with regard to the allocation of resources. Because it is so complex, it is literally impossible to predict the economic situation for the old in 2025.

One factor that will probably remain true is that economic well-being for the individual is closely tied to work or retirement. Since for most people, a big drop in income comes with retirement, it will be important to watch the supply and demand for workers. For the next few decades, with the enormous numbers of young people in our population, the proportion of older workers in the labor force will probably continue to decline. Up to the year 2000 there will be a continuing drop in age of retirement, and along with it, increasing problems for the society in maintaining the economic well-being of the old.

By the year 2025 we may have another turnabout, for with smaller numbers of the young, and with increasing health and longevity of the old, the proportions of older workers may rise again as their labor becomes needed again. This will be particularly true if the trend develops toward labor-intensive rather than energy-intensive production patterns — that is, where more man-hours of labor will be needed to make up for energy shortages. It will depend also on whether or not productivity increases in terms of output per man-hour.

At the same time, because there will be so many old-old people, the economic burdens on the society at large are likely to become greater. If old age continues to bring with it, sooner or later in the life of the individual, physical and mental deterioration, then the costs of health services, home and institutional care, and social services will become enormous. Questions are already being raised about the preservation of life, the quality of care for the terminally ill, the wisdom of using heroic measures to prolong life, and the question of euthanasia. These are excruciating problems, and they will grow ever more pressing. Some observers are now saying that we cannot avoid more warehousing of old people in the future; that with present value patterns and the change in women's roles, among other things, that we will be unable to provide tender loving care for the sick aged. Such care will not be purchasable outside the family, and it will be harder and harder to produce within the family.

What Will Be the Role of the Family?

Keeping in mind that "family" is not synonymous with "household," we can be sure that the four- and five-generation family will be the norm by the year 2000 and particularly so by 2025. Because of changing birth rates in the past, the person who will be old in 2000 will have more children and other relatives than an old person today, but their trend will be reversed thereafter, so that the person who will be old in 2025 will again have fewer children.

Another way of saying this is that people who are *presently middle-aged* have had many children, and when they grow old in 2000 they will have large family networks. But people who are *presently young* are having fewer children, and when they grow old in 2025 they will have small family networks. A sizable proportion will probably have no living kin at all.

Numbers of surviving children do not tell us, of course, about the interactions or patterns of assistance between parent and child, and predictions of the latter type are difficult. At present the data from a wide variety of studies show that the family has remained a strong and supportive institution for older people, despite the popular view to the contrary. Most old people today want to be independent of their families as long as possible, but when they can no longer manage for themselves, they expect their children to come to their aid. Not only do such expectations exist, but they are usually fulfilled. A complex pattern of exchange of services exists across generations, and both ties of affection and ties of obligation remain strong. Perhaps such family patterns will change by 2025 but we know that they have changed very slowly in the past, even when other kinds of social change have been rapid.

When it comes to living arrangements, there has been a marked trend toward separate households for older persons. This is due to rising levels of income (the generations move apart when they can afford it), to the greater availability of housing, and to the fact that the telephone and the automobile make it possible to maintain family ties without living under the same roof. Yet in 1970, the latest year for which good data exist, it was clear that the older the individual, and the sicker, the more likely he would be living with a child. (Of all persons aged 75+, one of five women — and one of 10 men — was living with a child.) It usually goes unnoted that at present for every older person in an institution, there are nearly three others living with a child.

It remains to be seen whether the trend toward separate households will continue. It is difficult to foresee whether the energy problem will affect residential patterns, whether it will result in more massing of persons in metropolitan areas or in more doubling-up of families. Either way there is likely to be more doubling-up of unrelated older persons for mutual care and companionship, and there are already increasing numbers of households in which an older person is living with an old-old parent. These latter instances may become more frequent, furthermore, if a more effective system of supportive social and home health services appears and if it leads to a decrease in the rate of institutionalization.

One thing is likely: that families will want more options in the settings and in the types of care available for an aged family member whose health is failing. Nursing homes may be necessary for a small part of the population, but many families are seeking ways of maintaining a frail old person in his own household or in the child's household, and the number of such families may increase in the coming decades, especially if the image of the nursing home remains as negative as it is now.

The future of the intergenerational family network will depend also upon changing attitudes toward marriage and divorce. Some observers believe that nontraditional forms of family life are spreading rapidly in the present middle-aged group as well as in the younger people, and that these will carry forward and affect the behavior of persons who are old in the year 2000 as well as those who will be old in 2025.

Part of the problem, of course, is the wide age range that we are referring to here as the young. The differences between a 15-year-old and a 40-year-old are immense (We tend to ignore the fact that a 25-year age range at the upper end of life encompasses the same immense differences, and we make a grievous oversimplification in lumping together all the persons over 65 as if they were one group.) It is this "young" age group, in any case, who are presently the most frequently involved in divorce, either as parents or as children, or who are living in other nontraditional families. While communes and nonmarried families presently constitute a very tiny proportion even of the under-30, it is by no means a tiny proportion of that group who will have grown up in single-parent families. (Today 1 out of every 6 children under 18 is living in a single-parent home.) Many more mothers are now working; there are fewer adults at home to care for the child; and there are other signs of fragmentation of the family with regard to its child-rearing role.

It remains to be seen if the same fragmentation will become true of the *parent-caring* role. Middle-aged children may continue to come to the aid of their aged parents in 2025 just as they are doing in 1975. It is even possible that intergenerational ties may become more, rather than less, important for old people in the future, for as other social institutions take over the financial support and health care of the aged, the family may become more important with regard to human values and the expressive side of life, that is, in providing lasting emotional ties and a sense of identity and self-worth for both older and younger members.

The Young-Old

One major development that does not appear directly from the trends described above — a development that in many ways may be more important than anything we have thus far considered — is the fact that a new group is now appearing in American society, a group we might call the "young-old." While age is not the important factor, this is the group that is drawn, roughly, from those aged 55 to 75.

Age 55 is beginning to be a meaningful age marker in the life-cycle because of the lowering age of retirement. The large majority of persons now retiring are doing so earlier than required by mandatory rules, and already, in the age-group 55 to 65, only 81 percent of men are in the labor force (compared to 92 percent in the next younger age group). We have already suggested that whether this trend toward earlier retirement continues in the future will depend upon a large number of factors: rates of economic and technological changes, the number of young workers, the number of women workers, and so on. But most observers predict that the trend will continue at least until 2000, so that an increasing number in this group will be retirees.

The young-old are already a relatively healthy group. Only a minority (we estimate it to be between 20 and 25 percent) have health problems that interfere with their major life activities.

The large majority of the men in this group, and more than half the women, are married and living with their spouses in their own households. About 80 percent own their own homes. They see their children frequently. And whether they are working or retired, they play an active role in their neighborhoods and in their communities.

The young-old are much better educated than their predecessors, and in a less disadvantaged position in comparison to the young. By

1990, for instance, half will have had more than a high school education and will have had some college or higher education. The movement toward life-long learning, the spread of education into many institutions other than the school (into the workplace, the museum, the library, into TV and other mass media), the mounting numbers of adults engaged in formal or informal educational programs — all this is already reducing the educational differences between age groups. There is no reason to presume that these trends will be reversed, so that by 2000 and 2025 we can anticipate that the young-old will be a relatively well-educated group.

They are already highly active politically — indeed, when income and education are controlled for, political participation is highest for this age group as compared to younger groups. Again there is no reason to presume that this trend will be reversed, so that by 2000 and 2025, when there will be so many more of them, we can expect that the political weight in the society will shift more in their direction.

Thus the young-old are already markedly different from the outmoded stereotypes of old age — and they will be even more so in the future.

A vigorous and educated young-old group will develop new needs with regard to the meaningful use of time. They will want a wide range of options and opportunities, both for self-enhancement and for community participation. Some will opt for early retirement; some will want to continue working beyond 65; some will want to undertake new work careers at one or more times after age 40. The young-old are likely to encourage economic policies that hasten the separation between income and work, with the goal of providing retirees with sufficient income to approximate their preretirement living standards.

The range of life patterns with regard to work, education, and leisure will probably grow wider. The needs of the young-old in housing, location, and transportation will be increasingly affected by the decisions they make with regard to the use of leisure time. The desire to find interesting things to do will lead them to seek environments which will maximize options for meaningful pursuits.

The young-old are likely to want what might be called an "age-irrelevant" society, one in which arbitrary constraints based on chronological age are removed, and in which all individuals have opportunities consonant with their needs, desires and abilities, whether they be young or old.

Overall, as the young-old articulate their needs and desires, the emphasis is likely to be upon improving the quality of life and upon increasing the choices of life-styles.

This is a very general prediction for the year 2000.

For the year 2025, most of these trends will probably have accelerated — with regard to health, education, political and community activity, and so on. One major difference between 2000 and 2025 will relate to the probability that there will be more old people and fewer young, and that older people will more often remain in the labor market and maintain the role of worker. This will be especially true if, as already suggested, there is a movement toward labor-intensive production and decreased supplies of energy, so that more workers will be needed to produce the goods of the society. Thus we are predicting that by 2025 the trend toward the appearance of a leisure class of young-old may be reversed, and people are more likely to stay in the labor market, perhaps up to the age of 75.

Whether or not this turnabout occurs in labor participation patterns, the young-old will nevertheless be increasingly articulate about their needs and desires. To the extent that there will be a change from the pursuit of affluence and material goods to the pursuit of meaningful ways of self-enhancement and community enhancement, there is no reason to assume that the young-old will not share fully in that change. Indeed, it is difficult to imagine the opposite, for it is not a vigorous, educated, productive group who become the shortchanged in any society; and it is surely not such a group who become the expendables.

It may happen finally that our terms "middle-aged," "young-old," and "old," will come to refer to different ages than now. We are already finding it awkward to speak of 65-year-olds as old, for most of them look so young and feel so young. Unless some major catastrophe does, indeed, befall the society; and unless we move toward a new Dark Age rather than toward an Equilibrium Society, so that health and health care become worse instead of better, and longevity declines rather than increases, there is little reason to presume that the "younging" of older people will not continue. And if it does, we may come to reserve the term "old" for those who are 75. Perhaps then we shall extend the term "middle age" upward to 75; or perhaps my term "young-old" may become more widespread — or perhaps a better term will be coined. The 21st century is likely to become, not a society oriented toward youth but one oriented toward the young-old.